# Economics
# and the Public Good

# Economy, Polity, and Society

The foundations of political economy—from Adam Smith to the Austrian school of economics, to contemporary research in public choice and institutional analysis — are sturdy and well established, but far from calcified. On the contrary, the boundaries of the research built on this foundation are ever expanding. One approach to political economy that has gained considerable traction in recent years combines the insights and methods of three distinct but related subfields within economics and political science: the Austrian, Virginia and Bloomington schools of political economy. The vision of this book series is to capitalize on the intellectual gains from the interactions between these approaches in order to both feed the growing interest in this approach and advance social scientists' understanding of economy, polity, and society. This series seeks to publish works that combine the Austrian school's insights on knowledge, the Virginia school's insights into incentives in non-market contexts, and the Bloomington school's multiple methods, real-world approach to institutional design as a powerful tool for understanding social behaviour in a diversity of contexts.

## Series Editors:

Virgil H. Storr, Research Associate Professor of Economics and Senior Fellow, F.A. Hayek Program for Advanced Study in Philosophy, Politics & Economics, George Mason University

Jayme S. Lemke, Senior Research Fellow, Mercatus Center, George Mason University

## Titles in the Series:

# Economics and the Public Good

## The End of Desire in Aristotle's Politics and Ethics

John Antonio Pascarella

ROWMAN & LITTLEFIELD

*Lanham • Boulder • New York • London*

Published by Rowman & Littlefield
An imprint of The Rowman & Littlefield Publishing Group, Inc.
4501 Forbes Boulevard, Suite 200, Lanham, Maryland 20706
www.rowman.com

86–90 Paul Street, London EC2A 4NE

British Library Cataloguing in Publication Information Available

**Library of Congress Cataloging-in-Publication Data**

Names: Pascarella, John Antonio, author.
Title: Economics and the public good : the end of desire in Aristotle's Politics and ethics / John Antonio Pascarella.
Description: Lanham : Rowman & Littlefield, [2022] | Includes bibliographical references and index.
Identifiers: LCCN 2021050044 (print) | LCCN 2021050045 (ebook) | ISBN 9781786608437 (cloth) | ISBN 9781538166321 (paperback) | ISBN 9781786608444 (ebook)
Subjects: LCSH: Economics—Political aspects. | Economic policy. | Common good. | Aristotle. Politics. | Aristotle. Nicomachean ethics.
Classification: LCC HB74.P65 P375 2022 (print) | LCC HB74.P65 (ebook) | DDC 330—dc23/eng/20211019
LC record available at https://lccn.loc.gov/2021050044
LC ebook record available at https://lccn.loc.gov/2021050045

♾™ The paper used in this publication meets the minimum requirements of American National Standard for Information Sciences—Permanence of Paper for Printed Library Materials, ANSI/NISO Z39.48-1992.

*Dedicated with love to Antonio D'Agnano and Myra Pascarella.*

# Contents

# Introduction

From the perspective of one's own life, everything "economics" encompasses appears beyond one's grasp. Talk about labor, money, markets, and international trade draws attention to a large-scale view of things that paradoxically look impersonal despite the naturally intuitive sense that human beings move economics, and economics move them. For someone who wishes to understand economics, it would seem reasonable either to consult the opinions of persons engaged in business, politicians and economists who craft economic policies, or scholars researching in the field of economics. But what if the nature of economics is more accessible? Is it possible to develop some sense of economics by beginning with one's own observations and opinions? According to Aristotle, one can discover a true sense of economics and its natural limits by beginning from these observations and opinions and choosing to think through what they reveal about one's own desire for the good.

When studying Aristotle's works in search of his economic teaching, one scholarly tendency is to focus on how economics as an academic discipline could benefit from a better understanding of his philosophy. Representative of this view are two books. The first is Scott Meikle's *Aristotle's Economic Thought*, which argues that "strife" over exchange value and market economy "has been the underlying cause of chaos in the interpretation of Aristotle" (1995, 5). The problem is twofold. First, contrary to Greeks' concerns with ethics, "In modern society based on market economy, swathes of the most important kinds of decisions have been removed from the field of ethics altogether, and transferred into the province of economics," and because economists hold that "economics is an independent science," they "view that the relation [between ethics and economics] is minimal or non-existent" (1995, 5). Second, through economists' "failure to observe the role of metaphysics in Aristotle's economic thought," they do not understand how his "category

1

distinction . . . between use value and exchange value is fundamental to his
analysis of wealth, exchange, and money," thus missing "the distinctive character of [his] economic thought and the analytic strength and coherence of its
insights" (1995, 19–20). For Meikle, the ethical problem within economics
reflects a metaphysical problem, and economists would benefit from studying
Aristotle's metaphysics.

A second book that retains some of Meikle's metaphysical emphasis while
leaning more heavily on the ethical side of Aristotle's philosophy is Ricardo
F. Crespo's *A Re-Assessment of Aristotle's Economic Thought*, which begins
by exhorting economists to "embrace their moral duty" and not approach
their science as a "technical task" by reading Aristotle and recognizing that
the "deepest and most relevant knowledge on any subject-matter is philosophical" (2014, 4). Attributing "political, social and economic crises" to a
"loss of . . . unity" between economics and "the whole of political society"—
a loss caused by a "divorce in the 19th century" of the "marriage between
economics and politics, indissoluble by nature"—Crespo declares it is time
for a "reconciliation" based on Aristotle's teaching that "if we do not have
the economy serve the *polis'* common good, we cannot judge if economics
is fulfilling its mission, and neither can we determine if individual economic
behaviors are just" (2014, 4–5). Like Meikle, Crespo blends technical work in
Aristotle's philosophy with research that is heavily conversant with literature
in the field of economics. This work is very helpful to scholars in philosophy and economics, but it does not capture the more personal character of
Aristotle's philosophy.

An excellent survey of the scholarship on Aristotle's economic teaching
comes from Nathan Dinneen's article "Aristotle's Political Economy: Three
Waves of Interpretation" (2015). The "first wave" consists of "attempt[s]
to classify Aristotle's economic thought," and its representative works are
Karl Polanyi's "Aristotle Discovers the Economy" (1968) and M. I. Finley's
"Aristotle and Economic Analysis" (1977) (2015, 96, 98–105). The "second wave" occurs "more explicitly among scholars of political philosophy
about the importance of the 'political' in Aristotle's political economy," and
includes Harvey C. Mansfield, Jr.'s "Marx on Aristotle: Freedom, Money,
and Politics" (1980), Abram Shulsky's "The Infrastructure of Aristotle's
*Politics*: Aristotle on Economics and Politics" (1991), and William James
Booth's *Households: On the Moral Architecture of the Economy* (1993)
(2015, 96, 105–117). The "third wave" focuses on "the role of economics
and occupations on the character of a regime's people and the regime itself,"
and its representative works are Judith Swanson's *The Public and the Private
in Aristotle's Political Philosophy* (1994), Victor Davis Hanson's *The Other
Greeks: The Family Farm and the Agrarian Roots of Western Civilization*
(1999), and Michael Chan's *Aristotle and Hamilton: On Commerce and*

*Statesmanship* (2006) (2015, 96, 117–141). All these works provide a help-ful big-picture view of economics and politics in Aristotle's philosophy, and without taking anything away from their contributions, this book wonders if there is a deeper level to Aristotle's philosophy bound within his examination of these things.

Consistent across the research on Aristotle's economic teaching is an engagement with two excerpts from the *Politics* and the *Nicomachean Ethics*. In the *Politics*, most interpretations focus on Book I, chapters 8–11, where Aristotle explores the relationship between "household management" (*oikonomia*) and "the money-making art" (*chrēmatistikē*), with some gesture toward how these economic pursuits relate to "the political art" (*hē politikē*) and the practice of politics. In Book V, chapter 5 of the *Nicomachean Ethics*, as part of his inquiry into "justice" (*dikaiosunē*), Aristotle considers the rela-tionship between what is just, worth, and exchange through the use of "legal-currency" (*nomisma*). According to Finley, these are the "only two sections in the whole Aristotelian corpus that permit systematic consideration," but because both draw readers into questions about "community" (*koinōnia*), neither constitutes "economic analysis" (1970, 5–18). Finley's response is to Joseph Schumpeter's definition of "economic analysis" as "the intellectual efforts that men have made in order to understand economic phenomena or . . . the analytic or scientific aspects of economic thought" by "deal[ing] with the questions of how people behave at any time and what the economic effects are they produce by so behaving; economic sociology deals with the question of how they came to behave as they do" (1970, 3). Finley's argu-ment is consistent with much of the research mentioned above in finding that it is not possible to isolate Aristotle's economic teaching from his political teaching.

If it is not possible to separate economics from politics in Aristotle's phi-losophy, the next question to consider is what parts of his political teaching are necessary to supplement his economic teaching. Although both Meikle (1995) and Crespo (2014) fold in some of Aristotle's arguments about the city, the good life, virtue, and happiness, the bulk of their work is with *Politics* I.8–11 and *Nicomachean Ethics* V.5. Scholars working in the field of political philosophy (or political theory) take a different approach, par-ticularly in their interpretations of *Politics* I.8–11. Examining "Marx's debt to Aristotle in part 1 of *Capital*," Mansfield argues that Marx eradicates "politics in the Aristotelian sense, which politics necessarily establishes some form of rule" (1980, 351). Essential to Mansfield's claim is the argument that "Aristotle's discussion of slavery [in *Politics* I.4–7] is more open-minded than any modern lecture on the subject that merely asserts the possibility of freedom," and this discussion is essential for demonstrating how political freedom requires a decision about ruling and being ruled, one whose natural precedent is in the soul and the body (1980, 356–357). The nature of ruling and being ruled is a central theme in Book I of the *Politics*, and the inquiry into slavery's importance for understanding political rule, acquisition, and the preservation of freedom is a theme most carefully developed in the works of two scholars in particular: Wayne Ambler's "Aristotle on Acquisition" (1984) and "Aristotle on Nature and Politics: The Case of Slavery" (1987), and Mary P. Nichols's "The Good Life, Slavery, and Acquisition: Aristotle's Introduction to Politics" (1983) and *Citizens and Statesmen* (1992, 13–51). The care Ambler and Nichols invest in attending to how Aristotle's inquiries into slavery and acquisition contribute to *Politics* I's broader concern with the nature of the city and rule contrasts sharply with the works of Meikle (1995) and Crespo (2014, 16), both of which omit these inquiries from their interpretation.

Beyond Book I of the *Politics*, scholars in political philosophy also follow household management and the political art back to Book VI of the *Nicomachean Ethics*, where both come under the umbrella of "prudence" (*phronēsis*). Early precedents for this approach are Leo Strauss's *The City and Man* (1964, 23–24, 28–29) and Harry Jaffa's chapter on Aristotle in the first edition of *History of Political Philosophy* (1963, 99–100). In line with Strauss and Jaffa's work, Shulsky follows Aristotle's thread in Book VI back to Book I's claim that the "political art" is "the overarching practical science" to which economics is subordinate. But there is a wrinkle to this argument, for in connecting politics and economics to prudence, Shulsky notes these things are "practical sciences," not theoretical sciences (1991, 77–78). Chan follows these readings, and emphasizes how prudence is essential because it "concerns itself with the good and moral virtue" (2006, 17). In the field of philosophy, Crespo comes to a similar conclusion about economics as a practical science and the role of prudence, with some emphasis on the importance of choice for virtue (2014, 48–49).

By virtue of the work, every interpretation of Aristotle must choose where to concentrate its efforts, and the preceding works all contribute to understanding how his philosophy speaks to scholars in the fields of economics, political science, philosophy, and political philosophy. While there is a benefit to specialized approaches in the search for Aristotle's economic teaching, there is also a cost in partitioning his arguments into what interests researchers in these fields. A more comprehensive interpretation of Aristotle's economic teaching remains unexplored, one that allows readers to study economics and politics without ever detaching this study from their own pursuit of the good.

Although a book on Aristotle's economic teaching is nothing new, this book differs from others on this subject by being first and foremost a close and careful commentary on the portions of the *Nicomachean Ethics* and *Politics* relevant for situating this teaching within the context of his political philosophy's comprehensive concern with the need for the good. This book does not aim to treat Aristotle's political philosophy in ways that bring him under the province of an academic discipline. Aside from this introduction, the book confines the academic debates over Aristotle's economic teaching to the end notes for the sake of allowing readers to immerse themselves in his texts. Though academics from various disciplines should find this book helpful, its intended audience is anyone who desires to learn Aristotle's economic teaching through the interpretation of primary texts.

There are textual reasons for focusing exclusively on the *Nicomachean Ethics* and the *Politics* to discover how Aristotle naturally roots economics within his political philosophy. To speak very generally, the *Ethics* examines "happiness" (*eudaimonia*) as the human good found in a life according to "virtue" (*aretē*), and the *Politics* studies the things of the city (*polis*), which encompass communities, regimes, citizenship, justice, and education. In Book X of the *Ethics*, Aristotle prepares readers for the *Politics* by calling for an inquiry into regimes and legislation to complete "the philosophy concerning the human things" (*hē peri ta anthrōpeia philosophia*) (1181b1–15). This passage suggests the *Ethics* and *Politics* are complementary works, and to treat one text in isolation from the other could lead readers to an incomplete human philosophy. Treating such philosophy as "political philosophy" stems from singular passages in each work. In Book VII of the *Ethics*, Aristotle identifies "the political philosopher" (*tou tēn politkēn philosophountos*, literally "the one who philosophizes about the political art") as someone who contemplates pleasure and pain as the architect of the "end" (*telos*) toward which people speak of what is simply good and bad (1152a1–3). In Book III of the *Politics*, in the context of defining the just as "a political good" and bound to equality and inequality, Aristotle declares the basis for equality and inequality "holds . . . political philosophy (*philosophian politikēn*)" (1282b14–23). Happiness, virtue, community, and justice are common themes in the *Ethics* and *Politics*, and since both works begin with politics' authoritative claims to the good—thus subordinating many pursuits (including economics) to its own ends—it is worth wondering what political philosophy thinks of these claims. What is the connection between defining justice through equality and inequality and the contemplation of pleasure and pain in relation to an end to which people look to declare each thing good and bad? Since economic inequality is one of the most persistent sources of disputes over justice in the history of politics, there is fruitful ground for seeking Aristotle's perspective as a political philosopher on the causes of these quarrels.

The need to understand economics in light of Aristotle's idea of political philosophy emerges from noticing what might at first seem to be a strange connection between the money-making art in *Politics* I.8–11 and the inquiry into "friendship" (*philia*) from *Ethics* VIII–IX. The Greek word for "the money-making art" is *chrēmatistikē*, derived from *chrēmata* ("property, money") and the plural form of *chrēma* ("a thing one uses or needs"), whose root is *chrē* ("need") (Liddell and Scott 1889, 893–894). By name, the money-making art is "the art of useful things," bound to some sense of need. In the Book VIII of the *Ethics*, the three forms of friendship are the "useful" (*chrēsimon*), the pleasant, and the good, but because it seems something good or pleasant comes from what is useful, only the good and pleasant are ends (1155b17–21).[1] Through understanding the money-making art as the art of useful things, it is possible to see how this art could pursue either the pleasant or the good as ends. If the political philosopher contemplates pleasure and pain as good or bad in relation to some end, then such a person's view of the effects of money-making in life would emphasize the competition between the good and the pleasant as ends.

The preceding argument connecting the linguistic roots of "the money-making art" to Aristotle's inquiry into friendship serves as the first glimpse into why interpreting his political philosophy requires a literal translation of his texts. Admittedly this invites its own set of difficulties, for most readers do not know how to read Attic Greek, a language that holds its own set of ambiguities that are difficult to render in English. In writing this interpretation of Aristotle's economic teaching, it quickly became apparent—and reiterated with the development of each part of the argument—that he is remarkably precise with his language, and capturing this precision (albeit with awkward translations) is vital for seeing the heart of his political philosophy. A recent scholarly precedent for this approach is the late Delba Winthrop's *Aristotle: Democracy and Political Science* (2019). In "A Note on the Translation," Winthrop makes her case for why "the *Politics* can and should be read literally in order to be understood fully" since the text "is intentionally written in an ambiguous manner" (2019, 203–204). As Harvey Mansfield writes in the foreword to his late wife's work, previous translators "did not reproduce Aristotle's ambiguities . . . foreclosing possibilities that Aristotle had left open. With a more literal translation a more imaginative interpretation becomes possible, indeed *necessary* . . . . Ambiguities must be explained . . . . The literal translation serves her argument, her interpretation; and the error of "previous translators" supports an error of interpretation" (2019, viii). Similar to Winthrop's discoveries with her literal translation of Book III of the *Politics*, this book's literal translation discovers "a more imaginative interpretation" of Aristotle's economic teaching.

The opening for friendship to ensure economics holds a natural home in Aristotle's political philosophy is evident in Mary P. Nichols's *Citizens and Statesmen*. Contrary to most research on Aristotle's economic teaching where the references to friendship are passing—often simply noting it bears on justice and community (Finley 1970, 8; Crespo 2014, 52, 54, 59;

Dinneen 2015, 112)—Nichols draws attention to friendship in two key areas of *Politics* I. First, Nichols notes how Aristotle opens the door to equality and freedom between masters and slaves by mentioning the possibility of friendship between them (1992, 23). Second, to conclude her interpretation of Aristotle's inquiries into acquisition, the money-making art, and household management in *Politics* I.8–13, Nichols suggests that friendship and the "political rule that originates in the family, at least in the best cases, is the natural foundation for Aristotle's politics," for this is open to freedom, thus demonstrating how "political life . . . can be a matter of choice" (1992, 33–35). Among the existing interpretations of Aristotle's economic teaching, Nichols is unique in seeing how these ties between friendship, freedom, and choice bear on economics and politics in his political philosophy.[2] This book also recognizes these ties, and builds on Nichols's work by showing how tightly Aristotle draws them together through his political philosophy's playful linguistic precision.

In Book VI of the *Ethics*, Aristotle defines human beings as a "beginning" or "first-principle" (*archē*) with "choice" (*proairesis*), which he characterizes as either "desiring intellect" (*orektikos nous*) or "thinking desire" (*orexis dianoētikē*) (1139b4–5). Earlier in Book I—before Aristotle introduces happiness to the *Ethics*—he observes that if there is some end "we ourselves wish for" on account of itself and all things for the sake of it, this would be the good, for it would ensure "we ourselves do not choose (*haireō*)" all things for the sake of another "without-limit" (*apeiron*), thus leaving desire "empty and vain" (1094a18–22). Two consequences emerge from these passages. First, because desire is a defining characteristic of human nature, a life without the good is "empty and vain." Second, since human nature is synonymous with choice, any account of human pursuits must reckon with choice and its need for the good as a limit.

With *Politics* I.8–11's inquiry into the money-making art, the problem of desire shows itself, but without any mention of "choice." The economic heart of the inquiry is the tension between "true wealth" (*alēthinos ploutos*) that is not without-limit, and a money-making art through which there does not seem to be a "limit" (*peras*) to wealth. The uncertainty regarding wealth's limits bears itself out in confusion over the work belonging to the "art of household-management" (*oikonomikē*) and the money-making art, and the source of this confusion is some people's "desire" (*epithumia*) being without-limit by acting as if money-making is the end of all things (1256b26–34, 40–1257a1, 1257b30–31, 40–1258a14). From the perspective of an impersonal (and perhaps even scientific) economic analysis, it would seem what is most essential in these arguments is the definitions of "wealth" put forth by the arts of household management and money-making. Yet Aristotle uses these arts' competing senses of wealth to move readers to think about their own desires and if they are without-limit on account of money-making. Aristotle's inquiry into the money-making art is not a study of economics, but, as Nichols suggests, an invitation to "self-knowledge," for "human beings' acceptance of their natural limits seems necessary for them to develop their highest natural potentials" (1992, 26–27).

But where can human beings find the natural limit to their desires, especially when economics offers them the possibility of acquisition without-limit? To say it is in knowledge of the good only begs the question of how one acquires this knowledge. Once again, there are clues in a literal reading of Aristotle's political philosophy. Confusion exists between the arts of household management and money-making because they hold a common "use" (*chrēsis*) of legal-currency, but for different ends. Legal-currency exists because all acquisitions have two uses: a "proper" (*oikeia*) use bound to what that thing is (like wearing a shoe), and an "improper" (*ouk oikeia*) use bound to the exchange of that thing. Within the "household" (*oikia*), there is no need for exchange because those living within it "form-community" (*koinōneō*) in all things. But the money-making art came into being according to *logos* (often translated as "reason" or "speech," but transliterated throughout this book) with the "providing" (*porizō*) of legal-currency to produce easier foreign exchange (1257b32–38, 1257a5–13, 19–37). Despite scholars of Aristotle's economic thought parenthetically noting the Greek word for "proper" (Meikle 1995, 54–55; Crespo 2014, 17), they do not consider if there might be significance to the kinship between *oikia/oikos* ("household"), *oikonomia* ("household management"), *oikonomikē* ("art of household management"), and *oikeios/oikeia* ("proper," "one's own"). How does one's view of economics change when one wonders if the acquisition and use of money holds a limit bound to a natural sense of what is—to play on the two meanings of *oikeia*—"properly-one's-own"? Justification for approaching *oikeia* in this way is evident first through Nichols's allusion to the natural freedom that exists within the household and familial friendship (1992, 33–35), and Winthrop's insistence on translating this term as "pertaining to the household . . . . Because Aristotle seems to use the household to stand for the human things as distinguished from the rest of nature, and for the training of souls for politics and philosophy under the guidance of philosophy rather than convention" (2019, 204). Together, these insights suggest philosophy is more at home in the household, and there is a more natural freedom in the friendship and community most closely bound to what is properly-one's-own.

Seeking Aristotle's economic teaching through careful attention to detail allows readers to discover how his political philosophy is simultaneously theoretical, practical, and deeply empirical. In *Politics* I.8–11, Aristotle reveals how "experience" (*empeiria*) is ambiguous in its effect on economics. For one, the money-making art through which there does not seem to be a limit (*peras*) to wealth arises by "some experience and art (*technē*)" concerned with producing the most gain (1257a1–5, b5–8). And yet, when the inquiry purportedly shifts from knowledge to use, Aristotle notes use is twofold, "hold[ing] on the one hand free contemplation (*theōrian eleutheran*), necessary experience (*empeirian anankaian*) on the other" (1258b9–11). With the latter passage, Aristotle hints at the inseparability of freedom, contemplation, and experience in use. Use reflects some understanding of what is properly-one's-own, which may not necessarily be free. This danger is perhaps most apparent in Aristotle's characterization of people who pursue the money-making art as if it is the end of all things as "making-an-attempt" (*peiraō*) at producing excess by "using" their capacities in ways that are not according to nature (1258a6–14). What is "experience" (*empeiria*) if not the continuous using of oneself to "make-attempts" (*peiraō*) at something? How can this experience be free?

Using the *Ethics*, it is possible to outline how Aristotle's political philosophy offers readers the free contemplative experience necessary for a true sense of economics' natural limits. In Book I, Aristotle seems to dismiss the young as "proper" (*oikeios*) listeners because they are "without-experience" (*apeiron*), only to revise this quickly and say that problem is not one of age but a "character" (*ēthos*) that does not "produce" (*poieō*) its desires according to *logos* (1094b23–1095a11). In Book VI, following a suggestion that household management or regimes are what people need to seek the good, Aristotle wonders how the young could be wise in the first-principles (*archai*) of mathematics but not "natural" (*phusikos*) ones, and he suggests it is because they "trust" (*pisteuō*) mathematical first-principles through "abstraction" (*aphairesis*), while natural first-principles are from "experience" (1142a7–20). Notice how the term for "without-experience" is the same as the term for "without-limit"—*apeiron*—a term used to describe the pursuit of wealth through the money-making art in *Politics* I.8–11 and the problem of "choosing" (*haireō*) without the good for desire in *Ethics* I.2. To live "without-experience" is to live "without-limit," but not in the sense that one has not yet performed certain actions. Those who live "without-limit" are those who fail to see their desires need *logos* of the good. This recognition prompts readers to return to Book I, where Aristotle likens *logos* proceeding toward or away from first-principles to athletes running toward and away from the "limit" (*peras*) of a racecourse (1095a17–b4). With the help of this image, readers can see that the experience (*empeiria*) most proper to human beings is one where they "attempt" (*peiraō*) to think and act "in" (*en*) the "limit" (*peras*) of the good, an experience that is most free when they choose to use *logos* to discover their desires' natural end.

The thesis at the heart of this book is that the authoritative concern of Aristotle's political philosophy is to provide readers the free contemplative experience necessary for seeing their enduring need for the good to limit their desires and choices, and his teaching on economics (and its relation to politics) is subordinate to this end. Though not explicit, the need for political philosophy is evident from the beginning of *Politics* I.8, where Aristotle states "one might be unprovided" (*aporeō*, a term that indicates philosophically being "at a loss") over the relationship between the arts of money-making and household management, initially distinguishing these arts by saying the money-making art "provides" (*porizō*) things and the art of household management "uses" them (1256a3–13). Through this experience of being "unprovided" about these arts, the inquiry eventually uncovers a difference between the art of household management that is not without-limit but holds a "boundary" (*horos*), and an unnecessary money-making art without such limits and boundaries (1258a14–19). There are many other "unprovided" matters in Aristotle's political philosophy, but this one serves to show that both political philosophy and economics (broadly understood as what concerns acquisition, exchange, and wealth within and between political communities) aim to provide for human needs. But the needs for which political philosophy provides are prior to economic needs, for the proper use of acquisition, exchange, and wealth reflects one's own understanding of the good. The advantage political philosophy holds over economics and politics is it can provide human beings a path to the good through the experience of being "without-provision" (*aporia*) and moving toward knowledge of this naturally desirable end.

For political philosophy to provide for this natural need for the good in economics, it must avoid being an "abstraction" (*aphairesis*), the Greek term for which means "away-from-choosing" (*apo-hairesis*). Book I of the *Politics* is an example of such an abstraction, for "choice" only appears once when Aristotle goes out of his way to set choice aside for that part of his inquiry (1252a28–30). Book VI of the *Ethics*—which receives attention for bringing economics under the authority of prudence—is also an abstraction. In addition to its definition of human beings and choice as "desiring intellect" or "thinking desire," Book VI contains the abstract argument that prudence requires intellect, which is itself "sense-perception" (*aisthēsis*) of first-principles as "unmoving first boundaries (*horōn*)" (1144b6–16, 1143a35–b5, 9–11). If *Politics* I.8–11 and *Ethics* VI are readers' primary sources for understanding Aristotle's economic teaching, the absence of "choice" from the former text and the heavily abstracted view of prudence in the latter conceal his political philosophy's provision for choice. Yet as the inquiry into friendship draws to a close in *Ethics* IX, Aristotle uses being unprovided over "love-of-self" (*philautos*) to help readers see they hold a naturally pleasant intellectual sense-perception of the good through which it becomes clear that there are "bounds" (*hōrismenōn*) to the life that is properly-one's-own (*oikeiōs*) (1168a28–1171a20). In short, the true natural sense of economics' boundaries is most evident through friendship, which always begins with a choice for the good that is properly-one's-own.

The centrality of friendship in Aristotle's political philosophy and his provision for the contemplative experience of drawing choice into the limit of the good governs the structure of this book's inquiry into his economic teaching. Chapters 1–3 begin where most research on Aristotle's economic thought concentrate their efforts (*Politics* I.8–11, *Ethics* I & VI). Chapter 1 examines Aristotle's account of the development of natural acquisition into the money-making art that eventually splits into natural and unnatural forms, with the unnatural form being the one that introduces the problem of desire being without-limit to the inquiry (*Politics* I.8–9). In chapter 2, the grounds for subordinating economics to politics come forth, after which Aristotle alludes to what philosophy could provide to economics and politics (*Politics* I.10–11). In these two chapters, the confusion between the arts of household management and money-making receive attention, and both draw on the prior inquiry into slavery (*Politics* I.4–7) to begin wondering how freedom could find its way to economic life. Chapter 3 takes up the authoritative claims of the political art and prudence over economics in *Ethics* I and VI, with careful attention to the questions Aristotle raises about the good and choice in Book I, and a rigorous look at how Book VI's account of the nature of choice and the search for truth compels readers to think deeply about what it means to study economics and politics as "sciences" versus arts. The questions raised within these chapters all aim to demonstrate why Aristotle's economic teaching is not one readers can isolate from his conception of political philosophy.

To show the authoritative concern in Aristotle's political philosophy is the good and not happiness, chapter 4 combines the *Politics'* inquiry into the natural growth of the city (I.2–3) with the *Ethics'* preliminary inquiry into happiness (I.4–5, 7–8) based on their common appeal to "self-sufficiency" (*autarkeia*). Whereas the *Politics* refrains from considering choice's relationship to self-sufficiency, the *Ethics* puts this front and center with the question about the best life for a human being. Within this inquiry, Aristotle points to an opening for the contemplative life to provide more completely for the human good than the life of pleasure, the political life, and the money-making life.

Chapters 5–7 work together to establish political philosophy's authoritative perspective on economics and politics. With chapter 5, *Ethics* VII's inquiry into pleasure becomes the basis for understanding all human pursuits as choices about pleasures and good things, and it is on these grounds that Aristotle introduces readers to "the political philosopher." In chapter 6, choice's vital role in forming and sustaining friendships becomes the lens for moving from the useful pointing toward the pleasant or the good as ends in Book VIII to the discovery of the naturally pleasant love-of-self and care for the intellect in Book IX. Since the money-making art is "the art of useful things," the true bounds of an economics defined by money-making will always reside in a true discernment of what is good and pleasant by nature, a discernment readily accessible in friendship. Chapter 7 carries this insight back into Book V's inquiry into justice, then returns to Book X. The reason for this move is because a key source of injustice is a mistake about pleasure and the good things that derives from misunderstanding love-of-self. In Book X, Aristotle provides another account of pleasure, one that draws upon friendship to show how the most pleasant activity is contemplative, thus preparing the way to claim happiness is the contemplative life that is the best because it is most self-sufficient. Here Aristotle reveals how to bring the use of external goods under the contemplative life's authority, suggests such a life is more attendant to what is properly-one's-own, and reveals limits to laws' effectiveness in providing for these cares. From this teaching, chapter 8 continues the interplay between *Ethics* V, VIII, and IX with emphasis on what these inquiries say about economic exchange. After showing how friendship provides a more natural view of the household and its freedom than justice, and further, demonstrating how friendship liberates people from a preoccupation with worth, the chapter concludes with an account of what Aristotle means in *Politics* III.12 when he claims the basis for equality and inequality that defines justice "holds without-provision (*aporia*) and political philosophy" (1282a14–23).[3]

With the link established between the political philosopher's contemplation of pleasures and pains in relation to the good *and* political philosophy's awareness that conflicts over justice flow from misconceptions about the good and pleasure for which only *logos* can provide, Chapter 9 reveals the limits to relying on economic concerns such as the distributions of property and wealth as remedies to political life's ills. The problem of desire is ever-present, and it belongs exclusively to political philosophy—not economics or politics—to provide for the persistent choice that is most properly-one's-own: the choice to live in the limit of the good.

# Chapter 1

# The Problem of the Money-Making Art in Aristotle's *Politics*

The sole sustained discussion about what contemporary readers would call "economics" in Aristotle's political philosophy seeks to answer one question: What is the relationship between "household management" (*oikonomia*) and the "money-making art" (*chrēmatistikē*)? Based on this inquiry's appearance in Book I of the *Politics*, those who search for Aristotle's economic teaching by reading this inquiry in isolation from the rest of his political philosophy risk arriving at the mistaken conclusion that the three things most important for understanding the nature of "economics" are acquisition, exchange, and community. Yet from the beginning of Aristotle's "economic" inquiry and its broad view of natural acquisition, exchange, and community, his work's philosophic character is apparent, and he invites readers to work closely with his text to see their enduring need to know the good—a need that forms the heart of his political philosophy.

To begin his inquiry into the money-making art in Book I of the *Politics*, Aristotle says, "But wholly concerning all of acquisition (*ktēsis*)[1] and the money-making art let us contemplate (*theōreō*) according to the guiding manner, since the slave also was some part of acquisition" (1256a1–3). From the start, Aristotle points to the contemplative character of his economic teaching. The money-making art is (along with slavery) part of acquisition, which subtly indicates that readers cannot see the whole of acquisition without contemplating the ties between Aristotle's inquiries into slavery (I.4–7) and the money-making art (I.8–11).[2]

Though bound together by acquisition, Aristotle's contemplation of the money-making art holds a different character than that of slavery, for with this art Aristotle begins—for the first time in the *Politics*—by stating "one might be unprovided" (*aporeō*, in the sense of perplexity)[3] over whether this art is the same as the "art of household management" (*oikonomikē*), part of it,

13

or subordinate to it. If subordinate, does the money-making art "hold-forth" (*parechō*)[4] tools to the art of household management, or the raw material the art of household management "brings to completion" (or "brings to an end," *apoteleō*)[5] through its own "work" (*ergon*)? In response to this question, Aristotle proposes an initial distinction between the arts of household management and money-making: left to themselves,[6] the money-making art "provides" (*porizō*) things while the art of household management "uses" (*chraō*) them (1256a3–13). With this beginning to his inquiry into the money-making art, Aristotle contrasts readers' first experience of being unprovided in contemplation with a seemingly definitive statement about this art's provision to the art of household management. The unstated bridge between these provisional statements concerns the nature of the art of household management's work, one bound to some end and readers' sense of how to use these arts of acquisition.

From the distinction between the money-making art's provision of things that the art of household management uses, Aristotle draws attention to a dispute concerning whether the money-making art is some part of the art of household management, or another form. If the "money-maker" (*chrēmatistikos*) contemplates from where "useful things" (*chrēmata*, which could also mean "property" or "money")[7] and acquisition come, and if acquisition and "wealth" (*ploutos*) encompass many parts, then there is a question whether the art of farming and in general the care of food and acquisition is part of the money-making art (1256a14–19). The common concern of the arts of household management and money-making is acquisition, but the dispute about these arts' mutual relation hinges upon clarifying what constitutes "wealth" and "useful things." As the name for the "useful things" indicates, *chrēmata* forms the basis for "the money-making art," *chrēmatistikē*. If the money-making art provides what the art of household management uses, money-making is likely subordinate to household management. Yet Aristotle does not draw this conclusion, choosing instead to leave open what constitutes the "wealth" and "useful things" that money-makers contemplate to provide for household management.

Aristotle's inquiry into the money-making art spans four chapters in Book I of the *Politics*. The first two chapters in this inquiry focus mainly on the dispute about what constitutes "wealth" and "useful things," with some reference to the initial "unprovided" questions concerning the relationship between the money-making art and household management (I.8–9). The second two chapters of the inquiry focus more on the money-making art's subordination initially to household management, then politics (I.10–11). The first two chapters of this book follow this division. In this chapter, a careful examination of Aristotle's inquiry into what acquisitions and useful things belong to the money-making art reveals its contemplative foundations while outlining the relationship between exchange and political community. Through considering the ways the arts of household-management and money-making are either by nature or not by nature, Aristotle uncovers human beings' fundamental need for a natural end to which they can direct these arts. By attending to the role of law in money-making in light of the inquiry into slavery by law, readers learn that although nature itself is incapable of directly providing this end to human beings, Aristotle gradually unfolds what characteristics of human nature seek this end. Through this discovery, readers begin to see how Aristotle's economic teaching depends upon his political philosophy's search for the good.

## NATURAL ACQUISITION, NATURAL EXCHANGE, AND COMMUNITY (*POLITICS* 1256A1–1257A30)

### Natural Acquisition (*Politics* 1256a19–b26)

Taking up the question of how farming and caring for food relate to the money-making art, Aristotle begins with observations from nature. Because there are many forms of food, there are many "lives" (*bios*) among animals and human beings. Since there is no living without food, the "differences" (*diaphora*) of food "produce" (*poieō*) many "different" (*diapherō*) lives among the animals, which are evident from how they are in herds or scattered, in whichever way "is advantageous" (*sumpherō*) toward food for themselves through being either carnivores, herbivores, or omnivores. From this, Aristotle concludes "nature" (*phusis*) "marked-the-boundaries" (*horizō*) of animals' lives toward the easiness and "choosing" (*hairesis*)[8] of such things, seeing that the same thing is not "pleasant" (*hēdus*) to each animal according to nature, but different, and the lives of herbivores and carnivores are "set-standing-apart" (*diistēmi*) from one another (1256a19–29). Though part of nature, Aristotle credits food and not nature itself with producing different lives for animals. What does belong to nature is "marking-the-boundaries" of animals' choosing of foods, a marking evident in the diversity of what foods are pleasant to various animals. From nature's choosing arise different (*diapherō*) lives among the animals regarding what foods are advantageous (*sumpherō*) for themselves, and this sets all the different animals apart from each other. To play on the literal meaning of the verbs Aristotle uses, nature's choosing simultaneously bears-together (*sumpherō*) animals in certain lives that bear-apart (*diapherō*) from each other. Since Aristotle begins this account by noting the lives of animals and human beings are similar in caring for food, it follows that human beings' choosing of what is pleasant will bear their lives both together and apart.

From animals' different lives in their care for food, Aristotle surveys the different human lives. Some human beings are nomads who live "without labor *(ponos)*" and "have leisure" *(scholazō)*, though it is necessary for them to change their courses for their herds. Other human beings live by hunting, the different types of which include piracy, fishing, or the hunting of birds and wild beasts. But the greatest class of human beings lives from the earth and cultivating crops. All these lives hold their "work" *(ergasia)* in relation to what is "natural" *(autophuton)* and do not themselves provide food through "exchange" *(allagē)* and "retail-trade" *(kapēleia)* (1256a29–b2). The first part of Aristotle's account of human lives is analogous to the different advantageous ways animals live toward food (i.e., as herds or scattered), though there are two differences between animal and human lives. First, the inclusion of piracy as a type of hunting does not put human beings neatly into the category of carnivores, herbivores, or omnivores, for pirates do not eat other human beings as food. Second, while Aristotle describes both animals' and human beings' lives as holding their work in relation to what is natural, the separation of these works from exchange and retail-trade leaves uncertain whether these latter human works are natural. This complicates thinking through what the human care for food requires when it comes to managing this care among themselves.

Aristotle next turns to what is pleasant in human beings' care for food, for they live pleasantly by mixing the different lives (i.e., nomad, farming, pirate, fisher, and hunter), filling up the life that is most in need what it happens to lack in the "self-sufficient" *(autarchēs)* as "need necessitates" *(chreia sunankazō)* (1256b2–7). Although animals live pleasantly according to the food they eat, human beings live pleasantly by mixing together different lives. This mixing is possible because human beings hold an awareness of need and necessity that spurs them to seek the "self-sufficient." But what is at work in this mixing of lives? Aristotle does not connect the arguments for his readers, but the common language of the "pleasant" points back to the idea of "choosing." Nature chooses how animals care for food (a wolf, for example, will always be a carnivore and need to hunt for its food to survive), while human beings can choose what foods they want to eat to live. Such choosing affects how human beings manage the care for food in relation to each other, and the character of this choosing depends on discerning the relationship between the pleasant and the self-sufficient.

After accounting for the different lives through which animals and human beings care for food, Aristotle brings acquisition back into the inquiry. From the time they first come to be to when they are complete *(teleioō)*, it is apparent that nature itself gives such acquisition as the care for food itself to all animals, for some animals bring forth together food with their young who do not "have the capacity" *(dunamai)* to provide for themselves, while others hold food in themselves (like the nature that is milk) for some time. As a result, it is clear that one must suppose for all the things that come to be that plants are for the sake of animals and the other animals are for the sake of human beings. While the tame animals are for the sake of "use" (*chrēsis*) and food, most but not all of the wild ones are for the sake of food and other helps that come to be from them (1256b7–20). With the return of acquisition, Aristotle's focus shifts from animal and human life to nature itself. The common acquisition that animals and human beings receive from nature is the care for food. This care, however, invites questions about nature, which reveals itself as a supposed hierarchy where plants provide food to animals, and animals provide food to themselves and to human beings. Once again, human beings usher in a distinct consideration, for in addition to living pleasantly through choosing different lives to provide for the self-sufficient in their care for food (a choosing that belongs to nature for animals), Aristotle reveals human acquisition holds a distinct concern: use. Through this development, readers must wonder not only how use fits into choosing's discernment of the pleasant and the self-sufficient, but what nature itself provides to inform human choosing.

To emphasize the need to contemplate nature's capacity to provide for choosing, Aristotle uses the preceding supposition about nature's hierarchy of acquisition to consider a hypothetical argument about war that brings art back into the inquiry along with political concerns, saying:

> If, therefore, nature produces nothing neither incomplete (*ateles*) nor in vain, necessarily for the sake of human beings nature produced all these things. And on account of this war by nature is an art of acquisition in a way (for the art of hunting is a part of this), and there is need to use [war] towards both beasts and human beings who naturally are such to be ruled (*archō*) but not willing, on the grounds that this war is by nature just (*dikaios*). (1256b20–26)

While the conclusion to this passage may shock some readers, it is essential to understand how it is a hypothetical argument that demonstrates the limits to thinking about human life solely in terms of acquisition. The first hint that Aristotle's argument is more contemplative than assertive is its heavily conditional nature. Starting with the initial condition of nature producing nothing "neither incomplete nor in vain," Aristotle's observations about the different lives through which animals and human beings care for food suggest they are "incomplete" because they continually need food to survive. If the hypothetical argument is to hold up, nothing nature produces can be "in vain," and the only way it appears one can save the argument is to reassert nature by necessity produces all things for human beings to acquire.[9] On its own, this argument is suspect given the assumption about the natural order

*Chapter 1*

of acquisition as it relates to food: some plants, after all, are not edible, and therefore animals and human beings would not need to acquire them. The argument remains viable, however, when one remembers human acquisition concerns both food and use.

At first glance, the appearance of "war" in a hypothetical argument about acquisition is a non-sequitur. Aristotle provides the opening for war to enter the argument by drawing on his statement about the supposed hierarchy of nature that human beings can use wild animals for other helps besides food. For the argument about war being "by nature just" to be true, one must concede an equivalence between "wild animals and human beings who naturally are such to be ruled but not willing." Aristotle's use of the phrase "on the grounds that" prior to his statement about naturally just war reveals this argument is not his own,[10] but belongs to others who wish to treat wild animals and human beings as objects of acquisition. For his part, Aristotle leaves this assumed analogy between wild animals and certain human beings unexamined, along with two political questions: "How does one 'rule' human beings?", and "What is just?". By leaving these questions open, Aristotle suggests natural acquisition is insufficient for providing perspective on politics.

The bridge between Aristotle's hypothetical supposition about nature's order and the argument others make about just war is an assumption about art. War seems to be "an art of acquisition in a way" by some kinship with the art of hunting. Aristotle recognizes this is not a self-evident proposition, hence why he qualifies the analogy with the statement "in a way." The qualification allows thoughtful readers to think of other uses for war aside from acquisition, such as the defense and preservation of what one possesses. Although the argument about war as a natural art of acquisition is dubious, it rests upon a true insight about nature, specifically, that hunting is a natural form of acquisition produced in the lives of some animals and human beings. Through art, human beings can use their naturally given capacity for acquisition in different ways than the animals. In this way, art shows itself as something human beings can use to produce something different than what nature gives (which in the present context is something as dangerous as war). To put it in a way that aligns with Aristotle's allusion to choosing in his outline of natural acquisition, it is through art that human beings choose to produce conditions different from those given by nature. This choosing concerns the pleasant, the self-sufficient, use, and—as the hypothetical argument about war and ruling suggests—the just. The inclusion of this last idea in the initial account of natural acquisition reveals what is strikingly absent from the inquiry up to this point: the city (*polis*) and political life. Though these things are about to emerge in Aristotle's inquiry into the money-making art, readers must bear in mind that they will not fully understand these things without seeing how they relate to choosing.

## The Natural Art of Exchange (*Politics* 1256b26–1257a19)

Following his overview of the things related to farming and the general care of food and acquisition, Aristotle turns to the art of acquisition, which takes two forms: one that is natural, and the other associated with the money-making art. Starting with the art of acquisition's more natural form, it is "according to nature part of the art of household management, insofar as there is need [for this] either to be present or to provide this so that there is present a store of such useful things that are necessary toward living, and useful to community (*koinōnia*) in a city or a household" (1256b26–30).[11] The natural relationship between the arts of acquisition and household management emerges conditionally: the art of household management needs the art of acquisition, though it is unclear if the art of household management naturally encompasses the art of acquisition, or if something else provides this art to household management. What the art of household management needs from the art of acquisition are the things necessary for living, but unlike the preceding discussion about acquisition and food, Aristotle qualifies the art of acquisition naturally related to the art of household management as providing what is useful for community in either a household or a city. The progression from acquisition related solely to food to community in the household or city suggests a more civilized view of acquisition. This shift in perspective is further apparent in no longer speaking of acquisition as a biological care for food, but an "art" that either needs to be present or provided to communities.

The introduction of community to Aristotle's inquiry into acquisition allows him to put forth a preliminary moral teaching that alludes to questions about political life's ends. After stating it seems that the things necessary for living that are useful to community in a household or a city constitute "true wealth" (*alēthinos ploutos*), Aristotle returns to the idea of "self-sufficiency" (*autarkeia*) to argue such acquisition (i.e., true wealth) is not "without-limit" (*apeiron*) toward to "good living" (*agathēn zōēn*). This runs contrary to Solon, a famous Athenian legislator who said no limit (*terma*) to wealth has been laid down for human beings (1256b30–34). Although the "self-sufficient" appears in Aristotle's earlier description of human beings' pleasant mixing (and implicit choosing) of lives in their needed care for food, this passage about true wealth is the first appearance of "self-sufficiency" since its introduction as the "end" (*telos*) of the city (1252b27–1253a1). Because self-sufficiency receives a more thorough examination in later chapters, for now it is enough to note that the first two passages about self-sufficiency in the *Politics* become the basis for introducing moral questions about ends. If self-sufficiency serves as the city's end *and* keeps the acquisition of "true wealth" from being without-limit toward "good living," then its nature transcends both politics and economics.

The reintroduction of moral questions within the inquiry into the money-making art brings an expansion of what constitutes wealth and an implicit basis for its limits derived from the example of the arts. Aristotle suggests there is a limit laid down to the other arts, for the size and quantity of an art's tool is not without-limit, and "wealth is a multitude of tools for household managers and politicians" (1256b34–37).[12] Considering this argument flows from a discussion about the natural form of the art of acquisition, Aristotle looks poised to assert there is a limit to this art. Instead, Aristotle concludes "there is some art of acquisition according to nature for household managers and politicians" (1256b37–39). This is a strange conclusion for two reasons. First, it avoids asserting a limit to the natural form of the art of acquisition.[13] Second, by limiting the conclusion to clarity about *some* natural art of acquisition, Aristotle indicates there is more to learn about this art and how household managers and politicians use it. One can attribute the indefinite nature of this art partly to the uncertainty of what tools are at the disposal of household managers and politicians, but a better explanation for Aristotle's odd conclusion may flow from the re-emergence of self-sufficiency and its allusion to the discussion of ends. Because Aristotle defines "true wealth" after placing the art of acquisition in relation to self-sufficiency toward "good living," it appears that arts stand in need of direction by ends.[14]

Why Aristotle refrains from concluding the natural art of acquisition has a limit to wealth becomes apparent with the inquiry's turn to the money-making art. Identifying the money-making art as another class of the art of acquisition, Aristotle notes this art's name is "just," and because of this art, there does not seem to be a "limit" (*peras*) to wealth and acquisition (1256b40–1257a1). The money-making art thus appears to contradict the argument that the quantity and size of arts' tools is not without-limit. While it is easy to see how money needs to be a reasonable size to use for exchange, it is more difficult to see why there should be a limit to how much money one acquires (though it remains true that the amount of money in circulation at any given time is finite). The challenge Aristotle sets up for subsequent arguments is to look at the money-making art in a way that shows why it appears there is no limit to acquisition and wealth, yet clarify how this understanding of the money-making art is incorrect. Increasing the challenge is the many who "customarily-consider" (*nomizō*)[15] the natural art of acquisition and the money-making art are the same. Though Aristotle concedes the two arts are close to one another, he adds that while the natural art of acquisition is by nature, the money-making art is not by nature and comes to be by some "experience" (*empeiria*) and art (1257a1–5). Here is a shift in approach to show acquisition and wealth have a limit: the first argument for this limit comes through the arts, but the second relies on nature. Going forward, one must search for the point where the money-making art departs from the limits set by the natural art of acquisition.

To address the confusion about wealth's limits in relation to the money-making art, Aristotle begins with the natural basis of exchange. Each "piece of acquisition" (*ktēma*) has a twofold use: the "proper" (*oikeia*) use belonging to that thing, and the "improper" (*ouk oikeia*) use involving the "exchange" (*metablētikē*) of one thing for another. For example, the proper use of a shoe is wearing it, and the improper use of a shoe is exchanging it. This example occasions the first appearance of something akin to commercial activity in the *Politics*, with a description of how a person who gives in exchange (*allattomenos*) a shoe for "legal-currency" (*nomisma*) or food from a person who is in need of a shoe uses the shoe improperly because it did not come to be for the sake of exchange (*allagē*) (1257a5–13).[16] Although Aristotle mentions legal-currency as a means of exchange, he does not draw attention to it. Instead, the focus remains on what is natural about exchange. The appearance of food alongside legal-currency as a means of exchange shows a progression beyond natural acquisition by focusing on the use of things, where one can choose to use something either for the sake of its proper or improper end.

From the twofold use of pieces of acquisition, Aristotle introduces the "art of exchange" (*hē metablētikē*) and its natural foundation. All things belong to the art of exchange, for its beginning was what is according to nature, namely, human beings holding more or less of things than is "adequate" (*ikanos*). From this observation, Aristotle concludes the "art of retail-trade" (*hē kapēlikē*) does not by nature belong to the money-making art, for it was necessary to produce an exchange (*allagē*) only so far as it was adequate (1257a13–19). A curious feature of this argument is how the money-making art holds an indeterminate position between the natural art of exchange and the art of retail-trade. Despite Aristotle's earlier statement that the money-making art's name is "just" because it seems from this art that there is no limit to wealth and acquisition, the distinction he draws between the money-making art and the art of retail-trade suggests the former art could align with the natural art of exchange, thus extending to all things and holding a limit to acquisition and wealth from the perspective of what is adequate. If this is true, then perhaps readers should withhold assenting to Aristotle's apparent assertion that the money-making art is not by nature.

## Natural Exchange and Community (*Politics* 1257a19–30)

At the same time as Aristotle alludes to a general, natural art of exchange, he points to an area this art does not reach, thus reiterating natural limits to wealth. In the "household" (*oikia*)—the first community—there is no work for the art of exchange.[17] Unlike the household where people "form-community" (*koinōneō*) in all things, the art of exchange occurs only where there are many households so that they can produce "mutual-giving" (*metadosis*)[18] as is necessary according to their needs. Aristotle adds barbarians still produce this exchange (*allagē*), often by exchanging (*katallassō*) useful things (*chrēsima*) with one another and no more (1257a19–28). The appearance of the household in this argument merits careful attention. By reminding readers that the household is the first community and noting the natural art of exchange occurs among many households, Aristotle recalls the natural progression of political communities from the household to the "village" (*kōmē*) in Book I's second chapter: the household is the community according to nature "set-standing-together" (*sunistēmi*) for every day,[19] while the village is the first community from many households that is for the sake of a non-daily use (1252b12–16). A couple questions emerge when comparing Aristotle's initial definitions of the "household" and "village" with his distinction between these communities regarding the natural art of exchange. First, why does Aristotle refrain from designating the community in which barbarians exchange useful things a "village"? Second, if the natural art of exchange holds no work within the household, what is the natural work through which each person within the household forms-community in all things? Aristotle does not provide direct answers to these questions in his inquiry into the money-making art, but through them, readers catch a glimpse of his important argument that exchange is not a necessary foundation for forming-community.

Underlying the questions about community and the art of exchange raised by the household is uncertainty about the naturalness of these things. Two prior arguments about the household need recollecting. First, the art of acquisition is part of household management because "living" (*zēn*) and "living well" (*eu zēn*) require the necessary things (1253b23–25). Second, the art of acquisition is naturally part of the art of household management because there is need for a store of useful things necessary for living that are "useful to community in a city or a household." Thus far in the *Politics*, the household holds a consistent relationship with what is necessary and useful. The household also holds a steady relationship to the city, which itself marks the coming to completion of political communities for the sake of self-sufficiency, the end that brings together both "living" and "living well." But the non-community of exchanging useful things among barbarian households complicates the picture, for Aristotle concludes this art of exchange is neither against nature, nor is it a form of the money-making art since it is a restoration of the self-sufficiency according to nature (1257a28–30). If households not in community with one another can restore self-sufficiency through the art of exchange, what does this mean for the city's claim to self-sufficiency?

To answer this question, one can work back from Aristotle's conclusion that the money-making art is distinct from the natural art of exchange because money-making does not take its bearings from natural self-sufficiency in necessary and useful things. The first steps in this argument come from the observation that every piece of acquisition has a "proper" and "improper" use. In the original Greek, the term for "proper" (*oikeia*) is nearly identical to the term for "household" (*oikia*).[20] The significance of the pun comes through the example of the barbarian households: the natural art of exchange provides for natural self-sufficiency by enabling each household to acquire the useful things it puts to proper use for its daily needs. Only in the context of community in the household are pieces of acquisition used according to their ends. In this respect, Aristotle adheres to an earlier assertion that the money-making art provides things that the art of household management uses.[21] The self-sufficiency according to nature from the natural art of exchange is only half the picture. Although exchange enables more extensive acquisition of necessary and useful things, the use of those things is the work of communities that think about what self-sufficiency entails.

Before turning to Aristotle's fuller examination of the money-making art, it might be helpful to outline how the preceding inquiry into natural acquisition and exchange presents a partial view of political life. The city is almost entirely absent from the inquiry, aside from the statement that the city (like the household) needs a store of useful things necessary for living. This statement appears at the end of a sequence of arguments that looks at human life solely from the perspective of acquisition, starting with food and working its way toward what is necessary for "good living." Aristotle's definitions of "true wealth" and "wealth" prompt arguments that neither the art of acquisition directed toward self-sufficiency nor arts' tools are without-limit. Implicit within this latter argument is the idea that arts need direction from their ends more than their own tools. With the natural art of exchange between households, Aristotle suggests arts receive their ends not from tools, but communities.

The gradual emergence of community in the inquiry further clarifies why Aristotle tests the limits of understanding human life in terms of acquisition with the specious argument that war is just by nature when used against wild animals and human beings who are such to be ruled but unwilling. No community appears in this argument, but as the inquiry into acquisition develops, both the household and the non-communal barbarian households engaged in natural exchange show the presence of the smallest form of community prevents human beings from thinking only of acquisition. At the very least, the household suggests living in peace is more natural to human beings than war. Though the arts of acquisition and exchange provide necessary things to the household, the art of household management's primary work seems to be holding together community within the household. And since it is in the context of community that Aristotle links self-sufficiency to "good living," it is apparent that political life gives human beings a way to live that is not dominated by the necessity of acquisition.


## THE MONEY-MAKING ART AND THE
## PROBLEM OF GAIN (*POLITICS* 1257A30–B31)

### Legal-Currency, the Money-Making Art, and Gain
### (*Politics* 1257a30–b4)

The money-making art's move away from the self-sufficiency sought by the natural art of exchange marks the beginning of Aristotle's close look at the money-making art. The money-making art came into being "according to *logos*" (which can mean reason, speech, argument, or rational account)[22] with an expansion of exchange beyond households close to one another. The use of legal-currency was provided out of necessity when more foreign sources of help came to be by importing those things of which there was need and exporting those things which were more than enough. Because it is not easy to carry each of the things that are necessary according to nature, people "set-down-together an agreement" (*suntithēmi*)[23] to give and to take something for exchanges (*allagē*). This new means of exchange belonged to the useful things (*chrēsima*) and held a "manageable" (literally "good changing of hands," *eumetacheiristos*) need or use (*chreia*)[24] toward living (like iron or silver) (1257a30–37). Though Aristotle is about to assert the exchange of legal-currency marks the beginning of the money-making art, a few ideas from the preceding argument merit careful attention. Although the natural art of exchange arises in accord with the self-sufficiency that is according to nature, the money-making art begins according to *logos*. While it is too strong to suggest *logos* and nature are at odds, one ought to wonder why the first appearance of *logos* in the inquiry into acquisition and exchange suggests a move beyond nature as a standard.[25]

Admittedly this argument is not entirely unexpected, for human beings' pleasure in mixing (and therefore choosing) the lives by which they acquire food so that each life acquires whatever it happens to lack in the self-sufficient suggests something like *logos* is at work.[26] Further evidence that Aristotle draws on this earlier argument appears in both passages' heavy emphasis on "use" and "need" that provides a helpful context for legal-currency's origins: legal-currency is ultimately a tool, and through *logos*, one sees its need derives from human beings' natural limit to carry the necessary things for the sake of exchange. While the limit to what one can carry for the sake of exchange is apparent, an open question about self-sufficiency remains from legal-currency's introduction: Does self-sufficiency necessitate acquisition through exchange with foreign sources? With a slight reframing of the question, its political importance is clear. Aristotle introduces foreign exchange immediately after the example of the independent barbarian households engaging in the natural art of exchange to provide for each household's self-sufficiency. If it is right to understand the household as a self-sufficient community, does the natural art of exchange among barbarian households point to the need for the self-sufficient communities of cities to engage in the art of exchange as well?

Though Aristotle leads readers to wonder about the necessity of foreign exchange for political life, his focus remains on explaining how the money-making art arises and eventually separates itself from the natural art of exchange. The materials for legal-currency were iron, silver, or other metals. At first, it was simply size and weight that marked-the-boundary of legal-currency, but in the end (*teleutaios*), a sign of this quantity came in the form of an engraved mark or stamp to dispense with measuring the metals (1257a37–41). Two related ideas lurk in the background of this argument: worth and *logos*. Within a short span of text, Aristotle shows how the worth of things exchanged shifts from the necessary things being exchanged, to different quantities of metals representing those necessary things, and finally to engraved marks or stamps that are signs of quantities of metals that represent quantities of necessary things.[27] Only *logos* could bring legal-currency to its end, for what is more removed from exchange yet tied to it than signs understood as quantities of necessary things? While nature provides necessary things, choosing to provide for their manageable exchange and determining their worth with legal-currency is a human work accomplished through *logos*.

From the progression of legal-currency toward its more manageable form, Aristotle turns to a division in the money-making art. Once legal-currency was provided for "necessary exchange" (*anankaias allagēs*), there came to be another form of the money-making art: "retail-trade" (*kapēlikos*). While retail-trade may at first have come to be simply equal[28] to necessary exchange, with experience it became more of an art concerning from where and how one will produce the most "gain" (*kerdos*) (1257b1–4).[29] With this argument, Aristotle settles on a distinction between two forms of the money-making art: the necessary exchange of necessary things according to nature through foreign imports and exports, and the retail-trade of legal-currency to produce gain. This distinction provides clarity about the earlier argument that suggests the money-making art is closer to the natural art of exchange (*hē metablētikē*) through which human beings produce necessary exchanges because they hold more or less of things than is adequate.[30] Necessary exchange shows there is a money-making art according to nature that holds a limit for acquisition. Retail-trade, however, is a different form of the money-making art that produces gain, something distinct from the exchange of naturally necessary things through the use of legal-currency. Consequently, Aristotle does not treat the money-making art as if it is simply against nature. If the money-making art facilitates necessary exchange, it is by nature. But if the money-making art produces gain through retail-trade, it is not by nature.[31]

The possibility for the money-making art to take either a natural or an unnatural form implies there is a choice in how the art comes to be. Unfolding the nature of this choice requires looking beyond Aristotle's inquiry into the money-making art in the *Politics*, though the account of this art's origin provides helpful clues. The natural precedent for the money-making art is the natural art of exchange that occurs between households that restores the self-sufficiency that is according to nature.[32] Both arts are alike in beginning from human beings naturally holding more or less of things than is adequate, but differ in three ways. First, the money-making art relies on unspecified foreign sources, not households (and implicitly communities) close to each other. Second, while self-sufficiency toward good living is the limit for the natural art of exchange, Aristotle does not carry this limit into his summary of the "necessary exchange" form of the money-making art. Third, while the natural art of exchange occurs through a direct exchange of the useful things, the money-making art occurs through the exchange of legal-currency. Insofar as Aristotle introduces the money-making art as coming into being according to *logos*, it is *logos* and not nature that provides the money-making art to human beings. Taken together, these three differences between the natural art of exchange and the necessary form of the money-making art show that while *logos* provides legal-currency to produce manageable foreign exchange, *logos* makes this provision without accounting for two natural things: community and self-sufficiency. This leaves readers to wonder what the consequences might be if *logos* fails to provide for community and self-sufficiency, and further, how it might be possible to provide for *logos* so that its provision of the money-making art is according to nature.

## Legal-Currency, the Art of Retail-Trade, and the Redefinition of Wealth (*Politics* 1257b5–31)

With the money-making art's two forms settled as either necessary exchange or the art of retail-trade, Aristotle returns to the idea of wealth, which provides an opening for community and self-sufficiency to offer perspective on the money-making art. In light of the art of retail-trade, Aristotle says, "On account of this the money-making art seems to be about legal-currency most of all, and its work to have the capacity itself to contemplate from where there will be a quantity of useful things (*chrēmata*): for it is productive of wealth and useful things" (1257b5–8). As is often the case with Aristotle's inquiry, what seems to be an argument's linear development is a revealing shift. Because of the art of retail-trade's development, it appears the money-making art's purpose is to produce the most gain in the form of legal-currency under the assumption that legal-currency is synonymous with "useful things" and "wealth." A similar assumption occurs at the beginning of Aristotle's inquiry into the money-making art when he raises the dispute over whether this art is some part of the art of household management, or another form. The dispute arises from the money-maker contemplating from where useful things, acquisition, and wealth come. Because acquisition and wealth encompass many parts, Aristotle wonders if the art of farming and in general the care of food and acquisition is part of the money-making art. Though both arguments concern contemplating useful things and wealth, careful readers should notice a change in the later argument: it omits "acquisition." This omission suggests why the art of retail-trade is the form of the money-making art that is not by nature, for in producing gain, this art could fail to provide for the care of food, an acquisition that nature itself gives to all animals and human beings.[33]

The preceding comparison between the two passages about what the money-maker and money-making art contemplate reveal Aristotle's fundamental concern with this art is how it affects contemplation. The far-reaching consequences of this contemplation are evident in the idea of wealth. Earlier, Aristotle defines "true wealth" as a store of things necessary for living and useful (*chrēsimos*) for community in a household or a city, and "wealth" as "a multitude of tools for household managers and politicians." Between these definitions, Aristotle presents competing arguments about limits to wealth. While the self-sufficiency of such acquisition as "true wealth" is not without-limit (*apeiron*) toward good living, Solon says there is no limit (*terma*) to wealth. This leads Aristotle to entertain the possibility that arts derive limits from the size and quantity of their tools not being without-limit.[34] Since the money-maker and the money-making art contemplate wealth, the distinction between "true wealth" and "wealth" uncovers contemplation's work in money-making concerns limits to the acquisition of wealth.

Taking some time to unfold Aristotle's grounds for the distinction between "true wealth" and "wealth" uncovers the different contemplative approaches to money-making. To begin, "true wealth" relates to community in a city or a household, while "wealth" relates to persons who in some way rule communities (i.e., politicians and household managers). Next, "true wealth" consists of things necessary for living and useful for community, while "wealth" is a multitude of tools neither deemed necessary for living, nor useful for community. The application of this distinction to legal-currency is immediately apparent: it is a tool used for the exchange of useful and necessary things, but on its own is neither necessary for living, nor useful for community because its sole purpose is to produce more manageable exchanges. This last point may be paradoxical considering the foreign exchange facilitated by legal-currency is analogous to the natural art of exchange that occurs between households.[35] Aristotle's definition of "true wealth" provides some clarification. What makes wealth "true" is clear ties to necessity: wealth is a form of acquisition, acquisition is necessary for living, and because living for nearly all human beings requires some form of community, wealth is useful to communities' capacity to help human beings live. In short, community provides the necessary context for understanding wealth's natural purpose. The separation of wealth from community enabled by legal-currency is a false understanding of wealth, one that mistakes a tool (a means) as an end. Community, in contrast, uses wealth in pursuit of self-sufficiency toward good living, thus providing an end that keeps one from thinking the acquisition of wealth is without-limit. Aristotle is consistent on this point: though households and cities need acquisition for the sake of self-sufficiency, acquisition is not what holds these communities together. Communities may use wealth, but it is not the foundation of community itself.

When holding Aristotle's definitions of "true wealth" and "wealth" alongside what the money-maker and money-making art contemplate, questions about the relationship between art and nature come into clearer focus. Aristotle introduces his distinction between "true wealth" and "wealth" by stating there is need for a form of the art of acquisition that is naturally part of the art of household management either to be present, or to provide this art so there is "true wealth" in a city or a household. Despite ambiguity over whether the foreign exchange facilitated by the legal-currency in the money-making art occurs between cities like the natural art of exchange occurs between households close to each other, Aristotle is clear that both the household and the city need an art of acquisition. The source of this art's need is nature itself, which does not equally distribute the necessary things.[36] Nature provides the need for exchange, but not exchange. It belongs to human beings to ensure there is an art of acquisition present to acquire the necessary things, an art they need to provide to their communities.

The confusion among arts of acquisition points to a foundation for the arts that provides a clearer path to aligning them with nature. Human beings' mixing of arts is akin to their pleasant mixing of lives for the natural acquisition of food. This mixing is similar to the way nature produces different lives among the animals, marking-the-boundaries of their lives toward the easiness and choosing of food. Nature's bounding is evident through the same thing not being pleasant according to nature for each animal.[37] To provide an art of acquisition that is according to nature and ensures wealth is not without-limit, one must provide for whatever it is in human beings that is responsible for choosing and the pleasant, something that is neither strictly with or without *logos*.

While legal-currency can distort the natural basis of wealth and the money-making art, Aristotle is careful to show this is not a necessary consequence of discovering legal-currency. On the one hand, wealth is "set-down" (or "established," *tithēmi*) as a quantity of legal-currency, and because of this, legal-currency seems to be the concern of the money-making art and the art of retail-trade. On the other hand, "legal-currency seems to be mere trash and altogether law (*nomos*), not at all by nature" (1257b8–11). Recall that the money-making art came into being according to *logos* out of the necessity to provide legal-currency to produce the easier foreign exchange of things necessary according to nature. If there are two possibilities for legal-currency—either provided according to nature, or not at all by nature—each possibility owes its origin to some *logos* that is either natural or unnatural.

To explain why legal-currency seems to be altogether law and not at all by nature, Aristotle notes that when those using legal-currency "change-the-setting-down" (*metatithēmi*, in the sense of changing something established) of the currency itself, it has no "worth" (*axios*), is not at all useful toward the necessary things, and someone who is wealthy in legal-currency often will be unprovided (*aporeō*) in necessary food (1257b11–14). The criticism of legal-currency is twofold. The first criticism relates to the currency itself. As the verb for "change-the-setting-down" (*metatithēmi*) indicates, legal-currency's worth is "set-down" (*tithēmi*), and therefore changeable by setting-down another form of it. Given how easy it is to render legal-currency worthless, there is something persuasive about treating it as trash with worth only through law. The second criticism of legal-currency points readers back to the development of acquisition. Though law sets-down legal-currency's worth, that worth derives from people providing legal-currency according to *logos* by "setting-down-together an agreement" (*suntithēmi*) to give and take for necessary exchange things like iron or silver that hold a manageable need or use toward living. Both wealth and legal-currency are things provided by being set-down, a work that needs *logos*. If legal-currency provides for necessary food and the exchange of things used or needed for living, the *logos* setting it down is according to nature. But if legal-currency's worth comes to be apart from necessary exchange, the *logos* setting it down is contrary to nature, leaving readers to wonder why the *logos* takes on this character.

The recognition that legal-currency should not be synonymous with wealth is also evident in myth. After noting it is strange "to be well-provided" (*euporeō*) in wealth but to "perish" or "destroy" (*apollumi*) oneself from hunger, Aristotle cites the example of Midas for whom all things "set-down-before" (*paratithēmi*) himself come to be gold through the insatiable greed of his prayer (1257b14–17). The myth of Midas has the advantage of showing readers' common awareness that there is more to wealth than legal-currency. Nevertheless, a more philosophic argument remains embedded within the mythical allusion. The term Aristotle uses for "set-down-before" (*paratithēmi*) reinforces the theme of wealth and legal-currency being things set-down. While law sets-down legal-currency's worth, for Midas, the destructive change in all things "set-down-before" himself comes through the insatiable greed of his prayer. Together, the two passages point to a deeper problem regarding legal-currency's worth. Though this worth can be set-down in law and seem to be nothing, it is not the laws that are destructive, but the character of the person who—on account of something insatiable in oneself that affects one's own *logos*—turns away from what is natural and necessary for living and destroys oneself.

The preceding examination of wealth and the money-making art allows Aristotle to clarify the art of household management's concern. The strangeness of being well-provided in legal-currency yet unprovided in food leads Aristotle to comment that others correctly (*orthōs*) seek some other wealth and money-making art. On the one hand, there is the money-making art and wealth that is according to nature, and this is the art of household management. On the other hand, there is the art of retail-trade that is productive of useful things not from all things, but through "change" or "exchange" (*metabolē*) of useful things (1257b17–22). The ambiguity of the term Aristotle uses for "change" or "exchange" builds on his attempt to show the money-making art and its use of legal-currency are not necessarily detached from human beings' natural need for acquisition. If developed far enough, the art of retail-trade can alter people's understanding of useful things' ends (i.e., not as living and good living, but gain). Presumably the art of household management can draw the money-making art and wealth back toward nature, though ambiguity returns over whether these two arts are synonymous.

Looking further into how the art of retail-trade comes to pursue the gain of legal-currency, Aristotle turns to the relationship between arts and their ends. Because the art of retail-trade is productive of useful things through their "change" or "exchange," "it seems to be about legal-currency, for legal-currency is an element and a limit of the exchange (*allagē*)" (1257b22–23).[38] Though there are several terms Aristotle uses for "exchange," his use of *allagē* in this passage indicates the term refers to the general act of things changing hands.[39] Thus, in the art of retail-trade, what changes hands is legal-currency, which comes to be "an element and a limit of the exchange" because it is a more manageable thing to carry and exchange than the things that are necessary according to nature. Within the art of retail-trade's exchange of legal-currency, the wealth from this money-making art—which, it bears repeating, is different from the money-making art defined by necessary exchange—is indeed without-limit (1257b23–24). This argument about the acquisition of legal-currency being a form of wealth without-limit appears to contradict Aristotle's earlier argument that implies the size and quantity of an art's tool limits the amount of wealth when understood as "a multitude of tools for household managers and politicians."[40] On the one hand, this argument stands on its own since there is no such thing as an infinite amount of wealth (while theoretically possible, it is practically true that nothing human beings produce is infinite). On the other hand, since the amount of legal-currency one acquires through the art of retail-trade is without-limit, tools' size and quantity is no longer a sufficient limiting principle for the arts.[41]

With tools' failure to limit arts now apparent, Aristotle turns to ends, saying:

> For just as the medical art is without-limit with respect to being healthy, and each of the arts is without-limit with respect to its end (on the grounds that they themselves most of all wish to produce that [end]), yet with respect to the things towards the end [they are] not without-limit (for the end [is] a limit to all of them), and thus there is not a limit to the end of this money-making art, and an end [is] such wealth and acquisition of useful things. (1257b25–30)[42]

Since the argument concludes with Aristotle asserting there is no limit to "such wealth and acquisition of useful things" in the art of retail-trade, it appears as if even ends are not limiting principles. Indeed, given the length of the argument, its conclusions are puzzling, and so each step of the argument requires careful attention. To start, Aristotle's observation about the medical art states something intuitive: the medical art always aims to produce healthy human beings, and there is no single point at which the medical art can stop producing healthy human beings because this need is always present. From the medical art, it follows that each of the arts is without-limit with respect to its end because it is the "wish" of each art to produce its respective end. In ascribing a "wish" to the arts, Aristotle alludes to a question worth keeping in mind: To what extent are arts capable of "producing" their ends? For example, if most human beings turn to the medical art because of illness or injury, does the medical art "produce" health in the patient, or restore the patient to the healthy condition that preceded the illness or the injury? The answer to this question may be implicit in Aristotle's discussion of how ends set limits to the means arts can use to "produce" their ends. Since the end of the medical art is health, certain things (such as poisonous and lethal substances) cannot "produce" health because they only produce sickness and death. Now, this does not preclude the possibility that the medical art can make advances in the means of promoting health. Indeed, in the millennia since Aristotle's writing, a limit to advances in medicines and treatments available to the medical art has yet to emerge. Still, the limit to all these means is they must promote health, otherwise they cannot be part of the medical art.

Turning to how these lessons apply to the money-making art, notice how Aristotle qualifies the money-making art he addresses as "this money-making art," which in the context is the art of retail-trade. Aristotle reinforces his choice to speak of one form of the money-making art by adding it is without-limit in relation to "an end" in an indefinite sense. In the case of the art of retail-trade, its end is "such wealth and acquisition of useful things," namely, legal-currency. While the art of retail-trade understands wealth and acquisition solely in terms of legal-currency, Aristotle's definition of "true wealth" as an acquisition whose self-sufficiency is not without-limit toward good living—combined with his presentation of the money-making art as initially associated with necessary exchange of useful things toward living—mean one could understand the money-making art in relation to ends that have natural limits not in the arts and their tools, but in certain ways of living.

With the relationship between arts and ends clarified, Aristotle solidifies the distinction between the money-making art and the art of household management. As opposed to the money-making art defined through the art of retail-trade that is without-limit toward its end of acquiring and producing legal-currency through the exchange of useful things, there is a limit belonging to the art of household management, for its work is not the money-making art's (1257b30–31). Aristotle's distinction recalls the first unprovided questions about the relationship between the arts of money-making and household-management concerning how the art of household management's work "brings to an end" and uses what the money-making art provides. The clarity Aristotle provides on the art of retail-trade's work sharpens the distinction between the natural and unnatural money-making art *and* shows there is more to discover about the art of household management's work. When Aristotle introduces the natural art of exchange, he states there is no work for this art in the household where people form-community in all things. With the natural art of exchange, people produce a mutual-giving as is necessary according to their own needs. While people produce exchange itself with the natural art of exchange, through the art of retail-trade, they produce useful things and wealth from the exchange of legal-currency. Whether the money-making art assumes its natural form for producing necessary exchange, or its unnatural form through which it produces the most gain of legal-currency, its work is productive in a way the art of household management's is not.

Through distinguishing the money-making art and the art of household management on the basis of work, Aristotle reveals the relationship between arts and their ends depends on contemplation. Whether it is the money-maker or the money-making art, both share the work of contemplating from where useful things and wealth come, though the art omits acquisition and the care for food when it becomes the art of retail-trade with its end of producing wealth strictly in the form of legal-currency. Although the preceding arguments settle distinctions between forms of the money-making art and state the art of household management's work is not the same as the art of retail-trade's, there is still confusion from Aristotle's statement that the art of household management is the money-making art and wealth that is according to nature. If the household is where people form-community in all things, and if the art of household management's work is to "bring to an end" and use what the money-making art provides through exchange, then the art of household management's contemplation must focus on a natural end that provides for community, a limit to the acquisition of wealth, and direction on its use.

## LAW AND THE CONTEMPLATIVE FOUNDATIONS OF ARTS AND COMMUNITIES (*POLITICS* 1253B1–23, 1255B37–1256A3, 1255A3–B4)

Before proceeding with how Aristotle alleviates the confusion between the arts of household management and money-making, it is worth looking back at his outline of the arts belonging to household management (*oikonomia*) from Book I's third chapter in the *Politics* to find a characteristic of community within the household that could establish limits to wealth and inform its use. After stating that it is apparent in the *Politics*' first two chapters from what parts the city is set-standing-together (*sunistēmi*), the fact that every city "composes" (*sunkeimai*)[43] itself from households means it is necessary to speak of household management, the parts of which are from the things that set-standing-together the household. The "complete household" (*oikia teleios*) is from slaves and free persons (*eleutheros*), and the first and smallest parts of the household are the master and slave, husband and wife, and father and children. Related to these three parts of the household are the arts of mastery, marrying, and child-bearing, with the latter two arts being without a name. But there seems to be some other art—calling itself "the money-making art"—that seems to some people to be some part of household management, and to others seems to be the greatest part of household management. How this holds is something "one-must-contemplate" (*theōrēteon*) (1253b1–14). Since its introduction to the *Politics*, Aristotle approaches the money-making art as a matter for contemplation in the context of community. Although the inquiry into the money-making art starting in Book I's eighth chapter imitates the art's introduction by setting it alongside other arts, before Aristotle introduces this art to his work, he begins by outlining the persons who set-standing-together the "complete household" (slaves or free persons). In contemplating the money-making art's relation to the art of household management, one must contemplate if it is natural for the art of household management's end to form-community with both slaves and free persons.

Between Aristotle's introduction of the money-making art to the *Politics* and his full inquiry into the money-making art is an inquiry into mastery and slavery. The placement of this latter inquiry suggests it is necessary for understanding how the money-making art holds in relation to the art of household management.[44] The ties between these two inquiries are explicit when one looks at how the inquiry into mastery and slavery ends alongside the way the inquiry into the money-making art begins. For the inquiry into mastery and slavery, Aristotle concludes that the art of acquisition—specifically, "the just" (*dikaia*) art of acquisition, which is either some "art of war" (*polemikē*) or an "art of hunting" (*thēreutikē*)—is different than the "sciences" (*epistēmē*) of mastery and slavery that concern the use and not the acquiring of slaves. It is in this manner that the inquiry marks-the-boundary concerning the slave and the master (1255b37–40).[45] Acknowledging that the difference between an art and a science receives attention elsewhere in Aristotle's political philosophy and is a subject for later chapters, for the purposes of distinguishing the art of household management from the money-making art, what is immediately relevant regarding community in the household is whether the acquisition of slaves is natural. In setting the "just" art of acquisition apart from the supposed sciences of mastery and slavery, Aristotle quietly makes the significant argument that there is an unjust art of acquisition associated with the sciences of mastery and slavery.

At the beginning of his inquiry into the money-making art, Aristotle says "let us contemplate" all of acquisition since the slave is some part of acquisition (1256a1–3). Looking back at the three arts related to household management in light of this passage, it is clearer why the arts related to the free parts of the household (i.e., the arts of marrying and child-bearing related to husbands, wives, and children) lack names while the art of mastery does not: of these parts of the household, only slaves are acquired. Though Aristotle does not say it here, the free parts of the household look to be natural in a way that slaves do not, in part because it is odd to think of spouses and children as acquisitions. Indeed, nature seems to provide the free persons of the household, while only art provides slaves. Slaves, then, might be products of some art of acquisition, an art that is just or unjust depending on whether it is according to nature. If the "complete household" is from slaves and free persons, yet slaves become parts of this household by an art of acquisition that is not according to nature, then it is possible that natural community in a complete household exists only among human beings who are free.

The just art of acquisition that could provide slaves to the household seems to appear early in Aristotle's inquiry into the money-making art through the hypothetical argument that draws an errant analogy between war, the art of hunting, and the art of acquisition on the grounds that war is just by nature when used against human beings who are such to be ruled but unwilling.[46] When looking at this argument with an eye toward how it connects to the prior inquiry into mastery and slavery, readers should wonder why Aristotle describes an art of acquisition that some think is just but does not draw the conclusion that this is how human beings acquire slaves. The absence of this conclusion combined with Aristotle's failure to mention any form of community in relation to this art suggests this acquisition is not part of the money-making art and the art of household management. To see why this is true, readers must look back to part of Aristotle's inquiry into slavery.

To set up his inquiry into slavery in the *Politics* (I.4–7), Aristotle describes how for some "being master" (*to despozein*) is against nature, for it is by law that one person is a slave, another free, but this difference is in no way by nature. On account of this, being master is in no way just, for it is "forcible" or "violent" (*biaion*) (1253b20–23). These conflicting arguments about whether being master is by law or by nature reappear in Aristotle's inquiry into the money-making art with the argument that legal-currency seems to be altogether law and not at all by nature. To arrive at this argument, Aristotle notes the money-making art's name is "just" because from this art (which is not by nature but comes to be by some experience and art) there does not seem to be a limit to wealth and acquisition.[47] According to both of these arguments, it is law that sets human beings against nature, in the first case regarding who is free and slave, and in the second case regarding wealth and acquisition. But while this tension arises from experience and art in the money-making art (specifically through the art of retail-trade supplanting the natural money-making art that facilitates necessary exchange), Aristotle does not place the blame on art itself in his inquiry into mastery and slavery, thus suggesting there is a common foundation for art and law.

The law in question about mastery and slavery emerges in the sixth chapter of Book I of the *Politics*, following the previous two chapters' respective inquiries into the nature of the slave, and from this, whether any human being is a master and slave by nature. These inquiries are important for later portions of Aristotle's inquiry into the money-making art and receive consideration in the next chapter, but their significance will be clearer by discovering the shared basis for art and law. Contrary to those who assert being slave is by nature are those who assert these things are according to law, for the law is some "agreement" (*homologia*, literally "same-*logos*") that those conquered by the stronger in war belong to the conquerors who are stronger.[48] Opposing this view of the just are many of those in the laws who move against it like they would move against a rhetorician with a "writ of illegality" (literally a "writing against-laws," *graphontai paranomōn*)[49] on the grounds that it is terrible if that which has the capacity to be forced is slave and ruled according to a "capacity" (*dunamis*) of the strong to be forceful and violent. Among the wise seem to be both views, and a cause of their dispute and what produces "exchange-upon" (*epallassō*) the *logoi* is some way in which "virtue" (*aretē*) happens upon abundant resources and itself has the capacity to be forceful or violent most of all, and the strong always "hold-over" (*huperochē*)[50] in some good. From this, it seems there is no force or violence without virtue, but the dispute concerns only the just, which for some seems to be "without-thought" (*anoia*) or "goodwill" (literally "good-thought," *eunoia*),[51] and to others seems to be the rule of the stronger (1255a3–19). The foundation for law is *logos*, and in this case, the *logos* supporting the law through which human beings become slaves according to force or violence disputes the just while side-stepping questions about virtue and what is good. The implicit assumption of the *logos* in question is that virtue is some good, but why this is true goes unexamined. For his part, Aristotle alludes to the problems this ignorance of virtue and what is good creates. If virtue has the capacity to be forceful or violent to enslave others through happening upon abundant resources, it is without-thought. If virtue has the capacity even without abundant resources, it is unclear if force and violence align with goodwill or good-thought. Finally, if virtue is nothing other than the rule of the stronger, one must wonder if it is only force or violence that makes virtue stronger. Whatever the case may be, Aristotle shows how people use some *logos* about the just to define virtue according to some good (i.e., abundant resources or being strong) that is thoughtless.

Bearing in mind "virtue" does not appear in the first two chapters of Aristotle's inquiry into the money-making art, readers can better sense how its absence in that inquiry is an echo of the dispute in *logos* that neglects the nature of virtue in his inquiry into mastery and slavery. Looking at the dispute about the just, Aristotle declares that if the *logoi* are set-standing-apart, the other *logoi* that there is no need for the better according to virtue to rule and to be master are neither "strong" (*ischuros*), nor do they hold what is "persuasive" or "trustworthy" (*pithanos*) (1255a19–21). Here Aristotle grants through *logos* that there is need for virtue to rule and to be a master, but does not grant virtue a capacity to enslave or be violent. Despite this ignorance of virtue, there are some wholly "holding-themselves-against" (*antechō*) others who set-down that the slavery according to war is just (supposing this is something just because law is something just), yet at the same time do not assert this (1255a21–24). For those who depend on law as the *logos* for the just through which they set-down slavery through war, they are hypocritical in ways that those who hold to a *logos* that declares a need for virtue to rule and be master are not. Before turning to how Aristotle addresses this hypocrisy, remember that he describes the money-making art as coming into being according to *logos* when people "set-down-together an agreement" (*suntithēmi*) to provide legal-currency for exchanges. Through this provision, wealth is eventually set-down (*tithēmi*) as a quantity of legal-currency, which seems to be law and not at all by nature.[52] From the perspective of Aristotle's inquiry into slavery, virtue's absence from the money-making art's provision of legal-currency according to *logos* may explain why it does not seem to be by nature.

The hypocrisy behind the law that sets-down slavery from war as just comes from the fact that the "beginning" or "rule" (*archē*) of wars itself admits of not being just, and no one would assert someone unworthy of being slave should be a slave. Because the well-born would then seem to be slaves through being taken and sold, they themselves do not "wish" (*boulomai*) to say they are slaves, but only the barbarians are. Such people, however, seek the slave by nature, something the inquiry sought from the beginning, for it is necessary for them to assert that some are everywhere slaves, and others are nowhere slaves (1255a24–32). Now Aristotle uncovers a source of the *logos* supporting slavery from war as just is some people's wish to determine who is worthy of being a slave. Because these hypocrites exempt themselves from their own *logos* and do not wish to be slaves (as if anyone has such a wish), Aristotle reminds readers that the only *logos* capable of consistently defining the slave is by nature.

But even this *logos* runs into problems from the manner in which the well-born "customarily-consider" (*nomizō*) they are this way everywhere but barbarians are only well-born at home (*oikoi*), as if there is something on the one hand simply well-born and free, and on the other hand not simply such. Whenever they say this, they mark-the-boundary of the slave and free *and* the well-born and badly-born by nothing other than virtue and vice, "thinking" or "deeming-worthy" (*axioō*)[53] that just as human beings come from human beings and wild animals from wild animals, so too are the good born from the good. Aristotle then concludes his observations in puzzling fashion, saying, "While nature itself often wishes to produce this, nevertheless it lacks the capacity" (1255a32–b4). In looking back over Aristotle's whole account of this argument for slavery according law, this conclusion shows how a *logos* (in this case of the just) can lead people to set-down laws about nature that nature itself does not support. People "wish" for nature to produce human beings in ways that align with their own laws or customs about worth—an idea that invites readers to wonder about the nature of the free, virtue, and good—only to discover nature cannot produce things according to their own wishes.[54]

For readers making their first pass through Book I of Aristotle's *Politics* seeking to understand how the arts of money-making and household management relate to each other, the digression above on the law regarding slavery may seem unnecessary. But these insights regarding law (*nomos*), *logos*, and

nature casts household management (*oikonomia*) in a new light when readers
see the term according to its literal roots as the "laws" or "customs" (*nomos*)
that are set-down to provide for the "household" (*oikos*). Legal-currency
(*nomisma*) seems to be altogether law and not at all by nature because when
people "change-the-setting-down" (*metatithēmi*) of the currency itself, it
has no worth, leading to the strange case of someone like King Midas being
well-provided in wealth but unprovided in necessary food. This is possible,
however, only through developing the art of retail-trade, extended experience
in which leads to people contemplating not how to provide for necessary
exchange, but producing the most gain.[55] This art (which many customarily-
consider to be the same as the natural art of acquisition) can change human
beings' contemplation because while it is something people see at work
through the law, its true foundation is *logos* working to provide for their
natural need for acquisition.

Like the different *logoi* concerning the just and slavery that Aristotle sets-
standing-apart, human beings set-standing-apart the different arts of acquisition (i.e., the natural art of exchange, the art of household management, the
money-making art, and the art of retail-trade). This is akin to how nature
sets-standing-apart the lives of animals by marking-the-boundary of their
lives toward the easiness and choosing (*hairesis*) of foods with the pleasant.[56]
The work of exchange and retail-trade is now clearly the work of art—of
*logos*—and the provision of these arts begins from human beings choosing
through *logos* to live either according to nature or contrary to nature. If there
is confusion about the arts of money-making and household management, it
originates in how people choose to provide for themselves, a natural work
that depends on the interaction between *logos*, the pleasant, and the arts.

## USE, HUMAN NATURE, AND THE CONFUSION
## BETWEEN THE ARTS OF HOUSEHOLD MANAGEMENT
## AND MONEY-MAKING (*POLITICS* 1257B32–1258A14)

Picking back up the thread of Aristotle's inquiry into the money-making art,
although he establishes the art of retail-trade works toward the end of acquiring legal-currency without-limit, the art of household management's end is
unknown. This uncertainty leads to some confusion over the two arts' ends,
for while the art of household management's work makes it appear necessary
for there to be a limit to all wealth, all those "engaging in money-making"
(*chrēmatizō*) increase legal-currency without-limit. The cause is these two
money-making arts' nearness to one another, exchanging-upon themselves
the use of the same thing (1257b32–36). The money-making art and the
art of household-management's exchange-upon use echoes the dispute

among the wise over the law about slavery according to law where there is exchange–upon the *logoi* because of virtue and some good.[57] What increases the confusion of the exchange–upon use is the art of household management's placement in the category of the money-making art, which is itself divided into a form bearing this name associated with necessary exchange, and the art of retail-trade that seeks to produce the most gain without-limit. This added confusion means use is insufficient for finding a firm distinction between these arts, forcing readers to look for something more fundamental.[58]

With use settled as the point of confusion between the arts of household management and retail-trade, Aristotle sets the stage for further thinking about the relationship between arts and ends. Whether it is the art of household management or the art of retail-trade, "It is a use of the same acquisition, though not according to the same [end], but of the one [use or art it is] another end, and of the other [use or art] increase [is the end]" (1257b36–38).[59] Once again, Aristotle casts doubt on the earlier argument that tools limit their arts,[60] for if tools truly limit their arts, then the arts of household management and the art of retail-trade would have the same limit since they use the same acquisition (legal-currency). Because those practicing the art of retail-trade increase legal-currency without-limit, it seems to some that increase is the art of household management's work, and they go "through-to-the-end" (*diateleō*)[61] supposing there is need either to preserve or increase the "substance" or "property" (*ousia*) of legal-currency without-limit (1257b38–40). Though Aristotle remains vague on the art of household management's end, readers know from the many arts of acquisition that there is distance between this art and the art of retail-trade. Between households is the natural art of exchange, which serves as the model for the foreign and necessary exchange facilitated by the money-making art. With experience, the money-making art becomes the art of retail-trade.[62] Through these many arts, the household— the first community in which there is no work for the art of exchange—can become subject to the art of retail-trade's end. But this exchange of the art of household management's work and end for those belonging to the art of retail-trade does not occur because of the arts themselves; rather, the exchange comes from people choosing to work in the art of household management as if it is the art of retail-trade.[63]

Since the confusion between the arts of household management and retail-trade hinges on the use of the acquisition of legal-currency, an earlier argument about the two uses of acquisition may help show how Aristotle's juxtaposition of these two arts allows readers to discover which is more natural. Every piece of acquisition has a proper (*oikeia*) and improper (*ouk oikeia*) use (i.e., the wearing of a shoe and the "exchange" of it, respectively). Notice the kinship between these terms and "the art of household management," *oikonomikē*. The proper use of a piece of acquisition seems tied to the household, the community according to nature set-standing-together for every day, whereas the village is a community of households for the sake of a non-daily use.[64] The household's need to use acquisitions is constant, but its need to acquire them is not. The proper use of things relates to this constant need, while their improper use is their exchange (*metablētikē*) provided by the money-making art. Households make use of acquisition through the money-making art as needed, but it is a mistake for those working in the art of household management to exchange the use of things from what is proper to their community's constant need for an improper use detached from this need. Since legal-currency relates to a piece of acquisition's improper use, a view of wealth bound solely to this does not necessarily correspond to useful things that communities need. This is significant because the word for the "money-making art" (*chrēmatistikē*) has at its root the term for "useful things" (*chrēmata*), which itself derives from *chrē*, "need" (Liddell and Scott 1889, 893). The natural foundation for the money-making art is human need, and this art is naturally useful when providing for this need. If some arts are necessary to provide for the related human needs of useful things and communities, then there must be an end that provides directly for human need.

Although details are scarce on the natural end Aristotle has in mind for the arts of acquisition and communities, he provides readers insights into what this end must address by considering two related mistakes people make regarding their own need. One cause for people exchanging the art of household management's work for the art of retail-trade's increase of legal-currency without-limit is their "setting-down-through" (*diathesis*, in the sense of "disposition")[65] themselves "to be serious" (*spoudazō*) more about living, but not living well. Because this "desire" (*epithumia*) is without-limit, they "desire" (*epithumeō*) the things productive of what is without-limit (1257b40-1258a2). This passage marks the first and only appearance of "desire" in Aristotle's inquiry into the money-making art, but its role is significant since this characteristic of human nature is partly responsible for confusion about the arts of household management and retail-trade. But desire alone does not cause this confusion about the arts, for it accompanies people being more serious about living than living well. These two ideas appear together in Book I of the *Politics*' fourth chapter when Aristotle first asserts the art of acquisition is part of household management because both living and living well are impossible without the necessary things, and prior to this, in Book I's second chapter with the statement that the city comes into being on the one hand for the sake of living, and on the other hand for the sake of living well.[66] In all these passages, whether the community is the household or the city, Aristotle speaks to the need to understand living and living well together, which suggests it is a mistake to think first of satisfying the needs of living, then discern what constitutes living well. Looking at all these passages together, readers see that the natural foundation for arts and communities is people "setting-down-through" themselves some disposition toward living and living well that incorporates desire, which is without-limit.

In finding the art of household management takes on the art of retail-trade's end (the increase of legal-currency without-limit) through desire itself being without-limit, Aristotle suggests this confusion about arts of acquisition is one instance of a much broader problem within human nature. The question concerns what human beings are "setting-down-through" themselves to encourage desire. The term for "setting-down-through" (*diathesis*) derives from the verb "to-set-down-through" (*diatithēmi*), whose root is "to-set-down" (*tithēmi*). In Aristotle's inquiry into the money-making art, legal-currency is something set-down in law that is either by nature or not by nature depending on whether it makes human beings well-provided or unprovided in necessary things. Because the money-making art comes into being according to *logos*, and since the art of household management and the art of retail-trade differ on whether wealth has a limit,[67] the fact that all art is *logos* means the cause of people's "setting-down-through" themselves either art's end is the interaction between *logos* and desire. In the present case, desire being without-limit finds its match in the art of retail-trade's *logos* that wealth is without-limit. While one could remedy this error by adopting the art of household management's *logos* through which it is necessary for there to be a limit to wealth, readers must be cognizant that the broader problem to which Aristotle alludes is the need to find a comprehensive *logos* that provides a limit to all desire.

Although the remedy to the desire for living that is without-limit would seem to be looking toward living well as the end, this too is insufficient. Because those who throw themselves toward living well seek the things toward bodily "enjoyments" (*apolausis*) that are apparently in acquisitions, all their "way of spending time" (*diatribē*) is money-making. From this comes the other form of the money-making art (i.e., the art of retail-trade) (1258a2–6). This mistake about living well is understandable. After all, human beings' bodily need for food is the natural foundation for all acquisition. The problem of bodily enjoyments creeps into the picture by turning human beings' pleasant mixing of lives that hold their work in relation to natural food in pursuit of the self-sufficient toward exchange and retail-trade.[68] In this way, the art and *logos* of retail-trade coopts human beings' naturally pleasant mixing of lives to displace the natural acquisition and care for food with money-making through the allure of bodily enjoyments.

Adding nuance to this mistake about living well, Aristotle specifies that the enjoyments people seek are in "excess" (*huperbolē*), and so they seek what is productive of excess enjoyment. If the money-making art does not have the capacity to provide this excess to those seeking it, they "make-an-attempt" (*peiraō*) at another cause using each of their capacities in a way that is not according to nature (1258a6–10). Though Aristotle introduces the problem of enjoyment as a bodily one, it is now about "excess," which reaches all human capacities. "Courage" (*andreia*), for example, produces boldness, not useful things (*chrēmata*). Similarly, the arts of generalship and medicine do not produce useful things, but victory and health, respectively. But to those who mistake living well as the pursuit of excess in enjoyments, they produce all things to be money-makings, as if this is the end toward which all things need directing (1258a10–14). The common ground between courage (which Aristotle does not present as a virtue here as he does in the *Nicomachean Ethics*)[69] and the arts is they are all human capacities that produce different ends for human beings. Money-making, however, supplants these ends, but how? In addition to the enticing nature of enjoyment, remember that the money-making art's work is "to have the capacity itself to contemplate" sources of useful things since it is productive of wealth and useful things. Through the art of retail-trade, it *seems* the money-making art's concern is legal-currency most of all.[70] Money-making becomes the end of all things and the basis for people using their capacities contrary to nature because the art of retail-trade provides the capacity to contemplate what produces excess, a capacity nature does not provide to human beings. Readers must wonder, however, what is the end that leads human beings to use their capacities according to nature, and how to provide this without seeking what produces excess enjoyment.

## CONCLUSION: THE MONEY-MAKING ART'S NATURAL BOUNDARY AND THE GOOD (*POLITICS* 1258A14–19)

Despite subtly opening his inquiry into the money-making art's horizons to the end toward which all things need directing, Aristotle draws narrow conclusions about the relationship between the arts of household management and money-making to close the first half of this inquiry. First, Aristotle concludes that the inquiry states what the "unnecessary money-making art" (*mē anankē chrēmatistikē*) is and the cause of its need or use (*chreia*). Second, the unnecessary money-making art is distinct from the necessary money-making art, an art of household management according to nature that concerns food, which is not without-limit but holds a "boundary" (*horos*) (1258a14–19). The "unnecessary money-making art" is the art of retail-trade that produces gain to increase legal-currency without-limit, and its cause is a combination of human beings "setting-down-through-themselves" a desire without-limit for living but not living well, or a view of living well that either seeks bodily enjoyments, or an excess of enjoyments. Though it is not surprising for Aristotle to present the art of household-management as the necessary money-making art, this conclusion differs in two ways from the arguments initiating it. First, whereas the art of household management makes it appear necessary for there to be a limit to all wealth, the distinction between the necessary and unnecessary money-making arts omits speaking of wealth in favor of food, the first natural acquisition. Second, to focus on this natural acquisition, Aristotle exchanges "limit" for "boundary," though the reasons for this change are not yet evident in his inquiry.

By distinguishing the arts of household management and retail-trade as necessary and unnecessary money-making arts, respectively, Aristotle obscures the status of the necessary exchange through which the money-making art (along with legal-currency) first comes into being out of necessity when exchange moves beyond households close to one another and there is need for more foreign sources of help. This obscurity seems tied to the status of the city in relation to the money-making art, with "city" only appearing once in the first half of Aristotle's inquiry in his definition of "true wealth," the acquisition whose self-sufficiency is not without-limit toward "good living."[71] But through describing how people's mistakes about living and living well cause the unnecessary money-making art, Aristotle reminds readers of how the city comes into being on the one hand for the sake of living, and other hand for the sake of living well. The precondition for this is a community of villages (which are themselves communities of households) "holding the limit of every self-sufficiency, so to speak," and it is partially on these grounds that self-sufficiency is—like nature—an end (1252b27–1253a1). In the chapters ahead, there is much to unpack regarding "self-sufficiency" in Aristotle's political philosophy. For now, readers should notice that while Aristotle is consistent in presenting self-sufficiency in relation to community in Book I of the *Politics*, when this idea appears in his inquiry into the money-making art, it seems to be toward another end, namely, "good living." The shift suggests there is something about the inquiry into the money-making art that moves human beings closer to nature's ends than Book I's inquiry into communities, and this shift may shed light on the city's relationship to the money-making art.

Aristotle's statement about self-sufficiency toward "good living" marks the only appearance of "good" (*agathos*) in his inquiry into the money-making art. Although Aristotle does not declare in this inquiry that the good is the natural end to direct human need, it is implicit in how the arts of household management and money-making "exchange-upon" one another through use of legal-currency (the former art making it appear that there is a necessary limit to wealth, and the latter art increasing wealth without-limit). The competing *logoi* of slavery by law "exchange-upon" one another because of virtue and "some good," yet these *logoi* do not hold up because when one looks to nature to see if the good are born from the good, one finds nature does not have the capacity to produce human beings in this way.[72] In discovering the art of retail-trade's cause resides in desire that is without-limit *and* seeking excess enjoyment by using one's own capacities not according to nature so that they are productive of money-making that is without-limit, readers learn that nature alone is not the cause of how human beings choose to live. Because all art is *logos*, Aristotle's uncovering of how human beings adapt themselves to the art of retail-trade's end shows they choose to live according to a *logos* that directs them toward some good that may or may not be according to nature. Is it not possible that there is a *logos* of the good according to nature toward which human beings can direct all things they do? Might the good itself provide a limit for their desires, and in this way be the "boundary" they need to hold? In searching for Aristotle's economic teaching in his inquiry into the money-making art, readers must be attentive to how this inquiry is part of his political philosophy's search for the good at which all things aim.

*Chapter 2*

# Liberating Household Management and Political Life from Money-Making

At the beginning of his inquiry into the money-making art in Book I, chapter 8 of the *Politics*, Aristotle presents two general sets of questions. The first set of questions concerns the relationship between the money-making art (*chrēmatistikē*) and the art of household management (*oikonomikē*), and the second set concerns the sources of acquisition (*ktēsis*), wealth (*ploutos*), useful things (*chrēmata*) that the money-maker contemplates (*theōreō*). In pursuing the second set of questions in the first half of his inquiry into the money-making art (I.8–9), Aristotle settles on a distinction between necessary and unnecessary money-making arts—the arts of household management and retail-trade (*kapēlikē*), respectively—whose different ends are evident in their use of legal-currency in ways that either hold there is a limit (*peras*) and boundary (*horos*) to wealth, or seek to increase wealth without-limit (*apeiron*). To arrive at this distinction, Aristotle shows these arts' foundations reside in human beings' "setting-down-through" (*diathesis*) themselves their desires (*epithumia*) and enjoyments as if money-making is the end (*telos*) of all things.[1] Only after this discovery does Aristotle turn to the first set of questions about the money-making art in his second half of the inquiry (I.10–11), an approach that suggests questions about the arts must find their way back to questions about human nature and its ends.

Initiating the second half of his inquiry into the money-making art, Aristotle seems to return to "the unprovided" (*to aporoumenon*) question from the beginning (*archē*) of the inquiry concerning whether the money-making art is part of the art of household management, but reframes it to ask if the money-making art belongs to the household manager (*oikonomikos*) or the politician (*politikos*), or if it needs to be present to him (1258a19–21).[2] Despite continuity in being unprovided about the money-making art at the start of each half of the inquiry, the second half's unprovided question not only shifts its focus toward persons practicing arts, but brings the politician into the mix. Drawing an analogy between the politician and the household manager, Aristotle introduces the "political art" (*hē politikē*) to the *Politics*, saying, "For just as the political art does not produce human beings, but takes them from nature (*phusis*) to use them, in this way nature needs to give over land, sea, or something else for food, and from these things, there is need to-set-down-through (*diatithēmi*) [them] as befits the household manager" (1258a21–25).[3] At first glance, this argument's conclusion looks simple: nature gives food to household managers for them to use in a way that aligns with the art of household management, in which case household managers practice the necessary money-making art that is not without-limit but holds a boundary. One could even take this argument as the logical conclusion to the account of how human beings pleasantly mix lives (*bios*) that hold their work (*ergasia*) in relation to what is natural to provide food in pursuit of the self-sufficient (*autarchēs*) as "need necessitates" (*chreia sunankazō*).[4] What complicates the argument is Aristotle's analogy between this natural acquisition that is supposedly the art of household management and the political art, for this invites readers to wonder what it means to take human beings from nature and use them just like they would take food from nature and use it.

Aristotle's unprovided question about household managers and politicians thus turns his inquiry into the money-making art toward questions of rule, compelling readers once again to be mindful of how this inquiry fits into Book I of the *Politics*' broader context. At the beginning of the *Politics*, after some preliminary observations about communities, cities, and the good (all of which receive careful attention in this book's fourth chapter), Aristotle says that those who suppose the "political-ruler" (or politician), "kingly-ruler" (*basilikos*), "household manager," and "master" (*despotikos*) are the same do not speak "nobly" (*kalōs*), for they "customarily-consider" (*nomizō*) that these rulers do not "differ" (*diapherō*) in "form" (*eidos*), but only in being over few or many, as if there is no difference between a big household and a small city (1252a1–13). Within Aristotle's inquiry into the money-making art, answering the unprovided question concerning whether this art either belongs or must be present to the household manager or politician requires accounting for how these rulers differ in form, a difference bound to the nature of how these persons rule.

In approaching economics and politics with a mind toward questions of rule, readers may naturally wonder what produces freedom in these practical matters. Although it seems freedom depends largely on the ordering of economic exchange and political communities, Aristotle aims to provide readers a deeper, natural sense of freedom in Book I of the *Politics*. By reading the second half of the *Politics*' inquiry into the money-making art (I.10–11) along with a more thorough look at the inquiry into slavery (I.4–7), readers learn that while acquisition and exchange are naturally subordinate to the rule of households and cities, economics and politics also need to be subordinate to human beings' natural sense of the good. Though freedom and slavery may manifest themselves in forms of rule, in Aristotle's political philosophy, their true beginning is within the human soul, and the use of economics and politics reflect a choice of how to live. The contemplative character of Aristotle's inquiries into money-making and slavery points to how political philosophy is necessary for the preservation of freedom in economics and politics, primarily through persistent and gentle reminders to readers that every practical pursuit depends on some *logos* of a good that may or may not be according to nature.

## THE ART OF HOUSEHOLD MANAGEMENT, THE POLITICAL ART, AND THE IDEA OF SUBORDINATE ARTS (*POLITICS* 1253B23–1254A17, 1258A19–34)

The first unprovided question in Aristotle's inquiry into the money-making art concerns whether this art is the same as the art of household management, part of it, or "subordinate" (*hupēretikē*). If subordinate, the nature of this subordination is unclear: Does the money-making art hold-forth (*parechō*) tools to the art of household management, or the raw material this art itself "brings to an end" (*apoteleō*) through its work (*ergon*)?[5] At the halfway mark of Aristotle's inquiry, the art of household management is a necessary money-making art distinct from the art of retail-trade (the unnecessary money-making art); the art of household management is also distinct from the money-making art that facilitates necessary exchange. But by describing the art of household management as a money-making art and leaving the status of the money-making art associated with necessary exchange uncertain, readers enter the second half of Aristotle's inquiry unprovided about the relationship between these two arts. Though there is good reason to think the money-making art is not the same as the art of household management, there is ambiguity over why this is true. Obscurity also remains regarding whether the money-making art is part of the art of household management. To gain clarity on these questions, it is helpful to focus on the questions about the money-making art's subordination in light of a fundamental insight about human life from Aristotle's inquiry into slavery.

In the first chapter of the *Politics*' inquiry into slavery (I.4), Aristotle sets out to determine what a slave is before taking up questions surrounding the slave by nature and law in the inquiry's subsequent chapters (I.5–6). Beginning with the observations that acquisition is part of the household (*oikia*) and the art of acquisition (*ktētikē*) is part of household management (*oikonomia*) because both living (*zēn*) and living well (*eu zēn*) are impossible without the necessary things, Aristotle draws an analogy between "the boundary-marked arts" (*hai hōrismenai technai*) and the household manager: just as it is necessary for the "proper tools" (*tas oikeias organas*) to be present for the arts to bring to an end their work, so too is it this way for the household manager. Tools are either "without-soul" (*apsuchon*) or "ensouled" (*empsuchon*), and the subordinate is a form of tool in the arts. From these observations, Aristotle concludes, "A piece of acquisition (*ktēma*) is a tool toward living, and acquisition is a multitude of tools, and the slave is some ensouled piece of acquisition, just as every subordinate [is] a tool before tools" (1253b23–33). If slaves belong among "a multitude of tools," they fit Aristotle's definition of "wealth"—"a multitude of tools for household managers and politicians"—from his inquiry into the money-making art. This also means that slaves do not fit Aristotle's definition of "true wealth"—"a store of such useful things that are necessary towards living, and useful to community in a city or a household"—a sort of acquisition whose self-sufficiency is not without-limit toward "good living" (*agathēn zōēn*).[6] If slaves belong to "wealth" and not "true wealth," they are neither necessary for living, nor useful to community in a city or a household. If slaves are present in the city or the household, it is because these communities' rulers mistakenly think they need slaves. If the self-sufficiency of "true wealth" is toward "good living," then the rulers who use slaves do not understand what makes life "good."

To see what household managers and politicians who make use of slaves misunderstand about "good living," it is necessary to consider what makes their understanding of life incomplete. After presenting the slave as a tool before other tools, Aristotle considers one condition under which there would be no need for slaves: if tools themselves either had the capacity "to be exhorted" (*keleuō*) or "have sense-perception beforehand" (*proaisthanomai*) of how to bring to an end their works (such as shuttles weaving by themselves or picks playing the cithara), then "ruling-artisans" (*architektōn*) would not need subordinates, and masters would not need slaves (1253b33–1254a1). Notice how Aristotle's argument emphasizes these rulers' needs for their subordinates, yet says nothing of the subordinates' need for rulers. Since arts exist to produce things, the comparison between masters and ruling-artisans suggests these rulers produce their own need for subordinates. While the need for the ruling-artisan is self-evident in the case of tools without soul because they do not have the capacity to hear exhortations or sense-perception, ensouled tools like the slave have these capacities, thus freeing them from the need for masters. Why, then, do masters think they need to produce slaves?[7]

The possibility that a deficiency in the masters leads them to think they need slaves becomes evident as Aristotle refines what it means for a slave to be a piece of acquisition through a distinction in tools, which are either "productive" (*poiētikos*) or "practical" (*praktikos*) in their use. While the use of a shuttle makes threaded products, with clothing or a bed, there is nothing apart from the use of these things (i.e., wearing or sleeping). Since "action" (*praxis*) and "production" (*poiēsis*) differ in form and need tools, it is necessary for tools to hold these differences. From this necessity, Aristotle concludes, "Life (*bios*) is action, not production, and on account of this the slave is a subordinate of the things towards action" (1254a1–8). From a distinction in tools through their uses, Aristotle uncovers something about the nature of human life and suggests masters make a vital mistake: through thinking they need to use slaves, masters reveal their own incapacity for action and living a truly human life.

Before seeing how Aristotle settles on the definition of the "slave," one should consider how echoes of this argument about life appear in the first half of his inquiry into the money-making art. In the account of natural acquisition, Aristotle suggests human beings choose to provide food through exchange and retail-trade, and such choosing (*hairesis*) involves the pleasant (*hēdus*). To produce more manageable exchanges, human beings provide legal-currency according to *logos*, though to exchange any piece of acquisition is an improper (*ouk oikeia*) use of that thing. Since the slave and legal-currency are pieces of acquisition that are practical and not productive tools, legal-currency is fit only for the action of exchange, not the production of gain (which is how the art of retail-trade misuses legal-currency).[8] If legal-currency becomes a means of production, it is because people using it choose a life that is not according to nature, likely going astray because of an errant *logos* about the pleasant.

From the slave being a subordinate of things toward action, Aristotle offers one further reflection on pieces of acquisition before defining the slave. The way people speak of a piece of acquisition is the same as how they speak of a part, which is not only part of another thing, but wholly belongs to another thing. On account of this, the slave is not only the master's slave, but wholly belongs to the master. From this, what the nature and capacity of the slave is clear, for the slave is a human being who—while a human being—does not by nature belong to oneself but to another person as a piece of acquisition, a tool that is practical and "separable" (*chōristos*) (1254a8–17). Aristotle frames this definition as a deduction about the nature and capacity of the slave from the preceding considerations about subordinate tools and pieces of acquisition, and it hinges upon the assumption that a human being can be a piece of acquisition and still be human. Consequently, Aristotle's definition stands or falls according to the nature and capacity of human beings. Ambiguity on these things is evident in the way Aristotle bridges his arguments about slaves as pieces of acquisition with remarks about how people speak of parts. If parts belong wholly to other things, how is it possible for a slave to belong wholly to a master while being separable? And if the slave must simultaneously be a piece of acquisition and a human being, is the master from whom the slave is separable also a human being?

The confusion about the slave's status as a piece of acquisition that is both a subordinate and part of the master adds complexity to the unprovided questions at the beginning of each half of Aristotle's inquiry into the money-making art. In the inquiry's first half, Aristotle questions if the money-making art is either part of or subordinate to the art of household management. In the second half, Aristotle hearkens back to this question while introducing the politician and the political art to the inquiry as analogous to the household manager and the art of household management.[9] The confusion about the nature and capacity of the slave as a part of the master provides a different character to these unprovided questions. Does the money-making art belong wholly to the art of household management and household manager *and* the political art and the politician, or is it a practical tool that is separable from these arts and rulers?

With these questions in mind, one can return to the unprovided matter that initiates the second half of Aristotle's examination of the money-making art. Elaborating on what it means for the household manager to-set-down-through what nature gives over for food as befits one's rule, Aristotle appeals to the weaving art which does not produce wool itself but only uses wool, and further, "knows" (*gignōskō*) what sort is useful and suitable, and what is poor and unsuitable (1258a25–27). The presence of the weaving art in this argument points back to Aristotle's discussion of using shuttles as productive tools in his inquiry into slavery, tools that would dispense with the need for both ruling-artisans and subordinates if they could bring to an end their works by themselves. Together, these two passages suggest that the weaving art knows how to bring to an end its works, knowing the tools and materials that are useful and suitable to produce its products. Broadly speaking, arts have knowledge of ends and means. But by drawing a comparison between the weaving art and the household manager, Aristotle brings further difficulties into his inquiry. If the weaving art is productive and not practical, does this mean the art of household management is productive? This is a strange conclusion in the immediate context since Aristotle's analogy follows his observation about how the household manager acquires food from nature. One wonders, then, if the analogy presents household managers as akin to ruling-artisans and masters who produce a need for subordinates and slaves out of a failure to understand that life is action and not production.

Recognizing the arts are once again a source of confusion, Aristotle concedes one might be unprovided over why the money-making art is part of household management while the medical art is not when there is need for those in the household to be healthy, just as there is need for living or some other of the necessary things. Although both the household manager and the "ruler" (*archōn*) see to health, there is a sense in which they do not since health is more the doctor's concern. In the same way, the useful things (*chrēmata*) are on the one hand the concern of the household manager, but on the other hand are not and belong to a subordinate (1258a27–34). The same ambiguity over parts and subordinates from Aristotle's inquiry into slavery finds its way into this argument that suggests the money-making art is subordinate to household management because this art holds a direct concern for the useful things not shared by household management. Presumably this means the money-making art is separable from household management, which reiterates the problem of whether something can wholly belong to another thing yet still be separable. Tied to this problem is how the argument begins with the household manager and the ruler in relation to health, presents the doctor as the ruler concerned with health, but concludes without naming the household manager's direct concern, nor the subordinate ruler of the useful things. This omission only heightens the problem of Aristotle's analogy between household managers and politicians, especially since he establishes these rulers differ in form at the beginning of Book I of the *Politics*.

Aristotle's use of the medical art in the preceding unprovided question encourages readers to look back to two arguments from the first half of the inquiry into the money-making art to understand the political questions at stake in the inquiry's second half. The medical art first appears as part of the argument that arts are without-limit toward their ends, an argument that allows Aristotle to assert the art of retail-trade is the form of the money-making art that is without-limit toward wealth and the acquisition of useful things understood in terms of legal-currency. The medical art's second appearance is as an example of an art turned away from its end of health toward money-making because people use their capacities in ways that are not according to nature to provide things productive of excess enjoyment for themselves. This serves as the conclusion to Aristotle's explanation for why people confuse the art of household management with the art of retail-trade by setting-down through themselves their desires and enjoyments in ways that are without-limit because they misunderstand both living and living well.[10] Whether it is the household manager, politician, money-maker, master, or slave, resolving the questions about parts and subordinates concerning these persons and the arts related to them depends on the nature and capacity of human beings, something explored more thoroughly in Aristotle's inquiry into whether slavery is by nature.

## HUMAN NATURE AND THE MONEY-MAKING ART'S NEED FOR POLITICAL RULE (*POLITICS* 1252A7–16, 24–33, 1253B14–23, 1254A17–1255A3, 1255B4–37, 1258A34–B8)

Because Aristotle establishes at the beginning of the *Politics* that people are wrong for customarily-considering that the politician (or "political-ruler"), kingly-ruler, household manager, and master do not differ in form,[11] readers should take this as his guidance for interpreting Book I. Within Book I's tenth chapter, the money-making art becomes a means for testing the nature of ruling for both the household manager and the politician. To gain a better view of how the rule of household managers and politicians differs in form through their relation to the money-making art, readers need to return to Aristotle's inquiry into slavery since he speaks of both the money-making art and slaves in relation to an art of acquisition that is part of household management. A close look at this inquiry is necessary since Aristotle provides a natural foundation for distinguishing a master's despotic rule from political rule, a distinction that allows household managers and politicians to rule themselves, their communities, and the money-making art with freedom.

Before taking up Aristotle's examination of what is a slave by nature, there are two arguments prior to this inquiry that merit careful attention for understanding how the character of his political philosophy must inform readers' search for his economic teaching. In the second chapter of Book I, Aristotle sets out to examine the city and distinguish the different forms of rulers from each other by proposing one might "most nobly" (*kallista*) contemplate things by seeing "the matters naturally-growing themselves" (*ta pragmata phuomena*) from the beginning (*archē*). Here Aristotle introduces two necessary "couplings" (*sunduazō*), the second of which is "ruler (*archon*) by nature and ruled (*archomenon*) [by nature][12] on account of preservation (*sōtēria*)," to which he adds the following explanation that introduces the ideas of master and slave to the *Politics*:

> For that which itself has the capacity to foresee with thought (*dianoia*) is ruler by nature and mastering (*despozon*) by nature, and that which itself has the capacity with its body [to labor *or* to produce][13] these things is ruled and by nature slave (*doulon*). On account of this, the same thing is advantageous to [or bears-together (*sumpherō*)] master (*despotēs*) and slave (*doulos*). (1252a24–33)

According to this argument, the ideas of what is "mastering" and "slave" are subsets of the naturally necessary coupling of ruler and ruled for preservation. All the terms Aristotle uses for "ruler," "ruled," "mastering" and "slave" are in their neuter gender, which suggests they do not refer human beings.[14] From this natural perspective, what is "mastering by nature" defines its claim to "ruler by nature" through thought, and what is "by nature slave" is the body that "labors" or "produces" what thought foresees.[15]

How this relationship between the ideas of "mastering" and "slave" does not necessarily apply to human beings is evident in the above-mentioned cases of tools that are subordinate to the needs of ruling-artisans (such as a shuttle for weaving), and the weaving art that knows what wool to use to produce its products.[16] The weaving art provides the "mastering" thought that foresees how the ruling-artisan, subordinates, and tools labor upon or produce woven products, thus making these things "slaves." Lest readers mistake this deduction as a defense of slavery, remember that Aristotle's argument in the first passage dismisses the ruling-artisan's need for subordinates and the master's need for slaves if the tools and human beings ruled by another could bring to an end their works themselves. This suggests that what is "mastering" and "slave" do not necessarily exist in separate human beings, but could be present in one person.

Though Aristotle defines the foresight of thought as "ruler by nature and mastering by nature," his description of that which either labors or produces the things derived from this thought as "ruled and by nature slave" is not parallel with its antecedent: while being dependent on the thought of what is ruler and mastering by nature makes something "by nature slave," it does not necessarily mean that thing is "ruled by nature." To see an example of this problem in the arts, remember that there is an art of acquisition by nature (which many customarily-consider to be the same as the money-making art) while the money-making art (in the form of the art of retail-trade) is not by nature since it comes to be by some experience and art.[17] If arts are thoughts that are rulers and mastering by nature, suppose one person chooses the natural art of acquisition's rule and mastering, and another chooses the art of retail-trade's. Each person is "ruled and slave by nature" to an art, but because the natural art of acquisition is the only art that is by nature, only the person who adopts this art would be ruled by nature.

The possibility that someone might not be ruled by nature should inform readers' interpretation of the last sentence where Aristotle—now speaking of persons—states "the same thing is advantageous to [or bears-together] master and slave." If what is mastering and slave are subsets of the necessary coupling of "ruler by nature and ruled [by nature]" for preservation, then preservation is "advantageous to [or bears-together] master and slave." Aristotle's argument only holds up by assuming that the persons who are masters and slaves correspond directly with what is mastering and slave by nature, an assumption he tests in the second chapter of his inquiry into slavery (I.5). Before examining this test, one should wonder why Aristotle first presents the master and slave as persons whose necessary coupling may be by nature, yet does not conclude it is "advantageous" or "bears-together" by nature.

This deserves some attention because this passage marks the first appearance of the verb for "to be advantageous" or "to bear-together" (*sumpherō*) in the *Politics*, a term central to the definition of the "the just" (*to dikaion*) in Book III. In Book I, shortly after Aristotle introduces the "advantageous" to the *Politics*, "the just" first appears in relation to *logos*, community, households, and cities. Following this argument, "justice" (*dikaiosunē*) enters the *Politics* within the question of whether the city can "complete" (*teleioō*) human beings—implicitly toward an end (*telos*)—through law.[18] Acknowledging all these passages receive closer examination as this book unfolds, this glimpse at the extensive reach of the "advantageous" in the *Politics* illustrates how ruler and ruled are essential for understanding households, cities, and their attendant arts, all of which are either by nature or not by nature depending upon whether they contribute to human beings' preservation.

As a test for how the "advantageous" illuminates ruler and ruled in ways that are either by nature or not by nature, consider its sole appearance in Aristotle's inquiry into the money-making art when he describes how nature "marked-the-boundaries" (*horizō*) of animals' lives toward the easiness and "choosing" of what is advantageous toward foods, thus producing "different" (*diapherō*) lives among them. This contrasts with human beings' ability to provide food either by mixing lives that hold their work in relation to what is natural, or resorting to exchange and retail-trade. As the first half of Aristotle's inquiry develops, readers learn how people customarily-consider the art of household management to be the same as the art of retail-trade and confuse these arts' works and ends through their common use of legal-currency, here uncovering the strange possibility of someone being well-provided (*euporeō*) in this form of wealth while going unprovided (*aporeō*) in necessary food and ultimately perishing.[19] Looking to these arts, human beings can choose to work in an art of that is advantageous toward the increase of legal-currency and not the acquisition of food. Through choosing the art of retail-trade as their ruler, human beings choose to be ruled by something advantageous toward their own ruin, not their preservation. To remedy this error, human beings must choose the rule of an art that is by nature, something that is apparent by looking to the art's end.

The second argument readers must consider before the examination of what is slave by nature comes at the end of Book I's third chapter after Aristotle says "one-must-contemplate" how the money-making art holds as part of household management.[20] To set up his inquiry into slavery, Aristotle says, "First let us speak of master and slave, so that we might see the things towards the necessary need (*tēn anankaian chreian*), and if we ourselves might have the capacity to take hold of some better knowing concerning these things than the current assumptions" (1253b14–18). Aristotle does not grant that "the necessary need" for master and slave is self-evident, and he asks his readers to be open to the possibility that there is something better to know about master and slave than what they "take hold of" from "current assumptions."[21] Aristotle asks his readers to seek some other way of knowing about master and slave because it seems to some that mastery (*despoteia*) is some "science" (*epistēmē*) that is the same as household management, political-rule, and kingly-rule. To others, "being-master" (*to despozein*) is against nature because "the slave" (*to doulon*) and "the free" (*to eleutheron*) are by law but do not differ by nature, hence being master is not just, for it is forcible or violent (*biaion*) (1253b18–23). While what constitutes a "science" for Aristotle requires looking elsewhere in his political philosophy (something this book's next chapter explores), at the moment readers should focus on how he retains the intellectual character of "being-master" in this idea's second appearance, now with "science" as that which "has the capacity to foresee with thought." Although Aristotle introduces "mastering" as "by nature" in the first argument, now he questions if "being-master" is by law and not by nature, here associating law with the forcible or violent, and the just with nature. The implicit question is if science's authority derives from nature or law.

A curious feature of Aristotle inviting readers into the search to know something better about master and slave is how "the free" first appears in the *Politics* immediately after reiterating a question about science and ruling that appears at the start of the book. After declaring those who customarily-consider there is no difference in form between the politician, kingly-ruler, household-manager, and master do not speak nobly by failing to see a difference between a big household and a small city, Aristotle adds there are other things people customarily-consider about the kingly-rulers and politicians that are not "true" (*alēthēs*). For the kingly-ruler, it is not true that one is such a ruler whenever "set-standing-upon or over" (*ephistēmi*) others by oneself. Similarly, it is not true that one is a politician whenever one is ruler and ruled in turn[22] "according to the *logoi* of such a science" (1252a7–16). In this passage, science is an insufficient standard for the politician, and in the later argument preceding the inquiry into slavery, science is insufficient for differentiating between mastery, household management, political-rule, and kingly-rule. If science cannot account for the differences in forms of ruling, then those seeking to understand how to differentiate mastery, political-rule, and household management must seek how human beings are free by nature.

## Discovering Political Rule's Free Character through the Natural Slave (*Politics* 1254a17–1255a3)

Following the definition of the slave through its nature and capacity as a human being who belongs to another by nature as a piece of acquisition that is a practical and separable tool at the end of Book I's fourth chapter,[23] Aristotle begins the fifth chapter by saying, "Whether anyone is by nature such or not, and whether it is better and just for anyone to be slave or not, but all slavery is against nature, one must examine after these things. And it is not difficult by *logos* to contemplate and to learn-accordingly from the things-coming-to-be" (1254a17–20). In addition to the untested assumption from Aristotle's definition of the slave that a human being can be a piece of acquisition and still be human, the turn to examining whether anyone is a slave by nature is another indication of his inquiry's contemplative character. Discovering the definition of the "slave" does not confirm the existence of human beings who are slaves.[24] Nor does this discovery answer if it is better, just, or according to nature for human beings to be slaves. All these things require philosophic contemplation, and while readers may initially think they are incapable of this, it is "not difficult" if they turn to *logos* to learn from "the things-coming-to-be." In this way, Aristotle provides a path to knowing something about master and slave that is "better . . . than the current assumptions," one that is open to everyone.[25]

Aristotle begins the *logos* contemplating the things-coming-to-be with "ruling" (*to archein*) and "being-ruled" (*archesthai*), which are not only among the necessary things, but the advantageous things, and from the moment things come to be, they are set-standing-apart (*diistēmi*) either into being-ruled or ruling (1254a21–24). The first part of Aristotle's argument recalls the necessary coupling of ruler and ruled through which he introduces the ideas of "mastering" and "slave" to the *Politics* and the advantageous relationship between master and slave. With the argument's second part, Aristotle diverges from the necessary coupling of ruler and ruled to set-standing-apart ruling and being-ruled from each other. The separation suggests ruling and being-ruled may not always couple in necessary and advantageous ways.

Without naming particular rulers, Aristotle states there are many forms of rulers and ruled, and further, the rule (*archē*) of better things over better ruled things is always better (like rule over a human being instead of a beast), for together they better bring to an end the work (*ergon*) that belongs to them. Supporting the idea that some work belongs to rulers and ruled, Aristotle explains how something "common" (*koinon*) comes to be from many things "set-standing-together" (*sunistēmi*), regardless of whether these things are "holding-together" (*sunechēs*)[26] or "divided-themselves" (*diaireō*). All things show from themselves ruler and ruled, and this is from the whole of nature present in the ensouled things, for even in the things that do not "hold-a-share" (*metechō*) of living (like harmony) there is some rule (1254a24–33). This passage recalls the four rulers whose differences in form are not customarily-considered, but now provides a loose standard for differentiating these forms through contemplating what makes ruler and ruled better through their common work (i.e., things holding-together or divided-themselves, ensouled things, and nonliving things). To see this general argument more concretely, remember Aristotle's argument that tools (which are either ensouled or without-soul) would not need ruling-artisans if they could bring to an end their works themselves.[27] The mutual need between ruling-artisans and tools is present because the former are rulers and the latter are ruled, yet neither can bring to an end their works unless they are set-standing-together. But if the necessary and advantageous things are not always present because ruling and being-ruled are set-standing-apart, how are rulers and ruled set-standing-together?

An undeveloped part of Aristotle's argument about ruler and ruled being set-standing-together to bring to an end a common work is the distinction between things holding-together and divided-themselves. While ruling-artisans and their tools are things divided-themselves, the next step in Aristotle's argument offers some clues about things holding-together, beginning with the observation that the "living-animal" (*zōon*) (elsewhere translated as "animal") is first set-standing together from soul and body, with the soul as ruler by nature and the body as ruled. From this, there is need to examine what is more by nature in things that hold according to nature, not things that "ruin" (*diaphtheirō*) themselves. Because of this, one must contemplate a human being best "disposed-through" (*diakeimai*)[28] in both body and soul, for in those who are either "wretched" (*mochthēros*) or hold wretchedly, it often seems the body rules the soul through holding "basely" (*phaulōs*) and against nature (1254a34–b2). Like his introduction of "ruler by nature and ruled" to the *Politics*, Aristotle describes the soul as ruler by nature but does not say the body is ruled by nature. With this new argument, Aristotle provides an example of how rule may not be by nature through wretched persons who seem to put their bodies wrongfully in place as rulers over their souls. In doing this, wretched persons hold themselves contrary to how nature set-standing-together all living-animals, which raises the question of how human beings come to hold themselves contrary to nature.

With the living-animal as an example of something holding-together, Aristotle provides a more refined natural precedent for different forms of rule. Reiterating that one can first contemplate despotic (*despotikē*, "of a master") and political rule in the living-animal, Aristotle says, "For on the one hand the soul rules the body with despotic rule, and on the other hand the intellect (*nous*) [rules] desire (*orexis*)[29] with political or kingly [rule]" (1254b2–6). Bearing in mind that Aristotle's argument only distinguishes forms of rule without defining which human beings might be masters and slaves, readers should focus first on outlining the distinction between despotic and political or kingly rule. If the "ruler by nature and mastering by nature" has the capacity to foresee with thought while "that which has the capacity with its body [to labor *or* to produce] these things is ruled and by nature slave," then the soul's rule over the body is despotic since the body has no thought or fore-sight on its own. But the soul's despotic rule over the body forms only part of the living animal's picture, one Aristotle complements with the intellect's political or kingly rule over desire within the soul.[30] Although the intellect and desire are within the soul that is perhaps separable from the body on account of its despotic rule, Aristotle does not encourage this conclusion. Rather, the soul, body, intellect, and desire form a whole that characterizes all living-animals that hold both despotic and political or kingly rule within themselves. What remains uncertain is the nature of the distinction between despotic and political or kingly rule.

As a corollary to the soul's despotic rule over the body and the intellect's political or kingly rule over desire, Aristotle says, "In this it is manifest that [it is] according to nature and advantageous for the body to be ruled by the soul, and for the passionate part (*pathētikos morios*) [to be ruled] by the intel-lect and the part holding *logos*, but from [being-ruled] equally (*isos*) or in the reverse [there is] harm to all" (1254b6–9). Reading this passage as parallel to the one in the paragraph above, political or kingly rule are distinct from despotic rule because they hold *logos*. This marks a refinement of the errors people make when they customarily-consider that the kingly-ruler is one who rules by oneself and the politician one who is ruler and ruled in turn according to a science's *logoi*. Although both rule by holding *logos*, this rule is not from a science. Furthermore, there is not ruling and being-ruled in turn between the intellect and the part holding *logos and* desire and the passionate part, for it is not "according to nature and advantageous" for desire and the passionate part to rule the intellect and the part holding *logos* either as equals or superiors. In support of this argument, Aristotle adds that the nature of tame animals is better than wild ones, and it is better for all the animals to be ruled by human beings so they "hit or happen upon" (*tunchanō*) their preservation. On top of this, since in animals the relationship of the male to the female is that of the "stronger" (*kreitton*) and ruler toward the "inferior" (*cheiron*) and ruled, nec-essarily it is the same toward all human beings (1254b10–16). The primary purpose of Aristotle's argument is not to make a sweeping statement about the order of nature, but to clarify why intellect must rule desire.[31] Left to itself, desire's nature is wild, untamed, and inferior, characteristics hostile to its own preservation. Desire stands in need of the intellect's stronger nature, a strength tied not to force, but holding *logos*.

After laying all the preceding groundwork about ruling and being-ruled, Aristotle defines as "slaves by nature" those set-standing-apart from others as far as soul from body and human being from beast. People are themselves disposed this way if their work is the use of the body and this is the best thing that comes from them. Despotic rule is better for such people, "For a slave by nature is one who has the capacity to belong to another (and on account of this belongs to another), and forms-community (*koinōneō*) in *logos* so far as to have sense-perception (*aisthēsis*) of it himself but not to hold it" (1254b16–23). Of the standards Aristotle lists for ruler and ruled in the preceding paragraph, only those pertaining to animals and human beings, souls and bodies hold in the definition of "slave by nature"; he does not say the "slave by nature" is set-standing-apart from other human beings in the same way as males and females, nor the stronger and the inferior.[32] Indeed, to define what persons might be "slaves by nature" in relation to other human beings, Aristotle has to set-standing-part ensouled animals, whose work is something common that derives from their being set-standing-together. Defining people as "slaves by nature" is possible only for those who break apart the whole of human nature.[33]

One of the errors in thinking there are human beings who are "by nature slaves" is apparent when readers compare this definition to a foundational characterization of human beings from the second chapter of Book I in the *Politics*. After "most nobly" contemplating "the matters naturally-growing-themselves" from the beginning to see communities' apparent natural growth from households, to villages, and cities (the nature and end of which is self-sufficiency),[34] Aristotle deduces that a human being is "by nature a political animal (*politikon zōon*)," in part because only human beings hold *logos*. Like animals, human beings have sense-perception of pleasure and pain and can signal these things through voice. But through *logos*, human beings can make apparent what is advantageous and harmful, as well as what is just and unjust. To this, Aristotle first adds human beings are the only animals to hold sense-perception of "what is good and bad, just and unjust, and other things," then closes by saying "community in these things produces a household and a city" (1253a9–18). Since this passage's role in Aristotle's inquiry into the natural growth of communities receives more thorough examination in a later chapter, the present focus is on the contrast between a human being who is "by nature a political animal" and one who is "slave by nature." To be a "slave by nature," a human being must not hold *logos* that provides sense-perception of the moral matters that produce community. The only sense-perception of the "slave by nature" is of the *logos* another person holds. This *logos* has nothing to do with what is advantageous and harmful, good and bad, or just and unjust; the sole concern of this *logos* that "forms-community" is the body's use, not community itself. To be a slave, then, is antithetical to political community's natural foundations in *logos*.

Since one of the conditions for Aristotle's inquiry into the slave by nature is the need to contemplate a human being best disposed-through in body and soul that holds according to nature, the contrast between a human being who is "by nature a political animal" and "slave by nature" shows the slave is a human being who does not hold according to nature, and therefore not a good model for a human being who is by nature. The next phase of the inquiry into the slave by nature supports this, for while animals "are subordinate"[35] to passions (and not by having sense-perception of *logos*), since both the bodies of both tame animals and slaves help with the necessary things, the "alternating-exchange" (*parallassō*)[36] of their need (*chreia*) is small (1254b23–26). Far from being a vigorous defense of natural slavery, by finding that the exchange in the need for slaves and tame animals is small, Aristotle tacitly questions why human beings need slaves to perform the bodily work that tame animals can do. Aristotle also implicitly questions why human beings would direct *logos* toward the use of slaves when tame animals can be subordinate for the same work through the passions. In this respect, those who dispose themselves to think they need to use slaves are wretched like a "slave by nature" is wretched.

To conclude his examination of natural slavery, Aristotle considers how nature itself testifies against the need for slavery in political life, saying:

> Nature itself wishes to produce differing bodies of free persons and slaves, the [latter] strong (*ischuros*) towards necessary use, the [former] correct [or straight (*orthos*)] and useless towards such works, but useful towards political life (which comes to be divided-itself between the needs of war and peace), though often the contrary happens, and some hold the bodies of free persons while others [hold] the souls. (1254b27–34)

Aristotle's statement about nature's wish undermines the existence of natural slaves in two ways.[37] First, despite setting the standard for the natural slave as a human being who is set-standing-apart from other people as far as the soul is from the body, the argument is primarily about the bodies of free persons and slaves. Second, by starting with differences in bodies between free persons and slaves but ending with souls, Aristotle invites readers to wonder what distinguishes a free soul from a slavish one. Without providing an answer, Aristotle's brief description of "political life" (*politkon bion*) provides a clue.

In the account of natural human acquisition, Aristotle distinguishes five lives (i.e., nomad, farming, pirate, fisher, and hunter) holding their work in relation to what is natural that people mix to fill up whatever each lacks in the self-sufficient from exchange and retail-trade.[38] Political life's absence from the five lives through which human beings care for food suggests acquisition does not define political life; the same deduction is possible from the failure to mention political life in relation to exchange and retail-trade, both of which occur between communities (either households or cities). But insofar as these five lives, exchange, and retail-trade all emerge as ways human beings provide food in contrast to nature's marking-the-boundaries of animal's lives toward what is advantageous in their "choosing" (*hairesis*) of food, political life's "dividing-itself" (*diaireō*) between the needs of war and peace suggests the mark of a free soul is how it chooses to address these needs.

Aristotle's final remarks in the examination of the natural slave raise further questions about the human soul and political rule. If human beings were born only differing in their bodies as images of the gods, it is apparent that everyone would assert those not born in this image would "be worthy" (*axioō*) of being slave. But if this is true about the body, it is much "more just" to mark-the-boundary with the soul, though it is not as easy to see "nobility" (*kallos*) of soul. From this, Aristotle concludes, "That there are therefore by nature some who are free persons and others slaves, it is manifest, and for these it is advantageous and just to be slave" (1254b34–1255a3). If bodies were the sole basis for distinguishing who is free from who is slave, no one would question who is worthy of being free and slave. But as living-animals, human beings are first set-standing-together with soul as ruler by nature over the body, so justly marking-the-boundary of who is worthy of being free and slave—of who is ruler by nature and ruled—requires seeing the soul. Because it is not easy to see the soul, the discovery that it is advantageous and just for free human beings to rule slaves does not justify slavery, but lays bare a fundamental political problem: among human beings, nature alone is incapable of differentiating ruler and ruled.[39]

Readers should consider how Aristotle's statement about nature's wish from the examination of what is slave by nature complements nature's wish from the investigation of what is slave by law. In that investigation, Aristotle considers the *logos* of those who argue that conquest in war by force or violence is by those who are strong (*krateō*) always holding-over (*huperechō*) others in some good, specifically virtue (*aretē*). Despite implying there is something persuasive or trustworthy to the *logoi* that the better according to virtue need to rule and to be master, Aristotle draws attention to the error of those who "customarily-consider" that human beings are either simply well-born and free, or they are not. Such people mark-the-boundary of slave and free *and* well-born and badly-born by nothing other than virtue and vice, deeming worthy that just as human beings and wild animals come to be from their respective species, so too are the good from the good. From this, Aristotle concludes, "While nature itself often wishes to produce this, nevertheless it lacks the capacity."[40] In examining the slave by nature, Aristotle observes it often happens that nature fails to produce human beings' bodies and souls to reflect the differences between slaves and free persons. With the investigation of what is slave by law, Aristotle retains nature's wish to produce human beings with differences between slave and free, but now shifts the terms from the use of bodies to virtue and vice, then adds nature "lacks the capacity" to make this happen. The shift to virtue and vice seems to answer the call from the inquiry into slave by nature for a "more just" way to mark-the-boundaries of free persons and slaves with the soul. But if nature "lacks the capacity" to mark-the-boundaries of souls with virtue and vice, what has this capacity?

## Household Management, Political Rule, and the Human Need to be Free (*Politics* 1255b4–37)

If there is no necessary need for slaves yet some people produce this need through arts of acquisition and practicing household management, then one must wonder why people go astray and how to correct their errors. Here the last parts of Aristotle's inquiry into slavery are relevant. To draw the inquiry into the slave by law to a close, following the discovery of virtue and vice as better ways of marking-the-boundaries of free persons and slaves than force or violence, Aristotle concludes that some *logos* holds in the dispute (for each side's *logos* includes virtue). Because the good are not born from the good like wild animals and human beings are born from each other, nature's incapacity to produce human beings in this way means there are not always some human beings who are slaves by nature and others who are free. But on account of the better according to virtue having a claim to rule and to be master, there is some marking-the-boundary that is advantageous and just where there is need for one person to be ruled and slave to another person who rules according to the natural rule of being master; bad rule, on the other hand, is "disadvantageous" (*asumphorōs*) to both master and slave (1255b4–9). Aristotle remains reluctant to bring "free persons" and "masters" together. Even if it is naturally advantageous and just for someone with virtue to rule and be master over someone with vice as a slave, Aristotle does not designate the master as a "free person" because the master and slave need each other for their mutual advantage.[41] While failure to practice this rule of being-master is disadvantageous and bad for both master and slave, Aristotle fails to say such rule is "good" for both master and slave, thereby implying good rule belongs only to free persons.

In the final statement from his inquiry into the slave by law, Aristotle emphasizes the master and slave's mutual need for each while providing a small glimpse into a way of understanding good rule. From the recognition that the same thing is advantageous for the part and the whole *and* the body and the soul, Aristotle describes the slave as some ensouled part of the master separable from the body. As a result, for those who are by nature "worthy-themselves," there is something advantageous and "friendship" (*philia*) for master and slave toward each other. But for those who are worthy of master and slave by law and force or violence, the contrary occurs (1255b9–15).

Although the advantageous carries into Aristotle's last reflections on the slave by law, the "just" gives way to "friendship," appearing for the first time in the *Politics* in an unlikely context. Because Aristotle explores the relationship between the just and friendship in the *Nicomachean Ethics* (a relationship that features prominently in this book's forthcoming chapters), for now it is sufficient to notice that friendship holds common ground with ruling, being-ruled, and the just through its connections to worth and the advantageous. What is perhaps most curious about characterizing the master and slave as a "friendship" is the open question of what makes such human beings naturally worthy of each other, and relatedly, to what extent this mutual worthiness resembles friendship. While the separate and ensouled nature of friends is self-evident, it is difficult to conceive of how friends are naturally parts of one another like the slave is a separable part of the master's body. A sign of this difficulty occurs in Aristotle's final observation that those who are worthy of master and slave by law and force or violence and not by nature experience the contrary of something advantageous and friendship. Despite naming the "disadvantageous" as contrary to the advantageous, Aristotle provides no idea for what is contrary to "friendship."

Because Aristotle's examination of the slave by nature closes with the subtle hint that only rule by free persons is good and follows this with the veiled suggestion that ruling and being-ruled by nature relate more to friendship than the just, readers must look for clues for how freedom and friendship could inform their understanding of acquisition, the money-making art, and household management. In the Book I's seventh chapter (the final chapter in the inquiry into slavery), Aristotle moves to take up the last consideration he mentions before initiating the inquiry—what sort of science mastery is—by returning to the four forms of rule. From the examinations of what the slave is, the slave by nature, and the slave by law, Aristotle asserts it is evident that mastery and political-rule are not the same, nor are all the other rules the same. While political rule is over persons who are free by nature, mastery is over slaves. Furthermore, "household management's rule[42] is monarchy (*monarchia*) (for every household monarchically-rules itself), while political-rule is of free and equal persons" (1255b16–20). Aristotle's careful separation of free persons from masters bears fruit with his assertion distinguishing political rule from mastery. Political rule is not just for free persons, but for free persons by nature; mastery, on the other hand, is for slaves, designated neither by "law" nor "nature." Aristotle thus suggests freedom—and therefore political rule—more naturally suits human beings than mastery.

Along with clarifying political rule's relation to free persons, Aristotle brings in monarchy's rule to shed light on the difference between political rule and household management's rule. The passage above contains the first appearance of "monarchy" in the *Politics*, and the only appearance of this rule in Book I. Whatever defines this "rule (*archē*) of one (*monos*)" is very faint in Book I; its sole purpose is to provide separation between household management and political rule. In its contrast with mastery's rule, political rule is for free persons. When compared with monarchy's rule, political rule shows itself as fit for persons who are both free and equal. At this point in the *Politics*, readers know only free persons (i.e., parents and children) are the natural parts of the complete household, not slaves. If household management's rule is monarchy and neither mastery nor political rule, then it is for free persons who are not equals. For now, Aristotle refrains from looking at rule within the household. By saying "every household monarchically-rules (*monarcheō*) itself," he applies monarchic rule strictly to the household as a whole community. Readers should couple this characterization of household management's rule with Aristotle's statement from the inquiry into the money-making art that there is no work for the art of exchange (*metablētikē*) within the household because the people in it form-community in all things. As for the art of exchange (which is neither a form of the money-making art, nor the same as the art of retail-trade), it only occurs where there are many households.[43] Because Aristotle seeks to disentangle the arts of household management and money-making from each other, his statement about household management's monarchic rule provides a clearer basis for the distinction. As an art of exchange between communities, the money-making art requires the presence of a rule that is not its own. As a monarchy, household management is a form of rule, not an art of exchange.

Following his tentative sketch of the difference between four forms of rule, Aristotle brings science back into the inquiry to reinforce the fundamental nature of ruling and being-ruled for human life. The master—like both the slave and the free person—receives such designation not according to science, but by "being" (*einai*) this way. With this caveat, there *might* be sciences of mastery and slavery. The science of slavery's concern would be in services (like cooking), for works are either toward things that are more "in-honor" (*entimos*), or more necessary. While the science of slavery is toward the more necessary things, the science of mastery is one of using slaves, not acquiring them. Aristotle adds this science "holds nothing great (*mega*) or revered (*semnos*)" since the slave needs to know how to produce, and the master needs to know how to command. To support his denigration of the science of mastery, Aristotle states people in "authority or power (*exousia*) do not badly-suffer (*kakopatheō*)[44] themselves" with these things, and while some steward takes hold of "the honor" (*timē*), they either "philosophize" (*philosopheō*) or "practice-politics" (*politeuō*) (1255b20–37). Working backward through the argument, Aristotle dispenses with any pretense to honor in the sciences of mastery and slavery. The aversion of those with authority or power to trouble themselves with these sciences is akin to the hypocrisy of those who assert slavery according to war is just, yet do not wish to say the same thing if they are ever conquered, bought, and sold as slaves.[45] Aristotle sets up this hypocrisy by strengthening the standards for mastery and slavery, for as sciences, both the master and slave need "to know" (*epistamai*) them. This undercuts the master's own claim to being master if one does not know the respective science, and undermines the degrading status of the slave as a piece of acquisition since such a person must know the science under which one labors. These criticisms unfold between Aristotle briefly directing readers toward "being," and precede the conclusion that philosophizing and practicing politics are honorable. The arguments' framing suggests philosophy and politics are closer to people's "being" than mastery and slavery, and therefore more natural.

Without ascending to the heights of philosophy and politics, there is a portion of Aristotle's inquiry into natural slavery worth revisiting since it sheds light on what he means by "being" in ways that are necessary for disentangling household management from money-making. In the living-animal that holds according to nature, the body rules the soul despotically; within the soul, the intellect and the part holding *logos* respectively rule desire (*orexis*) and the passionate part with political or kingly rule. These forms of rule are advantageous, but if all things subject to them are ruled equally or in reverse, it is harmful to all. If political rule is of free and equal persons, then within the soul the intellect and desire *or* the part holding *logos* and the passionate part stand as equals. Though given by nature as equals, these things within the soul are not "according to nature" until there is a ruler and ruled, when that which has the capacity to foresee with thought rules and bears-together that which has the capacity with its body to labor or to produce what belongs to thought. At the end of the inquiry into the money-making art's first half, Aristotle reveals the confusion between the arts of household management and retail-trade occurs through mistakes about living and living well that originate in desire (*epithumia*) and bodily enjoyments being without-limit and turning toward money-making that is productive of legal-currency without-limit as if it is the end for all things.[46] The danger the money-making art poses for household management and political rule is enslavement to bodily enjoyments and desires. If household management and political rule belong only to free persons who are free through being a certain way, then Aristotle must draw his readers toward being free by showing them an end better than money-making, one closer to philosophy and politics.[47]

## Nature as the Authoritative Source for Exchange (*Politics* 1258a34–b8)

To turn back to the second half of Aristotle's inquiry into the money-making art and its unprovided question concerning whether this art either belongs to the household manager or politician *or* needs to be present to him, readers should use the inquiry into slavery's statements about nature's wishes to see how the money-making art is unsuitable for drawing people toward being free. In the examinations of the slave by nature and by law, nature itself wishes but fails to produce human beings who are free and slave in body and soul. In the first half of the inquiry into the money-making art, after distinguishing the art of household management as a money-making art that is according to nature from the art of retail-trade that is productive of wealth that is without-limit through the exchange (*allagē*) of legal-currency, Aristotle declares arts are without-limit with respect to their ends "on the grounds that they themselves most of all wish to produce that [end]."[48] While nature fails to produce things according to its own wishes in the inquiry into slavery, the art of retail-trade shows the arts are capable of such production. As wretched as slavery is, there may be something more wretched about the art of retail-trade because it (like the other arts) wishes to produce an end, an idea that never appears in Aristotle's inquiry into slavery. In providing for the unprovided matter concerning the art of household management's relation to the household manager and politician, Aristotle must reveal how the money-making art's end derives from nature to show these two rulers how to rule freely.

At the beginning of the second half of Aristotle's inquiry into the money-making art, he states that the common ground shared by the political art and the household manager is both set-down-through (*diatithēmi*) what nature gives over to them. While the political art uses human beings, the household manager uses things from the land, sea, or something else for food. But food is not the household manager's sole concern, as there is also concern for the useful things (*chrēmata*) that belongs to a subordinate. In Book I's fourth chapter, Aristotle defines the subordinate as a tool before other tools, and the slave as a practical subordinate separable from the master who needs the slave like a piece of acquisition (*ktēma*), a tool toward living.[49] As a subordinate, the art of useful things (the money-making art, *chrēmatistikē*) is separable from the household manager, hence why the useful things are not the household manager's sole concern.

Between the first unprovided question about whether the money-making art belongs to the household manager or politician or needs to be present to these rulers *and* the answer that this art is subordinate to the household manager, Aristotle raises another unprovided matter about why the money-making art is part of household management while the medical art is not.[50] What may initially appear as a redundant question takes on a new character given the arts' wishes to produce their own ends, for the money-making art's subordination to household managers and politicians as rulers does not necessarily answer why this art should be subordinate to the art of household management and the political art. Like the household manager and the politician, the money-making art needs to know what it takes from nature to set-down-through these things correctly.

From the recognition that the useful things belong to the subordinate money-making art more than the household manager, Aristotle concludes that most of all there is need by nature for the money-making art to be present, for nature's work is to "hold-forth" (*parechō*) food to what has come into being, and all things' food comes from the remainder of what has come into being. On account of this, "the money-making art is according to nature for all things from fruits of the earth and animals" (1258a34–38). At first glance, it may appear as if Aristotle repeats his conclusion to the account of natural acquisition through which one must suppose all things (plants, animals, etc.) are for the sake of human beings, and further, that war is an art of acquisition justly used by nature against both wild animals and human beings who are such to be ruled but unwilling. Although Aristotle retains all things' need for food, there is no longer a hierarchy of acquisition. By setting the money-making art "according to nature" with the "fruits of the earth and animals," the need for human beings to mix different lives to attain the self-sufficient is no longer central to acquisition.[51] More importantly, with the money-making art according to nature, human beings are no longer objects of acquisition. Readers should understand this change not only as a function of Aristotle's developing clarity about the money-making art, but his introduction of the political art to the inquiry. The use of human beings belongs more to the political art than any art of acquisition, though the nature of the political art's use and its relation to the art of household management is unclear.

Through the regular pairing of the "political" with "household management" throughout his inquiry into the money-making art (coupled with the absence of mastery from this inquiry), Aristotle subtly signals these things share a common foundation in what makes human beings free. After the inquiry into slavery, readers know mastery is not for free persons, but political rule and household management's rule are. It is also evident that nature does not hold-forth some human beings as slaves, and even if it did, the natural need for the money-making art stems from the care for food. The need for such acquisition does not establish any claims to ruler and ruled. The definitions of "true wealth" ("a store of such useful things that are necessary toward living, and useful to community in a city or a household") and "wealth" ("a multitude of tools for household managers and politicians") do not support the presence of mastery within cities or households,[52] nor do they permit household managers and politicians to acquire human beings as slaves and rule them as masters. With the free communities of cities and households and their free forms of rule exercised by politicians and household managers, human beings' acquisition from nature becomes freer. Far from mastering nature, the money-making art allows for a free acquisition from nature *and* a free exchange of what nature provides with other human beings.

Although the presence of the money-making art allows political rule and household management to be free from the need for mastery, this art also bears with it a different threat to human beings' free communities and forms of rule. Reiterating that the money-making art is twofold, Aristotle states that while the art of household management is "necessary and praised," with the art of retail-trade "the exchange [or the art of exchange (*metablētikē*)][53] is blamed justly (for it is not according to nature but from each other)" (1258a38–b2). Although Aristotle opposes the praise given to the art of household management with the blame given to the art of retail-trade, he refrains from using the art of household management's necessary character to declare the art of retail-trade is unnecessary. The precedent for this argument is in the first half of the inquiry into the money-making art where—after describing legal-currency as something provided (*porizō*) for necessary exchange—retail-trade emerges as another form of the money-making art that may have first been simply equal to necessary exchange, but with experience became more of an art concerning how to produce the most gain.[54] If the art of retail-trade receives just blame, it is not because it is unnecessary, but because it misunderstands the nature of necessary exchange.

Aristotle's juxtaposing the art of household management with the art of retail-trade illuminates the latter art's error about necessary exchange. When "legal-currency" first appears in the *Politics*, it is in the twofold distinction between the proper (*oikeia*) and improper (*ouk oikeia*) uses of pieces of acquisition: the proper use is of something for what it is (like wearing a shoe), and the improper use is the exchange (*metablētikē*) of that thing. These two uses provide the basis for Aristotle describing how all things belong to the art of exchange (*hē metablētikē*) that begins according to nature because human beings hold more or less of things than is adequate. This art of exchange has no work within households, but only between many households that mutually give as is necessary according to their needs.[55] The term that appears in these arguments for "exchange" and "art of exchange" is unique because its root (*meta*) ties it to terms related to "change." Though exchange is an improper use of a piece of acquisition, the change of all things into exchangeable things follows from a recognition that nature neither distributes all things equally, nor does it provide for exchange. What distinguishes the natural art of exchange from the art of retail-trade is the latter art loses sight of how the things exchanged come first from nature, not the people offering them for exchange. The natural need that serves as the basis for this exchange is one most human beings experience within the household (*oikia*), a teaching embedded within the name for a piece of acquisition's proper (*oikeia*) use. The natural need for exchange, then, finds its home in community.

Through this just blame given to the art of retail-trade, Aristotle adds that "the art of usury" (*hē obolostatikē*)[56] is with "most good-*logos* hated because it is the acquisition of legal-currency from itself and not from the very thing for which it was provided. For it came to be for the sake of exchange (*metabolē*), but the interest itself produces more" (1258b2–5). Though Aristotle's criticism toward the art of usury is harsh, its primary purpose is to solidify how the art of household management is according to nature while the art of retail-trade is not. The argument hearkens back to Aristotle's account of how the money-making art came into being according to *logos* when people provided legal-currency out of necessity to make the exchange of necessary things from foreign sources through importing and exporting easier.[57] Seeing nature's lack of provision for necessary exchange, human beings provided legal-currency through *logos*. *Logos* is the bridge between the need for which nature does not provide and the legal-currency that human beings "set-down-together in agreement" (*suntithēmi*) through law to use to provide for their natural need. The acquisition of legal-currency is "according to nature" if it facilitates the exchange of necessary things people need to live. With the art of usury, the acquisition of legal-currency is not according to nature because this art severs legal-currency from the exchange it should facilitate to produce more legal-currency, not exchanges. The art of usury is with "most good-*logos* hated" because it severs legal-currency from the *logos* that provides for people's natural needs.

As Aristotle closes the sequence of arguments that demonstrate the natural need for the money-making art to be present to household managers and politicians, he offers a linguistic note about the art of usury that asserts nature's authority in money-making and community. "Interest" (*tokos*) takes its name from the likeness between offspring and the parents generating them. Because interest is legal-currency from legal-currency, it is "most of all contrary to nature among the money-making things" (1258b5–8). Interest has a natural precedent in parents' ability to generate offspring. On top of its departure from providing for natural need, the art of usury's deeper problem is it uses legal-currency to imitate human beings' natural generation. This insight relates to community in two ways. First, to begin Book I's second chapter, there are two necessary couplings and communities from which the household comes: male and female for the sake of generation, and "ruler by nature and ruled [by nature]" on account of preservation (1252a26–31, b9–10). Second, to conclude his characterization of human beings as political animals by nature, Aristotle says they are the only animals to hold sense-perception of good and bad, just and unjust, and adds that "community in these things produces a household and a city."[58] With these two arguments in mind, the art of usury and interest reveal how money-making could undermine community's natural foundations. For human beings, generation belongs by nature to the household and the preservation it ensures with ruler and ruled. This preservation is inseparable from human beings' holding *logos* and their natural sense-perception of what is good and bad, just and unjust. All these things exist together within households and cities, yet the art of usury shows how human beings could use legal-currency and money-making to abandon the *logos* necessary for preserving community.[59]

Using the art of usury to demonstrate the distance between the arts of house-hold management and retail-trade, Aristotle shows how the money-making art bears the seeds of some form of slavery in political and economic life. The nature and capacity of a slave is to belong to another as a subordinate piece of acquisition, as a practical and separable tool. Accordingly, the slave by nature is set-standing-apart from others as far as soul and body, forming-community in *logos* only so far as to have sense-perception of it without holding it, with the best work to come from such a person being the body's use.[60] Although nature does not produce human beings in this way, there is something that fits these characteristics of a slave by nature more than any human being: legal-currency. Human beings produce legal-currency, which is set-standing-apart from themselves by having neither soul nor body. Legal-currency is wholly separable from the body, holds no sense-perception of *logos* because it lacks soul, and its best work is use for exchange to provide people with what is necessary for themselves and their communities. Recall that Aristotle ends the first of half of his inquiry into the money-making art with an account of how people use their capacities in ways that are not according to nature by seeking through money-making what is productive of excess bodily enjoy-ments.[61] The person who turns to money-making that seeks the production of legal-currency without-limit as if it is the end of all things becomes slave to a tool without a soul. In failing to rule one's own body with one's own soul, one harms oneself, for one is no longer free. Political and economic life face a similar yet more far-reaching enslavement to those who fail to see money-making in all its forms needs to be subordinate to human beings who freely rule themselves and their communities with *logos* of what is good and just according to nature.

## CONTEMPLATION AND A FREE APPROACH TO ECONOMICS AND POLITICS (*POLITICS* 1258B9–1259A36)

Throughout Book I of the *Politics*, although Aristotle consistently maintains free persons are parts of the household (and, by the end of the inquiry into slavery, the only natural parts), he provides little direct insight into what characterizes a free human being aside from opposition to a slave. But at the beginning of his inquiry into the money-making art's last chapter, Aristotle says, "Since we have marked-the-boundaries of the things towards knowledge (*gnōsis*) adequately, there is need to go through the things towards use. All such things hold on the one hand free contemplation (*theōrian eleutheran*), necessary experience (*empeirian anankaian*) on the other" (1258b9–11). In looking back on Aristotle's inquiry into the money-making art thus far in this passage's light, its free character becomes apparent. To start, three of the inquiry's four chapters seek knowledge, which suggests knowledge needs to inform use. If one follows the inquiry's marking-of-boundaries, nature's marking-the-boundaries of animals' lives toward the easiness and choosing of food through what is pleasant becomes the basis for knowing not only how human beings pursue the self-sufficient by pleasantly mixing five lives that hold their work toward what is natural, but how they provide food through exchange and retail-trade. With the shift from size and weight to an engraved stamp marking-the-boundary of legal-currency's quantity, readers acquire knowledge of how the art of retail-trade emerges as a form of the money-making art that abandons necessary exchange to produce the most gain. With this knowledge, readers know the art of retail-trade is an unnecessary money-making art distinct from the art of household management, a necessary money-making art that is according to nature, concerns food, and is therefore not without-limit, but holds a boundary.[62] Through marking these boundaries, Aristotle helps readers in the inquiry's third chapter acquire knowledge of how the money-making art is subordinate to the needs of the political art and household management.

Only after a summary statement about knowledge does Aristotle speak to the money-making art's use, which is twofold: "free contemplation" and "necessary experience." For Aristotle, these two characteristics of use are complementary and inseparable. The use of anything requires both contemplation and experience, and the necessary use of things can only be free when subordinate to contemplation and the knowledge it provides. Since its introduction to the *Politics*, Aristotle carefully presents the money-making art (i.e., the "art of useful things") along with contemplation, starting with the statement that how the money-making art holds as part of household management is something "one-must-contemplate." To initiate the inquiry into the money-making art, Aristotle invites readers to contemplate all of acquisition, and in refining the first question about how the money-making art holds in relation to household management, observes the money-maker contemplates sources of useful things, acquisition, and wealth. Once readers discover the art of retail-trade, Aristotle reiterates how the money-making art seems to concern legal-currency most of all, contemplating through this art how to produce wealth and useful things. After going through the unprovided question of whether the money-making art belongs or must be present to the household manager or politician, readers know this art and legal-currency are subordinates through which rulers set-down-through what nature gives over as food to provide for the needs of themselves and their communities as befits household management and political rule.[63] Aristotle provides the *logos* spurring this contemplative work, one that prepares readers for an outline of a free approach to economics and politics.[64]

## Nature and the Use of the Money-Making Art (*Politics* 1258b12–39)

With "necessary experience" as the explicit focus of the last chapter in his inquiry, Aristotle enumerates the "useful parts" of the money-making art, beginning with "the experience concerning pieces of acquisition"[65] that encompasses which kinds are most "profitable" (*lusitelēs*), from where, and how (such as in the acquisition of horses, cattle, sheep, and other animals). The second "useful part" of the money-making art is farming grain and plants, and the last part consists of beekeeping and raising other animals (such as fish and fowl) that happen to help. These things are "parts and first thing[s][66] of the most proper (*oikeiotatēs*) money-making art" (1258b12–21). This enumeration of the "parts and first things" of the money-making art fills in Aristotle's earlier statement that "the money-making art is according to nature for all things from fruits of the earth and animals" that nature holds-forth for use. These natural things belong to "the most proper money-making art" because one uses them for what they are. The only exchange is between human beings and nature itself, which supports the argument above for why the art of household management (*oikonomikē*) is "necessary and praised."[67] The money-making art's "useful parts" are most properly the things nature holds-forth to households whose use of natural things always precedes their exchange.

From the "most proper money-making art," Aristotle moves to the art of exchange (*hē metablētikē*) and the three things belonging to it. The greatest is "commerce" (*emporia*), which has three parts: ship-owning, carrying cargo, and selling. These three parts differ because some either are safer than others, or provide more profit. The second thing belonging to the art of exchange is the "practice of usury" (*tokismos*), and the third is "wage-earning" (*mistharnia*), which involves either the "vulgar or mechanical artisans or arts" (*tōn banausōn technitōn* or *technōn*),[68] or those who are "without-art" (*atechnōs*) but useful only for their bodies (1258b21–27). In keeping with the idea that the art of exchange's name indicates a "change" (*meta*) in natural things' use from a proper to an improper one, readers see how this art changes all that belongs to it: commerce changes useful or necessary things into things shipped, carried, and sold for profit, the practice of usury changes useful or necessary things into interest, and the vulgar arts or physical labor change human works into wage-earning. In other words, the art of exchange changes useful and necessary things from how nature holds them forth into money-makers. Nevertheless, Aristotle's language describing commerce shows the natural basis for the money-making art. Like "interest" and "offspring" sharing the same term (*tokos*), "profit" (*epikarpia*) has at its root the term for "fruits of the earth" (*karpos*). Since one part of commerce provides profits from selling the "fruits of the earth" it carries with ships, one can think of profits as provided "upon (as *epi* indicates) the fruits of the earth." Consequently, despite Aristotle's criticism of the art of usury as contrary to nature, readers can see how commerce is according to nature. What remains uncertain is wage-earning's relation to nature.

Before addressing wage-earning, Aristotle introduces a third form of money-making that "holds some part [of the money-making art according to nature] and the art of exchange" and deals with the "unfruitful things" (*akarpōn*) that come from the earth that are useful, as in the case of cutting timber and the art of mining that have many classes and forms (1258b27–33). This middle form of the money-making art fills in a gap between the "necessary and praised" art of household management that takes hold of food from the fruits of the earth *and* the "justly" blamed art of retail-trade that leads human beings to take things from each other. These "useful" but "unfruitful" things account for a whole range of useful and natural things within the money-making art that are neither food nor legal-currency, yet make this art possible. Timber, for example, provides the raw material necessary for the ships employed in commerce, while the art of mining provides for the acquisition of metals used as legal-currency. Aristotle now resolves an unprovided question from the inquiry's first half, for by expanding on what nature holds-forth, the money-making art holds-forth both tools and raw materials to the art of household management.[69] Adhering to his overarching perspective that knowledge needs to inform use, these three forms of the money-making art all emphasize use in a way that makes it more natural to understand this art as "the art of useful things."

After summarizing the three forms of the money-making art and all that belongs to them, Aristotle seems to bring his inquiry concerning use to an abrupt stop, saying, "Now what concerns each of these things in general has been said, and while it is useful towards the works to-be-precise-in-*logos* (*akribologeomai*) itself according to each part in turn, to-spend-time-in (*endiatribō*) [this] is burdensome" (1258b33–35). Taken on its own, this passage appears to be a glib dismissal of necessary experience in the money-making art. But Aristotle references an earlier part of the inquiry with the verb for "to-spend-time-in," whose root explains how there are some people for whom all their "way of spending time" (*diatribē*) is money-making because they think living well is only about excess bodily enjoyments.[70] Through this connection, it is evident that Aristotle's intention in this later passage is not to dismiss the use or need for *logos* concerning works in the various forms of money-making art, but to limit how much time one spends with them. There is no doubt that money-making is necessary and useful, but it is burdensome if it becomes the sole concern of one's own *logos*.

What follows Aristotle's stated intention to keep things general is a list of superlatives of forms of work related to wage-earning. The "most artistic" (*technikos*) works have the least amount of "chance" (*tuchē*), the "most vulgar" or "most mechanical" maltreat the body, the "most slavish" (*doulikos*) make the "most uses" of the body, and the most "low-born" or "low-minded" (*agennēs*) have the least need for virtue (1258b35–39). Though these works all belong to wage-earning, Aristotle refrains from distinguishing them by the wages they receive; their worth is not monetary. Given the "most vulgar" and "most slavish" works overemphasize the body and stray from the need for virtue, the implicit dynamic is between free and slave. The argument recalls the examination of the slave by law where people fail to realize the need to mark-the-boundary of free and slave by virtue and vice.[71] Tellingly, the free contemplation of the money-making art's uses provides readers with the knowledge that what is "slavish" has nothing to do with whether human beings are masters and slaves by law or by nature, but how they use themselves for the money-making arts. If people wish to be free, they must see their own need for works in virtue.

The passage above contains the sole appearance of "virtue" in Aristotle's inquiry into the money-making art. Since virtue is prominent in the *Ethics* (and therefore appears more in this book's later chapters), it is sufficient to sketch its connections with Book I of the *Politics*' few insights into the character of free human beings. Art's apparent mitigation of chance is a helpful frame of reference, especially with all the arts of necessary and useful things in the present inquiry (i.e., acquisition, exchange, money-making, retail-trade, household-management, and the political). Chance is akin to human beings' need for acquisition because it is inescapable; they will never be free from it. But through the arts, people can work freely or slavishly to provide for their natural needs. As Aristotle says in the necessary coupling of ruler and ruled by nature for preservation, what is ruler and mastering by nature foresees with thought what the body as ruled and by nature slave labors on or produces. Though the examination of slave by law reveals the need for virtue to rule and be master, it does not rule by force or violence. Virtue's rule is most properly in the soul, where the intellect and *logos* rule desire and passion with political or kingly rule, forms of rule that—like household management's monarchic rule—suit only free persons.[72] There is no mastering of need, but one can escape becoming a slave to the force or violence of the body's needs by using virtue to bring desire under the intellect's rule, thus setting-down the foundation to use the money-making art freely.

## Philosophy, Money-Making, and the Tension between Economics and Politics (*Politics* 1258b39–1259a36)

The small opening for virtue that grows from Aristotle encouraging readers to contemplate far more than money-making in *logos* initiates a series of arguments that confirm the *Politics'* inquiry into the money-making art points beyond itself to richer questions in his political philosophy. To start, Aristotle refers readers who care to contemplate the various works in the money-making art to others who write on the subject, then suggests someone should bring together the stories of those who "succeed" or "hit the mark" (*epitunchanō*) in money-making, "for all of these things are beneficial (*ōphelimos*) to those who honor the money-making art" (1258b39–1259a6). Unlike his choice simply to name a couple of people who contemplate works in the money-making art, for those who "honor the money-making art," Aristotle chooses to tell the story of Thales of Miletus, a philosopher. This is an odd choice for an audience that supposedly "honors" the money-making art, for it likely does not honor philosophy. What seems strange at first becomes less so upon recalling Aristotle's earlier observation that people do not honor the works that might belong to the science of slavery as much as philosophizing or practicing-politics, an observation that closely follows the argument that people may find something advantageous and friendship when they are by nature worthy of each other. What connects these two arguments is the insight that people are free not according to a science, but through "being" (*einai*).[73] By bringing these arguments together, one can approach Aristotle's final arguments in his inquiry into the money-making art as attempts to draw readers into being by nature worthy of philosophy and politics.

With Thales, Aristotle introduces "wisdom" (*sophia*) to the account of the money-making art. Like virtue, wisdom does not appear until the end of the inquiry. Unlike virtue, Aristotle's story of Thales contains the only two appearances of "wisdom" in the *Politics*. Wisdom's first and penultimate appearance is in the peculiar context that the very thing some attribute to Thales' wisdom is money-making and something general (1259a6–9). This introduction does two things. First, since Thales follows Aristotle's exhortation to collect success stories for those who "honor the money-making art," he quietly introduces the possibility that wisdom is something honored as well, even if by mistake. Second, for those prone to wonder what wisdom is, its errant credit to Thales for money-making provides an opening to contemplate wisdom's nature. The next detail Aristotle presents about Thales is the reproach for his poverty on the grounds that "philosophy" (*philosophia*) is "not beneficial" (*anōphelēs*) (1259a9–10). This passage marks the first appearance of "philosophy" in Aristotle's *Politics*, thus entering the inquiry under reproach, yet poised for vindication out of a mistaken understanding that wisdom helps money-making. The argument that philosophy is "not beneficial" opposes Aristotle's statement that stories about success in money-making are "beneficial" (*ōphelimos*), which leaves readers to wonder if philosophy—the "love (as in friendship, *philia*) of wisdom (s*ophia*)"—is beneficial in a way that differs from money-making.

In describing Thales' money-making, Aristotle quietly leads readers to question what type of life is worth living. From astrology, Thales observed there would be a good olive harvest, so in the winter he gathered a few useful things (*chrēmata*) as "caution-money" (*arrabōn*) for all the olive presses in Miletus and Chios. When harvest season came, he rented out the olive presses for as much as he wished and brought together many useful things for himself "to point out it is easy for philosophers to be wealthy, if they wished, but this is not what they are serious (*spoudazō*) about" (1259a10–18). The last part of this story begs the question of what philosophers are serious about, which should lead readers curious about wisdom to inquire further into it. The language of "being serious" also echoes the earlier argument about people "setting-down-through" themselves a desire for living that is without-limit because they "are serious" more about living than living well. It is through this that they exchange the art of household management's work for the art of retail-trade's increase of legal-currency without-limit.[74] In both cases, "being serious" reflects a choice about living. Both philosophy and money-making are ways of living open to everyone. But while Aristotle describes those who turn the art of household management into money-making as going wrong through desire, he does not explain why Thales chose the life of philosophy. Together, these passages raise questions about how human beings become serious about living a certain way, questions that receive no resolution in Aristotle's inquiry into the money-making art.

Further evidence of Aristotle's intention to draw readers into the fundamental questions of his political philosophy arrives in his choice to find common ground between Thales the philosopher and cities. After reiterating the previous story is about how Thales produced a display of his wisdom, Aristotle defines such a general thing of money-making as "having some capacity to furnish for oneself a monopoly" (1259a18–21). Although Aristotle does not define "wisdom," he does reveal philosophers could create monopolies *if* they wished, even if they are not serious about such things. At the same time as Aristotle hints at wisdom and philosophy's extensive scope, he narrows that of money-making, stating that whenever cities are unprovided in useful things, they make a monopoly of things for sale to produce "revenue" (*poros*) (1259a21–23). Despite seeming to be a mundane statement about how cities use monopolies, there is an intriguing kinship between the word for "revenue" (*poros*) and the verb for "unprovided" (*aporeō*). When unprovided in useful things, cities see their need to produce revenue, and money-making has the capacity to provide this. But for what need does wisdom and philosophy provide? The first unprovided questions in Aristotle's *Politics* arise with the money-making art, and they concern how this art holds in relation to the art of household management, building toward the conclusion that the money-making art—the art of the useful things—is a subordinate to the art of household management and the political art. Situated within Book I's comprehensive concern with differentiating forms of rule, Aristotle's philosophic inquiry reveals the art of household management and the political art are by nature rulers, and the money-making art is by nature ruled.[75] Wisdom and philosophy, then, provide for the need to see ruler and ruled by nature, though why this is true is not evident in Book I.

For those invested in politics and economics, it might seem unnecessary to bring wisdom and philosophy to bear upon practical matters. To speak generally, one can deduce from Book I of the *Politics* that the practice of politics provides for the need of ruling and being-ruled within communities. Similarly, one can deduce the practice of economics is to provide for the acquisition of necessary things to human beings living in communities (whether households or cities) through exchange facilitated by legal-currency. The needs for practicing politics and economics are self-evident, and these needs will not provide for themselves while people contemplate their natures. But to rely exclusively on those who practice politics and economics as sufficient teachers in these matters assumes they know the truth about these things. The necessary experience of practicing politics and economics must be put to the test by someone seeking true knowledge of these matters: a philosopher.

The second and final story Aristotle tells in his inquiry into the money-making art is of a man from Sicily who from "some legal-currency set-down-in-deposit (*tithēmi*)[76] for himself" purchased all the iron from foundries. When "merchants (*emporoi*) from markets (*emporiōn*)" came to him, he alone sold the iron "without producing much excess of the price [or honor (*timē*)], but nevertheless took hold of one hundred talents from the fifty." Upon "perceiving" (*aisthanomai*) this himself, Dionysius "exhorted" (*keleuō*) the man to carry his useful things out from Syracuse, for he could not remain because he discovered revenue for himself that was "disadvantageous" to Dionysius' own "matters" (*pragmata*). Like Thales, the man from Sicily "employed art (*technazō*) so a monopoly came to be for himself" (1259a23–33). The kinship Aristotle draws between Thales and the man from Sicily in making monopolies accentuates the disparate fates of each man: Thales gains a reputation for wisdom through the useful things he brought together, and the man from

Sicily holds on to his useful things without a similar reputation. As a point of entry into the political dynamic at work in these stories, the term for "price" (*timē*) also means "honor," and it is out of an intention to appeal to those wish "to honor" (*timaō*) the money-making art that Aristotle provides these stories. Although Aristotle does not explicitly distinguish Thales from the Sicilian man in terms of honor, the two men are unequal in this regard. One explanation for this disparity is Thales' honor is not from his ruler, whereas the Sicilian man's dishonor stems from the conflict between himself and his ruler. But if the intention of these stories is to provide something beneficial to those who honor the money-making art, why does Aristotle's second story show a man who is successful at money-making run out of the city by his ruler? Would not such a story discourage people from money-making?

To make full sense of Aristotle's choice to close his inquiry into the money-making art with the conflict between the Sicilian man and Dionysius, his general concluding remarks on politicians and money-making provide a more concrete framework for contemplating the political questions at stake. Whereas Aristotle prefaces the stories of Thales and the Sicilian man to suggest they are helpful to those who honor the money-making art, after these stories, he says, "It is useful for politicians to know these things. For many cities there is need of money-making and such revenues, just as for a household, but more so. And because of this, some of those-practicing-politics practice-politics themselves on these things alone" (1259a33–36).[77] Aristotle's last thoughts on the money-making art are not about honoring it, but the relationship between politicians, cities, money-making, and households. These thoughts emerge from the story of a man whose money-making puts him at odds with his ruler. Aristotle's concluding remarks thus point in two directions: on the one hand toward the general relationship between money-making and politics, and on the other hand back toward the story of the Sicilian man and Dionysius. Looking back at this story in light of these conclusions unveils the need for the philosophic perspective on money-making and politics.

A key detail about the Sicilian man's story likely known by Aristotle's contemporaries but not immediately apparent to contemporary readers is Dionysius was a tyrant.[78] Tyranny—the worst "regime" (*politea*) in Aristotle's political philosophy—is a monarchy toward the ruler's advantage through "despotic-rule of the political community" (1279b6–7, 16–17). According to this definition, while tyranny is a form of despotic rule, the person who rules the political community as a tyrant does not see how a master's despotic rule differs from the politician's political rule. As monarchy, tyranny also entails some confusion about household management's rule, which explains why Aristotle summarizes the errors people make about the differences in four forms of rule as customarily-considering there is no difference between a big household and a small city.[79] Tyranny, then, is a complete collapse of forms of rule and community. Knowing this characteristic of tyranny increases the significance of the conclusion to Aristotle's inquiry into the money-making art. It is "useful" for politicians to know about money-making because their cities need money-making and revenues. Households (and household managers) have this need too, but to a lesser degree. Although this encourages thinking broadly of "economics" as the use of money-making to provide for households and cities, within Aristotle's political philosophy, this provision must be subordinate to the distinct forms of rule in the household and the city: first to household management's rule of free persons, and second to the city's political rule of free *and* equal persons.

Since being free is a common characteristic of household management's rule and political rule, looking at how Dionysius' tyranny exhibits despotic rule provides an indirect glimpse into a free approach to politics and economics. Dionysius "exhorts" the money-maker to carry his useful things out of Syracuse because the tyrant "perceives" (*aisthanomai*) these revenues are "disadvantageous" to his own matters. According to Aristotle's last words in his inquiry into the money-making art, Dionysius is guilty of practicing politics as if money-making and revenues are a ruler's sole concern. The fact that Dionysius (and all tyrants) do not understand politics comes in the last argument's subtle linguistic turn: despite beginning with the need for "politicians" or "political-rulers" (*politikoi*) to know about money-making and revenues, Aristotle refrains from characterizing those who "practice-politics" on these things alone as "politicians," instead relying on forms of the verb for "to practice-politics" (*politeuō*). As a tyrant, Dionysius "practices-politics," but he is not a "politician" or a "political-ruler." Dionysius' own hostility toward the money-maker's freedom is apparent by recalling Aristotle's argument that "ruling-artisans" (*architektōn*) would not need subordinates and masters would not need slaves if tools themselves either had the capacity "to be exhorted" or "have-sense-perception-beforehand" (*proaisthanomai*) of how to bring to an end their works. As Aristotle argues in response to the second unprovided question at the beginning of the inquiry into the money-making art's second half, though both the household manager and political ruler see to the useful things, they belong to a subordinate (the money-making art).[80] The money-maker in Sicily did not need to be exhorted to discover revenue, but had sense-perception beforehand of how to "employ art" himself to produce a monopoly. If the money-maker were free to practice his art, the revenue he produced would be useful to Dionysius and the city of Syracuse. But as a tyrant who rules despotically and not politically, Dionysius does not freely subordinate the money-making art to the political art, choosing instead to subordinate the money-maker as a slave.

Dionysius' judgment that his money-maker's revenues were disadvantageous (*asumphoros*) shows a deeper error about the free character of political
rule. At the beginning of his examination of the slave by nature, Aristotle's
*logos* begins by observing ruling and being-ruled are among the necessary
and advantageous things (*sumpherōn*), and all things that come-to-be are
set-standing-apart into ruling and being-ruled. Within the soul, it is "according to nature and advantageous" for the intellect and the part holding *logos*
to rule desire and the passionate part with political or kingly rule. From the
examination of the slave by law and virtue's claim to rule and be master
through *logos* and not force or violence, there is some marking-the-boundary
of natural rule that is advantageous and just; "bad" rule, in contrast, is disadvantageous.[81] As the term for "advantageous" indicates, ruling and being-
ruled are advantageous when the same thing "bears-together" (*sumpherō*)
ruler and ruled. Properly understood, money-making and revenues should
bear-together household managers and politicians, households and cities, rulers and ruled. But as Dionysius and the Sicilian man show, money-making
and revenue did not bear them together, and thus became disadvantageous.
In this story, rulers and ruled (and through them political communities) lose
their bearings not because of money-making itself, but Dionysius' tyranny
and its inherent ignorance of how *logos* is necessary for people to be free in
political and economic life.

How tyranny is senseless of political and economic life's naturally free
character is further evident if one takes Aristotle's description of the intellect's rule within the soul as holding *logos* as a cue to look back to his characterization of human beings as political animals by nature because they hold
*logos*. Through *logos*, people can declare what is pleasant and painful, make
apparent what is advantageous and harmful, and hold sense-perception of
what is good and bad, just and unjust; this sense-perception produces community in households and cities. As despotic-rule, tyranny is hostile to community in *logos*, for the slave does not hold *logos*, but forms-community only
so far as to have sense-perception of it.[82] In Syracuse, Dionysius' "perceiving" that the money-maker's monopoly is disadvantageous to his own matters reveals there is no community between these two men. Nor is there any
community in what is good and bad, just and unjust. In failing to provide for
these moral sensibilities and focusing solely on money-making and revenue,
Dionysius' tyrannical and despotic rule is bad for himself and those ruled by
him. Dionysius fails to learn the important lesson from those in "authority or
power" (*exousia*) at the end of Aristotle's inquiry into slavery who—seeing
the science of mastery "holds nothing great or revered"—give "the honor"
of this work to some steward while they either philosophize or practice politics.[83] Although Aristotle does not state it explicitly, Dionysius' rule could
be "good" and his money-maker's revenues useful to the city if he ruled as

a politician and freed himself from the work of money-making by producing a political community where he and his citizens ruled themselves and their community by holding the same *logos* of what is advantageous and just.

With the "advantageous" and its foundations in ruling and being-ruled, money-making, household management, and political rule all connect to central questions in Aristotle's political philosophy that suggest politics and economics are naturally inseparable. In Book III of the *Politics*, Aristotle defines "the just" (*to dikaion*)—"a political good" (*politikon agathon*)—as "the common advantage" (1282b17–18). Since there was no "common advantage" between Dionysius and his money-maker, there was nothing just, no political good, and no community. If cities and households need money-making and revenue, and what produces communities in cities and households is *logos* of what is just and unjust, then money-making and revenue must be subordinate to this *logos*. Money-making's incapacity to provide this *logos* is evident in how rarely what is "just" appears in Aristotle's inquiry into the money-making art. The first appearance is in the specious hypothetical argument that "war by nature is an art of acquisition in a way" that is "just" when used against wild animals and human beings "who naturally are such to be ruled but not willing." The second appearance is in Aristotle's description of the money-making art's name as "just" because it (unlike "some art of acquisition according to nature for household managers and politicians") makes it seem as if there is no "limit to wealth and acquisition." The final appearance is in the distinction between the "necessary and praised" art of household management and the art of retail-trade that is "blamed justly" since people's exchange through it is "not according to nature but from each other."[84] In each appearance, the just appeals to nature as establishing what is subject to acquisition and limits the extent of acquisition, yet nature's rule proves insufficient.

Why nature alone cannot rule acquisition with the just is also evident from the singular appearance of the "advantageous" in the inquiry into the money-making art with Aristotle's account of how nature produces different (*diapherō*) lives among animals that are advantageous (*sumpherō*) toward the acquisition of food, marking-the-boundaries toward the easiness and choosing of food through the pleasant, which thus sets-standing-apart the different animals from each other.[85] Nowhere in the examination of the money-making art and its unprovided questions about how this art holds in relation to household management does Aristotle speak of how human beings' own "choosing" rules acquisition in all its forms. The absence of this dimension is more glaring when one considers the contrast between acquisition that sets-standing-apart human lives from each other *and* the household that is a community set-standing-together (*sunistēmi*) for every day (whose only natural parts are free persons). Because every city is set-standing together from households, and since there is a common work whenever many things are set-standing-together as ruler and ruled, there needs to be an account of what human beings choose to hold in common as ruler and ruled that will provide for acquisition in ways that advantageously bear them together in community. The need for this account grows upon seeing how all human beings embody ruler and ruled *within* themselves (soul and body, intellect and desire, the part holding *logos* and the passionate part), and are often naturally born into households, communities that monarchically-rule themselves yet are parts of the city.[86] Neither household management and politics can be free, nor can they use economics (which encompasses all forms of acquisition) freely, without providing for human beings' capacity to choose to live in community and acquire all they need for political life.

## CONCLUSION: POLITICS, ECONOMICS, AND THE QUESTION OF THE GOOD (*POLITICS* 1282B14–23)

For Aristotle, politics and economics need philosophy to provide insight into the nature of choosing to be advantageous. This need for philosophy is clear when readers look at Aristotle's definition of "the just" as "the common advantage" in its full context:

> Since in every science and art a good is the end, a greatest ['good' or 'end'] is most certainly in the most authoritative of all these [sciences and arts]; this is the political capacity, and a political good is the just, and this is the common advantage, so it seems to all the just is something equal, and up to some point they agree with philosophic *logoi*, in which boundaries-were-marked concerning the ethical things (for they assert the just [is] something for some persons, and there is need for these to be equal for equal persons), but of what sort of things there is equality (*isotēs*) and of what sort of things there is inequality (*anisotēs*), there is need not to escape notice. For this holds without-provision (*aporia*) and political philosophy (*philosophian politikēn*). (1282b14–23)[87]

Whether it is a science, art, or capacity—things tied to household management, the political, and money-making in Book I of the *Politics*—all of them depend on "the end," which is "a good." Rather than working through the implications of all sciences and arts depending on a good as their ends, Aristotle focuses on "the just" as "a"—not *the*—"political good," which many think is "something equal." This suggests there is more than one "political good," and that there are non-political goods. Such a possibility accentuates Aristotle's assertion that "the most authoritative" science and art is "the political." Yet what is the source of "the political capacity's" authority? This is no small question since that authority supposedly explains why "the greatest [good or end]" belongs to the political capacity. Here readers should follow Aristotle's admission that the philosophic *logoi* marking-the-boundaries of the ethical things assert the need for equality and inequality through the just. But the basis for equality and inequality "holds without-provision," which in itself holds "political philosophy." This is the only appearance of "political philosophy" in Aristotle's *Politics* and *Nicomachean Ethics*, and it speaks to a need to look at these two works' approaches to the just and equality in light of the good.

If ruling and being-ruled are necessary and advantageous for all things, Aristotle's inquiry into the money-making art's near exclusive focus on the necessary things reveals economics provides an incomplete view of human life. As the myth of King Midas shows in the first half of Aristotle's inquiry, those who set-down wealth as a quantity of legal-currency could—if they change-the-setting-down of legal-currency's worth—make it useless toward the necessary things, leaving them well-provided in wealth but unprovided in necessary food.[88] In Book III of the *Politics*, four chapters before readers discover the basis for equality and inequality that "holds without-provision and political philosophy," Aristotle states what each regime is "holds something without-provision," and so it is "proper" (*oikeion*) for the person philosophizing "to look towards the doing (*to prattein*) and neither overlook nor leave something behind, but to make clear the truth concerning each thing" (1279b11–15). The philosophical is practical, and its view of regimes and acquisition—of politics and economics—does not separate the things done in these practical matters from the truth about them. Political philosophy looks at politics and economics knowing the acquisition of wealth affects the basis of equality and inequality—of the just—in regimes. But as Aristotle's inquiry into the money-making art shows, one cannot reveal the truth about regimes without first contemplating acquisition and wealth. Given the distinction between the money-making art that facilitates necessary exchange and the art of retail-trade that seeks the gain of legal-currency without-limit, not all forms of acquisition and wealth are good for human beings and regimes. The practical truth that political philosophy provides to politics and economics is the need to see these matters as pursuits of the good.

The unprovided question in the second half of Aristotle's inquiry into the money-making art concerning how this art holds toward household management and the political art suggests where to turn in the *Ethics* to begin seeing how his political philosophy draws politics and economics toward the good. In Book VI, household management and the political art appear in relation to "prudence" (*phronēsis*). The political art itself features early in Book I, which begins with Aristotle wondering if all things aim at the good. Books I and VI of the *Ethics* are necessary references not only because of their continuity in subjects with Aristotle's inquiry into the money-making art, but because they feature "choice" (*proairesis*), the nature of which derives from intellect and desire, and therefore relates to his model for political rule and what makes people free in Book I of the *Politics*. If it is "proper" (*oikeion*) for the philosopher to bring together practical matters with the truth, there must be something within philosophy that holds a kinship with household management (*oikonomia*), particularly when one needs to set-down-through what nature gives over to human beings for their use. As the name of "philosophy" and the first appearance of "friendship" (*philia*) in the *Politics* suggests,[89] the advantageous use of politics and economics depends on understanding the nature of friendship and all it reveals about how human beings choose to pursue the good.

*Chapter 3*

# Choice and the Intellectual Foundations of Politics and Economics

From the first two chapters of this book, it is clear that any attempt to discern the full scope of Aristotle's economic teaching solely through *Politics* I.8–11 misunderstands the character of his political philosophy. To some readers, it may seem sufficient to supplement the *Politics'* limited economic inquiry with parts of the *Nicomachean Ethics* that explicitly address economics. Using this approach, readers could look to Book I for a general account of the relationship between the political art (*hē politikē*) and household management (*oikonomia*), and Book VI for a glimpse into how these things are forms of prudence (*phronēsis*).[1] Readers who focus on economic exchange could also look to Book V's account of the just (*to dikaion*) and the worth of legal-currency (*nomisma*) (V.5).[2] Although these parts of the *Ethics* reveal some truths about economics, isolating them for the sake of gaining clarity on this subject conceals the depths of Aristotle's political philosophy and his authoritative concern with the good.

The fundamental flaw with relying upon Books I, V, and VI of the *Ethics* to complete Aristotle's economic teaching derived from *Politics* I.8–11 is these approaches ignore the nature of choice (*proairesis*) and human beings' enduring need for knowledge of the good. To see this deficiency (and how it eventually reveals the incompleteness of relying on Book V's account of the just to round out Aristotle's economic teaching), it is necessary to begin with a close reading of Books I and VI. While a cursory approach to Books I and VI may lead readers to conclude economics must be subordinate to politics for the sake of producing happiness (*eudaimonia*), careful readers will find that the practice of economics and politics is inseparable from choice, the nature of which is always in the limit of some good.

Aristotle's inquiry into the money-making art (*chrēmatistikē*) in Book I of the *Politics* concludes with him stating it is useful (*chrēsimos*) for politicians

(*politikoi*) to know what concerns money-making (*chrēmatismos*) and revenues (*poros*) because cities (*polis*) and households (*oikia*) need these things.
But because there is more need for money-making in the city, there are some
who practice politics (*politeuō*) by focusing exclusively on money-making.
One implication of Aristotle's observation is both cities and households need
to provide more for themselves than money-making. As for why there is
more need for money-making in the city than the household, the only hint in
Aristotle's inquiry of what he means by this comes in his statement that there
is no work (*ergon*) for the natural art of exchange (*hē metablētikē*) within
the household because those living in it form-community (*koinōneō*) in all
things; the art of exchange, in contrast, only occurs where there are many
households.[3] Despite this difference, Aristotle's inquiry concludes by suggesting communities hold more authoritative concerns than money-making
and revenues—than economics.

As the preceding chapter shows, the loss of what is advantageous
(*sumpheron*) between the tyrant Dionysius and the money-maker in Syracuse
points to questions about the just that emerge in Book III of the *Politics*.
These questions arrive along with the statement that every science (*epistēmē*)
and art (*technē*) depend on a good as the end (*telos*). Between defining "the
just" as a "political good" and "the common advantage" *and* on his way to
discovering the basis for equality and inequality "holds without-provision
(*aporia*) and political philosophy," Aristotle reminds readers of the philosophical *logoi* "in which boundaries-were-marked (*horizō*) concerning the
ethical things" since "it seems to all that the just is something equal."[4]
Although Aristotle gives readers a place to look for his *logos* about the just
and the equal, Book V's inquiry into justice (*dikaiosunē*) marks the halfway
point in the *Ethics*. Much like Aristotle presenting the question of the just
in light of the political capacity's (*dunamis*) pursuit of a good as its end in
Book III of the *Politics*, justice in the *Ethics* finds its place in an inquiry that
begins by raising questions about the good and the political art. Though both
politics and economics intersect upon questions about what is advantageous
and just, political philosophy holds the comprehensive view of these practical
matters that sees the just needs to account for equality and inequality together
in relation to the good.

The political art makes one appearance in Aristotle's inquiry into the
money-making art when he compares how the household manager (*oikonomikos*) must set-down-through (*diatithēmi*) what nature gives over for
food to how the political art takes human beings from nature to use them.
This leads Aristotle to raise questions about what ends properly belong to
arts, with the useful things (*chrēmata*) being on the one hand the concern of
the household manager, and on the other hand the concern of a subordinate
art (i.e., the money-making art). These questions about the arts flow from

Aristotle wondering—in line with the first unprovided (*aporeō*) question initiating the inquiry—if the money-making art either belongs to the household manager or the politician, or needs to be present to each ruler.[5] Within these passages, there are questions about the authority of these arts' rulers (i.e., the politician, the household manager, and the money-maker), and the authority of the arts themselves (i.e., the political, household management, and money-making). Aristotle also mentions other arts (such as the medical and weaving arts), which raises questions about the place of all these arts in the political community. Taken together, these passages leave readers to wonder what makes an art authoritative, an inquiry Aristotle takes up in Book I of the *Ethics* to show how the political art is the most authoritative of all arts.

Alongside Aristotle's inquiry into what makes the political art authoritative, there is some ambiguity over whether "the political" is an "art" or a "science." Readers catch a glimpse of this in the passage above from Book III of the *Politics* where Aristotle says the most authoritative science and art is "the political capacity." This suggests sciences and arts are both "capacities," albeit different kinds. While this ambiguity does not factor explicitly into Aristotle's inquiry into the money-making art, there is one passage in the discussion of slavery where he describes "mastery" and "slavery" as "sciences," but leaves it unclear if he speaks of the "art of acquisition" or the "science of acquisition" (*ktētikē*).[6] Nevertheless, Aristotle distinguishes between household management (*oikonomia*) and the art of household management (*oikonomikē*), retail-trade (*kapēleia*) and the art of retail-trade (*kapēlikē*). To the extent that those who study economics and politics approach each field as a science, it is worth wondering why Aristotle speaks of these fields as both sciences and arts.

What it means to understand politics and economics as "arts" versus "sciences" may seem like an academic matter that is irrelevant to those who practice each thing. The beginnings of the money-making art, however, suggest being an "art" leads to errors about its end. Aristotle distinguishes between some art of acquisition according to nature for household managers and politicians *and* the money-making art that does not come to be by nature, but by some experience (*empeiria*) and art; he also notes the money-making art's name is "just" because it is through this art that there does not seem to be a limit (*peras*) to wealth (*ploutos*) and acquisition (*ktēsis*). One needs to know these distinctions because many customarily-consider (*nomizō*) these arts are the same. Shortly thereafter, the art of retail-trade emerges as the form of the money-making art distinct from necessary exchange (*anankaias allagēs*) that (through experience) became more of an art seeking to produce the most gain (*kerdos*) from legal-currency.[7] Since these arts are all arts of acquisition, if some are by nature while others are not, it is not simply by virtue of experience or being an "art" that things hold differently in relation to nature.

What brings economics and politics together for Aristotle is *logos*, which appears twice in the *Politics'* inquiry into the money-making art. First, Aristotle describes the money-making art as coming into being according to *logos* when human beings—by setting-down-together an agreement (*suntithēmi*) through law (*nomos*)—provided (*porizō*) legal-currency out of necessity to produce easier exchanges of necessary things from foreign sources through importing and exporting. The provision of legal-currency shows how *logos* provides for naturally necessary exchange when nature itself does not. The second appearance of *logos* in Aristotle's inquiry comes after he asserts the art of retail-trade is "blamed justly" while the art of household management is "necessary and praised." In support of this argument, Aristotle claims the art of usury is "with most good-*logos* (*eulogos*) hated because it is the acquisition of legal-currency from itself" through interest rather than the exchange (*metabolē*) of useful things (*chrēsima*) "for which it was provided."[8] The hatred for the art of usury from good-*logos* suggests there is a bad-*logos* that confuses the arts of household management, money-making, retail-trade, and usury with one another, a *logos* that does not understand the nature of exchange.

Though Aristotle defines human beings as "political animals" in the *Politics* because they exclusively among other animals "hold" (*echō*) *logos*, this argument is a mere glimpse into what it means for *logos* to be at the foundation of his political philosophy. The most Aristotle reveals in this brief account is that through *logos* human beings hold sense-perception (*aisthēsis*) of what is good and bad, just and unjust, advantageous and harmful, pleasant and painful, and further, that "community in these things produces a household and a city."[9] What it means to "hold" *logos* and sense-perception through it is something of a mystery in the *Politics*, one that is central to Aristotle's inquiry into the political art in the *Ethics*. The broad nature of *logos* gives Aristotle's political works a philosophic character that does not reveal its practical implications without immersion in their theoretical questions. *Logos* is the foundation of all community, and the way a community holds *logos* is somehow akin to how each person holds *logos*.

The two communities that hold *logos* in Aristotle's *Politics* are the household and the city, and their attendant arts are the art of household management and the political art. In the *Ethics*, Aristotle brings these two arts together not only by asserting in Book I that the political art is authoritative over the art of household management, but in arguing in Book VI that household management and the political art are forms of prudence, a virtue related to action (*praxis*) and choice. This understanding follows brief accounts of science, art, wisdom (*sophia*), and intellect (*nous*), things that all hold ties to *logos*. When one holds the absence of "choice" from Aristotle's inquiry into the money-making art (and from almost all of Book I of the *Politics*)[10] up against its presence in the *Ethics'* considerations surrounding the political art and the art of household management, the *Ethics'* approach suggests it is closer to the foundations for politics and economics within human nature.

In focusing on how prudence—and through it politics and economics—depends on *logos* and choice, the authoritative nature of the good as the end in Aristotle's political philosophy comes forth. Though happiness seems to be the political art's authoritative end in the *Ethics*, it is not until the middle of Book I that happiness enters the inquiry. Prior to the first appearance of happiness, Aristotle raises questions about the good, choice, ends, and arts. Why, then, does Aristotle hesitate to take up happiness right away? Here the first mention of *logos* in the account of the money-making art from the *Politics* is instructive, for *logos* sits between natural acquisition and exchange on the one side, and the arts of money-making and retail-trade on the other. *Logos* thus relates to what is natural in economic life (acquisition and exchange), and to what is unnatural (legal-currency and gain, though the former is something provided to facilitate natural and necessary exchange). Readers should also recall that the art of retail-trade is without-limit (*apeiron*) toward its end of gaining wealth and acquisition in the form of legal-currency. By mistaking living well (*eu zēn*) for the pursuit of excess bodily enjoyments, people make an attempt (*peiraō*) through the art of retail-trade to use their capacities in ways that are not according to nature, as if money-making is the end for all things. In the first of these two arguments, Aristotle states "the end [is] a limit (*peras*) to all [arts]."[11] As a work of political philosophy, the *Ethics* is itself a *logos* with the capacity to provide a natural limit to politics and economics by drawing its readers into contemplating how the one end they need above all others is not happiness, but the good.

## ENDS AND THE POLITICAL ART
## (*ETHICS* 1094A1–1095A25)

### Approaching the Human Need for the Good
### (*Ethics* 1094a1–26)

Aristotle begins the *Ethics* with what appears to be a simple observation about arts and the good, saying, "Every art and every inquiry (*methodos*), and likewise action and choice, seems to aim itself at some good; on which account, nobly [or 'beautifully,' *kalōs*] they displayed-from [or declared-from (*apophainō*)] themselves the good, that at which all things themselves aim" (1094a1–3).[12] The temptation for readers is to think Aristotle presents a straightforward argument: if arts, inquiries, actions, and choices aim at some good, then "all things" aim at "the good." But there are at least two perplexing characteristics of this passage. First, if these pursuits aim at some good, does it follow that "all things" (presumably the whole cosmos) aim at the good?[13] The most Aristotle states is these pursuits themselves "nobly" or "beautifully" show the good is that at which all things aim. This leads to the second perplexity: Why does Aristotle present these pursuits as if they are capable not only of aiming themselves at some good, but "displaying" or "declaring" something about the good? The language suggests these pursuits have lives of their own, as if they are separable from human beings. For now, the question of the good belongs to human pursuits in the abstract, not human beings.

The opening sentence of the *Ethics* also sets up a parallel that gestures toward bringing human beings and their pursuits back together, for there is some kinship between art and action on the one hand, and inquiry and choice on the other. Though Aristotle has yet to define these terms more precisely, one can surmise that to produce or perform something with art is akin to performing some action. Similarly, choice is some sort of inquiry into an action. Aside from these parallels, it is reasonable to treat arts as depending on inquiries, and actions as depending on choices. In every case, there is some thinking at work that would be absurd to attribute to the pursuits themselves and not people thinking about those pursuits. This leaves readers to wonder why Aristotle holds back from examining how people's thinking guides their pursuits.

The detached character of Aristotle's opening arguments continues when he says, "Some difference (*diaphora*) displays itself among the ends: for on the one hand they are activities (*energeiai*, plural of *energeia*), and on the other hand some works beyond them" (1094a3–5). Aristotle's statements about pursuits and ends both complement and oppose one another, for although they both "display-from" (*apophainō*) or "display" (*phainō*) something about themselves, they reveal fundamentally different things: while pursuits aiming at some good apparently reveal the good is that at which all things aim, ends apparently reveal a "difference" among themselves. Despite introducing a difference between an activity and a work, Aristotle does not explore the nature of this difference, suggesting only that a work is beyond an activity. Further complicating the picture, Aristotle adds that in cases of ends where works are beyond activities, "there are some ends beyond the actions, [and] in these the works are naturally better than the activities" (1094a5–6). Activities and works now make their way into Aristotle's inquiry as ends, and though they seem to be akin to goods, the difference among ends makes it harder to assert all things aim at the good. The most readers learn for now is that works are "naturally better" ends than activities.[14]

From his statements about pursuits, the good, and ends, Aristotle turns to the arts and introduces the art of household management to the *Ethics*. Since there are many actions, arts, and sciences, it comes to be that the ends are many. Supporting this observation are the following arts and their ends: the medical art and health, the art of shipbuilding and a ship, the art of general-ship and victory, and the art of household management and wealth (1094a6–9). In this passage, "science" enters the *Ethics* amid increasing pursuits that increase the difficulties facing the opening statement about all things aiming at the good. Stepping away from the *Ethics* for a moment, remember that the connection between the art of household management and wealth is not so clear in the *Politics'* inquiry into the money-making art where Aristotle draws a distinction between "true wealth" and "wealth": the former is "a store of such useful things that are necessary towards living, and useful to community in a city or a household," and the latter is a "multitude of tools for household managers and politicians." This definition of "wealth" makes it possible to set-down a quantity of legal-currency as wealth, which leads to the absurdity of someone being well-provided (*euporeō*) in legal-currency and unprovided (*aporeō*) in necessary food. Through this problem, Aristotle distinguishes the art of household management's work from the art of retail-trade's: the former art is according to nature and its acquisition of wealth has a limit, while the latter art is not by nature and its acquisition of wealth is without-limit.[15] Because many customarily-consider the arts of acquisition, household management, money-making, and retail-trade are the same, it is evident that works and wealth provide a partially reliable means of differentiating these arts' ends, though one still needs some other end to see whether or not these arts' works and ends are according to nature.

To resolve the problem of many arts giving rise to many ends, Aristotle considers the possibility of bringing many arts under the authority of an "architectonic" (*architektonikos*) art. Speaking of cases where actions, arts, and sciences come under some one capacity—such as when bridle-making and other arts for the tools of horsemanship belong to the art of horseman-ship, an art which itself falls under the art of generalship along with every action fit for war—Aristotle suggests the ends of the architectonic capaci-ties are "more choiceworthy" (comparative of *hairetos*) than the ends of the capacities falling under them. In all these cases, it does not matter if the ends are actions, activities, or something else, as is the case in the sciences previ-ously discussed (1094a9–18). The emergence of architectonic arts seems to eliminate any need to discern whether ends are actions, activities, works, or something else, a need that is apparently vital to the sciences. But the example of the art of generalship subsuming the art of horsemanship should give readers pause. After all, even if the art of generalship uses the art of horsemanship for the sake of victory, does the art of horsemanship and all the arts under its purview aim primarily at victory in war, or another end? The practical problem of what makes something choiceworthy thus displaces the sciences' theoretical problem regarding the nature of ends. Despite the absence of "choice" from the _Politics'_ inquiry into the money-making art, the problem of many customarily-considering all the arts of acquisition are the same by subsuming them under the art of retail-trade's end suggests they see this art as more choiceworthy than the others. Choice, then, presents a more far-reaching practical problem: What makes the end of one activity, science, work, art, or capacity more choiceworthy than another?

Whereas the first chapter of the _Ethics_ detaches arts and ends from human beings, the second chapter returns to the question of the good with a more personal character with Aristotle supposing that if there is some end of actions that "we ourselves wish for" (_boulometha_, middle form of _boulomai_) on account of itself and all other things for the sake of this end, such an end would be "the good and the best (_ariston_, superlative of _agathos_)" (1094a18–19, 21–22). Now the question of the good emerges not from pursuits abstracted from human beings, but one's own actions. It is with this immediate concern that the good assumes its superlative status. The good ensures "we ourselves do not choose (_haireō_)"[16] all things for the sake of another thing without-limit, leaving desire (_orexis_) "empty and vain" (1094a19–21). As hinted in the passage above about architectonic arts, the practical problem for ends concerns why one end is worthy of choosing before others. With actions, choosing does not go without-limit, and neither does the desire animating it. Choosing is the bridge between human desire and ends, and it ensures desire does not go without-limit.

Given the good's potential to be the end that provides a limit to people's desires and actions, Aristotle invites readers to consider the need for the good, asking, "And therefore towards life (_bios_) would not the knowledge (_gnōsis_) of this good hold great weight, and just like archers holding a target, might we more hit upon the needful (_deontos_)?" (1094a22–24). By shifting the _Ethics'_ approach to the good from various pursuits to considering what it means to choose the good as the end for one's own actions and desires, Aristotle suggests knowledge of the good provides what is "needful" not simply for inquiries, arts, and sciences, but life itself. From this question about the need for the good, Aristotle proposes "one-must-attempt" (_peirateon_) an "outline" (_tupos_) that "gets a hold" (_perilambanō_) of whatever the good is and to which of the sciences or capacities it belongs (1094a24–26). Although Aristotle is about to examine why the good might belong to the political art, the passage above about architectonic arts and what is choiceworthy suggests sciences and capacities are insufficient for knowing what the good is. For that knowledge, readers must be attentive to all of Aristotle's outline in Book I.

Before turning to Aristotle's outline of the political art, one should see how his approach to people's need for the good in the _Ethics_ informs the first half of the _Politics'_ inquiry into the money-making art. In the _Ethics_, life's practical problem of leaving desire and choosing without-limit (*apeiron*) reveals why one-must-attempt (*peirateon*) to acquire knowledge of the good. In the *Politics*, people exchange the art of household management's work for the art of retail-trade's increase of legal-currency without-limit because of a setting-down-through themselves either a desire (*epithumia*) for living that is without-limit, or a view of living well that seeks what is productive of excess bodily enjoyments by making-an-attempt (*peiraō*) at money-making or some other use of their capacities that is contrary to nature.[17] In both texts, leaving desire without-limit produces practical problems. According to the *Ethics*, desire is "empty and vain" without the good, and the failure to provide the good to desire leaves one unprovided in what is needful for life. According to the *Politics*, a desire for living that is without-limit leaves one unprovided in whatever constitutes living well. But as this inquiry shows, living well may fail as an end when people do not see how their desire for excess bodily enjoyments may keep them from seeing that nature provides an end more suitable for using their capacities well. Despite the common problem of desire being without-limit in the *Ethics*' overview of people's need for the good and the first half of the *Politics*' inquiry into the money-making art, there is one major difference between the two examinations: Aristotle does not name "the good" as the end that provides this needful limit in the latter inquiry.

The absence of choice from Aristotle's inquiry into the money-making art underscores the good's near-total absence from this inquiry. The closest Aristotle comes to speaking of choice in this inquiry is in his account of natural acquisition with the description of how nature marks-the-boundaries of animals' lives toward the easiness and choosing (*hairesis*) of food through what is pleasant (*hēdus*). Human beings, in contrast, pleasantly mix different lives as need necessitates (*chreia sunankazō*) to acquire the self-sufficient (*autarchēs*). "Good" (*agathos*) appears only once in this inquiry when Aristotle declares the "self-sufficiency (*autarkeia*) of such acquisition [i.e., true wealth] towards good living (*agathēn zōēn*) is not without-limit."[18] Though implied, human "choosing" is never an explicit part of Aristotle's inquiry into the money-making art. To the extent that people's mixing of lives for the sake of acquisition is analogous to animals' different lives, the pleasant is part of what characterizes human choosing. An exclusively human part of choosing is self-sufficiency, which corresponds to need *and* is subordinate to what makes living "good." If one understands "economics" broadly as what concerns human acquisition, taking Aristotle's inquiry into the money-making art from the *Politics* in isolation from the rest of his political philosophy runs the risk of obscuring how people's choices about what is pleasant and self-sufficient toward the good precedes any use they make of the arts of acquisition in their lives.[19]

A glimpse of how the political art likely fails to provide for human beings' need for knowledge of the good comes from a peculiar characteristic of Aristotle's inquiry into the money-making art. In the first half of the inquiry (*Politics* I.8–9), Aristotle uses words related to limits—*peras* (limit) and *apeiron* (without-limit)—fourteen times.[20] The language of limits is absent from the second half of the inquiry (I.10–11), which begins with an analogy between the political art's use of human beings from nature to consider how the household manager sets-down-through what nature gives over for food. In examining how there is a limit to the art of household management's acquisition of wealth but not the art of retail-trade's, Aristotle remarks that every art wishes to produce the end toward which it is without-limit. If one compares arts' wishes with the *Ethics*' invitation to wonder about the good "we ourselves wish" for so that desire is not "empty and vain" because "we ourselves do not choose" all things without-limit, one sees how arts' wishes may be contrary to one's own. The political art's wishes merit attention given Aristotle's statements from the *Politics*' inquiry into slavery that nature wishes yet lacks the capacity to produce human beings who in body and soul are "useful towards political life" and free.[21] The truth manifest from the beginning of the *Ethics* but concealed in Book I of the *Politics* is that each person's actions in economic and political life begin with a wish for the good that provides a limit to one's own desires, choices, and actions.

## The Political Art (*Ethics* 1094a26–1095a25)

With the joint inquiries into the good and the sciences or capacities to which it belongs set, the political art makes its first appearance in the *Ethics* with Aristotle's tentative statement that the good "might seem to belong to the most authoritative (*kuriotatēs*) and most architectonic [science or capacity]; and such displays itself as the political [art] (*hē politikē*)" (1094a26–28).[22] At first glance, Aristotle appears to restate the *Ethics*' opening chapter's concluding argument that architectonic arts' ends are more choiceworthy than those under them. But after going through the need for the good from the perspective of one's own choices, this end now "might seem" to belong to the political art. Aristotle's change in approach to the architectonic arts on account of discovering each person's need for the good signals to readers that they should hold the political art's wishes up against their own to see which set of wishes is more likely to provide them a path to the needful knowledge of the good.

Aristotle's arguments for the "most authoritative and most architectonic" character of the political art start from the perspective of capacities and builds toward the good. With the capacities, the political art ordains whatever sciences are "needed" (or "used," *chreōn*) in cities, the kinds for each person to learn, and to what extent (1094a28–b2). The sciences have a twofold purpose under the political art's authority: to meet cities' needs or uses, and to ensure each person learns those sciences. Contrary to the view from one's own desire where knowledge of the good could help each person hit on what is needful, the political art's view is the cities' needs or uses govern what each person learns for the sake of using them. This contrast may explain why Aristotle briefly returns to the more personal voice to observe that "we see" the capacities "most-in-honor" (*entimotatas*, superlative of *entimos*)—such as the arts of generalship, household management, and rhetoric—fall under the political art (1094b2–3). Without discussing their ends, Aristotle recognizes that what most people notice about these three arts is they receive the most honor from cities. With respect to Aristotle's economic teaching, the most pressing question is if the city's use of the art of household management corresponds to this art's natural need. If every household monarchically rules itself,[23] there is likely a tension between the art of household management's end and the political art's, one with a precedent in whether the good derives from architectonic arts or one's own need to choose it.

Moving from the most-in-honor capacities and closer to each person's actions, Aristotle states that since the political art itself uses the remaining "[practical] sciences"[24] and "legislates" (*nomotheteō*) whatever things there is need to do and "to-hold-back-from" (*apechō*) oneself, the political art's end would "hold-concern-around" (*periechō*) the sciences' ends so that its end would be "the human good" (*ta'anthrōpinon agathon*) (1094b4–7). To use people for its own ends, the political art must (to play on the roots for the verb for "legislate") set-down (*tithēmi*) in law (*nomos*) what it needs them to do. How people act and hold toward the political art is now not a matter of what end they choose, but the political art choosing to set-down for them what they should do according to the end for which it holds concern. This raises an important question: Is the human good an authoritative end because it belongs to the political art, or is the political art authoritative because it aims at the human good as its end?

Whether the most authoritative thing is the human good as an end *or* the political art as a capacity leads into a conditional statement underscoring the tension between one's own need for the good and the city's needs. *If* the human good is the same for one alone and for a city, to have "taken hold of" (*lambanō*)[25] and "preserved" (*sōzō*) this for the city displays itself as greater and more complete (*teleioteron*, comparative of *teleios*), for while this is either "loved" or "something to be content with" (*agapēton*) for one alone, to do this for "nations" (*ethnos*) or cities is "nobler and more divine" (1094b7–10). All the comparative claims of the city regarding the human good—that it is greater, more complete, nobler, and more divine—rest on how the city "displays itself" (like ends and the political art) when taking hold of and preserving this good. Aristotle refrains from asserting the human good is the same for one person alone and the city, which puts greater emphasis on his conclusion to the second chapter of the *Ethics*, where he says, "Therefore the inquiry aims itself at these things, being something political [or some political art (*politikē tis*)]" (1094b10–11).[26] This broad statement leaves readers to wonder what "these things" encompass, with sciences, capacities, the human good, and the question of their relation to each person and cities all possible targets of the inquiry. All these questions are "something political," which suggests that whatever the political art ordains and the sources of its authority are not as straightforward as what it displays of itself. Considering one could read Aristotle's concluding statement as suggesting the inquiry is itself "some political art," the political things hold within themselves a more philosophical character than what they display.

The turn toward the human good and its apparent relationship to the political art contains the first appearance of *logos* in the *Ethics*, the third chapter of which begins with Aristotle stating "precision" (*akribēs*) is not the same in all *logoi*, just as it is not the same for "those working in a trade" (*dēmiourgoumenois*). The things to which the political art itself "looks" or "examines" (*skopeō*)—"the noble things (*ta kala*) and the just things (*ta dikaia*)"—"hold much difference and wandering (*planē*), so they seem to be by law only, not by nature" (1094b11–16). The expectations Aristotle sets for the precision of his own *logos* relate directly to the manifold character of the noble things and the just things. The goal of this *logos* is to reveal how these things are by nature. A similar problem appears in the first half of Aristotle's inquiry into the money-making art when he acknowledges that legal-currency seems to be altogether law and not at all by nature, even though this art came into being according to *logos* with the provision of legal-currency to produce easier foreign exchanges of necessary things. How "difference and wandering" characterize the just things is evident through how the money-making art's name in the first half of the inquiry is "just" because it—unlike "some art of acquisition according to nature for household managers and politicians"— makes it seem as if there is no "limit to wealth and acquisition." Yet in the second half of the inquiry, the art of retail-trade is "blamed justly" since the exchange is "not according to nature but from each other."[27] While the just is closer to law than to nature in the first argument (though the money-making art's name contrasts with what is according to nature), the just is more explicitly by nature in the second. Taken together, these arguments illustrate the difficulty in discerning what is just through *logos*.

Similar to the noble things and the just things, the good things hold some wandering too on account of the harm that comes to people through them, such as those who "destroyed" (*apollumi*) themselves through wealth, and others through courage (1094b16–19). Although wandering characterizes the noble, just, and good things, Aristotle does not declare that the good things hold "difference" among themselves. Whatever wandering the good things hold begins in people's relation to them. Aristotle's identification of wealth as a good thing is helpful since he makes the same point in the *Politics* with King Midas as the example of someone who "destroyed" himself through the insatiable greed of his prayer that all things set-down-before (*paratithēmi*) him turn into gold. Aristotle appeals to the tragic myth of King Midas to show the absurdity of being well-provided in wealth solely in terms legal-currency—whose worth is, like law, set-down (*tithēmi*)—while being unprovided in food and other necessary things. With the help of the *Ethics*, readers see those guilty of Midas' error about wealth misunderstand the truth about the good things. "True wealth," after all, is "a store of such useful things that are necessary towards living," and Midas' greedy prayer for gold (and others' greed for legal-currency) leads to the pursuit of wealth that is not good for living. A similar issue arises with courage, which Aristotle names in his inquiry into the money-making art as a capacity people use contrary to its nature to produce useful things (*chrēmata*), as if money-making is the end for all things.[28] Whether it is wealth or courage, the truest counter to people's own wandering about the good things is a *logos* that does not hold this wandering.

With the wandering of the things to which the political art looks established, Aristotle reiterates limits to his inquiry's precision. For the person who speaks about the wandering noble, just, and good things, Aristotle declares it is "something to be content with" (or "loved," *agapēton*) to point to "the truth" (*alēthēs*) roughly and in outline, and to draw conclusions in the same way (1094b19–22). This comment brings together two earlier statements about the inquiry's end. First, when Aristotle wonders about the need for knowledge of the good as the end to limit desire and action, he says one-must-attempt (*peirateon*) grasping what it is in outline. Second, as "something to be content with" or "loved," Aristotle likens his own imprecise *logos* about the truth to the good of one person alone, not that of cities and nations. It is not an accident that the first appearance of "the truth" in the *Ethics* brings these statements together, for Aristotle quietly instructs readers to understand that there are limits to the precision with which he—and any *logos*—can search for truth about the good.

From the reiteration of the imprecise character of his own *logos*, Aristotle makes a curious assertion about his intended audience. After stating precision should follow "the nature of the matter" (*hē tou pragmatos phusis*), Aristotle makes two seemingly redundant comments about "judging" (*krinō*), first saying one judges nobly the things one knows and is a "good judge" (*agathos kritēs*) of these things, then that a good judge "simply" (*haplōs*) is someone educated about all things (as opposed to a particular judge educated according to each thing). Because of this, "a young person is not a proper (*oikeios*) listener of the political art, for [such a person is] without-experience (*apeiron*) in the actions according to life, and the *logoi* [are] from these things and concerning these things" (1094b23–1095a3). With *logos*, the political art's concern is no longer the sciences through which it uses people to meet its own needs, but the actions every person chooses following their own wishes for the good. Yet at the same time as Aristotle brings the political art closer to each person's choosing of the good that cannot go on without-limit (*apeiron*), he seems to dismiss the young with the same term by declaring they are without-experience in the actions they need to be good judges in life. One wonders, however, if experience alone is "proper" for choosing the good in one's own actions. According to Aristotle's inquiry into the money-making art, this is likely not the case, for it is due to experience and art that the money-making art became the art of retail-trade through which it seems there is not a limit (*peras*) to wealth and acquisition.[29] More than experience, all people (not just the young) need *logos* of the good to limit life's choices and actions (of which the acquisition of wealth is a part).

To expand the scope of who is not a "proper" listener of the political art's *logoi*, Aristotle begins by observing the problem for the young is they follow the passions (*pathos*), and since the end is not knowledge but action, they will hear these *logoi* "vainly" (*mataiōs*) and "without-benefit" (*anōphelōs*). Such a problem is not primarily one of age, but a "character" (*ēthos*) living to pursue each passion. For people of this character, knowledge comes to be "unprofitable" (*anonētos*),[30] just as it is with those "without-self-restraint" (*akratēs*).[31] But for those who produce their desires (*orexeis*) according to *logos* and act in this way, there would be "much-benefit" (*poluōpheles*) to know what concerns these *logoi* (1095a3–11). In moving the focus from age to character, Aristotle quickly shows passion and desire do not pose problems strictly for the young, but affect people throughout their whole lives. While a general problem for one's own character, the passions and desires present an important challenge to political (and, through this, economic) life because of its more immediate affinity for action than knowledge. While it may seem that what is most beneficial in politics and economics is to be active in them, Aristotle suggests here that knowledge is itself beneficial for those who learn to produce their desires according to *logos*. The terms of this argument—when combined with the pun on *apeiron* ("without-experience" and "without-limit") in the previous passage—hearken back to the personal question about wishing for knowledge of the good as the best end so that desire is not "empty and vain." For politics and economics to be profitable and beneficial, people need to focus first not on actions or acquisitions, but acquiring the knowledge of the good through *logos* that produces a proper character for everything they pursue.

To conclude the *Ethics'* third chapter, Aristotle—looking back on "what it is we have set-down-first (*protithēmi*) ourselves" concerning the listener and how one must accept the *logoi* of the political art and the nature of its precision—declares this is all a prelude (1095a11–13). With this prelude in mind, readers can now see one passage from the *Politics'* inquiry into the money-making art as an attempt to draw them toward the free character necessary to benefit truly from politics and economics. The final chapter of this inquiry (I.11) begins by shifting from the first three chapters' emphasis on knowledge to use with Aristotle noting how *all* these things hold both "free contemplation" (*theōrian eleutheron*) and "necessary experience" (*empeirian anankaian*). After going through the parts of the "most proper money-making art" (*oikeiotatēs chrēmatistikēs*) and the art of exchange to see what is and is not according to nature, Aristotle states it is burdensome to-be-precise-in-*logos* (*akribologeomai*) concerning what is useful toward the money-making art's works (*ergasia*).[32] Recall that the first two chapters of the inquiry contemplate the natural limits to wealth and acquisition (I.8–9), which sets up the third chapter to consider how politicians and household managers may use the money-making art in ways that are according to nature (I.10). Aristotle's choice not to dedicate much time to precision in *logos* concerning the money-making art's works now shows itself as an echo of the *Ethics'* preference for knowledge of the good over experience. However imprecise a *logos* of the good may be, it is necessary to provide knowledge of a natural limit to one's own desires so that one is free to benefit from money-making and all economic matters.

After treating the above prelude as a digression, Aristotle begins the fourth chapter of the *Ethics* by saying, "Since every knowledge (*gnōsis*) and choice itself desires (*oregō*)[33] some good, let us say what it is at which the political art aims itself and what is the highest of all the practical goods" (1095a14–17). Rather than beginning from the arts and moving toward one's own desires, Aristotle now reverses course from the *Ethics'* first sentence and sets desire forth as what seeks some good to consider the political art's aim. From this perspective, the political art's aim is no longer the good or the human good, but "the highest of all the practical goods," which suggests a narrowing of the political art's good.[34] This occurs through the curious idea that knowledge and choice experience desire, something common to each person but not the arts. Once again, the *Politics* allows one to see a glimpse of how this passage aims to move readers toward a free character. In his inquiry into slavery, Aristotle describes political rule in the soul as the intellect and part holding *logos* respectively ruling desire and the passionate part. Later, Aristotle reveals political rule is of free and equal persons, while household management's monarchic rule is of persons who are free but not necessarily equal.[35] When looking at these passages in the *Politics* in light of the *Ethics'* prelude about the political art's *logoi* and its statement about knowledge and choice desiring some good as a precedent for determining the political art's practical good, readers can see that in order for rule to be free in the city and the household, desire and passion need to be ruled by intellect and *logos* of the good. If politics and economics need a free character to be beneficial, readers must find where the intellect, *logos*, the political art, and household management all come together in the *Ethics*.

Focusing on the practical good at which the political art aims itself, Aristotle observes that people "agree-in-*logos* among themselves" (middle form of *homologeō*, which implies "same-*logos*") that its name is "happiness" (*eudaimonia*), thus introducing this idea to the *Ethics*. Despite some consensus that happiness is living well and "doing and faring well" (dual meanings of *eu prattein*),[36] there are at least two disputes about what this means. First, between "the many (*hoi polloi*) and the wise (*sophoi*)," the many claim happiness is something visible and manifest like "pleasure" (*hēdonē*), wealth, or honor (Aristotle is silent on what the wise claim). Second, the dispute about happiness is not just among groups of people, but within the same person (like someone sick saying it is health, or a poor person claiming it is wealth). When people know their own ignorance of happiness, they "wonder" (*thaumazō*) at those who say something "great and beyond themselves." Finally, there are some who suppose there is some other good apart from the many good things that causes them to be good (1095a17–25). Without wading into each of these disputes, the practical question to emerge from them that is relevant to politics and economics concerns how pleasure, wealth, and honor are good things that contribute to happiness. Whether the dispute is between groups of people or within oneself, Aristotle leaves open the possibility that "the wise" may be able to sort through these disputes.

With happiness set as the highest practical good at which the political art aims and wealth featuring prominently in two arguments about the good things, it would be helpful to consider where the relationship between the political art and the art of household management stands at this point in the *Ethics*. In terms of authority, the art of household management (which is among the most-honored capacities) falls under the political art. Because the end of what is more architectonic is more choiceworthy than what falls under it, the political art's end of happiness is more choiceworthy than the art of household management's end of wealth, and wealth is something chosen for the sake of happiness. Although the perspective of the arts yields a hierarchy, the problem of people destroying themselves through wealth (and therefore other good things) suggests wealth is not simply one factor among many that one could add to the equation that produces happiness. And because some think wealth is happiness (either because they are provided or unprovided in it), ignorance of the nature of happiness only compounds the problem that people can destroy themselves with good things. From the perspective of Aristotle's political philosophy, understanding the ends at which the political art and the art of household management aim requires knowledge of the good things that one can acquire through contemplating the ends of one's own desires and choices.

In both the *Ethics*' introduction to happiness and the *Politics*' inquiry into the money-making art, Aristotle provides openings for how wisdom can draw politics and economics toward the good. In the *Politics*, Aristotle recounts the story of Thales to show that while he received reproach for his poverty on the grounds that philosophy is not beneficial (*anōphelēs*), his monopoly showed "it is easy for philosophers to be wealthy, if they wished, but this is not what they are serious (*spoudazō*) about." Surrounding this story are the only two appearances of "wisdom" in the *Politics*, and in both cases, Aristotle stresses that what Thales accomplished was a more general money-making thing, not wisdom.[37] The good by which some judge philosophy as not beneficial in this story is wealth, which is neither the good nor the end of philosophers' wishes. In the *Ethics*, it is the political art's *logos* of the good that could bear much-benefit (*poluōpheles*) to those whose proper (*oikeion*) character can produce their desires and passions according to it. After this, Aristotle suggests that the wise (unlike the many) see happiness is not something obvious like pleasure, wealth, or honor. Why this is true is not yet clear in the *Ethics*, though Aristotle's story of Thales and overview of the dispute about happiness both point to wisdom as providing a true view of what is beneficial.

The story of Thales ends with Aristotle stating that whenever cities are unprovided (*aporeō*) in useful things (*chrēmata*), they make a monopoly to produce revenue (*poros*). Immediately before Thales' story begins, Aristotle proposes someone should bring together stories of those who "hit the mark" in money-making, "for all these things are beneficial to those who honor the money-making art." The verb for those who "hit the mark" (*epitunchanō*) in money-making has at its root the same verb Aristotle uses to ask readers in the *Ethics* if they might "hit upon (*tunchanō*) the needful" in life's actions by holding knowledge of the good like archers holding a target.[38] Aristotle's path to showing cities' need to provide useful things and revenue through money-making thus begins with a brief statement that sets up money-making as the practical good for that inquiry. Between these two statements is Thales' story, one that Aristotle bookends with wisdom's ability to provide far more than revenue. In these passages from the *Politics* and *Ethics*, Aristotle alludes to wisdom being capable of providing the knowledge of the good necessary for hitting upon all that is needful in life, and in such a way that it provides what is good for each person and all practical pursuits (including politics and economics). How this is true requires turning to Book VI of the *Ethics*, where wisdom sits between accounts of choice, science, art, and intellect on the one

side, and the political art and prudence on the other. Through wisdom, readers
see politics' and economics' need for the good.


## PRUDENCE, THE POLITICAL ART, AND HOUSEHOLD MANAGEMENT (*ETHICS* 1099B29–32, 1102A5–31, 1104B30–1105A13, 1112A30–B12, 1113A15–B2, 1130B22–29, 1139A1–1142A30, 1143A35–B14)

To acquire some sense of the significance of Aristotle understanding the
political art and household management as forms of prudence in Book VI of
the *Ethics*, one should return to the lone appearance of the political art in the
*Politics'* inquiry into the money-making art. In this passage, Aristotle likens
the household manager setting-down-through the food nature gives over to
him to the political art taking hold of human beings from nature to use them.
The common characteristic of the household manager and the political art is
they both use for themselves things they do not produce (*poieō*).[39] If an art's
work is to produce something, what do the arts of politics and household
management produce? According to Book I of the *Ethics*, the political art
produces happiness, and the art of household management produces wealth.
If the political art is authoritative over the art of household management, the
latter art cannot produce happiness when left to itself. If this is true, economics (in the current sense of the word) could not produce happiness without
politics.

Through framing politics and economics as arts, an important question
emerges: What does it mean to produce happiness? Aristotle's inquiry into
the money-making art from the *Politics* yields no clues because it never
speaks of happiness. As for the *Ethics*, answering the question of how the
political art produces happiness requires first determining if this art should
prefer the good of one alone or the good of the city. But this only begs the
question of "What is happiness?", and it is not clear if the human good is the
highest of all practical goods, which many agree goes by the name of "happiness," yet disagree about what happiness is.[40] However foreign parts of
Aristotle's political philosophy appear to contemporary readers, from experience they are familiar with politicians proposing economic policies that they
claim will promote each person's own happiness *and* have the best aggregate
effect for their country. What Aristotle offers readers that makes him distinct
from politicians is a way to think about the human good in relation to the
natural and intellectual foundations of politics and economics.

Between the opening chapters of Book I and the account of prudence in
Book VI, Aristotle's few mentions of the political art point to these natural
and intellectual foundations. In the latter parts of Book I, Aristotle states

the political art itself "produces the greatest care" to produce "citizens" (*politas*) who are good and produce what is practical among the noble things (1099b29–32). Shortly thereafter, Aristotle says it seems "the politician according to the truth" (*ho kat'alēthian politikos*) labors and wishes to produce citizens who are good and obedient to the laws; he then adds that this aligns with the inquiry's choice (*proairesis*) to seek the human good and human happiness, which he defines in Book I as "some activity of the soul according to complete virtue (*aretēn teleian*)." This leads to the conclusion that politicians should know something about the soul just as someone performing medical treatment on the eye should know the whole body; the political art, however, is more honorable and better than the medical art (1102a5–23). What best captures the tension between these two passages appears in Book V's inquiry into justice, where—holding up on the one hand the education of the young toward "the common" (*to koinon*) having itself been legislated from the whole of virtue, and on the other hand the education by which each person is a good man simply—Aristotle wonders first if this education belongs to the political art or another art, then admits the possibility that being a good person and a good citizen are not the same in all cases (1130b22–29). The tension between what makes a good person and a good citizen suggests what is good does not always belong to law, which invites readers to wonder if what is good belongs to nature.

Between Book I setting the soul as the political art's concern and Book V's question about the relationship between the good person and the good citizen, Aristotle provides two related arguments about choosing and the political art that hint at how the good by nature could inform the pursuit of happiness in politics and economics. In Book II, Aristotle distinguishes "three things of choosing (*haireseis*)" from "three things of fleeing (*phugas*)": the former things are what is noble, advantageous, and pleasant, and their contraries are what is shameful, harmful, and "painful" (*lupēros*). In all these things, "the good person is accordingly-correct (*kataorthōtikos*), the bad person is errant (*hamartētikos*), most of all concerning pleasure. For this is common to all the animals, and to all things following under choosing, for both the noble and the advantageous display themselves as pleasant" (1104b30–1105a1). In the *Politics'* inquiry into the money-making art, the one mention of "choosing" is in the account of how nature produces different lives among the animals in ways that are advantageous through marking-the-boundaries toward the choosing of food with the pleasant. Though Aristotle next says human beings pleasantly mix lives as need necessitates to acquire the self-sufficient, he never speaks of their "choosing" in this inquiry.[41] By revealing that choosing is prone to error most of all through pleasure, the *Ethics* shows acquisition (and, by extension, economics) is good or bad according to how human beings choose to pursue the pleasant.

The political art—and every art, including those of acquisition such as household management, exchange, money-making, and retail-trade—is bound to the problem of pleasure in choosing when Aristotle observes how difficult it is "to fight" (*machomai*) pleasure, and "both art and virtue always come to concern what is more difficult. As a result and on account of this pleasures and pains concern all the matter for both virtue and the political art, so that those using these things well will be good, while [those using these things] badly [will be] bad" (1105a7–13). This passage provides valuable insight into the character of the political and economic arts in Aristotle's political philosophy. While the practice of politics provides for the needs of ruling and being-ruled within communities and the practice of economics provides for the acquisition of necessary things for people living in communities, Aristotle's political and economic arts respectively provide for how people choose to use pleasures and pains in ruling and being-ruled *and* all forms acquisition to acquire what is good for themselves and their communities. The kinship between art and virtue is they concern choosing what is good by dealing with pleasures and pains. With this in mind, recall that Aristotle refers to the *Ethics*' inquiry as "some political art," and the work's first sentence that states every art, inquiry, action, and choice seem to aim themselves at some good.[42] For Aristotle, every art holds a moral foundation in choosing the pleasant and the painful. As "some political art," Aristotle's political philosophy is an inquiry into the practical concerns of politics and economics that aims to show how to choose the good correctly through the proper uses of pleasures and pains in their arts.

What becomes apparent from examining Aristotle's inquiry into prudence are the limits in treating politics and economics as arts. When Aristotle describes the political art and household management as forms of prudence, he separates them from prudence in the proper sense, which concerns one's own good. As for how prudence relates to choice, science, wisdom, and intellect, because *logos* relates to all these things, readers should pay attention to how Aristotle uses his own inquiry to provide readers some experience in contemplating politics and economics within a philosophic *logos* of the good.

## Intellect and Desire, Choice, and Human Nature (*Ethics* 1102a26–31, 1112a30–b12, 1113a15–b2, 1139a1–b5)

In the opening chapter of Book VI, before Aristotle introduces prudence, he revises the *Ethics*' account of the soul from the first five Books as the inquiry turns away from the "moral" (*ēthikos*) virtues toward those of thought (*dianoia*). Hearkening back to Book I, Aristotle reminds readers that the soul has the part holding *logos* (*to logon echōn*) and the part without-*logos* (*to alogon*), then posits that "one-must-divide" (*diaireteon*) the part holding *logos*, saying, "Let us propose (*hupokeimai*) the [parts] holding *logos* are two, in one we contemplate such beings (*tōn ontōn*) whose first-principles (*archai*) do not admit themselves to hold otherwise (*endechontai allōs echein*), in the other [we contemplate] those things which admit [to hold otherwise]" (1139a1–8). The dividing Aristotle proposes by its very name implies a choosing (*hairesis*) within contemplation. But readers should be careful with how sharply they draw this division, for when Aristotle proposes back in Book I that "one-must-use" (*chrēsteon*) the "exoteric *logoi*" of the parts of the soul holding *logos* and without-*logos*, he acknowledges the possibility that boundaries-are-marked so that things may be "two in *logos* but naturally inseparable (*achōrista*)." This is in contrast to marking-the-boundaries of "the parts of the body and every thing divisible-into-parts (*to meriston*),"[43] though Aristotle adds the difference between these things does not matter in Book I (1102a26–31). The difference Aristotle draws is curious since the parts of the body are naturally inseparable, which suggests the soul is naturally inseparable. It is only through *logos* that the body and the soul are separable, and the same likely holds true with contemplating the things that either do or do not admit to hold otherwise.

Although the preceding divisions in the body and soul through *logos* initially appear to be purely theoretical matters, failing to attend to them has practical implications for politics and economics. Returning to Book VI's proposed divisions within the part holding *logos* and their respective contemplation, Aristotle says, "For towards the things of each class and of the parts of the soul each class [is] naturally towards each [part], if indeed the knowledge is present to these according to some likeness and proper-kinship (*oikeiotēs*)"[44] (1139a9–11). Aristotle's proposed division with the soul holding *logos* assumes a natural correspondence between the soul and various classes of things. Holding these divisions in knowledge alongside the soul's natural inseparability echoes Book I of the *Politics* where the definition of the "slave" as a human being who is by nature a practical and separable piece of acquisition (*ktēma*) leads into contemplating through *logos* how ruling and being-ruled (which are among the necessary and advantageous things) have a common work; this work exists in things that are either holding-together (*sunechēs*) or divided-themselves (*diaireō*). This *logos* discovers the political rule of intellect and the part holding *logos* over desire and the passionate part within the soul.[45] In body and soul, human beings are naturally holding-together, and their nature's inseparability means all their contemplation and the practical pursuits this informs continuously mix intellect, *logos*, desire, and passion. From this perspective, politics and economics are neither purely rational nor irrational. Central to Aristotle's teaching on the virtues in the *Ethics* is the idea of a *hexis*, a term that—by deriving from the verb for "to hold" (*echō*)—means "a holding."[46] The preceding passages all speak to a sense in which every facet of human nature holds-together in some way with *logos*. Since prudence is the *hexis* to which politics and economics belong, readers must pay careful attention to how Aristotle's political philosophy teaches that intellect and desire need to hold together toward the good in these practical pursuits.

With the parts of the soul setting up contemplation as the theme of Book VI, Aristotle outlines the relationship between intellect and action, starting with the assertion that the three things in the soul authoritative over action and truth are sense-perception, intellect, and desire (*orexis*). With respect to action, Aristotle dismisses sense-perception as a "beginning" or "first-principle" (*archē*)[47] because while beasts and human beings both hold sense-perception, beasts do not form-community in action (1139a17–20). Very quickly, Aristotle establishes action and truth are common to intellect and desire. This carries over to the next statement that likens affirmation and denial in thought to pursuit and fleeing in desiring. In light of the kinship between thought and desire, since "moral virtue [is] a *hexis* characterized-by-choice (*proairetikē*)," choice is "deliberate desire" (*orexis bouleutikē*), and if choice is serious, then the *logos* needs to be true and the desire correct, and further, what *logos* affirms, desire pursues; this, Aristotle asserts, is "the practical thought and truth" (1139a21–27). Before unpacking the important threads of the *Ethics* that come together in this passage, notice that Aristotle understands through choice that the "practical" is not merely the "expedient," but a form of thought that uses *logos* to bring desire to follow the truth.

A glimpse of what Aristotle's account of the practical thinking and truth means for economic and political life appears in his initial inquiry into "deliberation" (*boulē*) and choice from Book III of the *Ethics*. Not all things are subject to deliberation, but "we ourselves deliberate about the practical things up to ourselves." As opposed to the precise and self-sufficient sciences (like the one concerned with letters, where no one doubts how to write them), "we ourselves deliberate" in matters where things do not always come to be in the same way, which is the case in the arts of medicine and money-making. Deliberation extends to the arts and sciences where things are more doubtful, and the arts are more doubtful than the sciences (1112a30–b8). If the money-making art came into being according to *logos* by providing legal-currency out of necessity to produce a necessary exchange through which communities import the things they need and export the things of which there is more than enough, then deliberation in this art concerns the best way to import and export those things, and what form of legal-currency produces more manageable exchanges.[48]

Between these statements about deliberation's concern, Aristotle observes that "nature, necessity, and chance seem to be causes, and so too do intellect and all things through the human being" (1112a31–33). In the first half of the inquiry into the money-making art, nature's differences in food produce different lives among the animals toward such acquisition. There are similar differences in human lives, though they mix lives as need necessitates, and add exchange and retail-trade on top of natural acquisition. In the inquiry's second half, Aristotle initially describes nature as giving over things for food that the household manager needs to set-down-through and use for the sake of ruling the household, then refines this to say nature's work is to hold-forth (*parechō*) food, and concludes "the money-making art is according to nature for all things from fruits of the earth and animals." Shortly after Aristotle describes legal-currency's provision coming out of necessity, he differentiates between the money-making art that provides for necessary exchange, and the art of retail-trade that aims to produce the most gain. The sole mention of "chance" in the inquiry is in the statement that the most artistic works related to wage-earning have the least amount of chance. The cause that never appears in Aristotle's inquiry into the money-making art is the intellect, though he does describe the money-maker as someone who contemplates sources of acquisition, wealth, and useful things, and later, the money-making art's work as "the capacity to contemplate from where there will be a quantity of useful things: for it is productive of wealth and useful things."[49] Consequently, the *Politics'* inquiry into the money-making art does not directly account for how human beings' intellect affects the economic arts' work toward nature, necessity, and chance.

The *Ethics'* initial inquiry into deliberation also reveals something about choice and ends, for Aristotle says, "We ourselves do not deliberate about the ends but about the things towards the ends" (1112b11–12). Where, then, does the end come from? The end belongs to "wish" (*boulēsis*), which leads to the question if wish is for the good *or* "the apparent good" (*to phainomenon agathon*). The latter case invites the possibility that nothing wished for is by nature, but only seems to be good to each person. This prompts a distinction between the serious person and the many: whereas the serious person perhaps differs most in seeing the truth in each *hexis* and judges correctly, for the many, what is not good displays itself as good and they choose (*haireō*) the pleasant as good and flee pain as bad (1113a15–b2). Notice the kinship between "deliberation" (*boulē*) and "wish" (*boulēsis*). Choice—which precedes every action—depends on deliberation, which is always toward an end for which one wishes. As Aristotle presents them here, the ends of choice, deliberation, and action are either the good or the apparent good. The failure to judge the good according to the truth reiterates Book II's teaching that the good person is accordingly correct and the bad person is errant in choosing the pleasant (with the other two things of choosing being the noble and the advantageous). The only hint of how to avoid this error is to be a serious person, but it is not clear if the good person is the same as the serious person.

Setting aside that difficulty for now, Aristotle is careful not to undercut the idea that wish is for the good by nature, revealing instead that the wish seems to be errant because people choose the pleasant in ways that do not truly hold toward the good.

Returning to Aristotle's account of choice in Book VI, from his outline of how every *hexis* that is moral virtue needs the serious choice where desire pursues true *logos*, Aristotle provides an illuminating description of human nature. The first-principle or beginning (*archē*) of action is choice since this is from where the "motion" (*kinēsis*) comes, but choice itself derives from desire and *logos* for the sake of something. On account of this, there is not choice without intellect, thought, or a moral *hexis* (1139a31–35). Aristotle's understanding of action is simultaneously moral and intellectual; it is not merely the mechanical motion of desire,[50] but a common work of desire, *logos*, intellect, and thought. To define the nature of choice, Aristotle observes that thought itself "moves" (*kineō*) nothing, but thought that is for the sake of something and practical does, for this thought rules (*archeō*) the productive (*hē poiētikē*). While the producer produces for the sake of something, the thing produced is not (like an action) an end simply, for it is in relation to someone and something else (for example, if a carpenter produces a chair, the chair exists for the sake of someone sitting on it). The act, however, is for the sake "good-action" (*eupraxia*), and desire is for this end. From this, Aristotle concludes that "choice is either desiring intellect (*orektikos nous*) or thinking desire (*orexis dianoētikē*), and such a first-principle [or beginning, *archē*] is a human being" (1139a35–b5). Although both production and action are for the sake of an end provided by *logos*, actions relate more directly to human beings than productions because actions do not produce something apart from themselves. This is where Aristotle's statement about human beings as a "first-principle" or "beginning" becomes so vital. Behind the two descriptions of human beings is a question about what is authoritative in human nature: intellect or desire?

The discovery of human nature through choice by using a distinction between action and production provides a deeper insight into Book I of the *Politics'* gradual unveiling of economics' and politics' mutual need for free rule through aiming at the good by nature. From the inquiry into slavery, readers know that "Life is action, not production (*poiēsis*)," and further, that political rule requires intellect and *logos* to rule over desire and passion. Readers should also recall from this inquiry that nature's wish is to produce human beings who in body and soul are free and useful toward political life, yet it lacks the capacity to do this. Given the *Ethics'* account of choice, human beings are free or slave not because nature produces them in this way, but because they choose actions through which they become either free or slave. This insight bears directly on the two times Aristotle discusses "being serious" in his inquiry into the money-making art. In the first half of the inquiry, the reason why people exchange the art of household management's work for the art of retail-trade's is because of a setting-down-through them-selves to be more serious about living than living well. Because this desire (*epithumia*) is without-limit, they desire (*epithumeō*) the legal-currency that is productive of what is without-limit. In the second half of this inquiry, Aristotle uses the story of Thales to show philosophers could be wealthy "if they wished, but this is not what they are serious about." While there is an opening within Thales' story is to explain the end at which wisdom aims instead of money-making, Aristotle does not pursue it. Still, this unfulfilled wish from Thales' story is one that readers should hold against the art of retail-trade's wish to produce its own end.[51] Since there is a natural need and necessity for both ruling and being ruled *and* acquisition, politics and economics must work in common to provide for these needs. Because there is neither politics nor economics apart from human beings, it is necessary to provide them knowledge of the good so that their desires, choices, and actions in these things do not go on without-limit, thereby helping them to live freely. As Aristotle shows in Book VI of the *Ethics*, it is not any art or science that provides this needful knowledge, but wisdom.

## Prudence and Seeking the Good Things with Truth (*Ethics* 1139b11–1140b30)

With human beings as first-principles who combine intellect and desire, Aristotle concludes Book VI's second chapter by stating "the work of the intellectual parts [is] truth," and the *hexeis* "arrive at truth" (*alētheuō*) most of all with their respective virtues. Accordingly, Book VI's third chapter opens by revealing the five ways the soul arrives at truth: art, science, prudence, wisdom, and intellect (1139b11–17). This beginning moves away from the previous chapters' emphasis on parts of the soul to a broader view of how the whole soul arrives at truth. If intellect and desire are more tightly bound in human nature than *logos* suggests, it is likely that *logos* of the different ways of arriving at the truth is tightly knit as well. What gradually emerges in Aristotle's account of how the soul works and holds toward the truth is the centrality of the intellect to all human pursuits, one that has profound implica-tions for grounding politics and economics in a broad, natural context.

The first way the soul arrives at truth is science, something Aristotle defines both before and after his initial definition of prudence. Accordingly, only the parts of Aristotle's first definition that carry over to the second are necessary here. Supposing a need to speak precisely, Aristotle says, "We all assume (*hupolambanō*)[52] to know-scientifically (*epistamai*) ourselves the things that do not admit to hold otherwise," which means what can be "known-scientifically" (*epistēton*) is from necessity (*anankē*) and therefore "eternal" (*aidios*) (1139b18–24). While necessity relates to all these sciences—for all have some claim to being necessary for living—it is not clear that these sciences are eternal. After all, according to the parts of the *Politics* examined earlier, many potential political and economic sciences have nothing to do with the eternal: the forms of rule (i.e., political, kingly, household management, and mastery), slavery, the just art of acquisition, and the political capacity.[53] A hint of what may be both necessary and eternal comes when Aristotle shifts his definition of science to a "demonstrative *hexis*" that relies on first-principles and syllogisms, for a person knows-scientifically whenever one "trusts" (*pisteuō*) in any way and the first-principles are "known" or "familiar" (*gnōrimos*) to oneself (1139b25–36). If there is anything both necessary and eternal in science, it rests in first-principles. But this leaves readers to wonder about the nature of this trust they hold in science and, more importantly, how first-principles become known or familiar.

In moving from science to art, Aristotle returns to the distinction between things produced and actions that precedes his characterization of human beings as intellect and desire. Though both something practical and something produced both themselves admit to hold otherwise, since "we ourselves trust" in the exoteric *logoi* that there is a difference between production and action, there is a difference between "the practical *hexis* with *logos*" and "the productive *hexis* with *logos*." Because of this, neither *hexis* "holds-concern-around (*periechō*) the other, so that action is not production and production is not action" (1140a1–5). Although Aristotle refrains from mentioning first-principles, his appeal to readers' trust in exoteric *logoi* at the beginning of his examination of art echoes the need for trust that occurs where the examination of science ends. The distinction between action and production that defines life in Book I of the *Politics* and is instrumental to discovering human beings are (as first-principles) intellect and desire bears directly on *hexeis* with *logos* in the *Ethics*.

To see the significance of Aristotle's distinction between a practical and productive *hexis* with *logos* for his political and economic teaching, one should know that back in Book I of the *Ethics*, shortly after he settles on the preliminary definition of happiness as an activity of the soul according to virtue, he says, "Perhaps [there is] no small difference to assume the best thing [is] in acquisition (*ktēsis*) or use (*chrēsis*), and in a *hexis* or an activity" (1098b31–33). The *Politics'* inquiry into the money-making art—literally, the art of useful things (*chrēmata*)—begins with Aristotle saying "let us contemplate" this art along with what concerns all of acquisition.[54] The acquisitions throughout the inquiry are all that nature holds-forth (food, raw materials, etc.) and wealth (which encompasses these natural things, tools, and legal-currency), but whether these acquisitions truly provide for human needs depends on whether or not their use is according to nature. If there is a kinship between *hexis* and acquisition, then those who seek Aristotle's economic teaching must pay attention to how people's use of acquisitions depends on how they hold themselves through contemplation.

To acquire a better hold on the intellectual character of a *hexis*, readers should follow Aristotle's wondering if a *hexis* is "the best thing" in the passage above back to the first personal question of the *Ethics* about whether the good and the best thing is the end "we ourselves wish for" so that neither choosing nor desire are without-limit. To point to one's own need for the good, Aristotle asks, "And therefore towards life would not the knowledge of this good hold great weight, and just like archers holding a target, might we more hit upon the needful?" What it means to hold a target in this image is not having it in hand, but to hold it in sight. Because a *hexis* is with *logos*, one's own work in it depends on holding *logos* as an intellectual target. Though Aristotle insists on a distinction between a practical and a productive *hexis* in Book VI, recall how in Book I the political art's *logoi* concerning life's actions would be of much benefit to those who produce their desires according to *logos*. Furthermore, remember Book I's appeal to exoteric *logoi* about parts of the soul prompts the observation that things may be "two in *logos* but naturally inseparable."[55] As is now evident, politics and economics are both practical and productive pursuits, and their first-principle is human beings whose own *hexeis* all reveal how they hold toward the good.

Returning to Aristotle's examination of art in Book VI, his gradual refinement of its definition sheds light on how the various economic arts in the *Politics* reflect the ways people's own *hexeis* hold toward nature. Aristotle starts with an appeal to the "art of house-building" (*oikodomikē*) to reiterate how art is a productive *hexis* with *logos*, and states this is the same as a productive *hexis* with "true *logos*" (1140a6–10). The possibility that an art's *logos* is not necessarily "true" is something readers should keep in mind as Aristotle investigates the nature of art. Continuing to refine his definition, Aristotle notes every art's concern is "to artfully contrive" (*technizō*) and "to contemplate" something that admits of being or not being. The first-principle of such things is not in the thing produced, but the person producing it, thus "there is no art for the beings or the things coming to be from necessity, nor of the things according to nature, for these things hold the first-principle in themselves" (1140a10–16). The *Politics'* inquiry into the money-making art provides helpful examples for why there is no art for the things from necessity and according to nature. Animals' different lives in the acquisition of food reveal the same thing is not pleasant to them according to nature. The art of exchange (*hē metablētikē*) begins from what is according to nature (i.e., human beings holding more or less of things than is adequate), and so the need for its presence as part of the art of household management for the sake of self-sufficiency is according to nature. The money-making art came into being according to *logos* with the provision of legal-currency out of necessity to produce easier foreign exchange of things necessary according to nature, and this art remains according to nature when it provides for the exchange of the useful, fruitful, and unfruitful things that nature first holds-forth to human beings. Conversely, the money-making art is not according to nature when it becomes the art of retail-trade (the "unnecessary money-making art") that is justly blamed for seeking to produce wealth without-limit through the exchange of legal-currency. This unnecessary art begins with people mistaking living well as the production of excess enjoyment, leading them to use their own capacities in ways that are not according to nature.[56] In all these economic arguments, acquisition's necessity and the determination of whether or not its arts are according to nature does not come through any art, but a first-principle inherent to Aristotle's *logos*.

Before drawing his brief inquiry into art to a close, Aristotle reiterates art is necessarily production and not action, then notes art and chance concern the same things, citing the poet Agathon ("Good"), who says, "Art loves (*stergō*)[57] chance and chance [loves] art" (1140a16–20). The kinship between art and chance following on the heels of setting nature and necessity outside of art's concern recalls Book III's arguments that bring the arts under the authority not of nature, necessity, and chance, but intellect and desire working through human deliberation and choice toward ends for which they wish. Another sign of art's contemplative character is evident from Aristotle's brief account of wage-earning in the *Politics'* inquiry into the money-making art where those who are without-art (*atechnōs*) and slavish are useful only for their bodies, while the most artistic works have the least amount of chance. The need for exchange is present according to nature, but if human beings do not provide an art of acquisition to produce the exchange of necessary things, then it is a matter of chance whether they acquire what they need for natural self-sufficiency.[58] To play on the pun in Agathon's name, both art and chance can bear the good along with themselves, but only art falls under the authority of people's contemplation and desire of the good.

Following his playfully poetic view of the good, art, and chance, Aristotle concludes his account of art by saying, "Therefore art is, as has been said, some productive *hexis* with true *logos*, and artlessness (*atechnia*) the contrary productive *hexis* with false (*pseudos*) *logos*, concerning the·thing itself admitting to hold otherwise" (1140a20–23). Aristotle refines the argument above that art being with *logos* is the same as it being with true *logos*, now settling art in relation to true *logos* and artlessness with false *logos*. Though art remains a productive *hexis*, its definition's condition of "with true *logos*" aligns it with Book VI's characterization of "the practical thought and truth" that—in order for choice to be serious—"the *logos* needs to be true and the desire correct." Within the *Politics'* inquiry into the money-making art, the sole mention of what is "true" is Aristotle's definition of "true wealth" as "a store of such useful things that are necessary towards living, and useful to community in a city or a household." True wealth's self-sufficiency is not without-limit toward "good living," which starkly contrasts with the art of retail-trade that produces the possibility for someone to be well-provided in legal-currency and unprovided in necessary food.[59] In light of the *Ethics'* distinction between art and artlessness on the basis of true or false *logos*, Aristotle's distinctions among the arts of acquisition in *Politics* I.8–11 (i.e., art of exchange, necessary exchange, money-making art, and retail-trade) reveal these economic arts are true only if they provide what is necessary for good living. The art of retail-trade is therefore a false art, while all the other arts of acquisition are true. Insofar as people choose to abandon the true ends of the arts of money-making and household management through the art of retail-trade's false end, the *Ethics'* placement of art in the context of "the practical thought and truth" makes clear that the arts are either true or false according to people's contemplation of the good.

Moving from art to his preliminary account of prudence, Aristotle suggests contemplating whom "we say" is prudent. From this perspective, "The prudent person (*phronimos*) seems to be one who has the capacity to deliberate nobly concerning the good and advantageous things for himself, not according to a part (like the sorts of things towards health or strength), but the sorts of things towards the whole of living well" (1140a24–28). In Book I, Aristotle introduces happiness to the *Ethics* by noting all sorts of people "assume" it is living well and acting well, which leads to a brief account of how the many (as opposed to the wise) think it is pleasure, wealth, honor, or health.[60] But now in Book VI, the prudent person's concern with living well does not hold such a narrow focus, and is open to the good and advantageous things. Supporting the prudent person's concern with the whole of living well, Aristotle says, "A sign of this is that we say someone [is] a prudent person concerning something whenever towards some serious end one calculates [or reasons (*logizomai*)] well, of which there is not an art. As a result, a prudent person would wholly be the deliberative person" (1140a28–31). By identifying the prudent person with the deliberative person instead of an art, Aristotle brings the prudent person closer to the practical character of choice, and thus in more direct relation to the good than art.

Focusing on the prudent person's deliberative character, Aristotle works toward his first definition of prudence that distinguishes it from science and art. Deliberating neither concerns things lacking the capacity to hold otherwise, nor the things one does not admit to act on. If science is with demonstration yet there can be no demonstration when first-principles admit to hold otherwise, and if "there is no deliberating about the beings from necessity, then prudence would neither be a science nor an art: [not] a science because the act itself admits to hold otherwise, and [not] an art because action is another class from production. Therefore it remains for [prudence] to be a true practical *hexis* with *logos* concerning the good things and bad things for a human being" (1140a31–b6). The first definition of prudence adheres to Book VI's concern with the truth. Although Aristotle puts some distance between prudence and science, careful readers should note the act admitting to hold otherwise does not discount the idea of a first-principle that does not admit to hold otherwise informing the act. The shift from the prudent person's concern with "the good and advantageous things" to prudence's concern with "the good things and the bad things" bears this out, especially when one remembers Aristotle's implicit argument in Book I that the good things do not hold differences among themselves, nor do they wander (though some people can destroy themselves through the good things).[61]

From the first definition of prudence, Aristotle revisits the initial example of prudent persons and brings politicians and household managers into the inquiry. Aristotle first reminds readers that production's end is not the same as action's (i.e., good-action), then says, "Through this we ourselves suppose Pericles and those of this sort to be prudent, and that they themselves have the capacity to contemplate the good things for themselves and for human beings; we ourselves believe[62] such persons to be the household managers and the politicians" (1140b6–11). The inclusion of Pericles (the famous statesman who led the Athenian empire for the first two and a half years of the Peloponnesian War) alongside household managers and politicians invites readers to wonder if prudence is the same at the heights of political empire as it is within the household.[63] This supposed likeness in being prudent that many believe characterizes politicians and household managers recalls Book I's statement that taking hold of and preserving the human good for the city is greater and more complete, nobler and more divine, than doing so for one person alone.[64] In line with prudence's first definition, it seems contemplating the good things for oneself is the necessary precondition for taking hold of and preserving the human good in community (both households and cities).

From the connections between prudence and the rulers of households and cities, Aristotle considers how pleasure affects one's own understanding of the human good. In support of the preceding argument about prudent rulers, Aristotle says, "Thus we ourselves call[65] moderation (*sōphrosunē*) by its name, as preserving (*sōzō*) prudence (*phronēsis*). And it preserves such an assumption (*hupolēpsis*)" (1140b11–13). Moderation is the second moral virtue that receives detailed examination in the *Ethics* (III.10–12), and the appeal to its name here suggests this virtue people recognize within the household manager reflects the politician's more authoritative prudence. Aristotle's etymology for "moderation" also suggests prudence's concern with the human good depends on moderation, which means prudence is not a self-sufficient virtue. Through moderation, Aristotle brings pleasures and pains into the inquiry, saying, "For [it is] not every assumption that the pleasant and the painful ruin and distort, like whether the triangle holds or does not hold two right angles (*orthas*), but the things concerning acts" (1140b13–16). By comparing the practical and mathematical things, Aristotle shows that only certain forms of contemplating and calculating can help people know the good things for themselves. No mathematical formula provides clarity about the good things because people cannot contemplate what is good for themselves with pleasures and pains removed from the equation.

The ruinous effects of the pleasant and the painful prompt the return of first-principles to the inquiry. Acts' first-principles are their "that for the sake of which" (*to hou heneka*), but the first-principle does not display itself immediately to the person who ruins oneself through pleasures and pains, and therefore the need to choose (*haireō*) all things oneself and act through this does not display itself. From this, Aristotle concludes, "For vice is ruinous[66] of the first-principle. And so necessarily prudence is a true practical *hexis* with *logos* concerning the good things for human beings" (1140b16–21). Although Aristotle alludes to the role of ends in choosing with the "that for the sake of which," this argument hearkens back to Book II's distinction between the good person and the bad person where the former is correct and the latter is errant when choosing the pleasant. While there is room to wonder about how ends are first-principles in the early stages of Aristotle's inquiry into prudence, the present passage's concern with ruining oneself through choosing the pleasant and the painful illustrates how human beings are themselves acts' first-principles. Though it seems from this argument that the proper correction to vice's ruinous character comes through virtue, Aristotle opposes vice to prudence and its now-exclusive concern with the good things, dropping "the bad things" from the definition. The first-principle of prudence, then, is closer to the good things than virtue.

The insufficiency of virtue to help people choose the pleasant and the painful for the sake of becoming good is apparent in the conclusion to Book VI's fifth chapter. Unlike an art, there is no virtue of prudence (though prudence is itself some virtue). Also, "voluntarily erring [is] more choiceworthy" in art than prudence. Partly on the basis of these considerations, Aristotle's last description of prudence is that it is "not only a *hexis* with *logos*" (1140b21–30). If neither virtue nor art can fully lead the fight against pleasure, then the hopes Book II invests in virtue and the political art to manage pleasures and pains are partially misplaced. By combining the previous paragraph's implication that human beings are themselves first-principles with the question of what is choiceworthy in art, Aristotle's vague allusion to the *hexis* of prudence holding more than *logos* should point readers back to his definition of human beings through choice as a first-principle that is either desiring intellect or thinking desire. Though Aristotle uses the intellect to say more about the political art and household management in Book VI, the omission of desire from the account means two things for his political and economic teaching. First, readers must look elsewhere in the *Ethics* to discover where the intellect and desire come together (which does not happen until the inquiry into friendship). Second, if prudence emerges within an incomplete account of human nature, readers should not draw definite conclusions about politics and economics through it. Book VI's heavy emphasis on the intellect and relative silence on desire means the portrait of politics and economics to emerge from it is (to step outside of Aristotle's terminology for a moment) purely rational. This perspective inverts the problem of vice, for instead of desire ruining the first-principle that is a human being and holding the intellect back from displaying itself, overemphasis on the intellect holds desire back from displaying itself.

## The Intellectual Foundations of Politics and Economics (*Ethics* 1140b31–1142a30, 1143a35–b14)

With the mystery of Aristotle defining prudence as a *hexis* that is not only with *logos*, he revisits what constitutes science and begins to push the importance of the intellect and how it holds towards first-principles. Earlier in Book VI, Aristotle defines "science" as a "demonstrative *hexis*" that relies upon trusting and knowing or being familiar with first-principles of the things that do not admit to hold otherwise (i.e., things from necessity and eternal). Now, however, Aristotle says, "Since science is an assumption concerning the general (*katholou*) things and the beings from necessity, [and since] there are first-principles of the demonstrative things and of every science (for science [is] with *logos*), of the first-principle of what is known-scientifically there would neither be science nor art nor prudence" (1140b31–35). In this second definition of "science," it is no longer a *hexis* but an assumption, one that may or may not be subject to ruin by pleasures and pains. While the eternal things drop from the second definition, the nature of trust and familiarity in first-principles becomes more pressing. If science, art, and prudence are incapable of revealing first-principles, what is? *Logos* clearly has a role in the demonstrations from first-principles, but there is something more at work. Although such an inquiry appears to be an exercise in mere abstraction, understanding why Aristotle downgrades science from *hexis* to "assumption" is vital for seeing why there is a limit to the practical effects of political and economic sciences when compared to philosophy.

To bring the intellect forward as a viable path to the first-principles on which science depends, Aristotle elaborates on the problem for science, prudence, and art: while what is known-scientifically is demonstrable, the things of art and prudence admit to hold otherwise. On the grounds of demonstrability, the first-principles do not belong to wisdom either, for the wise person holds demonstration about some things (1140b35–1141a3). These arguments' underlying assumption is science does not concern what admits to hold otherwise. Aristotle casts doubts on this rigid view with a curious conclusion: "If the ways we arrive at truth and in no way deceive ourselves concerning the things that do and do not admit to hold otherwise [are] science, prudence, wisdom, and intellect, and three of these things do not themselves admit to be [such ways of arriving at truth] (and I say the three [are] prudence, science, [and] wisdom), then intellect itself remains to be of the first-principles" (1141a3–8). Alongside prudence, wisdom, and intellect, science now implicitly relates to things that both do and do not admit to hold otherwise. At the same time, readers should notice that (contrary to Book VI's third chapter) art is no longer among the ways of arriving at truth.[67] Along similar lines, Aristotle does not speak of these ways of arriving at the truth in relation to the soul, which confirms the earlier skepticism of Book VI's choice to divide (*diaireō*) the part of the soul holding *logos* on the condition that there may be a proper kinship (*oikeiotēs*) between parts of the soul and contemplation between things that do and not admit to hold otherwise. The need to understand the intellect's relationship to first-principles thus emerges amid two related shifts for science and art. Though science is no longer a *hexis*, it remains a way of arriving at truth; while art remains a *hexis*, it is no longer a way of arriving at truth. Considering one of the lessons from the *Politics* is the art of retail-trade corresponds to a view of living well that seeks what is productive of excess bodily enjoyments, readers should approach Aristotle's inquiry into the intellect and first-principles in the *Ethics* with a mind to finding how this contemplation prevents a productive error about the truth in economics.

The shifts in Book VI's accounts of art and science inform the beginning of its examination of wisdom that lays the foundation for revealing how the intellect holds in relation to first-principles. As a sign of an art's virtue, "we give" the name of "wisdom" to "the most precise arts." As for the sciences, because "we ourselves suppose" there are some wise people who are so wholly and not according to a part, wisdom would be "the most precise of the sciences. Therefore, there is need for the wise person not only to know the things from the first-principles, but to arrive at the truth concerning the first-principles. And so wisdom would be intellect and science, a science of the most honorable things holding a head" (1141a9–20). Precision in the arts is an insufficient basis for wisdom because "we suppose" people are wholly wise, but art is only a part of what human beings do. Precision in science is an insufficient basis for "wisdom" because science has no "head" without the intellect's ability to arrive at truth about the first-principles. To understand where Aristotle is about to take his examination of wisdom, recall that in Book I "we see" that the political art holds concern around the human good in part because the capacities most in-honor (which include the art of household management) fall-under its authority. With politicians and household managers as supposed models for prudence and contemplating the good things for themselves in Book VI,[68] it would seem that the most honorable things would be political. Yet what follows Aristotle's first definition of wisdom is a demotion of the political and economic things that encourages readers to look elsewhere to contemplate the good things for themselves.

Proceeding toward clarifying what the most honorable things are, Aristotle says, "For it would be strange if someone himself supposes the political art or prudence to be the most serious thing, if a human being is not the best of the things in the cosmos" (1141a20–22). Aristotle's statement is a microcosm of Book I's first four chapters and the tension between acquiring knowledge of the good through the most authoritative and architectonic art, *or* by contemplating one's own wishes, desires, and choices through a *logos* of life's actions. Book VI's turn toward the cosmos reaffirms the *Ethics*' opening sentence and the question it raises about all things aiming themselves at the good. In downplaying the political art, Book VI's examination of wisdom also holds happiness (the "highest of all the practical goods")[69] out of sight. The turn toward the cosmos is necessary because the human good is always contingent: if there is no cosmos, there are no human beings to contemplate their own good. To those who think politics and economics provide sufficient knowledge about the good, Aristotle must show why wisdom's contemplation of the cosmos is far more serious about these practical matters.

With the perspective of the cosmos in mind, Aristotle compares wisdom to prudence and the political art. From what people assert, while the wise concerns that which is always, prudence contemplates "the well-being" (*to eu*)[70] of each thing and is not the same from one thing to another. For example, what is healthy and good for a human being would not be the same for a fish. Through this, people assert some beasts (i.e., those holding the capacity for forethought in their lives) are prudent. Yet wisdom is evidently distinct from the political art, for if people say wisdom concerns things beneficial to themselves, there would be many wisdoms, for there is not one good concerning all animals, but one for each (unless there is one medical art for all beings). And it makes no difference if a human being is the best among the animals, for the nature from which the cosmos is set-standing-together is much more divine than a human being (1141a22–b2). Working from what people assert about wisdom, there does not seem to be a way to reconcile what is always the case with the well-being of each thing. Compared to the political art, this problem concerns what is beneficial to those under its authority (as is evident by how the political art differs from one city to another). Aristotle's last argument in this quotation, however, accomplishes something more clearly than the political art's introduction. At the end of Book I's second chapter, between declaring the political art holds concern for the human good and describing his inquiry as "some political art," Aristotle presents the hypothetical case that taking hold of and preserving the human good for nations and cities is "nobler and more divine" than accomplishing this for one alone. Like each person in relation to the political community's good, the political art's good diminishes in relation to the cosmos that are—like communities in the *Politics*—set-standing-together.[71] But in comparing the political art to wisdom and its view of the cosmos, the contemplation of what is more divine seems to depart from contemplating what is good and beneficial for each person. What good, then, is it beneficial to contemplate: one's own, the political art's, or the cosmos'?

From the differences between the political art and wisdom derived from what people assert, Aristotle defines wisdom as "science and intellect of the most honorable things by nature." Because of this, Anaxagoras, Thales, and other such wise persons are not said to be prudent, for they are ignorant of the advantageous things for themselves, knowing instead useless things, for "they do not seek [or examine (*zēteō*)] the human goods" (1141b2–8). Like its first definition before the digression on the political art and the cosmos, wisdom remains characterized by science and intellect of what is most honorable. But where wisdom initially appears as "the most precise of the sciences," it no longer holds this precision. At the same time, what is "most honorable" now relates to what is "by nature" in a cosmic sense. The problem for cosmic wisdom is that what is "by nature" is neither advantageous and useful, nor does it seek the human goods that concern the political art.

In contrast to wisdom's impractical character stands prudence and its concern with the human things and deliberating, for "we assert" the prudent person's work is to deliberate well about the practical good (not things lacking the capacity to hold otherwise, nor things of which there is not some end). Furthermore, "the prudent person [is] simply a good-deliberator skillful in aiming [or guessing (*stochastikos*)][72] at the best thing of the acts for a human being according to reasoning (*ton logismon*)" (1141b8–14). With the emphasis on deliberating, the contrast between prudent and wise persons is that the former are more suited for making choices (defined earlier as "deliberate desire") than the latter. The implication is that whatever good wisdom reveals is not practical for human beings whose nature is synonymous with choice (desiring intellect or thinking desire). The opening for the intellect in Aristotle's account of prudence comes with him emphasizing that prudence concerns not only the general, but needs to know or be familiar with what is "according to each thing" (*ta kath'ekasta*, i.e., particulars) since it is practical (hence why experienced people are more practical). On account of this, prudence is practical and holds both what is general and according to each thing, though "there might be something architectonic in here" (1141b14–23). This passage marks the penultimate appearance of what is "architectonic" in the *Ethics* (the two prior appearances of which are in Book I where the political art's claim to having an end that is more choiceworthy than everything under its authority bookends one's own need for knowledge of the good for life's actions that derive from wish, desire, and choosing).[73] In contrast to Book I, the current argument suggests what is architectonic in prudence is not an art.

Before seeing how Aristotle brings the political art and household management together under the *hexis* of prudence, some differences from the *Politics'* inquiry into the money-making art are worth bringing forward. The difference in what it means to contemplate the well-being and what is good for human beings as opposed to animals is reminiscent of the account of natural acquisition and the different lives animals and human beings live in the care for food. But where the only talk of "choosing" and what is advantageous in Aristotle's inquiry appears in his summary of acquisition to describe how nature produces animals' lives, in Book VI of the *Ethics*, the nature of human choosing is at the forefront of the inquiry. The appearance of Thales is also instructive, for in describing his money-making as "something general" distinct from wisdom, Aristotle suggests Thales discovered something beneficial, useful, and advantageous for himself. Thales was prudent, but perhaps not wise in his economic prudence. Like the *Politics*, an opening remains for wisdom to be beneficial in the *Ethics*, though it must not set its sights on the nature of the cosmos. Rather, wisdom should "seek or examine the human goods," but not like those who "seek or examine" what is productive of excess in money-making because they mistake living well for excess bodily enjoyments.[74]

The search for what is architectonic in prudence begins with Aristotle observing that prudence and the political art are the same *hexis*, but not the same being. Concerning cities, architectonic prudence is the "legislative art" (*nomothetikē*). As for the prudence concerning what is according to each thing, it holds the common name of the political art, and this is practical and deliberative, for a decree is the practical thing as "the last thing" (*to eschaton*). On account of this, they say only those (presumably those who make decrees)[75] practice politics themselves, for only they do these things, just like the artisans (1141b23–29). With the prior description of prudence setting its dual concerns as what is general and what is according to each thing pointing to "something architectonic," the legislative art seems to be the architectonic prudence that informs the practical prudence regarding decrees and their deliberation. But the conclusion Aristotle draws is not of prudence in harmony, but discord: if people say it is only those who deliberate and make decrees who practice politics, their prudence fails to follow the legislative art's architectonic prudence. But Aristotle drops the legislative art, which only appears one other time in the *Ethics* at the beginning of Book V's account of justice; after this passage in Book VI, it does not appear for the rest of the text. If the legislative art is not the architectonic thing prompted by the last definition of prudence, what is? Considering Aristotle brings the political art back into the inquiry as the same *hexis* as prudence, *hexis* is the authoritative thing needed to understand prudence and its political forms.

In developing the separate concerns of prudence for the city and prudence for each thing, Aristotle opens prudence's broader horizons. Aristotle starts by observing prudence seems most of all to concern oneself, and this is what holds the common name of "prudence." Of the other kinds of prudence, there is household management (*oikonomia*), "legislation" (*nomothesia*), and the political art, which is on the one hand deliberative, and on the other hand "judicial" (*dikastikē*). From this division in prudence, there might be one form of knowledge (*gnōsis*) that knows what is for oneself (which holds much difference), and it seems a prudent person knows the things concerning oneself, *and* ways of spending time (*diatribē*). Politicians, however, are "busy about many matters" (*polupragmōn*) (1141b29–1142a2). Aristotle quietly contrasts prudence's personal knowledge with prudence exercised in communities. Though there are differences in how one attends to all the things concerning oneself, personal prudence's concern is singular in its attention, and therefore more likely to provide for one's own needs. Household management, legislation, and the political art may each be more architectonic kinds of prudence, but they may fail to help one choose good ways of spending time. In the *Politics*, one such failure manifests in choosing to live as if every way of spending time is money-making.[76]

Giving more content to the knowledge that defines personal prudence, Aristotle comments on how people "seek or examine the good for themselves and suppose there is need to do this, and from this came the opinion that such people are prudent. Indeed, perhaps there is no well-being for oneself without household management or a regime. And for the things of oneself how there is need to manage a household [is] unclear and must be considered" (1142a7–10). The difference in concerns Aristotle initiates in this account of prudence takes more definite shape, with what is good for oneself tacitly set against what is good for others. Aristotle's last question about whether one's own well-being is possible without household management and a regime hints that the difference in knowledge is not as pronounced as some think. The question of how to manage a household moves away from the arts' perspective and comes down to the level of personal prudence. In this way, questions about regimes, the political art, and household management meet every reader at the personal perspective of their own good.

From the practical grounds of one's own good, Aristotle draws prudence back toward contemplation with a difference between the old and the young. A sign of the need to consider what managing a household entails appears in how the young can become skilled in geometry and mathematics and wise in these things, yet not seem to be prudent. In the first explanation Aristotle offers, what is according to each thing is only known or familiar through experience (*empeiria*), "for much time produces experience." Seemingly unsatisfied with this possibility, Aristotle then says one must consider how a child comes to be wise in mathematics but not what is natural (*phusikos*), suggesting it might be because mathematical things are through "abstraction" (*aphairesis*) while the first-principles of what is natural are from experience. The young do not trust (*pisteuō*) these natural first-principles, but they do trust those belonging to mathematics (1142a10–20). Aristotle's emphasis on the role of experience in prudence echoes his statement in Book I that the young are not proper (*oikeios*) listeners to the political art's *logoi* because they are without-experience (*apeiros*), which he quickly revises to state the error is less of age and more of living according to passion (*pathos*). For the political art's *logoi* to be beneficial, people must produce their desires according to *logos*.[77] Together, these two passages suggest a *logos* of the good concerning life's actions will be beneficial for those who trust in natural first-principles. As for why being wise in mathematics does not translate into practical prudence, Aristotle provides a subtle linguistic clue in the word for "abstraction" (*aphairesis*), which literally means "away-from-choosing" (a combination of the prefix *apo* and *hairesis*). Considering Aristotle's account of the money-making art deliberately takes part away-from-choosing, it should not surprise readers that such a general account of economic matters fails to provide the full knowledge necessary for exercising true economic prudence.

The young's lack of trust in natural first-principles prompts Aristotle to revisit how prudence and science stand in relation to each other, thus alluding to why it is difficult to produce desires according to *logos*. Science is not prudence because the practical is of the last thing, and:

> [Prudence] itself poses against [or corresponds with (*antikeimai*)] the intellect,[78] for while the intellect is of the boundaries (of which there is no *logos*), prudence is of the last thing of which there is not science but sense-perception, not of one's own private things (*tōn idiōn*),[79] but like we ourselves perceive the triangle is the last thing in mathematics: for here there will be a set-standing itself. But this [is] more sense-perception than prudence, but [sense-perception] of another form. (1142a23–30)

This passage sets up a paradoxical opposition and complementarity between prudence and intellect. Because prudence looks to the last things, it seems to be more sense-perception than science. Yet if sense-perception of the triangle is the last thing in the science of mathematics, it seems that prudence and intellect are not nearly as separate from one another as it first appears. In comparing practical sense-perception in prudence with mathematical sense-perception, Aristotle responds immediately to the challenge he presents about trusting natural first-principles. Both forms of sense-perception depend on the intellect, which holds within itself some sense of boundaries of which there is no *logos*.

To remove some of the mystery surrounding what it means to hold intellectual sense-perception of boundaries with no *logos*, remember that Aristotle ends his first half of the inquiry into the money-making art by declaring there is a distinction between the unnecessary money-making art and the necessary money-making art that is an art of household management according to nature concerning food that is not without-limit but "holds a boundary" (*echousa horon*). While the boundary of what each person can eat in a day varies, everyone has sense-perception of their limits (sometimes in retrospect), and *logos* is not necessary for revealing these limits. Of course, before Aristotle presents the bodily limit to the acquisition of food, he alludes to the intellectual limits to wealth's acquisition by finding errors about living and living well behind why people think money-making is the end of all things.[80] Living and living well are akin to the first-principles of science of which there is neither science, prudence, nor art. And if science is "an assumption concerning the general things and beings from necessity," every economic science concerning the necessity of acquisition must begin with an intellectual sense-perception that the boundaries for every form of acquisition are living and living well.

Shortly after Aristotle's paradoxical presentation of prudence and intellect, he brings them together with first-principles and ends. Contrary to his earlier presentation of prudence as concerned with the last thing and intellect with boundaries, Aristotle directs intellect toward the last things on both ends, for it (and not *logos*) is of both the first boundaries and the last things. This is most evident through the intellect's role either in demonstrations through syllogisms, or the practical things. In demonstrations, intellect is of "the unmoving (*akinētos*) first boundaries." In the practical things, intellect is of the last thing, what admits to be possible,[81] and the minor premise. These last things are first-principles of the that for the sake of which, for the general things come from what is according to each thing. Consequently, "there is need to hold sense-perception of these things, and this is intellect" (1143a35–b5). The unstated premise of the preceding line of argument is the sense-perception of what is relative to each practical thing helps establish the first-principles (i.e., the that for the sake of which) of future practical things. The key difference is Aristotle does not describe these first-principles as "unmoving" like syllogisms' first boundaries, though he likens intellect's sense-perception in action to sensing the minor premise of a syllogism. Where, then, could one find unmoving boundaries for actions?

From his observation about the intellect's sense-perception of practical first-principles, Aristotle notes these seem to be natural, and while no one by nature is wise, people seem to hold intellect by nature (1143b6–7). The question, then, is how people can hold intellectual sense-perception of first-principles by nature but not be wise by nature. One possible explanation comes from how "we ourselves suppose" intellect is something one holds during a certain time of life, as if nature is the cause. If this is true, there is need to hold-toward (*prosechō*) the opinions and demonstrations of experienced and older people, or prudent people, no less than demonstrations alone since these people hold an experienced eye and see correctly (1143b7–9, 11–14). Despite children not using their intellects as fully as adults, it is not so clear that there is some age when people use intellect and then it disappears. The underlying assumption seems to be that if nature is the intellect's cause, then it grows in human beings like a plant, flowers for a time, and withers away. Another assumption is that even if a person is not at the time of life that holds intellect, one could hold-toward those who do and imitate being prudent and experienced. But if this is true, nature is not the cause people suppose it is.

Lurking within the above supposition about holding intellect is the unstated problem of choice that a purely intellectual view of human nature sidesteps. Between the suppositions about nature and experience, Aristotle says, "And on account of this intellect [is] a first-principle [or beginning (*archē*)] and an end, for demonstrations are from these and concerning these" (1143b9–11).[82] Whether it is oneself or those who are experienced, older, or prudent, the first-principle and end toward which one holds oneself is the intellect. Because Aristotle teaches one should hold-toward both demonstrations and people making those demonstrations, there is no real division between demonstrative (or scientific) and practical contemplation. It should not escape readers' notice that the foundational nature of the intellect accompanies a less strict view of models for prudence: the earlier models in Book VI (i.e., politicians, household managers, the legislative art, the political art, and household management) now all give way to persons who hold intellect. In this respect, it is intellect and not any art that is "something architectonic" behind prudence. But insofar as human nature as a first-principle or beginning is desiring intellect or thinking desire, focusing solely on the intellect's role in the prudent pursuit of the human good fails to reckon with the other half of what governs choice.

Human nature's combination of intellect and desire increases the difficulty in holding oneself toward a true boundary for the acquisition of wealth. Although Aristotle only speaks of nature "choosing" animals' lives toward the acquisition of food, the evidence for nature marking-the-boundary in this way is through what foods are pleasant to each animal (differences through which animals are set-standing-apart from each other). For human beings, the pleasant resides in mixing lives as need necessitates to acquire the self-sufficient, and the self-sufficiency of true wealth's acquisition is not without-limit toward good living. Aristotle's account of natural acquisition alludes to nature marking-the-boundaries of human beings' lives by binding together the pleasant with how they choose to live, and they hold some intellectual sense-perception of self-sufficiency toward the good as its boundary. From the *Ethics*, readers learn the pleasant is the one of the three things of choosing (the other two being the noble and the advantageous) about which people are most errant, and through choosing the pleasant as good, they make it seem as if no one wishes for the good by nature. The pleasant and the painful are the intellectual perceptions of the pleasures and pains bound to each person's sense-perception, and by the pleasant and the painful ruining and distorting one's own practical assumptions, the need for practical first-principles to inform one's own choosing and actions never displays itself.[83] With these arguments from the *Ethics*, readers can see that the true source of confusion about the economic arts of acquisition in the *Politics* is an error in choosing the good that begins with a common misperception about the pleasant by intellect and desire.

The nature of choice means a rational science of politics and economics will prove insufficient in providing for human beings' practical and contemplative need for the good. To describe how prudence itself either "poses against" or "corresponds with" (*antikeimai*) the intellect, Aristotle likens prudence's sense-perception of the last thing in a practical matter to perceiving a triangle in mathematics, thus marking the moment where the perception is itself set-standing (*histēmi*). In Book I of the *Politics*, the household is the first community according to nature set-standing-together (*sunistēmi*) for every day, and the natural persons from whom it is set-standing-together are free persons (i.e., husband, wife, and children). Because every city composes (*sunkeimai*) itself from households, it is necessary to speak of household management and contemplate how the money-making art holds toward it. Every community requires ruler and ruled (a necessary coupling for preservation), for ruling and being-ruled are among the necessary and advantageous things, and there is a common work whenever they are set-standing-together. If part of every science is an assumption about things from necessity, then every political science concerns ruling and being-ruled, and every economic science concerns the acquisition of necessary things. Furthermore, if science arrives at truth concerning things that do and do not admit to hold otherwise, one must discern these complementary concerns.[84] For politics and economics, their respective necessities (ruling and being-ruled, and acquisition) do not admit to hold otherwise. What admits to hold otherwise in politics are the regimes and political arts formed in response to the necessity for ruling and being-ruled; for economics, the arts of acquisition and exchange that respond to the necessity for acquisition admit to hold otherwise. Though political and economic sciences can present people a set of assumptions for how to set-standing-together their communities where they use the arts of acquisition and exchange to provide what is necessary for their preservation, people will only choose to set-themselves-standing according to sciences if they perceive such things are good.

The great challenge that politics and economics must confront in theory and practice concerns how people choose the good without mistaking it for pleasure. This is present in Book I of the *Ethics*' early chapters where the problem of the political art's *logoi* being beneficial only to those who produce their desires according to *logos* leads into the many's definition of happiness—the highest practical good—as pleasure (and wealth or honor). In Book II, pleasures and pains are the common concerns of virtue and the political art. Pleasures and pains emerge in Book VI's examination of prudence when Aristotle appeals to the name of "moderation" as "preserving prudence" to suggest moderation preserves an assumption derived from contemplating the good things for oneself like household managers and politicians. This is necessary because pleasure and pain ruin the practical first-principles necessary for choosing how to act. Although "pleasure" and "pain" never appear in Book I of the *Politics*, the need to choose the good for the sake of free political rule is present in the political or kingly rule of intellect over desire from which it is manifestly "according to nature and advantageous for the body to be ruled by the soul, and for the passionate part [to be ruled] by the intellect and the part holding *logos*." Book VI of the *Ethics* clarifies why the intellect must rule desire, for in practical matters, the intellect's sense-perception of unmoving (*akinētos*) first boundaries informs the last things that admit to be possible in a potential action. The intellect's twofold sense-perception is the necessary foundation for choice—the first-principle of action from where motion (*kinēsis*) comes—for there is no choice without intellect, thought, or a moral *hexis*. As Aristotle shows at the beginning of the *Ethics*, precision in any *logos* of the human good runs up against the good things (which encompass wealth) holding some wandering on account of people destroying themselves through these things.[85] The good things wander—and seem to move—because people choose the pleasant instead of the good. Since the human good is the common concern of politics and economics, these practical pursuits will not be good and advantageous unless people hold an unmoving intellectual sense-perception of the good.

## CONCLUSION: WISDOM, EXPERIENCE, AND THE SEARCH FOR THE GOOD (*ETHICS* 1143B18–21, 1144A3–6, 1144B6–16, 1145A6–11)

An exclusive focus on "the political" and "economic" as arts and sciences in Books I and VI of the *Ethics* ultimately illuminates the question of what is authoritative in human nature. Though Aristotle presents intellect and desire together as the first-principle that is a human being in Book VI, only intellect receives the title of a first-principle (*archē*) and an end (*telos*).[86] This may seem to settle the question of what is authoritative in human nature within the context of the *Ethics*, but it is difficult to determine what practical conclusions flow from this insight. Given contemporary aspirations to study politics and economics as empirical sciences that work from observations about human behavior, it might appear irrelevant (and altogether impossible) to contemplate human nature. While Aristotle is neither a "Political Scientist" nor an "Economist" in the contemporary sense, his philosophy holds a deeply empirical character that is evident through how he uses words related to *empeiria*, "experience."

Embedded within *empeiria* are terms Aristotle employs in Books I and VI of the *Ethics* to suggest contemplative experience is practical and necessary for actions. The term for being "without-experience" (*apeiron*) also means to be "without-limit." In Book I, the problem of choosing being without-limit and not toward the good as its end leaves desire empty and vain, and so "one must attempt" (*peirateon*) an outline to take hold of whatever it is. Though it briefly looks like the young being without-experience in life's actions prevents them from being proper (*oikeios*) listeners to the political art's *logoi*, the true problem is a character not produced according to *logos*. In Book VI, after introducing wisdom and distinguishing it from prudence (the *hexis* to which politics and economics belong), Aristotle considers why the young are wise in mathematics but are not prudent. Although it initially seems the young are simply without-experience, the deeper issue concerns trust in first-principles: while trust in mathematical first-principles is through "abstraction" (*aphairesis*, "away-from-choosing"), trust in natural first-principles is through experience.[87] Aristotle does not give an account of this experience's character, but one can see its outline with the help of the preceding passages. To trust in the good as a natural first-principle, the *Ethics* immerses readers in the attempt (*en-peiraō*) to contemplate the good that is the necessary limit (*peras*) to their choices and desires, thus providing the philosophic experience (*empeiria*)[88] necessary for their well-being.

Readers catch glimpses of their practical need for wisdom as Book VI nears its end. Immediately following his account of intellect as a first-principle and an end, Aristotle admits one might be unprovided (*diaporeō*) over whether wisdom and prudence are useful, for while wisdom will not contemplate from which things a human being will be happy, prudence holds this way (though he wonders for what sake does someone need prudence) (1143b18–21). This is a strange question, for it asks if wisdom and prudence are useful without happiness. Although wisdom's contemplation seems detached from happiness, with prudence, Aristotle questions if there is need for happiness, the very thing Book I holds out as the good in the *Ethics*. This suggests happiness may not be the good, thereby prompting a closer examination of how Aristotle seems to set up the *Ethics* to seek happiness as its end.

Before returning to Book I and the inquiry into happiness in this book's next chapter, some final statements about wisdom and prudence in Book VI offer clues for approaching Aristotle's inquiry into happiness and virtue to seek the good and the best end by nature. Shortly after the unprovided matter of wisdom and prudence's use, Aristotle presents readers a new angle on the arts. Despite first declaring that neither wisdom nor prudence produce anything, Aristotle refines his statement to say wisdom produces happiness not as the medical art produces health, but as health produces health: "for being part of the whole of virtue (*tēs olēs aretēs*), to hold itself (*echesthai*) and to be active (*energein*) produces a happy person" (1144a3–6). Unlike the medical art producing health in a sick person, wisdom perpetuates itself in a person, for just as holding health is to be active in health, so too is holding wisdom to be active in wisdom. Here Aristotle expands the idea of what it means to produce something to holding oneself in a certain way, which differs from the arts producing something apart from themselves. Such an understanding of producing is more amenable to action than production, which brings it closer to what is more simply an end sought by the intellect and desire.[89]

At the same time as Aristotle points to holding and being active in wisdom as the key to understanding happiness, prudence—which concerns the good things for oneself—has no direct connection to happiness. Indeed, as Book VI nears its end, Aristotle downplays prudence in favor of "the authoritative good" (*to kuriōs agathon*) and shifts his attention to natural *hexeis*, noting these are harmful in both beasts and children when they are without intellect by likening a person without intellect to a strong body that falls because it does not hold sight. But, if this person takes hold of intellect, there is a difference in acting, and the *hexis* will be "authoritative virtue" (*kuriōs aretē*), which is not only distinct from "natural virtue" (*aretē phusikē*), but cannot come to be without prudence (1144b6–16). This division of virtue into the natural and authoritative is distinct from its initial division in the *Ethics* into the "intellectual" (*dianoētikē*) and the "moral" (*ēthikē*) (1103a4–5). By the end of Book VI, the key to prudence and virtue is intellect, and the intellect improves human beings' natural *hexeis*. While abstract, it is helpful to know that Aristotle's treatment of virtue in the *Ethics* is not constant. Rather, the work gradually moves toward discovering the intellectual foundations of practical matters, foundations necessary for discovering Aristotle's teaching on the relationship between politics and economics. The question that remains is where in Aristotle's political philosophy do these intellectual foundations take their most practical form.

Aristotle concludes Book VI with the argument that prudence is not authoritative over wisdom, stating this would be akin to the political art ruling the gods because it orders all the things in the city (1145a6–11). The portion of the *Ethics* that reveals the intellectual foundations of politics and economics through inquiring into what is good for oneself thus concludes by recalling how strange it is to suppose the political art and prudence are most serious in light of wisdom's recognition that human beings are not the best things in the cosmos. This insight leads to the definition of wisdom as science and intellect of the things most honorable by nature, and the problem of philosophers like Anaxagoras and Thales being wise but not prudent, ignorant of the advantageous things for themselves, knowing only useless things, and not seeking or examining the human goods. Yet at the end of Book VI, with prudence fully dependent on intellect and wisdom's capacity to produce happiness, Aristotle opens a new door for philosophy. Though readers know in the first definition of wisdom that science is trust and familiarity with first-principles, they do not learn there how the intellect is sense-perception of first-principles.[90] In thinking about the natural first-principles that are good for themselves, readers should rightly wonder what practical thing gives them the firmest trust and sense-perception of the good.

Though it seems throughout most of the *Ethics* that virtue and happiness offer the strongest trust in the good, neither of these things disentangles the good from pleasure. This work belongs to Aristotle's inquiry into friendship in Books VIII and IX, where he brings the useful (*chrēsima*) in relation to the pleasant and the good and helps readers understand these things not only in relation to themselves, but their friends and communities. According to its name, the money-making art (*chrēmatistikē*) is "the art of useful things," and is therefore bound to the attempt in Aristotle's political philosophy to distinguish the good and the pleasant as ends. As the first half of the *Politics'* inquiry into the money-making art demonstrates, while legal-currency is the limit (*peras*) of exchange in the art of retail-trade, people attempt (*peiraō*) to use their capacities contrary to nature and pursue the gain of legal-currency without-limit (*apeiron*) because their desires are without-limit due to a failure to understand the nature of living and living well. The acquisition of such wealth is contrary to that of "true wealth," the self-sufficiency of which is not without-limit toward "good living." Since self-sufficiency brings together living and living well as the city's end in Book I of the *Politics*,[91] and further, features prominently in Book I of the *Ethics'* consideration of what makes an end choiceworthy, it is necessary to examine this idea to see how Aristotle's political philosophy draws economics and politics toward being in the limit of the good through friendship.

*Chapter 4*

# Choice and the Limits of Self-Sufficiency as a Political and Economic End

After examining the arguments about the political art, household management, and prudence in Books I and VI of the *Ethics*, it is apparent that Aristotle's economic teaching is not something readers can extract from his political philosophy and present as an autonomous field of study.[1] The human need for knowledge of the good that first reveals itself in Book I deepens in Book VI with Aristotle's identification of human nature with choice (*proairesis*). There is not a single theoretical or practical pursuit in life that begins apart from choice, and for human beings, choice must always reckon with pleasures, pains, and some sense of the good.

The last hope for readers who wish to claim Aristotle's economic teaching resides wholly in Book I of the *Politics* is to assume self-sufficiency (*autarkeia*) is the city's end, and the arts of household management and money-making are subordinate to it. The problem with this approach is twofold. First, in Book VII of the *Politics*, happiness (*eudaimonia*) emerges as the city's end. Second, in Book I of the *Ethics*, self-sufficiency appears not in relation to community, but as an idea used to assess the status of happiness as an end. Readers could perhaps dispense with these difficulties by declaring economics and politics aim to produce happiness, but unless they reckon with all the difficulties in defining happiness in Book I and provide an honest accounting of how Aristotle finally defines happiness in Book X, they would not even scratch the surface of his political philosophy. To avoid this error, this chapter carefully examines Aristotle's arguments about self-sufficiency and the city in Book I of the *Politics*, and self-sufficiency and happiness in Book I of the *Ethics*. With the help of the *Ethics*, a surprise encounter with the money-making life prepares readers for contemplating how their own choice of the good in life is not subject to economics and politics, but a natural and pleasant sense of the good they experience in friendship (*philia*), the form of love that defines philosophy.[2]

As mentioned above, "self-sufficiency" is a common term in Aristotle's inquiries into political community in the *Politics* and happiness in the *Ethics*. In the *Politics*, self-sufficiency is the city's end (1252b27–34). In the *Ethics*, self-sufficiency is one of the reasons why happiness seems to be a complete end, for people choose (*haireō*) happiness on account of itself and it makes life choiceworthy (*hairetos*). Self-sufficiency also sheds some light on how human beings are naturally political (1097b1–21). Within the first half of the *Politics'* inquiry into the money-making art, the self-sufficiency of "true wealth"—"a store of such useful things that are necessary towards living, and useful to community in a city or a household"—"is not without-limit towards good living."[3] At first glance, it seems self-sufficiency is the end that unites politics and economics, with each person and every community seeking it. Yet an important distinction between the first of self-sufficiency's rare appearances in the *Politics* and the *Ethics* is the former work omits any mention of choice and happiness, which suggests self-sufficiency is not the common end of politics and economics.[4]

The need to understand self-sufficiency in relation to choice appears indirectly in the *Politics'* brief account of natural acquisition. Unlike nature marking-the-boundaries (*horizō*) of animals' lives toward the choosing (*hairesis*) of food through the pleasant (*hēdus*), human beings live pleasantly and provide food for themselves by mixing the different lives that hold their work in relation to natural things (i.e., nomad, farming, pirate, fisher, hunter), in each case filling up each life with whatever it happens to lack in the self-sufficient (*autarchēs*) as "need necessitates" (*chreia sunankazō*). These natural works are distinct from providing food through exchange and retail-trade.[5] Without drawing an explicit connection in this summary of natural acquisition, Aristotle ties human beings' sense of choosing the self-sufficient to the pleasant. Although providing for the self-sufficient in life and acquisition appears bound to need and necessity, the allusion to exchange and retail-trade *and* the natural sense of the pleasant in choosing point toward how all economic matters may depart from their natural boundaries.

Self-sufficiency's inability to limit each person's choices in acquisition from the perspective of the community's end is evident from the sole mention of "desire" (*epithumia*) in Aristotle's inquiry into the money-making art. In setting self-sufficiency as the city's end in Book I of the *Politics*, Aristotle folds "living" and "living well" into the definition. Shortly after this, Aristotle introduces the art of acquisition (*ktētikē*) as part of household management because living and living well are impossible without the necessary things. The first half of Aristotle's examination of the money-making art concludes with an explanation for why people exchange the art of household management's work for the art of retail-trade's increase of legal-currency without-limit. There are two causes of this mistake about these arts of acquisition: people either desire to be more serious about living than living well, or they think living well consists in excessive bodily enjoyments. From these mistakes through which people pursue money-making as if it is the end of all things, Aristotle settles on a distinction between the "unnecessary money-making art" (the art of retail-trade) and the necessary money-making art (the art of household management) that is according to nature, concerns foods, and is not without-limit but holds a boundary (*horos*).[6] Though the city, the household, and their respective arts of acquisition seem sufficient for informing how people seek living and living well, these things cannot speak fully to the end each person desires.

A brief look at the beginning of Book VII of the *Politics'* approach to the "best regime" (*politeia aristē*) confirms the necessity of viewing Book I's presentation of self-sufficiency as political community's end within the broader context of Aristotle's political philosophy. For those who want to produce the best regime, it is necessary to seek the "most choiceworthy life" (*hairetōtatos bios*) and whether this is the same for each person as it is in common. From a true "division" (*diairesis*) of things into the external, body, and soul, Aristotle notes that while the acquisition of external goods holds a limit, the "best setting-down-through" (*diathesis*, in the sense of "disposition") of soul is more useful and honorable than acquisition and the body, and so prudent (*phronimos*) persons should choose things for the soul's sake. On these grounds, Aristotle links happiness to virtue and prudence (*phronēsis*) since these things are more part of a person's nature than external goods, then tentatively concludes the best city is happy in the same way without going through all the "proper (*oikeion*) logoi" about this (1323a14–1324a4). In the first half of the inquiry into the money-making art, Aristotle describes the desire for living that is without-limit as a "setting-down-through" of oneself, which suggests this error relates to how people choose to live. To avoid this error about the money-making art's end, people need to know the most choiceworthy life that cares for virtue and prudence in the soul.

Aristotle confirms the need to return to the *Ethics'* examination of happiness and the most choiceworthy life in Book VII of the *Politics'* thirteenth chapter. "The well-being" (*to eu*) of all things comes through the correct posing (*keimai*) of actions' target and end, and the discovery of the actions bearing (*pherō*) toward the end. Recognizing that everyone aims at living well and happiness, Aristotle says, "We assert (and we ourselves marked-the-boundaries in the *Ethics*, if [there is] something beneficial in those *logoi*) [that happiness] is an activity and use of complete virtue" associated with the most noble actions and "the well-provided things" (*tas euporias*), not the retributions and punishments associated with just actions. Although they are from virtue, these just actions are "without-choosing [or choosing] of some bad thing," while noble actions from virtue prepare and generate good things (1331b24–1332a18).[7] The distinction Aristotle draws between the noble and the just (two things he ties to the political art in Book I of the *Ethics*)[8] hinges on the former things holding a stronger relationship to choice, the well-provided things, and the good things. This divergence between happiness and the just hints at why justice is also an insufficient end for politics and economics, for it is not bound to choice as strongly as happiness. What is closer to choice is *logos*. After describing the city as "serious" (*spoudaios*) when each citizen is serious through science (*epistēmē*) and choice, Aristotle states people become good and serious through nature, habit, and *logos*. The most important of these three things is *logos* since people can act contrary to their habits if something persuades them to hold better otherwise (1332a18–b11). Considering the connections between the most choiceworthy life, virtue, and happiness all depend upon the condition of "something beneficial" residing in the *Ethics' logoi*, readers should return to this text to see if it persuades them to hold better in how they choose to pursue their well-being.

About halfway through Book VI of the *Ethics*, the contemplation of well-being finds itself in the middle of a dispute between prudence and wisdom that seems to prove philosophers know useless things and do not seek human goods. Through this dispute, Aristotle reveals prudence, the political art, and household management are the same *hexis* (though with different concerns), and wonders if "the well-being of oneself" is possible without household management or a regime. One could reframe this part of Aristotle's inquiry to ask what provides more fully for human well-being: philosophy, or politics and economics? Within Book VI, prudence moves from a concern with both the good and bad things for human beings to the good things alone, all the while remaining "a true practical *hexis* with *logos*." The great obstacle to prudence that keeps people from choosing the good things is their ability to ruin their perception of their actions' first-principles through pleasures and pains.[9] While philosophy, politics, and economics all hold a common concern with well-being, the answer to what provides more fully for this comes down to what accounts more for choice. According to the *Ethics* and *Politics*, only philosophy produces a complete provision for choice.

In Book I of the *Politics'* final chapter, Aristotle states that household management is more serious about the virtue of free human beings than "the acquisition of soulless things . . . which we call wealth" (1259b18–21). For those who understand the sole concern of economics as the acquisition of wealth, Aristotle's description of household management (*oikonomia*) offers a sharp rebuke. Economics cannot be soulless, otherwise it is slavish. Although economics needs virtue, careful readers should hold Aristotle's statement in Book I up against his statement in Book VII that there are "two lives the human beings most loving honor (*philotimoi*) towards virtue appear to choose (*proaireō*)": the political and the philosophic, and there is "no small difference which of the two holds the truth" (1324a5–35). Since Book I of the *Politics* presents a "soulless" view of self-sufficiency in politics while Book I of the *Ethics* considers self-sufficiency to contemplate the good of the soul, it is the best idea for seeing how philosophy provides a comprehensive view of politics and economics by uncovering the way these practical pursuits rest upon a choice between pleasure and the good as ends for the best life.

## THE CITY AND SELF-SUFFICIENCY
## (*POLITICS* 1252A1–1253A39)

Like the *Ethics*, Aristotle's *Politics* begins with a statement that raises questions about the good, but with an emphasis on community:

> Since we see every city is some community and every community is set-standing-together (*sunistēmi*) for the sake of some good (for all do all things for the sake of what seems to be good), since on the one hand it is clear all [communities] aim themselves at some good, on the other hand the most authoritative of all [communities] and the one encompassing all the others [aims itself at] the most authoritative of all [goods] most of all. And this is what calls itself the city and the political community. (1252a1–7)

To help think through the relationship Aristotle establishes between communities and goods, recall the opening sentence of the *Ethics*: "Every art and every inquiry, and likewise action and choice, seems to aim itself at some good; on which account, nobly they displayed-from themselves the good, that at which all things themselves aim" (1094a1–3). Whereas Aristotle refrains from using the first-person voice in the *Ethics* until the second chapter's consideration of actions and desires,[10] he begins the *Politics* with what "we see" about cities and communities. Aristotle's focus is narrower in the *Politics*, starting not from arts, inquiries, actions, and choices, but community. Just as Aristotle moves from "some good" to the good as "that at which all things aim themselves" in the *Ethics*, the *Politics* moves from "some good" to "the most authoritative of all [goods]" that seems to belong to the city and the political community. The *Politics* thus brings the good down from the cosmos to find its home in political community. A final likeness between the two opening sentences is the sense in which the subjects in question—human pursuits in the *Ethics*, communities in the *Politics*—"aim themselves" at some good, giving them some agency independent of human beings. Here readers find a slight but significant difference toward the good: while the *Ethics* presents human pursuits as if they "seem to aim [themselves]" at some good, the *Politics* presents people and communities as aiming themselves at "what seems to be good." The use of "seems" in the *Ethics* calls into question the idea that human pursuits have the capacity to aim at some good of their own accord, but does not cast doubt on the target of these pursuits being some good. In the *Politics*, "seems" does not call into question communities' and people's capacity to aim themselves at some good, but casts doubt on whether people and communities aim at what is truly good.

The difference between how Aristotle's inquiries in the *Ethics* and *Politics* stand toward the good also comes forth in the alternate meanings for the different verbs he uses for "to aim" in each text. In the *Ethics*, the verb *ephiēmi* could mean "to long after, desire" (1889, 338). In the *Politics*, the verb *stochazomai* could mean "to endeavor to make out, to guess at" something (1889, 748). Accordingly, one could read the beginning of the *Ethics* as saying, "Every art and inquiry, and likewise action and choice, seems itself to desire some good," and the beginning of the *Politics* as indicating "all communities guess at some good," and "the most authoritative of all [communities] and the one encompassing all the others [guesses at] the most authoritative of all [goods]." Reading the "aim" of the *Ethics*' opening sentence as an allusion to desire anticipates why desire (*orexis*) and choosing need the "the good and the best end" in the text's first invitation to approach the good from a personal perspective. Though human pursuits seem to display the good from themselves, desire brings forth the possibility that the good *is* the best end. In contrast, the *Politics*' opening sentence presents communities as "guessing at" some good because communities lack desire. And because desire is part of choice (which as either desiring intellect or thinking desire defines human nature in Book VI of the *Ethics*),[11] readers need to be attentive to how the *Politics*' approach to communities in Book I lacks an account of political and economic life as choices about the good.

There is only one clue of where choice is at work in Book I of the *Politics*' outline of political communities. To correct the mistake of those who do not speak "nobly" because they customarily-consider (*nomizō*) there is no difference in the four forms of rule (political, kingly, household manager, and master)—in part because they do not distinguish a large household from a small city—Aristotle states it is necessary to divide (*diaireō*) the "set-down-together thing" (*to suntheton*, "compounded") into the "not-set-down-together things" (*tōn asunthetōn*, "uncompounded") that are the smallest parts of the whole from which the city composes (*sunkeimai*) itself. In this way, "we will see" better what relates to ruling and community, and if these things admit of "something artistic" (*ti technikon*) (1252a7–23). Despite seeming to be a mere setup for Book I's inquiry, Aristotle's conclusion to its first chapter suggests that what produces the city as a "set-down-together thing" is art. The inquiry that seeks to divide (*diaireō*) the city into its parts presumably discovers how the art that produces this community chooses (*haireō*) to set-down-together its parts. Aristotle begins the second half of his inquiry into the money-making art by noting a kinship between the political art using human beings from nature and the household manager who sets-down-through (*diatithēmi*) what nature gives over as food. The money-making art is subordinate to household management and according to nature when it holds-forth what nature provides as useful things (*chrēmata*), but contrary to nature when it becomes about the acquisition of legal-currency from itself and not necessary exchange.[12] As arts, politics and economics set-down-through human beings and acquisitions as given by nature to produce community and exchange. The unprovided question behind these arts in Aristotle's political philosophy is whether politics and economics choose to produce communities and exchanges that are according to nature.

A tool common to politics and economics is law (*nomos*). The money-making art came into being according to *logos* through the necessary provision of legal-currency (*nomisma*) that people set-down-together in agreement (*suntithēmi*) to give and take for exchanges of the things necessary according to nature. Through experience in the art of retail-trade, people set-down (*tithēmi*) wealth as a quantity of legal-currency, which seems to be altogether law and not at all by nature when a change-in-the-setting-down (*metatithēmi*, or "change in the establishment") of its worth makes it worthless. When this happens, someone wealthy in legal-currency could go unprovided in necessary food. In Book VI of the *Ethics*, Aristotle defines "art" as a productive *hexis* with true *logos*, and "artlessness" as a productive *hexis* with false *logos*. Though art initially appears as one of the five ways people arrive at truth, it disappears from this list when Aristotle repeats it, in part through the discovery that voluntarily erring is more choiceworthy in art than prudence; this discovery also leads to the statement that prudence is "not only a *hexis* with *logos*," which points to the role of desire in choice.[13] Both politics and economics rely on art to produce communities, exchanges, and legal-currency by setting-down laws for these things according to some *logos*. Through seeing how *logos* is "something artistic" behind the city as a set-down-together thing, readers glimpse how community is the work of choice.

Aristotle begins the second chapter of the *Politics* with a potential remedy for those who do not speak nobly about politics. Adhering to his focus on communities rather than forms of rule, Aristotle proposes "one might most nobly . . . contemplate" these things "if one looks to the matters naturally-growing (*ta pragmata phuomena*) from the beginning (*archē*)" (1252a24–26). This conditional framing encourages those who wish to approach politics with ruling to consider if nature's perspective is more noble. It is not clear, however, if this natural view of politics will be sufficient. Given this natural perspective, Aristotle states there are two necessary couplings of those who do not have the capacity to be without each other: female and male for the sake of generation, and ruler by nature and ruled by nature for preservation. The coupling for the sake of generation is not from choice, but "the natural aiming or desiring" (*phusikon to ephiesthai*) of all living things (i.e., plants, animals, and human beings) to leave behind another like themselves (1252a26–31). The omission of choice on account of nature's aiming or desiring implies that there is a more human view of this first necessary coupling, and further suggests there is no natural ruler and ruled (and therefore preservation) for human beings apart from choice.

With the two necessary couplings as his foundation, Aristotle presents a three-step development of communities. From the two necessary communities of male and female for generation *and* ruler and ruled for preservation comes the household, the community set-standing-together according to nature for every day. From the first community of a multitude of households comes the village, which is for the sake of non-daily use (*chrēsis*), and most of all according to nature looks like an offshoot of the household. After briefly considering how villages serve as models for cities, nations, and even gods under kings, Aristotle turns toward the city and self-sufficiency, saying:

> And from a multitude of villages [is] a complete community—a city—now holding every limit of self-sufficiency so to speak, coming-into-being itself on the one hand for the sake of living, and on the other hand being for the sake of living well. On account of this every city is by nature, if indeed also [are] the first communities. For this is an end of these [communities], and nature is an end; for such is each thing when the coming-into-being is completed, this we say to be the nature of each thing, just as of a human being, horse, and household. Still the that for the sake of which and the end [is] best, and self-sufficiency [is] both an end and best. (1252b12–1253a1)

A quick reading of the preceding arguments gives the mistaken impression that there is a natural growth from the household to the city, one that misses the arguments' contemplative character and the questions they raise about self-sufficiency and the natural limits and ends of community. Consequently, it is necessary to account for these questions to consider why the perspective of community remains insufficient for contemplating the nature of political life.

Although the *Politics* begins by introducing the city as the most authoritative of all communities, the account of communities naturally-growing toward self-sufficiency emphasizes what makes the city complete (*teleios*). The city is a complete community through the multitude of villages (i.e., communities of households) "holding every limit (*peras*) of self-sufficiency so to speak." From the inquiry into the money-making art, readers know each person, household, and community of households pursues self-sufficiency in natural acquisition and necessary exchange without any mention of the city; the lone appearance of the "city" in relation to the self-sufficiency of acquisition is in the definition of "true wealth." While living and living well characterize self-sufficiency as an end, when Aristotle describes how people's errors about living and living well stem from desiring what is without-limit, he does not bring in self-sufficiency as the end that will correct the way they throw themselves toward money-making as if it is the end of all things.[14] If the city is the most authoritative of all communities and aims itself at the most authoritative of all goods, why does its end of self-sufficiency fail to provide a limit to people's desires that helps them avoid pursuing money-making as their end? Together, these passages suggest Aristotle qualifies the limits of "self-sufficiency" with a "so to speak" because its scope extends to an end beyond political community.

Another clue for why readers must seek a different end for political community aside from self-sufficiency comes in the form of Aristotle's condition for the city being "by nature." Whether or not the city is by nature depends on whether the first communities (i.e., households and villages) are by nature, yet the city's end and nature seems to direct these communities' growth through the proposed analogy between a human being, horse, and a household. A notable difference exists between a horse and a human being on the one hand, and the household on the other: while the former two living things come into being in their infant states as wholes (i.e., a pony and a body) that grow into their mature forms (i.e., a horse and an adult) through their nature and not choice, the household requires at least two people as separate parts to choose to form the whole community. The household is also unique because it does not have a body like a human being and a horse. Indeed, a household cannot come into being without the art of house-building. The city is therefore not a whole in the same way as living animals are wholes, and it needs human beings to produce and preserve it through some art and end apart from self-sufficiency that is best for each person and political communities.

Self-sufficiency's failure to provide a complete end for political life leads to a turn toward human nature, with Aristotle saying:

> Therefore from these things it is clear that the city is of the things by nature, and that the human being by nature [is] a political animal (*politikon zōon*), and that the one without-city (*apolis*) through nature and not through chance surely is low, or stronger than a human being; just like the one reviled by Homer "without-brotherhood without-law without-hearth and home,"[15] for at the same time by nature such [a person is] one who desires (*epithumētēs*) war. (1253a1–6)

The city is now "by nature" because human beings are political animals by nature, which makes what begins as the most authoritative of all communities in the *Politics* subject to human nature. But the introduction of human nature to the *Politics* brings new questions into the inquiry concerning how a person could be without a city through nature (for it is easy to conceive how people lose their cities through chance, as in natural disasters). Aristotle's reference to Homer ties together the lack of brotherhood and law with a lack of hearth and home—the lack of the household necessary for generation and preservation. The foundation for generation is a natural aiming or desiring, and the foundation for preservation is the rule of thought (*dianoia*) over that which has the capacity to produce or labor according to thought. By this account, the household provides for human beings' natural desire for generation and the necessity for thoughtful preservation, while a person stripped of these things only desires war. An echo of this argument appears at the end of Aristotle's sketch of natural acquisition in the inquiry into the money-making art's first chapter through a specious analogy between war and an art of acquisition that takes it bearings about ruling and the just apart from any form of community.[16] Although the passage above links human beings' political nature to the city, these two arguments about war indicate the household provides the community necessary for ensuring desire contributes to necessary acquisition and peaceful preservation.[17]

Before Aristotle returns to self-sufficiency to provide more detail on what might mitigate human beings' desire for war, he finds a natural foundation for community in *logos*. In comparison to animals like bees or those living in herds, human beings are clearly more political, for "we say" nature produces nothing in vain, and humans are the only animals to hold *logos*. Though both animals and human beings can vocalize the painful and pleasant, through *logos*, human beings not only make apparent what is advantageous and harmful, but hold sense-perception (*aisthēsis*) of "what is good and bad, just and unjust, and other things; and community in these things produces a household and a city" (1253a7–18). Aristotle now subjects the city—the most authoritative political community that claims the most authoritative good as its end—to the authority of *logos* that is inseparable from sense-perception in human nature. The "just" and "unjust" thus first appear in the *Politics* not bound to communities and forms of rule, but the comprehensive nature of human sense-perception (which includes the pleasant and the painful, the advantageous and the harmful, and the good and the bad) that produces community in both the household and the city. Given the account in Book VI of the *Ethics* of the ruinous effects of pleasures and pains on the natural first-principles necessary for prudence, the description of the political art and household management as the same *hexis* as prudence, and the discovery of the intellect as sense-perception of first-principles, readers cannot hope to grasp Aristotle's full view of politics' and economics' natural foundations from Book I of the *Politics*.[18]

With the hint of the foundational role of *logos* in political community, Aristotle reconsiders the perspective of the city while providing a small opening to think of self-sufficiency in relation to choice, saying, "And a city is prior by nature to a household and each of us," just as it is necessary for a whole to be prior to a part. If the whole "abolishes" (*anaireō*)[19] itself, there will neither be hand nor foot except in the case of something having the same name (for example, speaking of a hand or foot made of stone), for these things will have been ruined. The ruin stems from the fact that what marks-the-boundary of all things is their work and the capacity, "therefore [it is clear that] the city [is] by nature and prior to each person, for if each is not self-sufficient when separated, then each holds like the other parts towards the whole. But if one does not have the capacity to form-community or needs nothing through self-sufficiency and [is] no part of the city, [that person is] either a beast or a god" (1253a18-28). Aristotle's argument begins with the city as "prior by nature to a household and each of us," but ends with the city as "prior *and* by nature." The shift suggests that while the city is prior to each person (likely because few people enter the world and live outside of the city), it may not be "prior by nature" in the sense that the city comes into being before all people. What prompts this revision is the conditional argument that each person's work and capacity is not self-sufficient when separate from the city. The possibility that there is a form of self-sufficiency in a human work apart from the city is present not only in this argument, but the statement about a whole "abolishing" (*anaireō*) itself, which literally means "to be without (*an*) choosing (*haireō*)." To assume being without the city ruins each person's work and capacity assumes they are not capable of choosing when separated from the city. Consistent with the attempt to view communities as naturally growing, choice remains absent from this account of political life.

Political community's constrained view of choice is further evident as Aristotle considers how law and the just contribute to the human work, saying, "Therefore while by nature [there is] the impulse (*hormē*) in all towards such community, the first person who set-standing-together [one is] a cause of the greatest goods. For just as a human being is best of the animals when completed, in this way [one is] worst of all when separated from law and what is just" (1253a29–33). As part of human nature, the impulse toward community in the city is incomplete. By implying this impulse receives completion through law and the just, Aristotle suggests it is *logos* that completes human nature. The question is if the just is the end *logos* needs to provide human beings for their completion, or if there is a better end. Gesturing toward something more comprehensive than the just, Aristotle concludes contemplating the natural growth of political community by introducing "virtue," "justice," and "injustice" (*adikaia*) to the *Politics*:

> For most difficult [is] injustice holding arms: and [to] the human being holding arms naturally fall prudence and virtue, [but] for these [arms] there is wont to use [them] towards their opposites. On account of this, [a human being is] most unholy and most savage without virtue, and towards sex and food worst. And justice [is] a political thing (*politikon*): for the just is an order of political community, and justice a judgment of the just. (1253a33–39)[20]

This argument suggests justice provides the prudence and virtue that naturally fall to human beings in their use of weapons. The bridge connecting virtue and prudence to justice are two naturally acquisitive desires (sex and food) necessary for forming community in the household. To couple for the sake of generation, male and female need to acquire each other; to couple for the sake of preservation, ruler and ruled need to acquire food. Virtue and prudence need to inform these acquisitions, yet Aristotle ends by speaking of justice. But in the *Ethics*, Aristotle does not declare justice is the same *hexis* as the political art. That description falls to prudence, a virtue that orients politics and economics toward the good things.

As Aristotle shows in Book VII of the *Politics*, the activity and use of complete virtue that mark-the-boundaries of happiness and generate good things through noble actions and well-provided things differs from the retributions and punishments associated with just actions that are without-choosing (*anairesis*). If one searches for how people make the choice (*proairesis*) to become good and serious, the most important thing to consider is *logos*.[21] Although Book I of the *Politics'* contemplation of communities' natural growth recognizes *logos* produces community in a city and a household, it does not present the human pursuit of self-sufficiency as a choice according to *logos*. The closest this inquiry comes to such a *logos* is in the assertion that the human being who is separate from the city is either a beast or a god. Designating such a person as a "beast" is possible because *logos* is the foundation for community. To act as if one lacks the capacity for *logos* is to be a beast. Opposed to this beastly person is the godly one who is no part of the city through needing nothing. Given the absence of choice in this political account of self-sufficiency, readers should wonder if this idea simply means "needing nothing." If such a condition is akin to being a god, it is a hyperbolic sense of self-sufficiency. Since politics and economics seek to provide for self-sufficiency, these pursuits need a natural understanding of this end, one informed by a *logos* fit for human choice.[22]

## SELF-SUFFICIENCY AND HAPPINESS (*ETHICS* 1095A14–1100B22, 1101A22–B9, 1102A5–26, 1112A13–17, 1113A9–14)

The second half of Aristotle's inquiry into the money-making art begins with an analogy between the political art and the household manager using what nature gives them (human beings and food, respectively) by setting-down-through these things with ruling arts. When Aristotle takes a closer look at household management to conclude Book I of the *Politics*, he distinguishes the virtue of free human beings from the virtue of soulless acquisition, which is wealth. The common characteristic of the political art and household management is their use of the human beings and acquisitions subject to their authority. If there is virtue in the arts of politics and economics, it will be apparent in how they use what nature gives them. With economics, readers learn from the *Politics* that people exchange the art of household management's work for the art of retail-trade's because both arts use the same acquisition (legal-currency) for different ends. Because the art of retail-trade seeks the increase of legal-currency without-limit, it seems to some that this is also the art of household management's end.[23] This confusion occurs in part because the arts of household management, necessary exchange, and retail-trade all fall under the umbrella of "the money-making art" (*chrēmatistikē*), which by its own name is the "art of useful things (*chrēmata*)." If "wealth" is the virtue manifest in the use of acquisitions according to nature, then virtue in economics resides in the character of the people using these things.

The opening chapters of the *Ethics* reveal the difficulties in finding virtue in how politics uses human beings. Unlike Book I of the *Politics* where Aristotle directs household management toward virtue, Book I of the *Ethics* introduces the art of household management's end as wealth on the way to positing the ends of architectonic arts are more choiceworthy than the arts falling under them. From this perspective, the art of household management is subject to the political art's authority over the human good, which is nobler and more divine when taken hold of and preserved for the city as opposed to one person alone. But the political art is not without its problems. For one, it seeks or examines the noble things and the just things that seem to be only by law and not by nature because "they hold much difference and wandering." The good things, however, do not hold this difference, and whatever wandering they hold derives from people who destroy themselves through the good things (like wealth). The unstated implication of Aristotle's argument is the good things do not seem to be by law, but are by nature.[24] After stating the political art's *logoi* would not be beneficial to those whose character is such that they fail to produce their desires according to *logos*, Aristotle declares the political art aims itself at happiness and outlines the disputes about what this is (including the observation that the many claim it is pleasure, wealth, or honor).[25] In addition to the lack of clarity over whether the political art seeks the good things, this art's preferred aim at the human good for communities and not each person is subject to all the disputes about the nature of happiness. Even if one supposes there is a connection between virtue and happiness, it is not clear from Book I of the *Ethics* that the political art's vision of happiness is naturally good for human beings.

Part of the quickly revised argument from the *Politics* that the city is "prior by nature to a household and each of us" is the assumption that "abolishing" (*anaireō*) the whole that is the city ruins the work and capacity of all its parts, with the human being who is not part of the city on account of self-sufficiency likened to a god. In the *Ethics*, the choiceworthy nature of happiness on account of self-sufficiency gives way to a consideration of "the human work" (*to ergon tou anthropou*) that is not entirely bound to the political art's choices about the good things (1097b15–25). From the *Politics'* inquiry into the money-making art, readers know that even if there is no work for the art of exchange (*metablētikē*) in the household, this does not stop people from importing the art of retail-trade's end into the household by using their own capacities in ways that are contrary to nature because they seek to provide for themselves whatever is productive of excess. Though this misuse of oneself stems from mistaking living well for the pursuit of excessive bodily enjoyments, it also demonstrates a failure to understand the exchange of all things is not their proper (*oikeia*) use.[26] The economic ruin of community in the household (*oikia*)—and political community at all levels—thus begins with an errant answer to the question most proper to oneself: For the sake of what good does one choose to live?

### The Good and Potential Choiceworthy Lives for Happiness (*Ethics* 1095a14–1096a10)

Aristotle's turn toward happiness as the political art's end in the *Ethics* sits between two general statements about the good that provide a helpful context for seeing the philosophic nature of his consideration of the lives to which happiness may belong. Prior to introducing happiness to the *Ethics*, Aristotle says, "Since every knowledge (*gnōsis*) and choice itself desires (*oregō*) some good, let us say what it is at which the political art aims (*ephiēmi*) itself and what is the highest of all the practical goods" (1095a14–17). Aristotle likens the political art's aiming to knowledge and choice's desire for some good using the same verb that appears as a substantive in Book I of the *Politics* to describe the "natural aiming or desiring" (*phusikon to ephiesthai*) behind the necessary coupling of male and female for the sake of generation that is not from choice. There are some desires sown into the nature of living things that drive them with or without *logos*, though for human beings the desire is deliberate and a choice is serious when *logos* is true.[27] The political art is closer to these desires than the political community and the city, for the latter two things' aim "guesses" at some good. Contrary to contemporary rational sensibilities, Aristotle proposes one can know how knowledge itself is capable of desire by considering how each person and the political art choose to aim at happiness.

After outlining the disputes about happiness and the good, Aristotle moves toward a question about first-principles (*archai*) by stating it is "more vain" to examine all the "opinions" (*doxa*) about happiness rather than those that are either most prevalent, or "seem to hold some *logos*." Briefly digressing from these opinions, Aristotle praises Plato for being "well . . . unprovided" (*eu aporeō*) over whether the "road" (*hodos*) in *logos* is to or from first-principles, just as in a racecourse one goes from the athletic judges, to "the limit" (*to peras*), and back. While "one-must-begin" (*arkteon*) from "things known or familiar" (*tōn gnōrimōn*), such things have two senses—"the things known to ourselves," and the things known "simply" (or "in one way," *haplōs*)—and so Aristotle concludes one must begin from "the things known to ourselves" (1095a17–b4). Although the immediate implication of Aristotle's approach is his inquiry aims to discover what is known simply, the appeal to Plato and the image of racecourse suggests a freer form of philosophic movement in *logos* in relation to first-principles.

In Book VI, Aristotle describes the young as wise in mathematics because they trust (*pisteuō*) such first-principles through abstraction (and therefore "away-from-choosing," *aphairesis*), while at the same time not seeming to be prudent because they do not trust natural first-principles that become known or familiar from experience (*empeiria*). This problem recalls the seeming dismissal in Book I of the young as proper (*oikeios*) listeners to the political art's *logoi* because they are without-experience (*apeiron*), when in truth the problem is a character that does not produce desires according to *logos*. This practical failure has an intellectual beginning, for without knowledge of the good, choosing (*haireō*) goes without-limit (*apeiron*), desire remains empty and vain, and one's own life does not hold the target through which one might hit upon the needful.[28] Since Book I's *logos* of the good and happiness immerses readers in the practical choice of the good, they should approach it as the beginning of Aristotle's attempt (*peiraō*) to provide contemplative experience through which they fully come to know and be familiar with the limit (*peras*) of the good.

Adhering to the opinions about happiness that seem to hold some *logos*, Aristotle observes that from the lives of the many and the most vulgar, it looks like they assume (not without-*logos*) that the good and happiness are pleasure, and thus "they love (*agapaō*) the life of enjoyment (*ton apolaustikon*)." To this Aristotle adds there are three lives "most of all holding-before

(*proechō*)" the others: the one of enjoyment, the political, and the contemplative (*theōrētikos*) (1095b14–19). In directing the good and happiness toward
pleasure, Aristotle sets the life of enjoyment in relation to an end; as for the
political and the contemplative lives, he does not introduce them with an end.
The life of enjoyment should remind readers of the mistake about living well
from the *Politics'* inquiry into the money-making art through which people
attempt to provide excessive bodily enjoyments (*tas apolouseis*) through the
acquisition of legal-currency without-limit, as if money-making is the end of
all things.[29] With these two arguments about enjoyments from the *Ethics* and
the *Politics*, one should approach Aristotle's discussion of the lives in which
happiness may reside with an eye for how pleasure (especially in money-
making) draws one back to questions about the nature of ends.

Aristotle's comparison between lives begins with what appears to be a glib
dismissal of the life of enjoyment with pleasure as its end, for he describes
the many choosing (*proaireō*) the life of fatted beasts as showing themselves
to be "all-completely (*pantelōs*) servile, though the many hit upon *logos*[30]
through those in positions of authority (*tas exousias*) having the same passions (*homoiopatheō*) as Sardanapallus" (1095b19–22).[31] Though the inclusion of "the many" connects the life of enjoyment to the life of fatted beasts,
neither "enjoyment" nor "pleasure" are explicit parts of the argument. The
life of fatted beasts that Aristotle derides as completely servile is, at best, a
narrow portion of enjoyment or pleasure, one that only concerns food (the
most natural acquisition).[32] What makes the *logos* for the life of fatted beasts
compelling is not the *logos* itself, but the example of people in the most
prominent (and often political) positions living a servile life. Since Aristotle's
standard for the opinions of happiness that he examines is that they hold some
*logos*, he quietly undermines the claim that one should follow *logos* because
it comes from someone in authority. Rather, readers should look to the *logos*
through which they hit upon the needful—the *logos* of the good.

In contrast to the many, Aristotle brings in people who are "refined
and practical" seeking honor, "for this [is] nearly an end of the political
life. But [this] displays itself as too superficial for the sought-for thing (*to
zētoumenon*), for it seems to be more in those who honor than those honored,
but we divine (*manteuomai*) ourselves the good to be something properly-
one's-own (*oikeion*) and hard-to-take-away (*dusaphaireton*)" (1095b22–26).
Unlike the life of enjoyment and its tie to pleasure, Aristotle quickly calls
into question the political life's end of honor through something "we divine."
Though the nature of this "divining" is vague, it is some sense of the good
being properly-one's-own through an implicit perception that it is something
people "choose" (*haireō*), and therefore "hard-to-take-away" (*dusaphaireton*). For those who seek honor, the good is always subject to others choosing
to honor oneself. Like the way Aristotle undermines the life of enjoyment

by alluding to the need to hit upon the good in *logos*, the good undermines honor's claim as the end of the political life. But unlike the many hitting upon *logos* for their servile end through the lives of others in positions of authority, the *logos* that questions honor arises from the view of choosing the good that is more properly-one's-own.

With honor, Aristotle considers the relationship between virtue and political life. Honor also displays itself as a deficient end because "it looks like people seek honor to trust that they themselves are good, and so they at least seek to be honored themselves by those who are prudent (*phronimos*), and among those knowing (*gignōskō*) them, and for virtue; therefore it is clear that (at least according to these persons) virtue is stronger," and one could assume this is more of an end for the political life (1095b26–31). Bearing in mind that Aristotle has more to say about virtue and the political life, notice that virtue's role in this argument is to uncover how people seek to trust they are good, thereby reinforcing the need to see the good as something people choose to be properly-one's-own. The search for this trust in the good being properly-one's-own points readers to Book VI's argument for the need to experience trust in natural first-principles, an argument that begins with Aristotle wondering if people can be prudent and seek the good and well-being for themselves apart from household management (*oikonomia*) or a regime.[33] Although each person, economics, and politics all seek the good, the trust in the good that all persons naturally seek in their choices is proper not to their communities, but themselves.

Recognizing the good as bound to the choices that are properly-one's-own, Aristotle arrives at the tentative conclusion that virtue shows itself to be "more incomplete (*ateles*)," for it seems one could hold this and either be asleep or without action throughout life. Nor would anyone call happy those who "suffer ill" (*kakopatheō*) or the greatest misfortunes (1095b31–1096a1). Aristotle does not reveal the significance of this last criticism of virtue until later in Book I, but it anticipates an important argument likening the *hexis* and activity (*energeia*) of virtue to acquisition and use; this argument appears after examining self-sufficiency, choiceworthy ends, and political life. The natural need for sleep and the necessary presence of chance in all human things suggests the practical choice of the good behind politics and economics must honestly account for human beings' natural limitations.

Despite stating his intention to examine three lives, Aristotle—seemingly out of nowhere—brings in the money-making life (*chrēmatistēs*) for a brief consideration immediately following a passing glance at the contemplative life, saying:

> Third is the contemplative [life], of which we ourselves will produce the investigation in the following things. But the money-making [life] is something forced

[or violent (*biaios*)], and it is clear that wealth [is] not the sought-for good (*to zētoumenon agathon*), for [it is] useful for the sake of another thing. On account of this, someone might assume the things said before are more ends, for these are loved (*agapaō*) through themselves. But the former things do not display themselves as ends, and indeed many *logoi* are thrown down against these, therefore let these things go. (1096a4–10)

Aristotle's criticism of the money-making life is twofold, taking aim first at the life itself, then its end. The rejection of the money-making life is a hybrid of the rejections of the political life and the life enjoyment. Although Aristotle does not dismiss pleasure as an end, he dismisses the life of enjoyment as fit for fatted beasts. The opposite occurs with the political life, for Aristotle does not dismiss this life itself, but challenges whether its ends (honor and virtue) are complete. In complete opposition to the money-making life is the contemplative life, which receives neither criticism nor an end from Aristotle. This juxtaposition is likely deliberate. In Book I of the *Politics*, Aristotle describes the money-maker as someone who contemplates sources of acquisition, useful things, and wealth. After discovering the art of retail-trade, the money-making art's work seems to concern legal-currency most of all, contemplating sources of useful things to produce wealth without-limit.[34] Money-making holds within itself a contemplative character, though it errs in holding money-making—a form of acquisition—as all things' end.

How the surprise opposition between the money-making and contemplative lives reflects Aristotle's attempt to provide readers philosophic experience in the good becomes clearer by using Book I of the *Politics* to make sense of the money-making life's "forced" or "violent" nature. Aristotle's inquiry into the money-making art begins by establishing that acquisition is naturally pleasant for both animals and human beings, though only the latter hold a sense of the self-sufficient. At the end of this inquiry's first half, Aristotle describes how the art of retail-trade owes its origins to people seeking to produce excess bodily enjoyments for the sake of living well out of a failure to understand that the provision and proper use of legal-currency is to facilitate the exchange of necessary things, not the production of wealth. For those who think of human life solely in terms of acquisition, they suppose all things nature produces (whether plants, animals, or other human beings) exist for them to acquire, consume, or use (with war seeming to be a just art of acquisition). In the second half of this inquiry, Aristotle describes the most slavish works as those that make the most uses of the body. These works stand in stark contrast to the free (*eleutheran*) contemplation that accompanies necessary experience in the money-making art's use. To seek constant acquisition is to think solely of the body. Such contemplation produces slavishness in politics and economics through setting-down laws concerning the acquisition of slaves (which is forcible or violent) and the production of wealth without-limit (something bound to the force of acquisition).[35]

Although the *Ethics'* inquiry into the lives people choose for happiness leads to a blanket dismissal of lives as ends, there are three things Aristotle refrains from criticizing: pleasure as an end, the political life, and the contemplative life. If lives are not ends, the remaining candidates for "the sought-for good" are the good, happiness, and pleasure (the three goods from the beginning of the inquiry into lives). Aristotle's examination of the life of enjoyment suggests pleasure is not only bodily, and his examination of the political life suggests the good that is "the sought-for thing" is "properly-one's-own and hard-to-take-away." The contemplative life—the investigation of which is something readers will produce along with Aristotle's throughout the *Ethics*—holds the promise of uncovering the good and pleasure that is properly-one's-own because this life avoids the money-making life's error of using oneself slavishly. With the money-making life, Aristotle rejects wealth as an end and "the sought-for good" because it is useful for something else. Although the political art seems most choiceworthy and authoritative because it determines whatever sciences and capacities are "needed" or "used" (*chreōn*) for the noble and divine purpose of taking and preserving the human good for cities and nations, looking at practical matters in terms of how people choose to live provides a freer view of these things through the contemplative life. Of course, since Aristotle describes his own inquiry as "some political art," it is not surprising that Book I of the *Ethics* brings the practical choices behind politics and economics under the authority of the good.[36]

## The Practical Good and Self-Sufficiency (*Ethics* 1096a11–1098b8, 1103b26–1104b3, 1138b20–34)

Between the inquiry into the lives most associated with happiness and the consideration of why happiness is a complete end on account of self-sufficiency, Aristotle—on his way to reasserting the need to search for the practical good—introduces "friends" (*philoi*)[37] to the *Ethics* alongside the singular appearance of "philosophers" (*philosophoi*). Initiating a short look at the idea of the good, Aristotle proposes it might be better to examine what is "general" (*kathalou*) and be unprovided (*diaporeō*) in how people speak of it, though this is arduous because "those to introduce the forms [are] friends. But perhaps it might seem to be better and needed—at least for preservation of the truth—to abolish (*anaireō*) the things that are properly-one's-own (*ta oikeia*), especially for those being philosophers, for both being loved (*phileō*), [it is] pious to honor the truth first" (1096a11–17). Aristotle's cautious statement raises a general question about how philosophy—the love (*phileō*) and friendship (*philia*) of wisdom (*sophia*)—needs to honor the truth and what is properly-one's-own, with philosophy seeming to hold what is properly-one's-own in lower esteem. While this statement may at first appear to have nothing to do with politics and economics, within Book I, readers should recall Aristotle's observation in the political life that "we divine ourselves the good to be something properly-one's-own (*oikeion*) and hard-to-take-away (*dusaphaireton*)." In Book VI, the criticism of Anaxagoras and Thales is they are wise but not prudent because they know useless things (like the divine nature of the cosmos) and "do not seek [or examine] the human goods." In the *Politics'* inquiry into the money-making art, Aristotle recounts how many mistakenly attribute wisdom to Thales' general money-making through monopoly, and in the process acknowledges the reproach against philosophy that it is not beneficial.[38] Taken together, these passages suggest that there is a form of philosophy that—like politics and economics—provides for what is properly-one's-own and the human good through seeking and loving the truth through friendship.

Without going through every unprovided matter concerning the general idea of the good, it is sufficient to collect some of the insights that anticipate friendship's vital role in a philosophy that provides for human beings' natural need to choose the good in politics and economics. Aristotle begins by acknowledging the many ways people speak of "the good," applying it to beings like the god and intellect, things such as the virtues, and toward things like the useful. There are some things that are good according to themselves (like prudence), others good on account of these (the beneficial things), and things good in both ways. After considering why an idea of the good would be a vain form, Aristotle reminds readers that the inquiry seeks the good that is practical and "acquirable" (*ktēton*) by a human being, and suggests it might be better (and with good-*logos*) for arts and sciences to know and be familiar with the good by holding it as a pattern. Aristotle then concludes with an unprovided (*aporon*) matter over whether there is something beneficial in arts' practitioners contemplating the idea of the good, with the example of a doctor looking to the health of each human being as evidence against this (1096a24–1097a14). In Aristotle's political philosophy, politics and economics not only hold a common concern with practical and acquirable goods, but share a contemplative character derived from their common foundation in the human intellect and prudence. As a result, all the political and economic arts and sciences are pursuits of the good that naturally begin with choice.

With the standard for the practical and acquirable good in mind, Aristotle—invoking a phrase from his discussion of the money-making life—returns to "the sought-for good,"[39] which in every action and choice is the end. If this end is for all actions, it is the practical good. With the *logos* arriving at the practical good, "still one-must-attempt (*peirateon*) to clarify this more"

(1097a15–25). Whether it is the inquiry into the lives people choose or the general idea good, "the sought-for good" in Aristotle's *logos* is the practical good that is the end of all actions and choices. Although Aristotle rejects the money-making life and its end, its direction toward what is acquirable (wealth and what is useful) is practical in a way that the contemplative life does not seem to be. But with the emphasis back on choice, Aristotle aims to use *logos* to provide practical experience in contemplating the good as an end.

In settling on the sought-for good as the practical good, Aristotle considers the nature of ends not from the perspective of the first chapter's distinction between works and activities,[40] but choice. Some ends "we ourselves choose" (*hairoumetha*) on account of other things, "like wealth, an aulos, and on the whole tools, thus it is clear not all [ends] are complete (*teleia*)." The best thing, in contrast, is simply complete, sought and chosen according to itself and never for something else, which is what happiness seems to be. Indeed, while "we ourselves choose honor, pleasure, intellect, and every virtue on account of themselves . . . we ourselves also choose [them] for the sake of happiness, assuming through these things we will be happy. But no one chooses happiness for the sake of these things, nor wholly on account of another thing" (1097a25–b6). In the *Politics*, the first unprovided question about the money-making art partially concerns whether this art is subordinate to the art of household management by holding-forth (*parechō*) tools to it. Aristotle also defines "wealth" as "a multitude of tools for household managers and politicians," and suggests there are limits to arts because the size and quantity of their tools is not without-limit.[41] This argument eventually proves insufficient in the *Politics*, though Aristotle refrains from using the *Ethics'* argument that wealth is an incomplete end because it is a tool people choose to use for the sake of happiness. Since readers know "choice" is absent from the *Politics'* inquiry into the money-making art, they must see how Aristotle provides a more complete view of politics' and economics' limits through their choice of ends.

In support of the idea that happiness seems to be a complete end, Aristotle adds this appears to be the case "from self-sufficiency, for the complete good (*to teleion agathon*) seems to be self-sufficient. But we say 'the self-sufficient' [is] not for oneself alone, living life alone, but for parents, children, a wife, and on the whole friends and citizens, since by nature the human being [is] political. Of these things, one must take hold of some boundary," otherwise they will stretch toward parents, descendants, and friends of friends without-limit (1097b6–13). In Book I of the *Politics*, the city seems to achieve its end of self-sufficiency apart from choice by "holding every limit of self-sufficiency so to speak." The city also seems necessary for the human work, for if the city abolishes (*anaireō*) itself, this will ruin the persons and households who are part of it; further, the person who "needs nothing through self-sufficiency and [is] no part of the city . . . [is] a god."[42] In the *Ethics* and the *Politics*, "self-sufficiency" is necessary for understanding political community, though the *Ethics* speaks of the persons forming communities (parents, children, and citizens) more than the communities themselves (households, villages, and cities). The *Ethics* also counters the *Politics'* god-like view of self-sufficiency that suggests people could need nothing. In both cases, the *Ethics* approaches self-sufficiency with a natural sense of how human beings choose (*haireō*) to live.

Although the *Ethics'* introduction to self-sufficiency alludes to political life's boundaries, Aristotle does not discuss these boundaries when "self-sufficiency" appears in Book V's inquiry into justice and Book X's final account of happiness. Perhaps unexpectedly, Aristotle's brief discussion of these boundaries appears in the ninth chapter of Book IX's inquiry into friendship where—in considering the number of friends a happy person needs—he takes a more natural view of why a friend seems choiceworthy. Knowing friendship's natural perspective on boundaries provides context for how Aristotle defines "the self-sufficient" in Book I, saying, "The 'self-sufficient' we set-down as that which taken alone produces life choice-worthy [and sufficient (*arkion*)][43] and in need of nothing, and such a thing we ourselves suppose to be happiness" (1097b14–16). At first, Aristotle's description of the self-sufficient as producing life so that it is "in-need of nothing" (*mēdenos endea*) seems to align perfectly with the *Politics'* god-like self-sufficiency that "needs nothing" (*mēden deomenos*). But given the *Politics'* exclusion of choice from its account of self-sufficiency, the *Ethics* provides a richer argument. While the *Politics* and the *Ethics* each question if it is ever possible to need nothing, the *Ethics'* approach to self-sufficiency presents the idea that the complete good as an end might ensure choice is in need of nothing. What remains unclear is if happiness is truly the complete good.

Aristotle's final argument for happiness as the complete and self-sufficient good indicates there is more to learn about the nature of happiness. Even when not counted together with all things, happiness is the most choice-worthy, and is more choiceworthy when counted together "with the least of the good things, for a holding-over (*huperochē*) of the good things comes to be what is set-down-in-addition (*to prostithemenon*), and the greater of good things [is] always more choiceworthy. So happiness displays itself as something complete and self-sufficient, being an end of the practical things" (1097b16–21). Though this argument affirms the choiceworthy nature of happiness, it leaves readers to wonder why it is more choiceworthy than the other good things. At best, readers can deduce happiness is a practical end, but how ends bear upon the good things is uncertain from establishing that such an end is "complete and self-sufficient."

Though short, Aristotle's account of self-sufficiency in Book I of the *Ethics* hints at how choice holds a stronger sense of political and economic boundaries than communities and all the arts of acquisition. In the *Politics'* inquiry into the money-making art, right before the argument that the size and quantity of a tool limits an art, Aristotle states that with "true wealth"—"a store of such useful things that are necessary towards living, and useful to community in a city or a household"—"the self-sufficiency of such acquisition is not without-limit towards good-living." Although the first half of that inquiry concludes with a reiteration of wealth's external limits through the statement that the art of household management is necessary and according to nature concerning food (which is not without-limit but holds a boundary), what precedes that conclusion is a description of how people exchange the art of household management's work for the art of retail-trade's by a setting-down-through (*diathesis*) themselves of a desire for living that is without-limit and not serious about living well. With the help of the *Ethics*, readers can see this setting-down-through oneself of an errant desire by which one goes through-to-the-end (*diateleō*) increasing legal-currency without-limit reflects a poor choice of how to live.[44]

The *Ethics'* brief treatment of self-sufficiency also indicates how provision for choosing the good is necessary for a free politics and economics. In Book I of the *Politics*, those who exchange the works of the arts of household-management and retail-trade are akin to those who exchange *logoi* regarding the law that sets-down slavery according to war as just on the grounds that the strong hold-over others in some good (namely virtue) and thus have the capacity to be forceful or violent most of all in the acquisition of slaves. Because Book I of the *Politics* withholds choice from its view of political and economic life, it cannot inquire into why people choose to acquire slaves, although the inquiry into the money-making art suggests seeking this acquisition is a poor choice. Book I of the *Ethics*, however, suggests that choosing the complete good (which is supposedly happiness) is more authoritative than holding-over others in good things. Aristotle does not come around to this insight about happiness in the *Politics* until Book VII, with the best setting-down-through of the soul with virtue and prudence being more useful than acquisition since these things are more bound to a person's nature than external goods.[45] This contrast between the *Ethics'* and the *Politics'* approaches to happiness reveals freedom in political and economic life does not begin with the structures of communities and exchanges, but the *logos* and choice of the good that forms them.

For those who wish for self-sufficiency to provide a complete view of the good, Aristotle dashes these hopes by admitting it is not enough to say happiness is the best thing since people already agree (*homologeō*) on this. From the recognition that it is "requisite" or "longed after" (*potheō*) to speak of what happiness is, Aristotle turns to "the human work," proposing that if the well-being of an art's work or action is in the work itself, perhaps one could set-down a human work apart from the arts. This work cannot be the living associated with nourishing, growth, and sense-perception because these are common to plants and animals, which leaves "some practical [living] of that which holds *logos* (*tou logon echontos*), and this on the one hand [is] as what trusts-upon (*epipeithēs*)[46] *logos*, and on the other hand as what holds and itself thinks. But we say this [living is][47] twofold and one-must-set-down (*theteon*) what is according to activity, for to say this seems more authoritative" (1097b22–1098a7). Like Book I of the *Politics*, self-sufficiency in the *Ethics* prompts a discovery of human beings' distinctive political nature through holding *logos*. While the *Politics* emphasizes how human beings hold sense-perception of what is pleasant and painful, advantageous and harmful, good and bad, and just and unjust—with community in these things producing a household and a city—the *Ethics* seeks a deeper sense of holding *logos*. Where the *Politics* introduces human beings holding *logos* through how "we say" nature produces nothing in vain, the *Ethics* wonders about *logos* itself being vain, either because one's character follows passion and desire, or one examines every opinion on happiness, or seeks an idea of the good that is neither practical nor acquirable.[48] In searching for the human work through the activity that *seems* more authoritative, Aristotle invites readers to contemplate what practical *logos* they can hold, think about, and trust in their lives.

Aristotle's tentative elevation of activity leads to a heavily conditional argument that anticipates Book VI's move to bring prudence—and, through this, politics and economics—under wisdom's authority. *If* the serious person's work is like the human work but distinct by setting-down-in-addition the holding-over and well-being of that work, then "we set-down a work of a human being [as] some living, and this [as] an activity of soul and actions with *logos*, and it belongs to the serious man [to do] these things well and nobly, and bring to completion (*apoteleō*) each thing according to the proper virtue (*tēn oikeian aretēn*)." *If* things are this way, then the human good is an activity of the soul according to virtue (and according to the best and most complete if there are many virtues), and in a complete life (1098a7–20).[49] Although activity retains its apparently authoritative place in the human good, the argument implies there are many virtues that are not all "proper" to the human work, and thus do not all provide for the human good that is properly-one's-own.

In Book III, Aristotle describes the serious person as someone who sees the truth in each *hexis* and judges correctly, wishing for the good as the end and choosing (*haireō*) the good instead of the apparent good by not mistaking the pleasant as the good. In Book VI, choice is serious and desire is correct when both follow true *logos*. With wisdom, Aristotle denies that prudence and the political art are the most serious thing, and after discovering the intellect holds the trustworthy sense-perception of the natural first-principles on which prudence depends, suggests wisdom is useful and produces happiness for the person holding and being active (*energein*) according to it. Through this last argument, Aristotle speaks of "the authoritative good" and states that natural *hexis* and virtue do not become "authoritative" without intellect.[50] From this summary view of what is "serious" in Books III and VI, readers see two things Aristotle omits from the argument introducing the serious person to the *Ethics*. First, *hexis* does not yet complement activity. Second, the serious person's *logos* is not set-down as "true." Nevertheless, the path toward these arguments does emerge in Book I, and in such a way as to prepare readers to learn over the course of the *Ethics* how the virtue that is properly-one's-own and the foundation for a complete life that produces a proper use of politics and economics is the intellect and its natural sense-perception of the good.

How Aristotle sees his own *logos* as providing for the authoritative human good is evident from an implicit choice he offers readers for approaching the *logos*. Characterizing the preceding account of the human work, the serious person, and virtue as an outline of the good, Aristotle says it might seem to belong to everyone to articulate "the things holding nobly in the outline, and time is a good discoverer and coworker (*sunergos*) of such things" (in the arts, for example, people set-down-in-addition what is lacking). But here readers need (*chrē*) to remember to seek the precision proper (*oikeion*) to the inquiry, prompting a comparison between how the carpenter and the geometer seek out "the right angle" (*hē orthē*): the former seeks what is "useful (*chrēsimon*) towards the work," while the latter seeks "whatever it is and what sort it is, for [one is a] contemplator (*theatēs*) of the truth" (1098a20–32). For those readers curious about what it means for the human work to be an activity of the soul with *logos*, Aristotle invites them to be coworkers with his own *logos* of the good. But how precisely readers will work with Aristotle's *logos* is their choice: Will they be practical and seek what is useful about the good, or choose to be theoretical and contemplate the truth about the good? While readers are free to choose their own approach, they need to be serious about seeking the good proper to the *logos*.

Aristotle's reminder of the need to seek the precision proper to a *logos* of the good bears with it a return to the question of how to seek first-principles. There is not one way to seek the cause in all things, and with first-principles (*tas archas*), it is adequate to point them out nobly, for there are different ways to contemplate them (like induction, sense-perception, and habituation). Consequently, "One-must-attempt (*peirateon*) to go after each [of the first-principles] as is natural to them, and one must be serious how to mark-the-boundaries nobly, for they hold great weight towards the things following them. For the first-principle [or beginning] seems to be more than half of the whole, and many of the sought-for things come to be manifest through this" (1098a32–b8). Though Aristotle outlines the choices readers face in seeking the precision proper to the inquiry and first-principles, they should not overlook how his philosophic *logos* is free to search for the good from both the practical and theoretical perspectives, and further, is free to contemplate first-principles as is natural. Aristotle's statement about the search for first-principles recalls Book I's first question about the personal need for knowledge of the good as the end that "holds great weight" because it prevents choosing from going without-limit (*apeiron*), leaving desire empty and vain. This vital question about the need for the good now merges with Plato's well-unprovided question about whether *logos* should proceed toward or from the limit (*peras*) of first-principles.[51] In their search for the practical and acquirable good that is naturally and properly-one's-own, readers need to attempt working with the *Ethics' logos* to gain theoretical and practical experience (*empeiria*) in the limit of contemplating the good.[52]

A quick look ahead to Books II and VI demonstrates the natural inseparability of the practical and theoretical character of the *Ethics'* search for the good. In Book II's second chapter, Aristotle—seeming to draw a hard line between the practical and the theoretical—states the present examination of virtue is not for the sake of contemplation and knowing what sort of thing virtue is, but becoming good. It is therefore necessary to examine actions since these are authoritative over the *hexeis* that come to be. To maintain this practical focus, Aristotle adopts the commonly posed notion that actions are according to "correct (*orthos*) *logos*," though "whatever it is . . . and how it holds towards the other virtues" is something to speak of later. Aristotle then reminds readers that a practical *logos* is imprecise, for actions and the advantageous things hold nothing stable. And because a general *logos* cannot precisely account for what is according to each thing, one-must-attempt to help the *logos* (1103b26–1104a11). Like the geometer who contemplates the truth by seeking "whatever [the right angle (*hē orthē*)] is," one who seeks to know "whatever [correct (*orthos*) *logos*] is" can trust that Aristotle aims to contemplate the truth of this common notion later in the *Ethics*. While some may think they can approach Aristotle's *Ethics* and dispense entirely with contemplating the truth about correct *logos*, the general character of any practical *logos* means readers will need to attempt to provide specific actions and advantageous things to the *logos* for the sake of becoming good through virtue. Regardless of whether readers seek what is useful or the truth in the *Ethics*, they necessarily become coworkers and co-contemplators with Aristotle's *logos*.

When one compares what follows from Aristotle's statement about helping the practical *logos* in Book II with the introduction to Book VI, one sees a crucial example of the *Ethics' logos* proceeding from and toward the limit of the good. In Book II, Aristotle introduces the famous teaching of virtue as a mean by saying, "Therefore one must contemplate this first, that such things [i.e., the virtues] are themselves naturally ruined by deficiency (*endeia*) and excess . . . while the proportionate things (*ta summetra*) produce, increase, and preserve" them (something "we see" with food in relation to health, or gymnastic exercise in relation to strength). For example, in relation to fear and pleasure, "the mean" (*hē mesotēs*) preserves courage and moderation, and the same holds for the other virtues and activities (1104a11–b3). Though this argument's immediate concern is the virtues, it sheds some light on politics and economics. In Book I of the *Politics*, the naturally necessary coupling of ruler and ruled is for preservation. Later, in the inquiry into the money-making art, the art of retail-trade's work of preserving or increasing the substance of legal-currency without-limit displaces the art of household management's acquisition of food that holds a boundary. In Book I of the *Ethics*, the political art's claim to the good rests upon the condition that the city's taking hold of and preserving the good for cities and nations is nobler and more divine than doing so for one person alone.[53] Politics and economics both seek to provide for preservation, the former through ruling and being ruled, and the latter through acquisition. The unique problem economics poses for politics is some forms of acquisition encourage the production and increase of substances that ruin human beings and communities instead of providing for their preservation, and the only proper remedy for correcting this problem dwells within *logos*.

The introduction to Book VI of the *Ethics* and its inquiry into prudence (part which involves contemplating the prudent person's deliberation about the good and advantageous things) challenges Book II's supposition about correct *logos* in ways that compel readers to make their way back to Book I's outline of the good. To begin Book VI, Aristotle says, "Since earlier we happened to have said that there is need to choose (*haireō*) the middle (*to meson*), not the excess or the defect (*elleipsis*),[54] but the middle that is as correct *logos* says, let us divide (*diaireō*) this" (1138b18–20). Contrary to how he first presents the mean as what preserves the virtues in Book II, Aristotle starts Book VI with an emphasis on what it means to choose that which preserves something. Though this introduction applies to the virtues, the language is more general. Once again, Aristotle plays on the verb for "choosing," suggesting one cannot choose the middle needed for preservation without "dividing"—literally, to go "through (*dia*)-choosing (*haireō*)"—correct *logos* itself.

The need to determine the nature of correct *logos* is apparent from deficiencies in its own account in the *Ethics*. To explain what it means to choose correct *logos*, Aristotle observes how in all *hexeis* there is some target to which a person holding *logos* looks and either loosens or tightens (an act akin to tuning a stringed instrument or a bowstring).[55] In such cases, the boundary (*horos*) of the means between excess and defect is according to correct *logos*. But the problem with saying there is need to choose the middle term according to correct *logos* is that this statement is "true but not at all clear, for in all the other cared-upon things (*tas allais empimeleiais*), as far as there is science," to hold this alone would not lead to someone knowing more. Thus, "there is need concerning the *hexeis* of the soul not only to be truly speaking of this, but marking-the-boundary (*diorizō*) of whatever correct *logos* is and some boundary (*horos*) of this" (1138b20–34). From later arguments in Book VI, readers know the boundaries of correct *logos* are first-principles of which there is neither *logos* nor science, but intellectual sense-perception. But this account is (like mathematical first-principles) an abstraction (*aphairesis*) and away-from-choosing, and it raises a question about how the intellect is natural.[56] The only sensible approach to the boundaries of correct *logos* is to follow Aristotle's image of looking to the target back to its first appearance in Book I where knowledge of the good is akin to archers holding a target. Yet Book VI deepens this sense of what holding a target and *logos* have in common through the inclusion of *hexeis* (literally, "holdings"). If holding *logos* is like tuning a musical string, then just as a properly tuned string holds a certain musical note in itself, so too does the person looking to the target of the string's proper tuning hold one's own *hexis* in tune with the correct note. The *logos* holds this tuning, but the act of tuning requires work from the person holding *logos* that is inseparable from choosing what is good.

Aristotle's statement about the lack of clarity in speaking about correct *logos* and how this applies to the sciences contains theoretical and practical consequences for those seeking true knowledge about politics and economics. In Book I of the *Ethics*, the argument that happiness seems to be the complete good on account of self-sufficiency leads into a search for the human work because it is not enough to say happiness is the best thing without inquiring into what it is. Ironically, the whole presentation of self-sufficiency as the end and nature of the city in the *Politics* rests on declaring "self-sufficiency [is] both an end and best" without investigating what it is.[57] To the extent that politics and economics as sciences respectively care for preservation through ruling and being ruled *and* acquisition, knowing that self-sufficiency is their common end and boundary could be true and yet provide nothing to help those engaged in their activities choose what is good. Because Book I of the *Politics* approaches self-sufficiency in community and the acquisition of wealth as abstractions from choice, it cannot provide natural boundaries to these things. The *Ethics*, on the other hand, suggests there is a boundary to self-sufficiency, and that friendship holds within itself a sense that neither community nor acquisition can go without-limit, thus making these things good for human beings.

## The Good Things, Happiness, and Pleasure (*Ethics* 1098b9–1100b22, 1101a22–b9, 1102a5–26, 1112a13–17, 1113a9–14)

Returning to Book I's inquiry into happiness, Aristotle follows his encouragement to be theoretical and practical coworkers with his *logos* and its natural search for first-principles by refining his account of the good things. After a musical note about the truth in *logos* singing together while the false is dissonant, Aristotle says, "The good things distribute (*nemō*) themselves in three ways: on the one hand we speak of the external, and on the other hand of those concerning soul and body, and the goods concerning the soul we say are most authoritative and most of all good, and we set-down actions and activities belonging to the soul as concerning the soul" (1098b9–16). Before proceeding, readers should recall Book I's third chapter and the observation that precision in *logoi* should follow "the nature of the matter," a condition through which Aristotle introduces the character that is proper (*oikeion*) for hearing the political art's *logoi* and benefiting from them. Pointing to the truth roughly and in outline is something loved (*agapēton*) because the noble things and the just things to which the political art looks "hold much difference and wandering, so they seem to be by law only, not by nature." The good things also hold some wandering on account of the harm that comes to people through them (like those who destroyed themselves through wealth or courage).[58] With his current focus on the good things, Aristotle sets the search for the practical and acquirable good among the good things that are by nature, authoritative, and do not belong solely to the political art.

In setting-down the goods of the soul as most authoritative, Aristotle takes a summary view of happiness before raising a question challenging one of the account's key assumptions. To say happiness is an activity of the soul agrees (*homologeō*) with opinions of the ancients and those who philosophize. It is also correct (*orthōs*) to speak of some actions and activities as ends to ensure the end does not belong to the external goods. By setting happiness as a good concerning the soul, it sings together with several earlier arguments that present the happy person as living well through good-action (*eupraxia*), as well as the arguments through which happiness seems to be virtue, prudence, and some wisdom, either with pleasure or not without pleasure. To all these things, one could add prosperity in external goods. Taking stock of these opinions, Aristotle concludes it is with good-*logos* that they are not wholly in error but accordingly correct in some way (1098b16–29). Knowing the prominence of prudence and wisdom in Book VI and the problem pleasure poses for truly seeing the practical first-principles on which one's own choices depend,[59] readers must look for clues in Book I that reveal how Aristotle will find a proper place for pleasure in living well. On top of this problem, notice the resistance to setting-down happiness among the external goods, yet the *logos* not wishing to close the door entirely on such goods being part of happiness. Economics is not wrong for holding an interest in acquiring external goods, but it is incorrect if it assumes these are authoritative goods.

The preceding *logos* sings together with those who say happiness is either virtue or some virtue. But in saying happiness is an activity according to virtue, Aristotle wonders, "Perhaps [there is] no small difference to assume the best thing [is] in acquisition or use, and in a *hexis* or an activity." While a *hexis* admits of being present without bringing to completion (*apoteleō*) anything good (like when someone is asleep),[60] the activity will act well from necessity. Just as it is not the noblest and strongest who win the Olympics, but those who compete, so the noble and good things in life come to those acting correctly (1098b30–1099a7). Aristotle's introduction of *hexis* to the *Ethics* initially appears to confirm the seemingly authoritative status of activity in the human work. But the Olympic analogy is not simple, for even if the noblest and strongest people abstain from competition, they remain the noblest and strongest. Their nobility and strength is akin to a *hexis*: it is something they hold that one cannot take away from them even if it may not be—to play on a literal reading of "activity"—in-work (*en-ergeia*). Also helpful here is the *Politics'* distinction between the proper and improper uses of pieces of acquisition: the proper use is of an acquisition for what it is (like wearing a shoe), and the improper use is the exchange of an acquisition.[61] If the best acquisition in life might be a *hexis*, does it have proper and improper uses? And how would this *hexis* hold toward activities?

Though Aristotle seems to abandon the distinction between *hexis* and activity by turning to pleasure, his first sketch of pleasure in the *Ethics* foreshadows how one may acquire a *hexis*. Continuing his look at the lives of Olympic athletes, Aristotle says:

> And their life is pleasant according to itself. For while to take pleasure (*hēdomai*) itself belongs to things of the soul, for each what is pleasant [is] towards what one is said [to be] a lover of such and such (*philotoiutos*), like a horse for the lover of horses (*philippos*), and spectacle for a lover of spectacle (*philotheōros*), and in the same manner the just things for the lover of the just (*philodikaios*) and wholly the things according to virtue for the lover of virtue (*philoaretos*). (1099a7–11)

Within Book I's eighth chapter, this description of pleasure belonging to the soul affirms the authoritative place of goods of the soul. The argument also subordinates external goods (i.e., horses and spectacles) to the goods of the soul through the love belonging to friendship, *philia*. Readers should follow this more favorable argument about pleasure back to Book I's dismissal of pleasure as the end for the completely servile life of enjoyment that the many choose (*proaireō*) because they have the same passions as those in positions of authority.[62] Through friendship, pleasure finds a home in the soul, and all the things toward which one chooses to live hold a common beginning.

While friendship and the experience of pleasure subordinate external goods to those of the soul, the nature of the just things and the virtues requires a more careful examination. Looking at the character of the many, Aristotle observes:

> Now for the many the pleasant things fight themselves through such things not being pleasant by nature, but for the lovers of the noble (*philokaloi*) the things pleasant by nature are pleasant, and such [are] the actions according to virtue, as they are pleasant to such people and according to themselves. So their life in no way needs the addition (*prosdeō*) of pleasure as some appendage, but holds pleasure in itself. (1099a11–16)

Using the opposition between the many and lovers of the noble, Aristotle suggests what is pleasant by nature "holds pleasure in itself" and does not need the addition of pleasure like the pleasant things that fight themselves for the many. When Aristotle introduces happiness to the *Ethics* earlier in Book I, he sets the many's claim that happiness is either pleasure, wealth, or honor against the wise, though he never says what the wise claim happiness is. These competing claims precede Plato's well-unprovided question about seeking first-principles in *logos*.[63] For the moment, the actions according to virtue sought by lovers of the noble mark Aristotle's first attempt to articulate what things are pleasant by nature. And although the *Ethics'* inquiry into moral virtue sets the noble as its end in Book III (1115b12–13), recall that Book II establishes the noble is (along with pleasant and the advantageous) among the three things of choosing (*hairesis*), and the challenge of fighting pleasure belongs to both virtue and the political art. According to Book III, the many fail to see the truth about each *hexis* and choose the pleasant as the apparent good. In Book VI, to support reading "moderation" (*sōphrosunē*) as "preserving (*sōzō*) prudence (*phronēsis*)," Aristotle describes how pleasures and pains ruin people's perception of the first-principle for the "true practical *hexis* with *logos* concerning the good things" for their lives.[64] Despite positing in Book I that the mean produces, preserves, and increases the virtues while excess and deficiency ruin them, friendship seems to be the *hexis* that holds a better sense of what is naturally pleasant in life.

Continuing his preliminary inquiry into virtue, pleasure, and happiness, Aristotle makes a grand statement about happiness that prompts a return to considering the place of external goods in a happy life. For those spoken of as good, no one would say this if such persons "do not delight (*chairō*) in noble actions," just as no one would say someone is just or liberal by not delighting in just or liberal actions. On the condition that these actions are noble and good if the serious person judges them—and contrary to the Delphic inscription that marks-the-boundary to say "Noblest [is] the most just, best (*lōston*) to be healthy; but most pleasant naturally to hit or happen upon something for which one has *erōs* (*eraō*)"—Aristotle says "we assert" happiness is best, noblest, and most pleasant because these things are all present in the best activities (1099a17–31).[65] The Delphic inscription marks the first of the rare appearances of *erōs* in the *Ethics*, a love that appears almost exclusively within the inquiry into friendship in Books VIII and IX.[66] There is no way within Book I of the *Ethics* for readers to grasp the significance of the difference between friendship and *erōs*, but they can see that both forms of love bear some relation to pleasure.[67] This difference emerges alongside the subtle suggestion that what is most just is not best, noblest, and most pleasant. In this context, it appears that happiness "needs the addition of the external goods . . . for it is either impossible (*adunaton*) or not easy to do the noble things without-resources (*achorēgēton*)" like tools, friends, wealth, and political capacity (or "power," *dunamis*). From things looking like they need the addition of "good days" (*euēmeria*), happiness is either "good fortune" (*eutuchē*) or virtue (1099a31–b9). Though life does not need the addition of pleasure, it does need the addition of external goods. The inclusion of friends along with tools, wealth, and political power places them among things both economics and politics can provide for happiness. But if friendship and its natural pleasure belong to the soul, there are things in life that economics and politics cannot provide.

From the uncertainty over whether happiness comes through good fortune or virtue, Aristotle states one may be unprovided over whether happiness is either something "learned (*mathēton*), from habit (*ethiston*), or from some other practice (*askēton*), *or* according to some divine portion or through chance." Acknowledging what concerns the gods is more proper (*oikeioteron*) to another examination, to learn or practice virtue is more divine, and virtue could be capable of becoming common to many through learning and care if they are "not maimed towards virtue." This leads to a puzzling conclusion:

> And if in this way it is better to be happy than through chance, [it is] good-*logos* to hold in this way, if indeed the things according to nature similarly both hold noblest, [and] in this way naturally, and likewise in this way with the things according to art and every cause, and most of all the things according to the best [art or cause]. To turn over the greatest and noblest thing to chance would be excessively unharmonious. (1099b9–25)

The constant in Aristotle's conditional argument is the noblest and best things hold according to nature. What differs is the cause of things holding in this way, which is either nature, art, or chance. In Book III of the *Ethics*, arts (including the money-making art), sciences, intellect, and "all things through the human being" emerge as deliberative causes toward ends in practical matters.[68] This teaching follows Aristotle asking what choice (*proairesis*) is, tentatively characterizing it as "with *logos* and thought" through its name being "that which may be taken before other things" (*on pro heterōn haireton*), and later summarizing its outline within Book III as some "deliberate desire" toward ends (1112a13–17, 1113a9–14). In Book VI, Aristotle defines choice *and* the beginning or first-principle (*archē*) that is a human being as either desiring intellect or thinking desire. Prior to this definition, Aristotle distinguishes the practical from the productive, and he applies this distinction to *hexeis* in the brief inquiry into art that follows his definition of human nature. At the end of this inquiry, he uses the poet Agathon—whose name means "good"—to describe the affinity between art and chance. Returning to Book I, when Aristotle presents happiness as "the highest of all the practical goods," his allusion to those who suppose there is some other good that causes many good things to be good leads into Plato's well-unprovided matter of how to know and become familiar with first-principles in *logos*.[69] Whether it is happiness, politics, or economics, wherever human beings act as causes, these things will only hold according to nature if people choose to pursue the good according to nature as their end, and this choice is inseparable from some *logos*.

Though Aristotle's primary purpose for raising the unprovided question about the cause of happiness is to set a working definition of this idea for the *Ethics*, his next series of arguments demonstrates why such a definition is vital for politics and economics. With happiness belonging to the best art or cause instead of chance, the sought-for thing (i.e., that happiness is some activity of the soul according to virtue) is manifest from the *logos*. And as for "the remaining good things [the external and bodily goods], on the one hand [it is] necessary [for some] to be present, and on the other hand [for others to be] coworkers and naturally useful as tools." These things also agree (*homologeō*) with setting-down the political art's end as best earlier in Book I, for this art cares most to produce citizens who are good and produce practical noble things, and only human beings can form-community in activities of the soul (1099b25–1100a4). The first time "the sought-for thing" appears in the *Ethics* is with the rejection of honor as the end for a happy life on the grounds that "we divine ourselves the good to be something properly-one's-own (*oikeion*) and hard-to-take-away (*dusaphaireton*)." In the surprise appearance of the money-making life, Aristotle rejects wealth as the "sought-for good" because it is useful for the sake of another thing. Later, following the implicit choice between the carpenter and geometer (i.e., seeking what is useful or contemplating the truth) as an approach to being a coworker with the *Ethics' logos* and attending to the precision proper to the inquiry, Aristotle tells readers they must attempt (*peirateon*) to search for first-principles as is natural, for the sought-for things become manifest through them.[70] Aristotle's *logos* manifests the authoritative good of the soul, and if readers are coworkers with this *logos*, they can form-community so that the external and bodily goods necessary for happiness will be "present . . . [and] coworkers and naturally useful tools." Though politics and economics seek to produce happiness through community and acquisition, they are always subordinate to people's natural choice of the good that is properly-one's-own that precedes all political and economic activity.

The final stretch of arguments about happiness in Book I paradoxically allude to the authoritative nature of choice in the pursuit of political and economic self-sufficiency while providing a sobering lesson on the role of chance and the limits of one's own choices in life. After suggesting the political art could produce happiness in its citizens and the city, Aristotle adds that there is need for both complete virtue and a complete life, though life still admits of many changes from chance and "great mishaps" (*sumphora*) that make it difficult to "proclaim" (*chraō*) someone is happy. Related to this is the question about whether it is possible to consider someone happy while living, or if one "needs (*chreōn*) to see an end." Recognizing this raises questions about the honors, dishonors, good-actions, and misfortunes of descendants, Aristotle adds "these things hold-forth (*parechō*) without-provision," largely because the inquiry assumes happiness is "lasting" (*monimos*) and not subject to change and chance. But being unprovided in these questions witnesses to the *logos* that finds the activities of the soul according to virtue are authoritative over well-being, for even though human life needs the addition of chance, these activities seem more lasting than sciences, and living this way is most "holding-together" (*sunechō*). By acting and contemplating things according to virtue, the happy person will handle chance nobly and harmoniously, and the sought-for thing will be present (1100a4–b22). There is no escaping chance in life, and the best one can hope to do is hold-together in such a way that one's own acting and contemplating is of things that are more lasting than change and chance. Part of what holds-forth the question without-provision that prompts this teaching are descendants, who appear earlier alongside friends in Book I's argument that the complete good and the self-sufficient that are choiceworthy on account of themselves hold some boundary and do not go without-limit.[71] Even with chance, how one's own life, politics, and economics hold-together depends on the end each chooses.

To see how friendship best illuminates the foundational choice of the good in politics and economics, there are two final arguments to consider from Book I of the *Ethics*. First, in the eleventh chapter, Aristotle admits that it would be "exceedingly friendless (*aphilon*) and contrary to opinions" to deny friends and descendants affect happiness, though to divide (*diaireō*) this would be without-limit (*aperanton*). Speaking generally and in outline, Aristotle includes being unprovided in whether there is something good in common with those who died, but concludes friends' good or bad actions neither produce nor "take away" (*aphaireō*) one's own happiness (1101a22– b9). This brief argument suggests a need to account for friends in a happy life, though choosing to do more than outline such things would produce an abstraction (*aphairesis*) from how one chooses to pursue happiness.

The second relevant argument occurs at the beginning of Book I's final chapter, where Aristotle—after reiterating "happiness is some activity of the soul according to complete virtue"—proposes contemplating virtue to contemplate happiness better, "For it seems the politician according to the truth has labored most of all concerning this, for he wishes to produce citizens good and obedient to the laws." If this investigation of the soul belongs to the political art, it would be "according to the choice from the beginning" of the inquiry that seeks the human good and human happiness (1102a5–26). Whereas Aristotle earlier states the political art cares to produce citizens who are good and produce the practical noble things, the politician's wish to produce good and happy citizens leads to the replacement of the noble things with obedience to the laws. Any care the political art holds for producing good and happy citizens begins with some wish for this end. The realization of this wish requires each person within the community to choose the things bearing toward this end, and the nature of such choices is more visible in friendship than politics and economics.

## CONCLUSION: PLEASURE, FRIENDSHIP, AND ARISTOTLE'S APPROACH TO A FREE POLITICS AND ECONOMICS

Using Book I of the *Ethics* as a guide, it becomes clear why the search for Aristotle's economic teaching within his political philosophy must look not to the pursuit of political and economic self-sufficiency, but the natural desire for friendship and the good. When the *Ethics'* inquiry into happiness turns toward the good things, the life that "holds pleasure in itself" is evident through friendship's love (*phileō*) and "in no way needs the addition of pleasure as some appendage" contrasts with needing the addition of external goods, good-days, and chance. This argument about pleasure through which contemplation of the soul comes about at the end of Book I begins with the question over whether the best thing is a *hexis* or an activity, an acquisition or use. In Book I of the *Politics*, the money-making art ("the art of useful things") is one of several arts of acquisition (the art of household management, the natural art of exchange, the necessary money-making art, and the art of retail-trade). Although Aristotle never speaks of human choice in the *Politics'* inquiry into the money-making art, he describes human beings as pleasantly mixing lives in pursuit of the self-sufficient as "need necessitates" (*chreia sunankazō*), states the self-sufficiency of true wealth is not without-limit toward good-living, and declares the natural art of exchange between households restores the self-sufficiency that is according to nature. With the argument about the mixing of lives, Aristotle is careful to set these natural works apart from exchange and retail-trade. Similarly, with the natural art of exchange, Aristotle notes this art is not a form of the money-making art.[72] In both cases, the *Politics'* inquiry into the forms of economic acquisition abstracts from choice and the human work.

The case for the political art's authoritative claim over the human good in Book I of the *Ethics* requires assuming that architectonic capacities' ends are more choiceworthy than what falls under them, and this art sets-down through the laws which sciences are used or needed (*chreōn*) in cities, who should learn them, and how people in the city should act. According to this preliminary argument, it seems everything one uses or needs for the human good requires subordination to the political art's practical choices. Yet when the political art returns in Book I's later chapters, its care to produce happiness for its citizens runs into a need for complete virtue and a complete life that raises questions about how to "proclaim" (*chraō*) someone happy and the "need (*chreōn*) to see an end." Through being without-provision in these questions, readers discover with *logos* that, in life, activities of the soul hold-together more lastingly than sciences.[73] Whereas Book I starts by positing the political art provides the good one uses or needs to be happy, it ends by affirming the activity (and therefore use) of the soul according to some virtue one acquires produces happiness. The crucial inquiry between these arguments is the consideration of self-sufficiency as the complete good that holds a boundary revealed by friendship and human beings' political nature. In Aristotle's subsequent inquiry into the good things, the human work, *hexis*, and activity, it is friendship that draws readers into contemplating what is naturally pleasant to the soul.

One way to illuminate a consistent political and economic teaching in Aristotle's political philosophy is to see how these arguments about the good things appear in arguments about prudence in the *Ethics* and the *Politics*. In Book VI of the *Ethics*, Aristotle describes prudence, the political art, and household management as the same *hexis* that seeks the good and well-being for oneself. Aristotle next invites readers to wonder if this well-being needs household management or a regime, and opens the door to considering how one comes to trust the experience of natural first-principles that one does not come to know through abstraction (*aphairesis*). In Book VII of the *Politics*, happiness depends on virtue and prudence because these things belong to a person's nature according to the true division (*diaresis*) of things into external, body, and soul, with acquisition and external goods holding a limit set apart from the more useful and honorable setting-down-through (*diathesis*) of the soul. Later in Book VII, all things' well-being depends on "the correct posing of actions' target and end, and the discovery of actions bearing towards the end." Happiness relates to "the well-provided things" from virtue that generate good things, and on this basis, cities are serious when each citizen is serious through science and choice. This seriousness of character depends on how each person's nature and habits hold toward *logos*.[74] As sciences and arts, no matter how well politics and economics provide insight into the things people need and use for their own well-being, the use of these capacities requires people to choose them, and this choice depends on trusting the good that *logos* holds out to them.

In Book I of the *Politics*, the common association of community and acquisition with use uncovers how the choice of the good is necessary for preserving the free character of politics and economics. Attempting to contemplate the natural growth of communities on the way to presenting self-sufficiency as the city's nature and end apart from choice, after establishing ruler by nature and ruled by nature form one of two couplings necessary for preservation, Aristotle defines the household as the community according to nature set-standing-together for every day (*pasan hēmeran*), and the village as the first community of many households that is for the sake of a non-daily use (*chrēseōs . . . mē ephēmerou*). The necessary and natural art of exchange that serves as a precedent for the money-making art (*chrēmatistikē*) and derives from the improper use of every piece of acquisition relates to the community defined by use (the village). The household (*oikia*), on the other hand, is a community not defined by use, hence why the name for the "proper" (*oikeia*) use of pieces of acquisition derives from the household, and further, why there is no work for the art of exchange in the household. In Book I of the *Ethics*, following the quiet introduction of a conflict between friendship and *erōs* over pleasure, happiness appears to need the addition of "good days" (*euēmeria*) among external goods like tools, friends, wealth, and political capacity.[75] While it would seem politics and economics make the authoritative provision for preservation and happiness, the inclusion of friends among these goods, the insufficiency of defining the household through use, and the natural role of pleasure in the human work all demand readers look deeper into human nature to discover the proper use of politics and economics for a good life.

From the *Politics*' examination of the slave by nature, Aristotle provides a glimpse into the natural foundations for a free politics and economics within the soul. In a *logos* contemplating whether it is good, just, and according to nature for someone to be a slave, Aristotle states ruling and being-ruled are among the necessary and the advantageous things. Within this inquiry—and after identifying nature with what is best and political rule with intellect and the part holding *logos* respectively ruling desire and passion—Aristotle finds the exchange in the need (*chreia*) for tame animals and slaves is small. Furthermore, he concludes that while it would be advantageous and just for a master to rule a natural slave, nature does not (despite its wishes) produce human beings who are naturally free and slave in body and soul. In this way, Aristotle demonstrates that while one can theoretically conceive of how mastery and slavery is just and advantageous, such forms of ruling and being-ruled are not necessary. The co-working of intellect and *logos* within the soul to produce political and therefore free rule over desire and passion suggests how the good is necessary for a free character in community and acquisition. When Aristotle distinguishes mastery from political rule and household management's rule in the final chapter of this inquiry, he argues the science of using slaves differs from that of acquiring them; he also denigrates mastery on the grounds that people prefer philosophizing or practicing-politics to exercising mastery. Bridging these arguments is a distinction between ruling and being-ruled either according to science or being.[76] The existence of mastery and slavery attests to pursuits of what is just and advantageous that are neither necessary nor according to nature. Since mastery and slavery concern acquisition and use in life, they reveal how politics and economics can produce slavish and illiberal acquisitions and uses of the things naturally necessary for preservation.

To produce freedom and liberality in politics and economics, Aristotle looks neither toward community nor acquisition, but friendship. In the *Politics'* examination of slavery by law, there is exchange in *logoi* about slavery being just because some assert those who hold-over (*huperochē*) others in some good like virtue have the capacity to be forceful and violent through happening upon resources (*chorēgias*). Despite setting-down a law that declares slavery according to war is just, Aristotle shows this *logos* depends upon the existence of natural masters and slaves. This inquiry concludes with Aristotle acknowledging there is something advantageous and friendship between those by nature worthy of being master and slave, though nature itself does not produce such human beings. Because the case for slavery by law hinges upon the acquisition of resources, it recalls the *Ethics'* argument that happiness needs the addition of external goods (friends, wealth, and political capacity) that act as tools, "for it is either impossible or not easy to do the noble things without-resources (*achorēgēton*)."[77] In the *Politics'* inquiries into slavery by nature and by law, the advantageous respectively appears alongside the just and friendship. In the former case, what is just and advantageous does not coincide with what is naturally necessary. In the latter case, friendship and what is advantageous may be by nature, but they are not necessary. The possibility of friendship even between master and slave shows both are worthy of a naturally freer life.

The "advantageous" (*sumpheron*) only appears once in the *Politics'* inquiry into the money-making art with the description of nature marking-the-boundaries of animals' lives toward the advantageous choosing (*hairesis*) of food with the pleasant. Similarly, the sole mention of the "disadvantageous" (*asumphoros*) is in the story of the Sicilian money-maker exiled from Syracuse by the tyrant Dionysius. According to Book II of the *Ethics*, the advantageous is among the noble and pleasant as three things of choosing, and all the matter of concern for virtue and the political art is using pleasures and pains to become either good or bad.[78] When it comes to acquisition and household management, Book I of the *Politics'* silence on the role of pleasures and pains in choice points to a glaring omission in its economic teaching.

This omission of pleasure and choice also affects Book I's political teaching, for while Aristotle acknowledges early on that law and the just are good for those who set-standing-together political community, it is not until Book III that he defines the just as "the common advantage." With this definition, he points back to Book V of the *Ethics' logoi* about justice and tells readers that the basis for equality and inequality "holds without-provision and political philosophy." If the just is something advantageous and the choice for the advantageous involves the pleasant, political philosophy must have something to say about pleasure. Book I of the *Politics* contains a veiled hint of this when, after stating self-sufficiency is the nature and end of the city, Aristotle describes human beings as political animals because they hold *logos*. Through *logos*, people hold sense-perception of the pleasant and the painful, advantageous and harmful, good and bad, and just and unjust, "and community in these things produces a household and a city." In Book I of the *Ethics*, the good things (as opposed to the noble and just things) do not differ and are by nature. When Aristotle divides external goods from those of the body and the soul, he states the souls' goods are most authoritative, presents pleasure as belonging to the soul, and binds it to the form of love that defines friendship.[79] While it seems the advantageous and the just provide the authoritative perspective on economics and politics, political philosophy sees these things begin with a choice concerning pleasure and the good. Thus, to acquire a complete understanding of what is advantageous and just in economic acquisition and political community, one must follow Aristotle's teaching on pleasure, political philosophy, friendship, and happiness in Books VII through X of the *Ethics*.

*Chapter 5*

# Political Philosophy, Pleasure, and the Good Things

Whether it is the *Politics'* inquiries into natural acquisition (I.8) and the natural growth of the city toward the end of self-sufficiency (I.2), or the *Ethics'* inquiries into the good, the political art, happiness, and self-sufficiency (I.4–5, 7–8), or the examination of prudence as it relates to the political art and household management (VI.5), readers always encounter some need to reckon with pleasure in contemplating their practical pursuit of the good. When thinking broadly about economics and politics, an honest accounting of individuals' pursuits of goods and pleasures may seem beyond the scope of any reasonable inquiry. But in Aristotle's political philosophy, a full understanding of economics and politics does not come through looking at people's choices in the aggregate. Rather, economics and politics—and indeed *all* human pursuits—begin with personal choices about goods that are inseparable from a natural desire for pleasure. In Book VII of the *Ethics*, Aristotle reveals political philosophy's mutual concern with the good and pleasure, and by the end of this inquiry, prepares readers to see through friendship how their own choice of the good is at the heart of all human things.

One of the central tensions in Aristotle's political philosophy is the relationship between one's own good and the political community's good. In the early stages of the *Ethics* and *Politics*, Aristotle seems to emphasize the political community's good over one's own. In the *Ethics*, the political art taking and preserving the human good for cities and nations displays itself as more complete, noble, and divine than doing so for one person alone (though this is something "loved," *agapēton*). In the *Politics*, Aristotle introduces the city as the most authoritative political community, and shortly thereafter defines the city as the complete community "holding every limit of self-sufficiency" because it is supposedly the end and nature of the first two communities (i.e., the household and the village). By approaching the *Ethics* and the *Politics* as works of political philosophy, it is reasonable to want to focus on the extent of the political community's authority. Though this is undoubtedly a concern for Aristotle, readers should remember that before he turns to the political art in the *Ethics* and names the city as the most authoritative community in the *Politics*, he states how all human things aim at some good. The *Ethics*, however, goes further in its opening sentence than the *Politics*, presenting the good as that at which all things aim themselves.[1] The question of the good is the first question in Aristotle's political philosophy, and readers cannot understand his teaching without engaging it.

Aside from the *Ethics* preceding the *Politics*, there is an important clue in Book III of the *Politics* that compels readers who wish to understand the nature of political community to return to the *Ethics*' inquiry into friendship (*philia*). The city, according to Aristotle, is not just a community of place, not "doing injustice" (*adikeō*),[2] and mutual-giving (like the barbarian households exercising the natural art of exchange from Book I's inquiry into the money-making art).[3] Though it is necessary (*anankē*) for these things to be present, the city is "a community of living well and households and families, for the sake of complete and self-sufficient living . . . [that is the] work of friendship, for the choice of living-together (*suzaō*) [is] friendship" (1280b29–39). The proper foundation for the city and its political and economic self-sufficiency in Aristotle's political philosophy is friendship, and the foundation for friendship is choice. Accordingly, if readers wish to understand politics and economics as the work of friendship, they must first discover the nature of the choice to form friendships.[4]

With choice as the foundation of friendship and political community, Aristotle throws readers back to Book VI of the *Ethics* and the discovery that "choice is either desiring intellect (*orektikos nous*) or thinking desire (*orexis dianoiētikē*), and such a first-principle [or beginning, *archē*] is a human being." As for what guides choice, it is desire and *logos* for the sake of something. Back in Book III, Aristotle establishes that for the sake of which is an end, which belongs to wish (*boulēsis*). With wish, Aristotle raises the question of whether this is for the good or the apparent good. Whereas many choose the apparent good because pleasure deceives them and they choose the pleasant as good and flee pain as bad, the serious person judges the good for each *hexis* according to the truth. The difficulty of choosing the good according to the truth as an end in wish shows itself earlier in Book II with the bad person choosing errantly because of pleasure. After asserting art, virtue, and the well-being of something concern what is most difficult, and furthermore, the most difficult thing to fight is pleasure, Aristotle concludes all the matter of concern for both virtue and the political art is using pleasures and pains to become good or bad.[5] These two arguments from Books II and III indicate the problem-facing choice—and therefore intellect, desire, and the whole of human nature according to Book VI—concerns disentangling the good and pleasure as ends.

In Book VI of the *Ethics*, politics' and economics' common need to distinguish the good from pleasure as an end is a small part of the inquiry into prudence. According to Aristotle, prudence and the political art are the same *hexis*, and household management (*oikonomia*) is a kind of prudence too. Prudence is neither a science (*epistēmē*) because acts admit to hold otherwise, nor an art since action differs from production; this leaves prudence as "a true practical *hexis* with *logos* concerning the good things and bad things for a human being." From this definition, Aristotle turns to people said to be prudent (like Pericles, household managers, and politicians), describing them as having the capacity to contemplate the good things for themselves and human beings. The nature of this contemplation is evident in the name of "moderation (*sōphrosunē*)"—which means "preserving (*sōzō*) prudence (*phronēsis*)"—since it preserves practical assumptions (*hupolēpsis*) about the good things. It is in this context that Aristotle finds a new way to present the problem pleasures and pains pose to contemplation of the good things. Pleasures and pains do not ruin every assumption like mathematical ones (which Aristotle later describes as "abstractions" and therefore are "away from choosing," *aphairesis*), but only practical ones (which he later associates with what is natural as opposed to the mathematical). But ruin through pleasures and pains extends further than assumptions, for vice is ruinous of the first-principle through which one needs to choose all things. From this, Aristotle concludes that prudence is "necessarily . . . a true practical *hexis* with *logos* concerning the good things for human beings."[6] Notice the subtle shift in the definitions of prudence bookending this account of its contemplation: though it seems prudence contemplates both what is good and bad for human beings, its true concern is the good things. Because politics and economics need moderation to preserve their prudence, the true source of moderation is contemplation of the good things.

Although Book VI identifies politics and economics with the *hexis* of prudence, Book I alludes to how Books VII through X work with Book VI to provide for the comprehensive contemplation of the good things that is not subject to ruin through pleasures and pains. Prior to situating happiness among the good things, Aristotle asks readers to attempt (*peirateon*) to contemplate first-principles in the manner that is natural to them and seek the precision proper (*oikeion*) to his *logos* as coworkers by presenting an implicit choice between being either practical carpenters who seek what is "useful towards the work," or theoretical geometers who are "contemplator[s] of the truth." Among the external goods, bodily goods, and goods concerning the soul, happiness takes its place among the most authoritative goods concerning the soul. From this perspective, Aristotle raises questions about the relationship between *hexis* and activity, describes the soul's relationship to pleasure in terms of friendship's love (*phileō*), and concedes happiness' need for external goods (which include friends, wealth, and political capacity).[7] Coming out of Book VI, its intense concentration on the soul necessitates moving back toward bodily and external goods to see the good things as a whole. Book VII's inquiry into pleasures and pains begins with Aristotle saying "we will produce another beginning (*archē*)," and ends by summarizing the account as stating what pleasures and pains are *and* how some of them are among the good things, others among the bad things. Aristotle then concludes Book VII by saying, "In the remainder we will speak concerning friendship" (1145a15, 1154b32–34). Though this seems to be a non-sequitur, it is truly an extension of the tie Book I establishes between friendship and pleasure in the search for the good things.

Readers should view Aristotle's invitation to "produce another beginning" in Book VII in light of Book VI's conclusion that prudence and the political art are not authoritative over wisdom (*sophia*).[8] In Book VII's eleventh chapter, Aristotle introduces "the one who philosophizes about the political art" (*tou tēn politkēn philosophountos*, henceforth "the political philosopher")[9] as someone who contemplates pleasure and pain. Through this contemplation, the political philosopher is the "architect" (*architektōn*) of the end toward which "we speak" of each thing as simply (*haplōs*) bad or good (1152b1–3). The *Ethics'* initial case for the good as the best end and its choiceworthy status rests on how the political art *seems* to be "the most authoritative and the most architectonic" capacity. In the middle of this case for the political art is a view of the good that proposes it is the best end because knowledge of it ensures each person's desire and choosing do not go without-limit, thus allowing one to hit upon what is needful in life.[10] The existence of an architectonic art presupposes an architect, and such an art's choice about the good in life necessarily reflects its architect's choice. Though politicians and household managers practice the political and economic arts, the political philosopher sees these arts' ends more clearly than their practitioners, for the political philosopher views these practical pursuits from the authoritative perspective of one who is a friend (*philos*) of wisdom (*sophia*).

At first glance, appealing to the philosopher's perspective seems to contradict Aristotle's observation in Book VI that philosophers such as Anaxagoras and Thales do not receive recognition for being prudent because they are ignorant of the things advantageous to themselves, knowing only useless things (*achrēsta*) and not seeking the human goods. The appeal to the political philosopher also seems to run up against Book I's presentation of philosophers as people who seem to abolish (*anaireō*) the things that are properly-one's-own (*ta oikeia*, which include friends) for the preservation of the truth (which is also a friend).[11] Before the introduction of "the political philosopher" in the *Ethics*, there are only hints of how philosophy may be practical by speaking with clarity on the good and bad things for human beings in relation to the good as an end. With "the political philosopher," however, Aristotle can begin to show how to seek the good as an end through contemplation, and further, how this contemplation of the good is practical for caring for the choices and things that are properly-one's-own. The greatest competition the good faces as an end is from pleasure, and it is through friendship that Aristotle addresses and resolves this conflict.

Though Aristotle's inquiry into friendship holds important insights into the nature of economic exchanges and how these relate to justice and political community, since the foundation for both political community and friendship is choice, readers must focus first on how his inquiry into friendship teaches them how to choose the good over pleasure as the end of their actions in caring for what is properly-one's-own. By weaving together threads from Books VII and X's inquiries into pleasure with Books VIII and IX's arguments for the good as the best friendships' end over the next several chapters, clarity emerges on how to pursue the good things. Of great interest for discerning Aristotle's political and economic teaching is the relationship between the useful, the pleasant, and the good in this stretch of the *Ethics*, especially since the money-making art (*chrēmatistikē*) is "the art of useful things." Because one cannot understand the useful things apart from Aristotle's moral teaching on pleasure and the good, one must work with this teaching to discover the true natural limits of economics and politics.

## *HEXIS* AND TRUST IN *LOGOS* (*ETHICS* 1105A17–19, 1105B9–18, 1145A15–27, 1145B8– 14, 1146B24–35, 1147A10–B19)

With his introduction to Book VII as "another beginning," Aristotle's turn toward pleasures and pains begins with a paradoxical departure from *and* continuation of the *Ethics'* main questions about the good and the political art. The departure comes with Aristotle starting not with things one should choose, but three forms of things concerning character that one should flee: vice, being without self-restraint (*akrasia*), and "beastliness" (*theriotēs*). The opposites of the first two things are virtue and "self-restraint" (*enkrateia*); as for the opposite of beastliness, Aristotle "sets-down-against" (*antitithēmi*) it a *hexis* that is some "heroic and divine" virtue (1145a15–27). While *hexis* is a natural carryover from Book VI's concluding arguments for intellect and prudence making natural *hexeis* into authoritative virtue, character allows Aristotle to use self-restraint to return to an important theme about the political art from Book I. In comparing the self-restrained person to the person without self-restraint, the former seems to be someone "abiding in reasoning (*logismos*)," while the latter "departs from reasoning." The person without self-restraint acts through passion, while the self-restrained person knows the desires (*epithumia*) are base and does not follow them through *logos* (1145b8–14). Book VII retains Book VI's sense that *hexeis* are ways the soul admits to hold otherwise in relation to reasoning and *logos*. The person without self-restraint acting through passion instead of *logos* recalls Aristotle's statement in Book I that the political art's *logoi* are not beneficial to those whose characters follow passion and fail to produce their desires (*orexeis*) according to *logos*. Though Aristotle introduces this argument by declaring the young are not the proper (*oikeios*) listeners for the political art's *logoi*,[12] the turn away from age to character as the source of the problem prefigures his focus on character in Book VII. What is clear in Book VII that is not apparent in Book I is character reflects one's *hexeis*, which themselves reflect the relationship between one's own desires and *logos*.

Although self-restraint and its absence are the most prominent subjects in Book VII of the *Ethics*, Aristotle does substantial work with *hexis* and pleasure prior to his introduction to the political philosopher that is helpful for understanding his economic teaching. One of the first issues is whether the person without self-restraint acts contrary to "true opinion" or science, though it turns out there is no difference to the *logos* because the fundamental problem is a slight trust (*pisteuō*) in either thing. With science, what it means to know-scientifically (*epistamai*) is twofold, for a person could either hold science and not use it, or hold it and use it. The difference comes down to whether the person holding science contemplates it (1146b24–35). Through science, readers learn that contemplation is a form of use. As the art of useful things, the money-making art is a form of contemplation. This fits Aristotle's characterization of the money-maker in Book I of the *Politics* as someone who contemplates the sources of acquisition, wealth, and useful things, and his later characterization of the money-making art's work as the capacity to contemplate sources for a quantity of useful things understood as the gain (*kerdos*) of legal-currency without-limit through the art of retail-trade. The turn toward the production of gain owes its origins to people setting-down-through themselves (*diathesis*) mistakes about living and living well on account of desires (*epithumia*) and bodily enjoyment through which they use their own capacities in ways that are contrary to nature, as if money-making is the end of all things. In the last chapter of the *Politics'* inquiry into the money-making art, Aristotle characterizes the money-making art's use as holding "free contemplation" (*theōrian eleutheran*) and "necessary experience." This final part of Aristotle's inquiry contains the only two appearances of "wisdom" in the *Politics* when he discusses how many mistakenly attribute wisdom to Thales' money-making. Within this story, Aristotle mentions the reproach against philosophy that it is not beneficial.[13] If contemplation is the use of a science through trust, and if an economic science's use requires both free contemplation and necessary experience, the philosophic experience that the *Ethics* provides in contemplating the good would be what is most necessary for trusting and using an economic science so that it is beneficial.

Aristotle suggests how the beneficial use of science requires philosophic contemplation by considering what it means to hold science as a *hexis*. Much like Book I's introduction to *hexis*, to hold science in this way (like an acquisition) and not use it is akin to a person being asleep (which in Book I's terms is not working in the activity of science).[14] But now in Book VII, Aristotle adds a problem regarding *logos*, noting it is not a sign of holding a science to state its *logoi*, for both those who are in the passions and first learning something can speak like this. Instead, "there is need to naturally-grow-together (*sumphuō*) [with the *logos*], but this needs time" (1147a10–24). The natural complementarity of *hexis* and activity comes forth in this passage. For a science to be a *hexis*, the acquisition of its *logos* must couple with its use, and one must naturally-grow-together with the *logos* over time so that even one's own passions follow it. A precedent for this argument appears in Book II when—in being unprovided (*aporeō*) over how one becomes virtuous—Aristotle criticizes the many for fleeing to *logos* instead of acting virtuously, supposing this is what it means to philosophize, be serious, and care for the soul so that they hold well (1105a17–19, b9–18). For any *logos* to be beneficial (regardless of whether it is philosophic, economic, or political), its true and natural acquisition requires producing one's own desires and passions according to it—to hold it as a *hexis*.

Seeking a natural cause for a person being without-self-restraint, Aristotle considers an instance where two conflicting general opinions are present: either one needs to taste all sweet things, or one should not taste sweet things. When a person with these opinions faces the authoritative sense-perception of something sweet before oneself, if that person is without self-restraint, desire (*epithumia*) for what is pleasant leads and the first opinion becomes active (*energein*), leading one to act against correct *logos*. To loosen this ignorance so that the person without self-restraint becomes someone with scientific knowledge, Aristotle appeals to a *logos* from "those who study nature" (*phusiologōn*)[15] that reveals being without self-restraint occurs in relation to science because "the last boundary" (*ton eschaton horon*) is neither known-scientifically nor seems to be known-scientifically like what is general, but is "sense-perceptible" (*aisthētikē*). When someone either does not hold a science's general opinion, or holds it without it being known-scientifically, that person is like someone either asleep or drunk (in which case one only speaks of the scientific *logos* without applying it). By not being authoritative in actions, "the authoritative science" does not seem to be present (1147a24–b19). By this account, the condition for naturally-growing-together with *logos* requires bringing sense-perception of actions' last boundaries under the authority of a science's *logos*. In Book VI, every science begins with trusting first-principles that are known or familiar (*gnōrimos*) to oneself. In practical matters, prudence relies on the intellect's joint sense-perception of first-principles as boundaries of which there is no *logos* and the last things relevant to every action.[16] When one looks at what holding a science as a *hexis* requires in light of these arguments from Book VI, one sees the interworking of intellect, desire, pleasure, and *logos* within human nature.

To move toward a practical sense of naturally-growing-together with *logos* and holding one's desires in relation to it as a *hexis*, remember Book VI's argument that the young do not trust in the experience (*empeiria*) of natural first-principles, yet become wise in mathematics because they trust its first-principles through abstraction (*aphairesis*). Aristotle introduces this problem by raising a need to consider if there is well-being for oneself without household management (*oikonomia*) or a regime (*politea*). In Book I—after acknowledging it would be vain to examine all the opinions about happiness instead of those that "seem to hold some *logos*"—Aristotle praises Plato for being well-unprovided over whether beginning with what is known or familiar in a *logos* concerning first-principles requires moving toward or away from them as a limit (*peras*). As Book VI shows, pleasures and pains ruin practical first-principles, not mathematical ones. Book III anticipates this argument with the account of how people wish for the apparent good instead of the good by nature because they choose (*haireō*) the pleasant as good and flee pain as bad.[17] As a *logos* attempting to provide philosophic experience in the limit of the good, Aristotle's *Ethics* can only produce practical benefits by helping readers trust their perception of the good while growing into a true sense of what is pleasant.

## PLEASURE AND THE GOOD THINGS
### (*ETHICS* 1147B20–31, 1148A4–32, 1148B15–24, 1149A34–1150A8, 1150B29–36, 1151A11–19)

Book VII's inquiry into pleasure begins with a distinction relevant to politics and economics. The things that produce pleasures are either the necessary things (*ta anankaia*) or the choiceworthy things (*ta haireta*), with the choiceworthy things holding either according to themselves, or excess. The necessary things that produce pleasure are the bodily things such as food and sexual need (*chreia*), and the choiceworthy things that produce pleasure are victory, honor, wealth, and the other good and pleasant things (1147b20–31). A curious feature of this distinction between the things that produce pleasure is how Aristotle refrains (at least initially) from saying the necessary things hold excess like the choiceworthy things, for is it not possible for someone to go to excess in food and sex? This is especially odd given the observation in Book I of the *Politics* that without the prudence and virtue that naturally falls to them, human beings are most unholy and most savage when it comes to food and sex. The remedy to this problem seems to be justice and political community,[18] yet these do not enter the picture in the *Ethics'* account of pleasure. What accounts for this absence? And why would these things not be necessary for addressing the choiceworthy pleasures of victory, honor, and wealth?

With sexual need and food as necessary things that produce pleasure, Aristotle recalls two natural arguments from Book I of the *Politics*. First, one of the two necessary couplings needed to form the household is male and female for the sake of generation. Aristotle presents this coupling not from choice (*proairesis*), but "the natural aiming or desiring" (*to phusikon ephiesthai*) of all living things. Second, in the account of natural acquisition, Aristotle compares how the pleasant indicates the ways nature marks-the-boundaries of animals' lives toward the choosing of food with human beings' pleasant mixing of lives holding their work toward what is natural in pursuit of the self-sufficient as need necessitates. In what is necessary for community and acquisition, pleasure is naturally more fundamental to each than justice. As for the choiceworthy things that produce pleasure, remember that Book I of the *Ethics* initially subordinates the arts of generalship and household management and their respective ends (victory and wealth) to the political art with the human good as its end.[19] With Book VII's focus on the choiceworthy things, the good and pleasant things now display themselves as more foundational than the political art and justice.

Two quick adjustments following Aristotle's distinctions between the things that produce pleasure tie together the moral questions facing these things in the *Politics'* inquiry into the money-making art and the *Ethics'* opening inquiry into happiness. Starting with the bodily things, the person who pursues their enjoyments and an excess of their pleasures and flees the pains concerning taste and touch contrary to choice and thought (*dianoia*) is someone without self-restraint (1148a4–10). In acting contrary to choice and thought, one acts contrary to human nature understood as a first-principle (*archē*) consisting of intellect and desire, for one lives solely as a body. In Book I of the *Politics*, the soul and thought should rule the body as a master, the intellect should rule desire (*orexis*) with political or kingly rule, and both the intellect and the part holding *logos* should rule the passionate part, for this is advantageous for the whole of human nature. Together, these arguments shed new light on the problem of the person who supposes living well entails turning all things into money-making to seek what produces an excess of bodily enjoyments.[20] With the help of the *Ethics*, the money-making art's turn toward gain begins with a misunderstanding about the nature of necessary pleasures.²¹ If one could bring the necessary pleasures under the authority of choice—the authority of intellect and desire—one could avoid the excesses of these pleasures.

With the choiceworthy pleasures, Aristotle hints at how *logos* can correct the problem with choosing an excess of pleasure. Some desires (*epithumia*) and pleasures are among the noble and serious things—"for some of the pleasures [are] by nature choiceworthy"—some are contrary to these, and others are between these, namely, useful things (*chrēmata*), gain, victory, and honor. In all these desires and pleasures, "there is no blame for being affected (*paschō*) by, desiring (*epithumeō*), and loving (*phileō*) them," but for going to excess and being more serious about these good and serious things than there is need to be, which is contrary to *logos* (1148a22–32). This last argument recalls the first moral error that causes people to exchange the art of house-hold management's work for the art of retail-trade's gain of legal-currency without-limit: a desire without-limit that is serious about living but not living well.²² What is unclear in the *Politics'* inquiry into the money-making art that is evident in the *Ethics'* inquiry into pleasure is that *logos* is necessary to ensure the pursuit of the choiceworthy pleasures is good. The inclusion of both the useful things and gain (two things that are part of economic life) among the choiceworthy desires and pleasures that are neither noble and seri-ous nor their contraries raises the question about what types of things these are, though they do seem to fall among the good and pleasant things. If the good and pleasant things are choiceworthy (as is evident in the lack of blame for being affected by, desiring, and loving them), readers should wonder which of these dispositions is most likely to be amenable to acting according to *logos*. Back in Book I, when Aristotle's inquiry into happiness turns to the good things and introduces the distinction between activity and *hexis*, taking pleasure belongs to the things in the soul, and what is pleasant for each person are such things for which one holds the love (*phileō*) belonging to friendship (*philia*).²³ Aristotle thus continues to build the argument that friendship is necessary for bringing the good and the pleasant things in accord with nature through *logos*.

How neither *hexis* nor desire are sufficient for bringing the good and pleas-ant things in accord with nature through *logos* appears in two brief arguments Aristotle makes on his way to revealing vice is a problem that begins in the intellect. Shifting away from necessary and choiceworthy pleasures, Aristotle states there are some things pleasant by nature either simply, or according to the classes of animals and human beings. Other things are not pleasant by nature, but become pleasant either through mutilations, habits, or wretched natures that one can see through the *hexeis* resembling them (such as the beastly *hexis* of cannibalism) (1148b15–24). Aristotle's account of natural acquisition in Book I of the *Politics* suggests the acquisition of food is simply pleasant by nature to both animals and human beings. Human acquisition is distinct from animals' not only because they can mix lives that hold their work toward what is natural, but because they can provide food through exchange and retail-trade. These two forms of acquisition that are not directly bound to pleasure like the acquisitive lives show where art can affect human *hexeis*, for acquisition admits of being either according to nature or contrary to nature in the same way as human *hexeis* admit of being virtuous or beastly. This is possible because with desire, "if *logos* or sense-perception says that [it is] pleasant, it impels (*hormaō*) towards the enjoyment" (1149a34–b1). The pleasant affects both *logos* and sense-perception of desire, things all bound together in choice and human nature. In Book I of the *Politics*, the coworking of *logos* and sense-perception in community appears with the statement that the person who first set-standing-together community is "a cause of the greatest goods" by helping complete the natural impulse (*hormē*) toward community with law and the just. The consequence for acquisition of leaving such an impulse without *logos* and community appears early in the account of natural acquisition with the specious argument that "war is by nature an art of acquisition in a way . . . [when used] towards both beasts and human being who are naturally such to be ruled but not willing." Despite its claim to being just, this view of acquisition detached from *logos* and community is beastly because it is like the human being who lacks the capacity to form-community.[24] To live a human life, the natural impulses, desires, and pleasures at the foundation of politics and economics need to hold a trustworthy sense of the pleasant that only Aristotle's *logos* of the good can provide.

Despite acknowledging there is something fearful to human beings with beastly *hexeis*, these are not as bad as vice. Following a distinction between human, natural, and beastly desires and pleasures, Aristotle reiterates that moderation and licentiousness concern only the human and the natural, for animals do not hold choice or reasoning. Although both human beings and animals can be "set-standing-out (*existēmi*) from nature," vice in human beings ruins the better thing within in them because it holds a beginning or first-principle in the intellect. In this respect, vice and what is bad in a human being is ensouled while what is bad within beasts is without-soul (1149b27–1150a8). The intellect's work with natural desires and pleasures through choice and reasoning is the beginning of virtue and vice. Aristotle reveals the full implications of the soul holding vice shortly after this passage, describing the vicious person (as opposed to the person without self-restraint) as one who "abides in choice" and whose "wickedness" (*ponēria*) is holding-together (*sunechēs*) while going unnoticed. With this discovery about vice, Aristotle acknowledges the way "we have been unprovided" (presumably by focusing on being without self-restraint) does not hold (1150b29–36). Though Book VII begins with character and attempts to hold back the nature of intellect and choice, these arguments about vice's intellectual beginnings in relation to natural desires and pleasures suggest Aristotle now aims to provide a more complete view of how the natural *hexeis* and virtues become authoritative virtue under intellect and the authoritative good, something to which he alludes at the end of Book VI.[25]

With the discovery of vice's intellectual origin, Aristotle returns to human beings' need to trust in first-principles. The person without self-restraint pursues an excess of bodily pleasures contrary to correct *logos* without having been persuaded or trusting (*peithō*) to do this, so one could persuade such a person to trust correct *logos*. But this does not occur with the licentious person, for while virtue preserves the first-principle, wretchedness ruins it. In actions, the first-principles (i.e., that for the sake of which) are akin to mathematical hypotheses that *logos* does not teach; rather, such teaching falls to "either natural or habitual virtue to have correct opinion (*orthodoxeō*) concerning the first-principle" (1151a11–19). A similar argument appears in Book VI when Aristotle argues that pleasures, pains, and vice ruin practical first-principles, not mathematical ones.[26] A curious inversion happens in these two arguments: Book VI omits speaking of virtue's ability to preserve first-principles while describing the ruinous work of vice, yet Book VII speaks of virtue preserving first-principles while omitting "vice" as what ruins first-principles. Book VII's appeal to virtue would be more at home in Book VI's account prudence, just as Book VI's appeal to pleasures and pains would be more appropriate in Book VII. The constants in these two arguments are not virtue and vice, but first-principles, pleasures, and pains. Although virtue and vice are prominent themes in the *Ethics*, these rest upon the natural foundations of first-principles, pleasures, and pains. But while the experience of pleasures and pains is self-evident, it seems that of practical first-principles is not, for how do people experience what *logos* does not teach?

To understand the forthcoming turn to the political philosopher in Book VII, a look back to Book I clarifies how Aristotle's mysterious teaching that there is no *logos* of first-principles is vital to his understanding of politics and economics. Cautioning against demands for the same degree of precision in all *logoi*, Aristotle discusses how the noble things and the just things that concern the political art "hold much difference and wandering, so they seem to be by law only, not by nature." The good things also hold some wandering (but no differences) on account of the harm that comes to some people through them (as is evident from people who, like King Midas in the *Politics*, destroy themselves through wealth). Shortly after this observation, Aristotle praises Plato for being well-unprovided over whether *logos* should proceed toward or away from the limit (*peras*) of first-principles. Later in Book I, these statements about precision in *logos* and first-principles merge when the search for "the proper virtue" (*tēn oikeian aretēn*) for happiness precedes Aristotle's advice to seek the precision proper to his inquiry and to attempt (*peirateon*) to go after first-principles as is natural to them. Though readers have a choice of how they want to be coworkers with Aristotle's *logos* by seeking "the correct thing" (a literal reading of *hē orthē*, "the right angle") either as carpenters looking for what is useful or geometers looking to contemplate the truth, from the philosophic perspective, there is no need to divide what is useful from contemplating the truth.[27] In Book VII, it becomes clear that the reason why the good things by nature become destructive and hold some wandering is people choosing to seek an excess of the pleasure these things produce. If these good things are destructive in one's own life, they are also destructive in political and economic life. To state this in *logos* is insufficient, for in all practical pursuits, their truest limit abides in choosing the good. This choice requires experience, one Aristotle's *logos* attempts to provide by helping readers trust their own contemplation can hold an abiding sense of the good.

## THE POLITICAL PHILOSOPHER'S CONTEMPLATION OF PLEASURES AND PAINS (*ETHICS* 1152B1–1153B25)

Book VII's introduction of the political philosopher as one who contemplates pleasures and pains as the architect of the end toward which people speak of things as simply bad or good affirms the inseparability of the practical and the theoretical in Aristotle's *Ethics*. Although Aristotle states in the beginning of Book II that his inquiry into virtue is not for the sake of contemplation but becoming good, he introduces correct *logos* only to leave its nature open, and encourages readers to attempt (*peirateon*) to help the imprecise practical *logos*. In the next chapter, Aristotle describes how people become good or bad depending on how virtue and the political art use pleasures and pains. What it means to use pleasures and pains looks different in Book VII than it does in Book II in light of the description of a person holding science as a *hexis* as one who uses the science by contemplating it through a trust formed by naturally-growing-together with the *logos* over time.[28] If contemplation is use, the political philosopher's contemplation of pleasures and pains suggests what is useful and true form a whole.

The acquisition of this holistic view of human life is of great significance for Aristotle's economic teaching given how the *Politics* shows the money-making art—the art of useful things—can become unnatural and unnecessary through the use of legal-currency in the art of retail-trade. This form of the money-making art makes it possible to abandon the acquisition of "true wealth" ("a store of such useful things that are necessary towards living, and useful to community in a city or a household"), the self-sufficiency of which is not without-limit toward good living. Although Book I of the *Ethics* leads readers to think the political philosopher is the architect of happiness, recall that the recognition of happiness as a "complete and self-sufficient . . . end of the practical things" that holds-over all the other good things gives way to examining the human work that requires holding *logos*, which *seems* to belong more authoritatively to an activity of the soul.[29] The opening this passage provides for *hexis* and *logos* informs Book VII's inquiry into pleasure that subordinates happiness to the political philosopher's search for clarity on the status of the good and pleasant as ends.

Following the political philosopher's introduction, Aristotle presents three views of pleasure and the good that set the stage for the remainder of Book VII. For some, no pleasure seems good, for the good and pleasure are not the same. For others, some pleasures seem good, but most are base. And finally, even if all pleasures are good, they do not admit to be the best thing (1152b1–12). Despite the choiceworthy things that produce pleasure appearing among the good and pleasant things earlier in Book VII, these three views all seek some separation between pleasure and the good. To challenge the views that pleasure is neither good nor the best thing, Aristotle says the good is twofold: on the one hand there is the good simply, and on the other hand the good for some person. From this it follows that natures and *hexeis* are good in these two senses (1152b25–28). A sense of how this argument keeps the good and the pleasant together comes through the example of wealth: it is good simply, though it is possible that someone (like King Midas) could destroy oneself in the pursuit of wealth. As for Aristotle's pairing of natures and *hexeis*, he notes the good is on the one hand an activity, and on the other hand a *hexis*, and whatever settles a natural *hexis* pleases incidentally (like medicine and health). In contrast to this incidental pleasure, "there is the activity in the desires of the remainder of *hexeis* and natures since there are pleasures without pains and desires, such as the contemplative activity belonging to the nature not being in-need" (1152b28–1153a2). Contemplation now emerges as an activity that persists in human nature even when other *hexeis* are unsettled or in-need, though it is fair to wonder to what nature and *hexis* the contemplative activity belong, and further, if this nature can truly never be in-need.

As Aristotle's inquiry into pleasure develops, the connections between pleasure, *hexis*, and activity grow. Pleasures are "activities and an end" that belong to using things, "and not all [pleasures are] an end of some other thing, but of the things leading into the completion (*teleiōsis*) of their nature." On account of this, pleasure is "an activity of the *hexis* according to nature" (1153a7–14). The description of pleasure as an end and an activity bound to "the *hexis* according to nature" refines several arguments from Book I of the *Ethics*. Despite initially positing a difference among ends (i.e., works and activities), the subsequent discovery of the human work as an activity of the soul reveals ends must hold some other form. What precipitates the discovery of the human work is the stipulation that the inquiry seeks the practical and acquirable good for a human being. The sought-for good then becomes the end for every action and choice, and through this, self-sufficiency defines the complete good as that which produces a choiceworthy life in need of nothing. The major question within the examination of happiness as the human work is whether "the best thing [is] in acquisition or use, and in a *hexis* or an activity." With this question, Aristotle finds life "holds pleasure in itself" through the love (*phileō*) people hold in the soul towards external goods.[30] If pleasure is "an activity of the *hexis* according to nature," then the use and acquisition of the good as an end must naturally hold in this way, though how this is true requires understanding the nature of friendship.

With the idea of the sought-for good, readers receive a glimpse of the political and economic significance of these arguments about pleasure, *hexis*, and activity. Between the arguments above from Book VII about the contemplative activity and pleasure, Aristotle distinguishes what is pleasant simply and by nature from the delight and pleasure that accompany the "restoring (*anaplēroō*) and set-standing-accordingly (*kathistēmi*) of nature" (1153a2–7). Before Book I's inquiry into the lives holding-before others in their claim to happiness, Aristotle describes how many (as opposed to the wise) claim happiness is pleasure, wealth, or honor. Along similar lines, he notes how those who are sick claim happiness is health, while those who are poor say it is wealth. Both pleasure and wealth have restorative senses, and wealth's briefly appears in Book I of the *Politics* when Aristotle concludes the natural art of exchange (*hē metablētikē*) between households is not a form of the money-making art, but a restoration (*anaplērōsis*) of the self-sufficiency according to nature. Though there are times when such restorations are necessary, they are not always choiceworthy. This insight seems to guide Book I of the *Ethics'* inquiry into happy lives. To choose (*proaireō*) the life of pleasure associated only with the bodily acquisition of food is beastly and servile. The political life's pursuit of honor as the "sought-for thing" is insufficient because "we divine ourselves the good to be something properly-one's-own (*oikeion*) and hard-to-take-away (*dusaphaireton*)." And as for the money-making life, wealth is not the sought-for good because it is useful for something else. Only the contemplative life remains untouched, though its natural end and pleasure go unexamined in Book I. Although Book I of the *Politics* attempts to present self-sufficiency as the end and nature of the city that ruins the human work if this community ever abolishes (*anaireō*) itself,[31] Book VII of the *Ethics* teaches that the completion of human nature belongs not to politics and economics, but choosing the natural pleasure of the contemplative life.

Pleasure's need for the good as an end comes forth in Book VII with an argument comparing health and money-making. After noting a mistake some make about pleasure, activity, and the authoritative good, Aristotle criticizes those who claim pleasant things are base because they lead to sickness. Such a claim is the same as stating healthy things are base toward money-making. The error here is supposing the pleasant and healthy things are base according to themselves when they are only base in their direction, something apparent in the possibility that even contemplating can harm health (1153a14–20). According to these arguments, the pleasant things, healthy things, and contemplation all need a proper context. The statement about the healthy things and money-making is of special interest since the first half of the *Politics'* inquiry into the money-making art closes with Aristotle describing how people use the medical art for the end of money-making because they seek living well through excessive bodily enjoyments.[32] Whether it is the pleasant things, the healthy things, money-making, or contemplation, they all need the authoritative direction that only the good can provide.

To clarify the preceding argument about pleasure, Aristotle returns to the idea of a *hexis*, saying pleasure does not impede prudence or any *hexis*, but only pleasures belonging to another *hexis*, for the pleasures from contemplating and learning produce more contemplating or learning. Since pleasures are bound to *hexeis*, it is with good-*logos* that pleasures and activities are not the works of arts. At best, arts are only of capacities, though it seems the arts of aromas and cookery are arts of pleasure (1153a20–27). The natural capacities to which the arts of aromas and cookery relate are the sense-perceptions of touch and taste, both of which hold pleasure in themselves. If these arts produce any pleasure, it is through someone acquiring and using the perfumes and foods produced by them. It is no different with the money-making art and legal-currency, though its most damaging effects are on contemplation. This teaching on pleasure, however, provides a remedy. Because the pleasure of contemplating produces only more contemplation, the contemplative activity and the *hexis* of contemplating are naturally self-sufficient, producing nothing outside of themselves. With contemplation, Aristotle offers a clearer sense of something to which he alludes in Book I, namely, how happiness belongs to a life that "in no way needs the addition of pleasure as some appendage, but holds pleasure in itself." But insofar as such a life is human, it still needs the addition of external goods (which include friends, wealth, and political capacity).[33] Because this last argument arises through an implicit tension between *erōs* and friendship regarding the pleasant, it is evident that understanding the subordination of political and economic self-sufficiency to contemplative self-sufficiency requires knowing the nature of friendship.

Aristotle's gradual refinement of pleasure's natural context as an activity of a *hexis* according to nature further immerses readers in the political philosopher's contemplation of pleasures and pains for the sake of determining the end toward which things are simply bad or good. Describing the prudent person as someone pursuing a life without pain, Aristotle distinguishes the simply good pleasures from the bodily ones characterized by desire (*epithu-mia*), pain, and excess. Next, recognizing there is agreement (*homologeō*) that pain is bad, Aristotle refines this argument, separating pain that is simply bad from pain that is an impediment. The question then becomes how pleasure is something good and possibly the best thing, even if some pleasures (like some sciences) are base. In this context, Aristotle proposes pleasure could be the best thing and most choiceworthy if it is the unimpeded activity of the best and most choiceworthy *hexis*: happiness. Yet while the happy life is with good-*logos* pleasant and complete, happiness still seems to need the addition of bodily goods, external goods, and chance. With respect to chance, Aristotle notes even good-fortune is an impediment, and perhaps it is not just to call it this, "for the boundary of [good-fortune] is towards happiness" (1153a27–b25). What emerges from this line of argument is the overarching question about the nature of the simply good pleasures that differ from bodily pleasures admitting of desire, pain, and excess. Understanding the nature of this pleasure is essential since it could provide an anchor to the pleasures of acquisition that can become base and produce similarly base economic sciences. After all, Aristotle does not dispense with the need for bodily and external goods that the economic sciences provide. Like Book I of the *Ethics*, his only hesitation concerns chance, which he resolves by establishing external and bodily goods are coworkers with the good of the soul that is happiness. Through being without-provision about chance in that inquiry, Aristotle recognizes the soul's activities are authoritative over well-being, for they are more lasting and holding-together (*sunechō*) than the sciences.[34] At this point in Book VII, however, Aristotle is silent about the soul's goods, and although he speaks of happiness as a boundary in life, its claim rests on one's own natural sense of choosing the best thing.

## *LOGOS*, PLEASURE, AND HUMAN NATURE (*ETHICS* 1153B25–1154B34)

Whether happiness can be the boundary and end for the best life now depends on what type of pleasure it is. Seeing that neither the same nature nor the same *hexis* is the best or seems to be the best, Aristotle observes that all things do not pursue the same pleasure, though all things do pursue pleasure (1153b25–31). This argument partially hearkens back to the first sentence of the *Ethics* and the idea that the good is that at which all things aim themselves, with the crucial difference that Book VII's argument about pleasure does not speak of "aiming." This omission may not be accidental, for "choice" is also absent from the present argument, yet Book I begins with choice seeming to aim itself at some good as well.[35]

Next, Aristotle wonders if it is possible that all things do not pursue the pleasure they suppose or assert they pursue, but the same pleasure, "for all things by nature hold (*echō*) something divine." The bodily pleasures, however, have taken hold of the "inheritance" (*klēronomia*) of the name of "pleasure" because people often turn toward these and all things hold-a-share (*metechō*) of them, and so people suppose these are the only pleasures because they are known or familiar (*gnōrimos*) (1153b31–1154a1). Two subtle arguments are at work here that point back to the political philosopher's concern with ends. First, there is a tension between all things holding something divine by nature and the bodily pleasures inheriting the name of "pleasure." The term for "inheritance" (*klēronomia*) implies that the law or convention (*nomos*) of pleasure is at odds with its nature. This is not to say the bodily pleasures are unnatural, but that there is ignorance of pleasure's full nature. Second, in saying that the reason why the *nomos* of pleasure does not provide a full account of its nature is the bodily pleasures being known or familiar to people, Aristotle recalls the well-unprovided question in Book I about how to approach first-principles in *logos*, settling on approaching them from "the things known or familiar to ourselves."[36] If many people know or are familiar with the bodily pleasures, Aristotle's own *logos* may use these to move toward the first-principle and end of which the political philosopher is the architect.

The problem the bodily pleasures pose for a full understanding of pleasure's nature prompts a question about the choice between what is good and bad. Acknowledging that it would be strange for the happy person not to live pleasantly, Aristotle proposes examining the bodily pleasures from the perspective of those who say noble pleasures are "intensely (*sphodra*)[37] choiceworthy," but the bodily pleasures are not. One challenge that emerges from this perspective is the way that some *hexeis* admit of an excess of the bodily goods and, through this, pleasure. While the person pursuing an excess of bodily goods is base, the baseness is not on account of pursuing necessary pleasures since all delight in cooked foods, wine, and sex, but pursuing these pleasures contrary to how one needs to pursue them. With pain, however, people not only flee excess, but the whole of it (1154a1–21). Despite Book VII's earlier distinction between necessary and choiceworthy pleasures, this argument suggests those who pursue the noble pleasures may be wrong to think the necessary pleasures are not also choiceworthy. As bodily goods, the necessary pleasures are firmly among the good things. This makes Aristotle's turn toward pain important, for the question is why pains contrary to the bodily pleasures are wretched and therefore bad (for pain is the contrary of pleasure, and since bad is contrary to good, pain is bad) (1154a10–11). What is at stake is pain's status as a bad thing, something necessary for the political philosopher to contemplate since his end is the standard for determining what is simply bad and simply good.

Before further examining the relationship between pleasure and pain, good and bad, Aristotle considers what produces trust (*pistis*) in *logos*, saying:

> Now there is need not only to say the truth but the cause of the false too (for this contributes towards the trust), for whenever a good-*logos* displays something displaying itself as the truth that is not true, it produces more to trust in the truth; consequently, one must say through what the bodily pleasures display themselves as more choiceworthy. (1154a22–26)

The need for trust in the truth of good-*logos* about choiceworthy (*hairetos*) pleasures recalls Book VI and the young's need for wisdom and trust in the experience of natural first-principles that differs from their trust in mathematical abstraction (*aphairesis*).[38] By declaring how his own *logos* can help readers trust in the truth about the nature of pleasure and why it is good, Aristotle signals how his work of political philosophy aims to provide them with the contemplative experience they need for trusting in the natural first-principles necessary for their own good.

The first reason why bodily pleasures display themselves as more choiceworthy is because they expel pain. Some pleasures do not seem serious either because they are of a base nature (either from birth in beasts, or habit in base human beings), or because they are cures for a deficient nature completing (*teleioō*) itself. Another reason why the bodily pleasures seem choiceworthy is because they are intense to those without the capacity to delight in other pleasures. The nature of the many, for example, holds delight solely in these pleasures, which is harmful. Those who study nature witness in animals who always labor how seeing and hearing are painful, though eventually they are "habituated-together" (*sunēthēs*)[39] with these things. This is like how the young dispose-through (*diakeimai*) themselves as they increase. For some, things are pleasant because they are like drunks. For others, their nature is melancholic and always needs a cure, and they become licentious and base because they oppose a contrary or chance pleasure to an intense desire (*orexis*) (1154a26–b15). According to this argument, the bodily pleasures appear more choiceworthy through nature and habit's disposing of pleasures, pains, and desires. An important clue for what Aristotle omits from this account comes in the form of those who study nature (*phusiologōn*), who appear earlier in Book VII to explain how people fail to hold science as a *hexis*. Rather than naturally-growing-together (*sumphuō*) with *logos*, it is not active because the sense-perception and desire for the pleasant is more authoritative than the *logos* that turns one away from the pleasure. Nature and habit's need to come under the authority of *logos* appears in Book VII of the *Politics* with the argument that all things' well-being requires the correct posing (*keimai*) of actions' target and end. For cities to be serious, each citizen needs to be serious through

science and choice. Aristotle then states human beings become good and serious through nature, habit, and *logos*, with *logos* being the most important since
people can act contrary to their habits if *logos* persuades them to hold better
otherwise.[40] In light of this argument, the search for serious pleasures in Book
VII of the *Ethics* demands engaging choice through *logos*. But as the *Politics*
suggests, what makes each citizen serious from the city's perspective may
diverge from what naturally makes human beings good.

Because Book VI of the *Ethics* defines human nature through choice
as either desiring intellect (*orektikos nous*) or thinking desire (*orexis
dianoiētikē*), the implicit failure in Book VII to dispose-through desire, pleasures, and pains with *logos* of the good indicates that provision for the intellect
is necessary for completing human nature. Instead of the tendency to set aside
*logos* and oppose an intense desire with bodily pleasure, Aristotle turns to the
pleasures without pains. Not only are these pleasures without excess, but they
are pleasant by nature because they produce actions that are by nature. Such
pleasures differ from the cures that are pleasant incidentally (1154b15–20).
By implying bodily pleasures admit of excess, Aristotle refines a prior argument that suggests only choiceworthy things (like victory, honor, and wealth)
hold excess, not the necessary things.[41] The return of pleasures without pains
recalls the definition of pleasure as "an activity of the *hexis* according to
nature" that leads into the completion of something's nature. On the way to
this definition, Aristotle distinguishes what is good simply from what is good
for some person. Whereas activities are simply good, whatever is pleasant by
settling a natural *hexis* (like medicine is for health) is not simply good, but
good for the sick person. The one example Aristotle provides for a simply
good activity is the contemplative one belonging to the nature that is not in-
need.[42] The present discernment of what is pleasant by nature reflects a sense
of what is simply good, one that resides not in a distinction between what is
necessary and choiceworthy, but what completes one's nature.

As soon as Aristotle opens the door for pleasures by nature that are simply
good, he acknowledges a difficulty that confirms Books VI and VII of the
*Ethics* are incomplete but complementary accounts of human nature, saying,
"The same thing [is] not pleasant through the nature of ourselves not being
simple . . . and so subject to ruin (*phthartos*)."[43] The terms of this argument
are vague, establishing only that whenever one of these things in human
beings' non-simple nature acts, it is contrary to the other thing by nature. And
whenever one "makes equal" (*isazō*) these natures, the acting seems neither
painful nor pleasant, while "if the nature of one were simple, the same action
will always be most pleasant" (1154b20–25). The political and economic
significance of this obscure account of human nature is not readily apparent
without remembering Aristotle's etymology of "moderation" as "preserves
prudence" in Book VI, for it preserves practical first-principles from ruin

through pleasures, pains, and vice. Preceding this argument is the observation that people suppose household managers and politicians are prudent; after this argument is the statement that there is no virtue for prudence like there is for art because it is more choiceworthy to err voluntarily in art. With this last observation, Aristotle concludes prudence is "not only a *hexis* with *logos*." If politics and economics derive from prudence, because prudence is not strictly rational, neither politics nor economics can be strictly rational. In Book VII, the first-principle in human nature that vice ruins is the intellect, for human beings are set-standing-out (*existēmi*) from nature through vice (which is itself ensouled).[44] By seeing how ruin begins within the soul, one cannot conclude that human nature is not simple in the sense that there is a divide between the body and the soul, and that politics and economics must divide their provision for these needs accordingly. To be simply good for human beings, politics and economics must see the whole of what preserves human nature.

Aristotle's final argument about pleasure in Book VII provides an example of a simple nature that initially seems to be an impractical conclusion, but is in truth a starting point for the complete view of human nature that begins to emerge in Books VIII through X of the *Ethics*. Unlike human beings, "the god always delights in a single and simple pleasure, for not only is there an activity of motion (*kinēsis*) but of absence of motion (*akinēsia*), and pleasure is more in rest than in motion."[45] Opposed to this godly view of pleasure is an unnamed poet who says, "Change (*metabolē*) of all things is sweet,"[46] a statement Aristotle attributes to "some wickedness, for just as a change-able human being [is] a wicked person, so too [is] the nature itself needing change, for [it is] neither simple nor decent (*epieikēs*)" (1154b26–31). A helpful context for this argument opposing the god's activity of pleasure that is without motion to a nature needing change is Book VII's earlier account of the vicious person as someone who "abides in choice" and whose wicked-ness goes unnoticed while holding-together (*sunechēs*). Through this insight just beyond the midpoint in Book VII, Aristotle acknowledges that the way the inquiry into natural desires and pleasures had been unprovided does not hold.[47] The paradox of a changeable nature is its activity holds-together in motion (presumably from one pleasure to the next), whereas human nature would be best when its activity holds-together without motion from one pleasure to another. Yet to teach human beings to become more like the God whose nature is not akin to their own would seem to be a poor way to pro-vide what their nature needs, in part because they can choose to be wicked while the God cannot. At the same time, human beings can also choose to be decent, and it is through this choice that they can discover how to provide fully for their nature.

Rather than being a mere musing about the divine, Aristotle's description of the God's nature as "decent" holds great weight for understanding his political and economic teaching. As the inquiry into justice nears its end in Book V of the *Ethics*, the decent and "decency" (*epieikeia*) are at the heart of a question without-provision (*aporia*) regarding the seriousness of justice, for the decent is better and stronger than the just. Similarly, in the later chapters of Book IX's inquiry into friends, the decent person emerges amid being unprovided (*aporeō*) regarding the need to love (*phileō*) oneself. Through a contrast with the serious person, the decent person becomes a model for choosing to what is best for the intellect in friendship, thus providing a natural view of what is good and pleasant in life by forming-community in *logos* and thought within a bounded sense of the good.[48] Since politics and economics are naturally bound to community, the superiority of decency to justice and its personal sense of community within friendship suggest the decent holds a more natural view of ruling and acquisition than the just. A hint of this appears in Book VII of the *Ethics* with the way Aristotle opposes the decent nature to the wicked person (*ponēros*), whose very name derives from the verb for "labor" (*poneō*). In Book I of the *Politics*, what is ruled and by nature slave is "that which itself has the capacity with its body [to labor (*ponein*) *or* to produce (*poiein*)]" whatever that which is ruler and mastering by nature foresees with thought.[49] Much like Book I of the *Politics* works to show there is a freer way to live toward ruling and acquisition in community than mastery and slavery, the opposition between the wicked and the decent suggests human beings can choose to live a good, pleasant, and less laborious life by coming to know the true nature of friendship.

## CONCLUSION: POLITICAL PHILOSOPHY, PLEASURE, AND FRIENDSHIP'S NATURAL VIEW OF ECONOMICS

How friendship stands ready to provide philosophy's authoritative perspective on the good as the natural boundary for politics and economics is evident in how Book VII's laborious nature in need of change (*metabolē*) finds its counterpart in the natural art of exchange (*hē metablētikē*) from the *Politics*. This art of exchange appears after Aristotle defines the improper use (*ouk oikeia*) of a piece of acquisition as its exchange for something else (such as exchanging a shoe rather than wearing it). With a piece of acquisition's improper use set down as its exchange, Aristotle introduces the art of exchange as beginning according to nature from human beings holding more or less than what is adequate and producing their exchanges as necessary. This art of exchange has no work in the household, but occurs among many households so they can make a mutual-giving according to their needs.[50] As its name indicates, the natural art of exchange needs to change all things into exchangeable items. Though this change is naturally necessary, if it is possible to produce all things into exchangeable things, they are no longer "simple" in their use. This is the foundation of the tension in the money-making art between what is natural and unnatural: the need to exchange things is simple and according to nature, but in using all things as means of exchange to remedy nature's unequal distribution of them, it is possible to depart from their proper use.

How the "change" in "exchange" departs from nature is further evident in the origins of the money-making art and legal-currency. Against those who set-down (*tithēmi*) wealth as a quantity of legal-currency, Aristotle notes that legal-currency seems to be altogether law and not at all by nature through the change-in-the-setting-down (*metatithēmi*) of legal-currency's worth making it possible for someone well-provided (*euporeō*) in this form of wealth to go unprovided (*aporeō*) in necessary food. Despite legal-currency seeming to be unnatural, its provision (like the money-making art) was according to *logos* and out of necessity when people set-down-together an agreement (*suntithēmi*) to give and take legal-currency in exchanges (*allagē*) because it is not easy to carry all the things that are necessary according to nature.[51] By this account, the money-making art is natural and necessary, but whether its use of legal-currency is according to nature depends on the *logos* providing this art.

With the help of Book VII of the *Ethics*, it is now possible to see that the true cause for the money-making art's turn away from nature is an errant choice of pleasure as the good. Part of the first unprovided question in the *Politics'* inquiry into the money-making art concerns whether this art is a subordinate that holds-forth (*parechō*) tools to the art of household management. In the second half of this inquiry (I.10), Aristotle returns to this unprovided question and concludes there is need for the money-making art to be present to both household managers and politicians to set-down-through (*diatithēmi*) what nature holds-forth as food and useful things (*chrēmata*). While the art of household management is necessary and praised, the art of retail-trade justly receives blame since its exchange (*metablētikē*) is not according nature. Along these lines, the art of usury receives hatred with good-*logos* since "it is the acquisition of legal-currency from itself and not from the [exchange (*metabolē*)] for which it was provided." The groundwork for this argument comes from the end of the first half of the inquiry into the money-making art (I.9), where the cause of confusion between the art of household management through which there is a necessary limit to wealth and the art of retail-trade that seeks the increase of legal-currency without-limit is these arts' exchange-upon (*epallassō*) the use (*chrēsis*) of legal-currency for different ends. This change within the arts does not occur apart from human beings setting-down-through (*diathesis*) themselves a view of living well that seeks what is productive of excess in bodily enjoyments using their own capacities for money-making as if this is the end of all things. In the last arguments from Book VII of the *Ethics*, Aristotle explores why an excess of bodily pleasures seems more choiceworthy and concludes that this mistake about what is best in life begins with an incomplete view of one's own nature.[52] Because Aristotle omits choice from the *Politics'* inquiry into the money-making art, readers need the *Ethics* to see that economic pursuits become unnatural through the failure to subordinate pleasure to the pursuit of the good.

The persistent ties between choice, pleasure, and the good throughout the *Ethics* that begin to come together with Aristotle's introduction of the political philosopher in Book VII suggest how the most natural perspective on economics and politics belongs to political philosophy. In Book I of the *Politics*, the attempt to contemplate political community by "look[ing] to the matters naturally-growing from the beginning (*archē*)" yields only three mentions of the "pleasant": first among the things of which human beings hold sense-perception and produce community through *logos*, then in the natural lives for both animals and human beings in the acquisition of food. In the cases of acquisition, Aristotle presents nature as marking-the-boundaries of animals' lives toward the choosing of food with the pleasant, yet never speaks directly of human choosing even though the pleasant bears upon how they mix lives to provide for the self-sufficient as need necessitates. Within this summary view of human acquisition are two statements that take on a different character given Book VII of the *Ethics'* insights into pleasure. First, of the five human lives holding their work toward what is natural, only the nomadic is "without labor and comes to be at leisure (*scholazō*)." Second, the work of exchange and retail-trade is set apart from the natural works, though such works require labor and are not at leisure.[53] As the *Ethics* shows, there is no choosing apart from the pleasant, and the pursuit of the self-sufficient is no exception. Whether the work is toward what is natural or exchange and retail-trade, human beings' pursuit of economic self-sufficiency requires choosing these works and confronting how pleasure affects these choices. For the economist whose sole concern is acquisition, one's perspective remains bound to the labor of acquisition with no sense of leisure. But for the political philosopher who uncovers the full natural scope of choice with pleasures, pains, and the good, one sees the need to subordinate all economic concerns to a way of life that is without labor and at leisure.

An outline of the political philosopher's contemplation of pleasures and pains as the architect of the end toward which all things are simply good or bad appears in Book VII's two mentions of "those who study nature" (*phusiologōn*), who by their very name provide a *logos* of nature (*phusis*). The first appeal to those who study nature comes before the political philosopher emerges. In this case, readers learn how the desire (*epithumia*) and sense-perception for something pleasant as "the last boundary" becomes more authoritative than the *logos* against that pleasant thing. The second appeal to those who study nature comes after Aristotle introduces the political philosopher. In this instance, the bodily pleasures appear more choiceworthy because the young who dispose-through themselves the perpetual seeking of the pleasant are akin to the animals that always labor for whom the sense-perceptions of seeing and hearing are painful until being habituated-together (*sunēthēs*) with these things. An important bit of context for this second argument comes in what immediately precedes the first appeal to those who study nature, where Aristotle teaches that the *logos* of a science does not become a *hexis* until one naturally-grows-together (*sumphuō*) with it.[54] Since Book I of the *Politics* suggests human beings hold sense-perception of the pleasant and the good through *logos*, whatever pain the young experience as they labor to naturally-grow-together with the *logos* of the good life does not negate the truth that it would be good for them to choose this.

In Book VII of the *Politics*, nature, habit, and *logos* appear along with change to show how political philosophy can provide for what is good in politics and economics. Between nature from which all human beings first need to naturally-grow and the *logos* that could persuade them to hold otherwise stand habits, and these produce either worse or better change (*metaballō*) in the body and soul. But for the naturally-growing things to be beneficial, the habits must symphonize with *logos*. Like exchange, the need for change within human nature is not necessarily contrary to nature or wicked (*ponēros*). But if one's aim is well-being, one needs some labor (*poneō*) in correctly posing (*keimai*) actions' end *and* discovering the actions bearing (*pherō*) toward that end so that one does not always need to change. The richness of Aristotle's philosophic perspective on the need to harmonize nature, habit, and *logos* for economic and political well-being appears faintly in Book I of the *Politics* when—to introduce the need to contemplate how household management and the money-making art hold toward each other—he observes that every city composes (*sunkeimai*) itself from households whose only natural parts by the end of Book I are free persons (i.e., parents and children). To refute the idea that nature produces slaves, Aristotle proposes that one needs to examine things that hold according to nature, not those that ruin themselves, and so one must contemplate the human being best disposed-through (*diakeimai*) in body and soul. Such a nature is one where intellect and the part holding *logos* rule desire (*orexis*) and passion with political or kingly rule.[55] The beginning of political and economic well-being is not acquisition and rule, but correctly posing the end for these activities. This work is impossible without providing for human choice, which cannot be free without intellect and desire naturally-growing-together toward the good.

From the preceding overview of pleasure's connection to central economic and political themes in Aristotle's *Ethics* and *Politics*, Book VII's concluding turn from pleasure toward friendship no longer looks like the non-sequitur it seems to be on first reading. Opposed to the young in Book VII who dispose-through themselves pleasure against an intense desire is the statement in Book I that the proper (*oikeios*) listener to the political art's *logoi* are those whose characters are such that they produce their passions and desires according to *logos*, for in this way, such *logoi* are beneficial. In Book VI—which concludes with the assertion that neither prudence nor the political art is authoritative over wisdom—after defining wisdom as "science and intellect of the most honorable things by nature," Aristotle states that philosophers like Anaxagoras and Thales are not said to be prudent because they are ignorant of the advantageous things for themselves and know useless things instead of the human goods. But after raising the question of how the young trust in the experience of natural first-principles (as opposed to those of mathematical abstractions that are "away from choosing," *aphairesis*), Aristotle observes that prudence poses itself against or with (*antikeimai*) intellect, which is itself sense-perception of boundaries and first-principles. As Book VI nears its end, the authoritative good and prudence require the intellect, for without this, natural virtue cannot become authoritative virtue.[56] The problem with Book VI is that it lacks the practical context in which readers can grasp how the intellect informs prudence, virtue, and their pursuit of the human good. And while Book VI alludes to the ruinous effects of pleasure on the soul and Book VII clarifies that pleasure ruins the intellect as well, taken together, these two inquiries fail to teach readers how to choose the good with a clear sense of what is truly pleasant.

Although Aristotle chastises Thales in the *Ethics* for knowing only useless things, he receives praise in the *Politics* for showing through his money-making that philosophy could be beneficial for those who wish to be wealthy. Nevertheless, though Thales occasions the only two mentions of "wisdom" in the *Politics*, these occur with Aristotle's insistence that Thales' money-making is something general and not wisdom, for philosophers are not serious about being wealthy. The question Aristotle's account of Thales raises concerns how philosophy is beneficial. A kinship between philosophy and economics is present in Book I of the *Ethics* with Aristotle likening *hexis* and activity in the human soul to acquisition and use, an analogy that gives way to using the love bound to friendship (*phileō*) to understand how the soul holds toward pleasure. Though Book VII explores how *hexis* and activity naturally hold pleasure, this inquiry prepares readers to examine the nature of friendship in Books VIII and IX. This inquiry begins by establishing three forms of friendship—the useful (*chrēsima*), the pleasant, and the good—with the useful quickly giving way to a choice between the pleasant and the good as ends.[57] Since the money-making art (*chrēmatistikē*) is by its name the "art of useful things (*chrēmata*)," for economics to be truly beneficial, it must learn how political philosophy provides a proper sense of how to choose the good according to nature through friendship.

*Chapter 6*

# Friendship and the Natural Foundations of Politics and Economics

If one tries to think of natural limits to political and economic life, it might seem fitting to adopt a large-scale perspective and focus on political communities and the exchanges that occur within and between them (i.e., the perspective of *Politics* I.1–3, 8–11). Yet from the beginning of the *Politics*, Aristotle does not conceal from readers that politics and economics share a common foundation in the pursuit of some good. Here readers face a choice: they can either confine their search for the political and economic good to the *Politics*, or consider how the pursuit of the good in that text relates to the *Ethics*. Given pleasure and choice are rare in Book I of the *Politics* yet vital to the *Ethics'* search for the good, the textual analysis from the preceding chapters should sufficiently demonstrate that the search for politics' and economics' natural limits within Aristotle's political philosophy must work with these two texts together. As a political philosopher, Aristotle's perspective is comprehensive, but not because of his work's scale. What makes Aristotle's political philosophy comprehensive is his recognition that the true natural limits of politics and economics are accessible to all human beings through understanding the goods they choose in life, and the nature of these choices is most evident not in contemplating community and exchange, but friendship.

Outside of Aristotle's political philosophy, the idea that friendship (*philia*) is necessary for discovering the natural limits of politics and economics seems strange.[1] But within the *Ethics*, Books VIII and IX approach the goods common to political and economic life from the perspective of the goods people choose to seek in friendship. Although the human good is implicit in Book VI's inquiry into prudence and Book VII's inquiry into pleasure, these inquiries hold a divided view of human nature. According to Book VI, a human being is—as a first-principle or beginning (*archē*)—synonymous with choice (*proairesis*), which is either desiring intellect (*orektikos nous*)

197

or thinking desire (*orexis dianoiētikē*). But human nature and choice do not move (*kineō*) themselves. Whether it is production or action, the motion (*kinēsis*) of desire and thought (*dianoia*) always needs *logos* for the sake of an end (*telos*).[2] Taking this argument as a guide, readers can see Book VI as focusing on the intellect while Book VII concentrates on desire, with neither inquiry providing a complete view of human nature. In Books VIII and IX, however, intellect and desire come together in friendship, the natural foundation of which is forming-community in *logos* and thought for the sake of some good.

From the beginning of Book VIII, Aristotle outlines human beings' need for friendship in the context of the good things, saying, "For [friendship] is either some virtue or with virtue, but still [it is] most necessary in life. For without friends no one would choose (*haireō*) to live, even when holding all the remaining good things" (1155a3–6). There is a subtle demotion of virtue at work in this passage, for it is friendship that is "most necessary in life," not virtue. Friendship's necessity through no one choosing to live without it *and* its placement among the good things recalls how Book VII begins with a distinction between necessary and choiceworthy pleasures that disappears as the inquiry shifts to searching for a trustworthy *logos* about what is simply good and pleasant for completing human nature. This search produces Book VII's juxtaposition between the god's simple and decent (*epieikēs*) pleasure in the activity of what is without motion (*akinēsia*) and human nature, which is not simple and subject to ruin when needing change (*metabolē*). With human nature vaguely left as non-simple, Aristotle concludes Book VII by declaring that since the inquiry states how pleasures and pains are among the good and bad things, it remains to speak about friendship. What enables the shift from the necessary and choiceworthy pleasures to what is simply good and pleasant is the introduction of the political philosopher who contemplates pleasures and pains as the architect of the end toward which people speak of things as simply good or bad.[3] Through friendship, the political philosopher can provide *logos* of the good that moves human beings' non-simple nature and choices toward the end that ensures all activities in life are without motion and do not need change.

Political philosophy's subordination of economics and politics to friendship and the good begins with Aristotle's observation that those who are wealthy and acquire (*ktaomai*) rule and "dynasty" (*dunasteia*) seem to need (*chreia*) friends since there may not be any benefit to such prosperity if one takes away (*aphaireō*) a good-work (*euergesia*). Conversely, Aristotle wonders if one could guard and preserve prosperity without friends, and further, if friends are the only thing to which one can flee in poverty and misfortune (1155a6–12). This initial case for why no one would choose to live without friends refines arguments about pleasure from Book VII and external goods from Book I in ways that show friendship approaches the good from a more fundamental angle than virtue and happiness. When Aristotle names wealth as a choiceworthy pleasure in Book VII, friendship is absent from that inquiry's account of the good and pleasant things.[4] In Book I, Aristotle presents a threefold distribution of goods (external, soul, and body). Though goods concerning the soul are most authoritative and happiness is such a good (for it seems to be virtue, prudence, or wisdom, and it is either with pleasure or not without pleasure), prosperity in external goods is something one could add to the good-*logos* defining happiness. These external goods are tools, friends, wealth, and political capacity.[5] Book VIII's introductory argument about the human need for friendship rests on assuming that the acquisition of wealth and political rule as external goods form the authoritative context for friendship. But what sort of good friendship is remains an open question. At the very least, readers know from Book VII that friendship is not pleasure, and that friendship has some capacity to provide for the beneficial acquisition, use, and preservation of wealth and political rule.

After mentioning friendship's contribution to "thinking" (*noēo*) and noble actions, the friendship that looks to be by nature for parents and offspring, and the sense when wandering in travel that every human being is properly-one's-own (*oikeion*) and a friend, Aristotle turns to justice (*dikaiosunē*), saying:

It looks like friendship holds-together (*sunechō*) cities, and legislators (*nomothetēs*) are more serious concerning this than justice: for like-mindedness (*homonoia*) looks to be something similar to friendship, and they aim themselves at this most of all and standing-faction (*stasis*)—being most hateful— they drive out. And while those who are friends do not need justice, those who are just themselves need the addition (*prosdeō*) of friendship, and of the just things the most [just] seems to be for a friend (*philikon*). (1155a12–28)

All these arguments suggest friendship naturally extends to many things. For politics and economics, what is interesting is how the sense of what is properly-one's-own in wandering immediately precedes observations about cities. In Book I of the *Politics*, the household (*oikia*) is the first community from which cities compose themselves, and it is through that inquiry's interest in household management (*oikonomia*) that Aristotle declares one must contemplate how the money-making art holds as some part of household management. The statements above from the *Ethics* allude to friendship being the common ground between what is properly-one's-own and cities. Legislators' apparent greater seriousness about friendship is evidence that those who by their name set-down (*tithēmi*) law (*nomos*) recognize justice does not hold-together cities, in part because it fails to eliminate standing-factions. Why this is true is not clear, though justice needing the addition of friendship holds a clue. Back in Book I, the love (*phileō*) bound to friendship reveals how the soul holds toward pleasure, and lovers of the noble (*philokaloi*) not needing the addition of pleasure contrasts with happiness needing the addition of external goods to do the noble things. Pleasure belongs more to friendship than to the good associated with it, for to love in life is pleasant according to itself, and one could hold this love toward many things (including the just, noble, or virtue).[6] If friendship provides for the beneficial acquisition, use, and preservation of wealth and political capacity, it is because friendship is more fit than politics and economics to aim pleasure toward what is proper and good in life.[7]

As Aristotle's introduction to friendship moves toward its conclusion, he continues drawing readers to questions about the good and pleasure from Book I with statements about the noble and *erōs*. To start, friendship is not only necessary but noble on account of the praise for "those who love-friends" (*philophiloi*), and to have "many-friends" (*poluphilia*)[8] seems to belong to the noble things. People also suppose good men and friends are the same. From here, Aristotle surveys a wide range of proverbs about friendship. Among those proverbs seeking a "more natural" (*phusikōteron*) view, two include earth and the heavens having *erōs* for one another through rain, one finds "opposition [is] advantageous (*sumpheron*)," and another asserts that "from the differing things (*diapherontōn*) [come to be] noblest harmony." But these "unprovided matters" (*aporēma*) from nature are not proper (*oikeia*) to examining the human things concerning characters and passions. With this human focus, Aristotle wonders how many forms of friendship there are, noting that those who suppose there is only one form because it admits of more or less do not trust (*pisteuō*) in an adequate sign (1155a28–b16). In Book I, the possibility that the political art's *logoi* are proper and beneficial to those who produce (*poieō*) their passions, desires, and characters according to *logos* emerges from Aristotle observing that the political art examines the noble things and the just things that "hold much difference and wandering, so they seem to be by law only, not by nature." The good things do not hold these differences, though there is some wandering on account of the harm that comes to some people through them (like those who destroy themselves through wealth).[9] Book VIII's intention to focus on characters and passions suggests friendship is proper for discerning what is naturally good for human beings despite some wandering in the forms of friendship.

To first-time readers of the *Ethics*, it is difficult to see that the preceding line of argument is an outline for how Books VIII and IX gradually unveil friendship's natural boundaries and, through these, those of economics and politics. Contrary to Book VIII, Book IX's tenth chapter begins with Aristotle wondering how many friends one should produce, asserting that it is "an impediment towards living nobly" to have "more" (*pleōn*) friends "than the adequate things towards the life that is properly-one's own (*ton oikeion bion*)." This is most evident with friends toward use (*chrēsis*), for it is "laborious" (*epiponos*) and "concerns superfluous work" (*periergon*)[10] to serve them, thus there is no need for such friends. As for friends toward pleasure, there are few of these (1170b20–29). To say it is a laborious work to produce friends is an "economic" argument in a contemporary sense of the term. At the same time, careful readers must see Aristotle's philosophic sense of economics, especially with what is "properly-one's-own" recalling "household management" (*oikonomia*), and "use" being at the root of the "money-making art" (*chrēmatistikē*, literally the "art of useful things"). While economics and politics may hold out the promise of producing many friends through exchange and community, such a promise is neither needed nor adequate for the life that is properly-one's-own. That life itself is the foundation for this argument should remind readers of Book I's inquiry into the lives fit for happiness where Aristotle dismisses the life of pleasure bound to bodily enjoyment as servile, the political life bound to honor on the grounds that the good is properly-one's-own, and the money-making life and its end of wealth since it is useful for the sake of something else. The only life untouched is the contemplative life, which holds an implicit promise to aim pleasure, what is properly-one's-own, and the useful toward the good.[11] The inquiry into friendship fulfills this promise, revealing the holistic nature of the contemplative life by showing how human beings can choose to love the good.

An important thread connecting the above arguments from Books VIII and IX about friendship concerns *erōs* and what is more natural. Just as Book VIII's more natural views of friendship include *erōs*, Book IX's criticism of the life with many useful friends emerges after Aristotle puts forth a more natural view of friendship, and this criticism receives support from *erōs* and an appeal to the decent person (1170a13–b20, 1171a8–20). In Book I, Aristotle presents the serious person who judges and marks-the-boundary (*horizō*) of happiness as what is best, noblest, and most pleasant in opposition to the Delphic inscription that associates what is noblest with what is most just, and what is most pleasant with *erōs*. A key divergence in these two approaches to marking-the-boundaries of happiness is Aristotle's hint that happiness is not "most just." In Book VII of the *Politics*, Aristotle proposes that those who want to produce the best regime must seek the most choiceworthy life. But in following how the *Ethics* marks-the-boundaries of happiness, Aristotle finds the just actions neither align with the well-provided things (*tas euporias*), nor do they generate good things because they are "without-choosing [or choosing] of some bad thing." On account of this insight, Aristotle alludes to a difference in the choice to be either good or serious. Although Book III of the *Politics*' definition of the just as "the common advantage" makes it seem that justice provides the authoritative perspective on politics and economics, this definition rests on a judgment about the foundation for equality and inequality that "holds without-provision and political philosophy." Furthermore, in Book V of the *Ethics*, the decent calls into question the seriousness of justice. Something similar happens to the serious person and the noble in Book IX of the *Ethics* with the decent person's love-of-self (*philautos*).[12] By the end of the *Ethics*' inquiry into friendship, the natural foundation of politics and economics turns out to be love-of-self, the sole provision for which is proper to political philosophy's work of separating the good and pleasure as ends through *logos*.

## THE THREE FORMS OF FRIENDSHIP AND THE LIBERAL LOVE OF THE GOOD (*ETHICS* 1155B17–1159B21)

Although Book VIII's introduction to friendship quietly points to the *Ethics*' questions about the good and pleasure, the preliminary account of the forms of friendship reasserts these questions' primacy. Aristotle begins with readers knowing or being familiar (*gnōrizō*) with "the lovable" (*to philēton*), which is either what is good, pleasant, or useful. But since it seems something good or pleasant comes from what is useful, the good or the pleasant would be lovable as ends. As for whether people love the good or the good for themselves (or, put another way, what is simply good versus the apparent good), Aristotle sets this to the side since the lovable thing in each case is the apparent thing (1155b17–27). Surrounding this approach to the useful are two clues for how the examination of friendship is central to Aristotle's political philosophy. First, the appeal to what is known or familiar recalls the praise for Plato being well-unprovided over whether *logos* should proceed toward or from first-principles as its limit (*peras*). Although Aristotle proposes beginning with the known or familiar things (*tōn gnōrimōn*), because these things are known either "simply" or "to ourselves," he begins with what is known "to ourselves" and examines the four lives with a claim to happiness. Second, in Book III, Aristotle wonders if wish is for the good or the apparent good, for it is possible that nothing wished for is by nature, but only what seems good to each person. To resolve this difficulty, Aristotle defers to the serious person's judgment that sees the truth in each *hexis* and chooses the pleasant as good.[13] With friendship, the distinction between the good and the apparent good is not an abstraction but a choice bound to how friends live. In this way, the *Ethics*' persistent competition between the pleasant and the good as ends finds a practical and familiar context.

Because both the "useful" (*chrēsimon*) and the "money-making art" (*chrēmatistikē*) hold the common root of "need" (*chrē*), Aristotle's subordination of the useful to the good and pleasant as ends means the reduction of "economic" life to money-making is a failure to see its proper end. This failure is present in the unprovided matter that sets into motion the *Politics'* inquiry into the money-making art, where Aristotle wonders if this art is either part of or subordinate to the art of household management (*oikonomikē*). If subordinate, does the money-making art hold-forth (*parechō*) tools to the art of household management, or the raw material that the art of household management brings to completion (*apoteleō*) through its work (*ergon*)? The second half of this inquiry reframes this question to ask if the money-making art belongs to household managers and politicians (the rulers of households and cities), or if the art needs to be present to them. In the end, while the useful things (*chrēmata*) concern the household manager, these things belong to the subordinate money-making art that is according to nature when it provides for the exchange of the things nature holds-forth, but contrary to nature when it becomes the art of retail-trade (where exchange is from each other) and the art of usury (which acquires legal-currency from itself despite its provision being for the sake of exchange).[14] In light of this overview, the greatest matter without-provision in economic and political life concerns subordinating the use of money-making to the preservation of community in households and cities. To complete this work, "economics" must dwell upon the boundaries marked by its namesake, the art of household management (*oikonomikē*).

How political philosophy can provide economics with a natural sense of its boundaries through friendship is evident in the way Aristotle binds what is "proper" (*oikeia*) to what is "adequate" (*ikanos*) in the *Politics* and *Ethics*. In Book I of the *Politics*, after distinguishing a piece of acquisition's (*ktēma*) proper use for what it is (like wearing a shoe) from the improper use of exchange (*allagē*), Aristotle declares that while all things belong to the art of exchange (*metablētikē*) that begins according to nature from people holding more or less of things than is adequate, because it is necessary to produce an exchange only so far as is adequate, it does not belong by nature to the money-making art. An intellectual sense of what is adequate appears in the final chapter of this inquiry where Aristotle states that since the examination adequately marks-the-boundaries toward knowledge (*gnōsis*), there is need to go through what is toward use, for all these things "hold on the one hand free contemplation (*theōrian eleutheran*), necessary experience (*empeirian anankaian*) on the other."[15] According to these passages, a complete view of economics brings together free contemplation and necessary experience to bear upon the proper use of acquisitions.

In the *Ethics*, the contemplative sense of what is adequate finds its proper character in search of the good as a first-principle. Book I upholds the serious person as the model for the human work as an activity of the soul because this person "brings to completion each thing according to the proper virtue (*tēn oikeian aretēn*)." Next, Aristotle asks readers to be coworkers (*sunergon*) with the *logos* and alerts them to the need (*chrē*) to seek the precision proper to the inquiry, leaving them with the choice of whether they will be carpenters seeking what is "useful towards the work," or geometers who are "contemplator[s] of the truth." In contemplating first-principles (*tas archas*), "it is adequate to point them out nobly," and one-must-attempt (*peirateon*) to go after them as is natural and mark-the-boundaries nobly. When reading this passage along with the praise for Plato being well-unprovided about proceeding toward or away from first-principles as the limit (*peras*) in *logos*, one sees an implicit promise of philosophic experience being both practical and theoretical. This promise reemerges in Book VI where, following a statement that ties well-being to prudence in either household management or a regime, Aristotle describes the young being wise in mathematics but not prudent as a function of their trusting (*pisteuō*) in the mathematical first-principles through abstraction (*aphairesis*), yet failing to trust in the experience (*empeiria*) of natural first-principles. While Book VI and its inquiry into prudence does not provide practical experience of these first-principles, Book VIII's opening chapter suggests the inquiry into friendship can, for its examination of the forms of friendship begins with Aristotle admonishing those who think there is only one form that admits of more or less as not trusting in an adequate sign.[16] Friendship—like all things subject to human choice—begins with a first-principle, and early in Book VIII, the pleasant and the good hold the strongest claims to being the most proper first-principle for a free life.

Aristotle's early summary of what friendship entails suggests what an economics bound solely to the useful fails to provide in life. There is no friendship toward things without-soul (*apsuchōn*) since there is neither "returned friendly-affection" (*antiphilēsis*), nor wish of the good from such things. For example, it is laughable to wish for good things for wine, though one might wish for the wine to preserve itself so one may hold it. This prompts Aristotle to observe that such a wish is something people speak of as goodwill (*eunoia*), which many have toward those they assume are either decent or useful (1155b27–1156a5). Though there is no mention of legal-currency in this humorous remark about wine, applying this argument to the *Politics'* inquiries into acquisition and money-making suggests how friendship can move human beings toward what is free in life. The examination of slavery begins with Aristotle establishing that household managers need the proper tools (*tas oikeias organas*) to bring to completion (*apoteleō*) their work since neither living nor living well are possible without the necessary things. Tools are either ensouled or without-soul, and through this distinction, Aristotle defines a slave as "some ensouled piece of acquisition," with the qualification that pieces of acquisition are tools toward living (but not living well). In the examination of the money-making art, the art of retail-trade's use of legal-currency leads some to suppose they must go through-to-the-end (*diateleō*) to preserve or increase the substance (*ousia*) of legal-currency without-limit (*apeiron*), thus exchanging the art of household management's work for the art of retail-trade's. The causes of people setting-down-through themselves (*diathesis*) to live this way are mistakes about living and living well that seek desires (*epithumia*) and bodily enjoyments without-limit.[17] To pursue money-making as if it is the end of all things is to live without-soul and not be free. But through friendship and a sense of what is decent, there is a free way to seek the preservation and increase of what is useful in life without impoverishing the soul.

In the first look at useful and pleasant friendships, Aristotle indirectly outlines how friendship holds a complete sense of the good. Because people love and "feel-affection" (*stergō*)[18] for something good for themselves, in useful and pleasant friendships the love is not for the other person, but for something useful or pleasant that the other person provides (*porizō*). These friendships are "easily-dissolved" (*eudialutos*) because these friends do not "remain" (*diamenō*) the same. Useful friends tend not to remain the same because they seek the advantageous and are pleasant to one another only when they hold the hope of something good and beneficial. Consequently, useful friends do not live-together (*suzaō*) and do not need the addition (*prosdeō*) of their pleasant association (hence why people set-down this friendship with foreigners). As for why friends for the sake of pleasure do not remain the same, Aristotle observes how the young seem to seek these friendships most of all because of passion, through which they live with "sudden-change" (*metapiptō*) in the pleasant and are prone to *erōs* that gives them a wish "to pass the days" (*sunēmereuō*) and live-together with their friends, yet this love (*phileō*) quickly ceases (often on the same day) (1156a6–b6). This argument tacitly maintains not only the competition between the good and the pleasant as ends, but holds the good is more authoritative than the useful and the pleasant. The common ground between useful and pleasant friendships is they seek something good, but these goods are not lasting. Pleasure is also part of useful and pleasant friendships, but is deficient because it fails to encourage the friends to live-together. With the useful friendships, the pleasant follows what is advantageous. With friendships of pleasure, the problem seems to be an incomplete understanding of what is pleasant, rooting it solely in changing passions. Together, these passages suggest there is a form of friendship where the love of what is advantageous, good, and beneficial remains the same, is not susceptible to sudden-change, and encourages friends to live-together.

With this outline of useful and pleasant friendships' deficiencies, readers can use the *Ethics*' arguments about pleasure and the good to see the *Politics*' approach to economic life in a different light. In Book VII of the *Ethics*, Aristotle divides what is pleasant by nature simply from things that become pleasant through mutilations, habits, or wretched natures (which are all evident in certain *hexeis*). For human beings, both *logos* and sense-perception impel (*hormaō*) their desires toward the pleasant, a truth that anticipates Book VII's conclusion that human nature is not simple and does not experience the single decent pleasure of the god's activity that rests in the absence of motion. Instead, human nature is subject to ruin and laboriously-wicked (*ponēros*) when needing change (*metabolē*). The question of what is pleasant by nature simply versus what is not informs Book VIII's early hesitance to separate the good simply from the apparent good since people love each thing. In Book I of the *Politics*, the acquisition of food is naturally pleasant for animals and human beings. But while nature marks-the-boundaries of animals' lives toward the advantageous choosing (*hairesis*) of food with the pleasant, "choosing" is absent from human beings' pleasant mixing of lives holding their work toward what is natural in pursuit of the self-sufficient as need (*chreia*) necessitates. Similarly, though Aristotle mentions human beings providing food through exchange and retail-trade as distinct from these lives, he takes some time to introduce the idea that the provision of legal-currency and production of exchange through the money-making art came about according to *logos* to provide for necessary exchange. With experience, this exchange became more of an art concerned with producing the most gain, leading retail-trade away from being simply equal with necessary exchange.[19] While "choosing," "pleasure," and the "advantageous" never appear together Book I of the *Politics*, Books VII and VIII of the *Ethics* make clear that all arts of acquisition and exchange begin with a choice of the good or the apparent good that is inseparable from *logos* and pleasure.

The importance of friends' living-together and the inherent pleasure of friendship helps illuminate how money-making can produce a fractured view of political and economic life. In Book III of the *Politics*, Aristotle denies that the city exists solely for the sake of mutual-giving (*metadosis*) and not committing injustice, defining it as "a community of living well and households and families, for the sake of complete and self-sufficient living." The city is the "work of friendship," which itself is "the choice of living-together." Aristotle omits discussing this choice in Book I of the *Politics*, though its attempt to look at communities naturally-growing (*phuō*) from the beginning suggests how money-making corrupts the choice to live-together. Whereas the household is the community set-standing-together for every day (*hēmera*), the village (a community of households) is for a non-daily (*mē ephēmeros*) use. A multitude of villages forms a city, the nature and end of which is self-sufficiency. In raising the first unprovided matter concerning the money-making art's work, Aristotle distinguishes the money-making art from the art of household management on the grounds that the former art provides what the latter art uses. But the money-making art has no work in the household where people form-community (*koinōneō*) in all things, for this art's natural precedent is the art of exchange that begins among many households producing mutual-giving as is necessary according to their needs. Because this art restores the self-sufficiency according to nature, it is not the money-making art (although this art begins with the necessary provision of legal-currency to produce foreign exchange).[20] By taking its bearings from the natural art of exchange that works between households and extending this to cities, the money-making art's work cannot truly inform living-together within the household. The non-daily use of exchange is insufficient for teaching human beings how to form-community daily in all things within the household. With friendship, however, there is a wish to pass the days together (*sunēmereuō*) and live-together, and understanding the nature of this wish is necessary for ensuring the money-making art's use contributes to the preservation of community in households and cities.

In contrast to useful and pleasant friendships, Aristotle introduces the "complete" (*teleia*) form of friendship that prepares the way for Books VIII and IX to move toward a natural sense of the good in the *Ethics*. The complete form of friendship is between those who are good and similar according to virtue. Because virtue is stable, these friends wish for the good things for each other and remain good since they hold this way according to themselves, and each friend is good simply, good for the friend, and beneficial. Such friends are also pleasant simply and for each other, for the actions that are properly-one's-own (*oikeia*) and other such things are according to pleasure. Yet complete friendships occur between few people and are rare, needing-the-addition of time and being habituated-together (*sunēthēs*) to guarantee that each friend appears lovable and trusted (*pisteuō*), for while people quickly wish to produce "the proofs of friendship" (*ta philika*), they are not friends until they are lovable and know this (1156b7–32). These characteristics of complete friendship unite what is simply good and pleasant with what is good for each person through what is properly-one's-own. The trust necessary for complete friendship shows how Aristotle's political philosophy aims to provide for this. In Book I's consideration of the political life's claim to happiness, virtue looks like it provides for people's need to trust that they are good out of the recognition that "we divine ourselves the good to be something properly-one's-own and hard-to-take-away (*dusaphaireton*)." In Book VI, following the identification of the political art and household management with the practical *hexis* of prudence that seeks the good and well-being for oneself, Aristotle asks how people can trust in the experience of natural first-principles, for this needs something more than time and is not a matter of abstraction (*aphairesis*).[21] As Aristotle's *logos* seeks the foundation for trust in friendship, readers should consider how it provides trustworthy experience of the good as the natural first-principle in all choices and practical pursuits.

After introducing the complete form of friendship, subsequent comparisons to useful and pleasant friendships begin to establish an authoritative sense of the good and lay the groundwork for later arguments in the *Ethics* regarding the limits to politics' and economics' capacity to produce well-being. The likeness between useful, pleasant, and complete friendships is the friends come to hold something good. Of the three forms of friendship, the useful is the most expansive, something Aristotle reveals through *erōs*. Unlike friendships of pleasure that require taking pleasure in the same thing, "lover" (*erastēs*) and "beloved" (*erōmenos*) have different pleasures: the lover in seeing the beloved, and beloved in the lover's attendance. Nevertheless, "lovers" (*erōtikoi*) can exchange (*antikatallassomai*) the profit that is useful and advantageous to themselves since they are friends to this and not to each other, though the friendship dissolves when the profit disappears. If many lovers remain friends, it is through feeling-affection for their character (*ēthos*) from "habituation-together" (*sunētheia*) and being of the "same-character" (*homoēthēs*) (1156b33–1157a16). An economics defined by money-making is useful and advantageous to a wide range of people because it has no need to account for what is more personal in life. The descriptions of lovers' friendship to profit demonstrates they hold a "useful part" of "necessary experience" in the money-making art (i.e., what pieces of acquisition are most profitable) independent of their erotic attachment.[22] From this example, economic friendship understood as the useful and advantageous exchange of money for the acquisition of profit seems liberated from concerns with pleasure and character.[23]

Although useful friendships extend the farthest, they are also the most tenuous because they dispense with an essential natural foundation for economic and political life in Aristotle's political philosophy. In keeping with their separation from character, useful friendships (like those of pleasure) can form between the decent and the base, for the delight in these friendships follows the benefit. But useful and pleasant friendships fall short of the trust belonging to what is worthy (*axioō*) of "true friendship" (*alēthōs philia*) that "does not listen to calumny" (*adiablētōs*) and is not subject to doing injustice (*adikeō*). After citing cities that seem to be allies for the advantageous as an example of useful friendships, Aristotle concludes that friendship between the good is the authoritative (*kuriōs*) form, while useful and pleasant friendships are likenesses insofar as there is some good in each (1157a16–32). What characterizes all friendships is trust in some good. In complete and true friendships, the trust is in each friend being good. In useful and pleasant friendships, the trust is in the benefit of some useful and pleasant good. Within these arguments is an implicit comparison between "true friendship" and useful friendships like alliances that suggests such foreign connections are subject to injustice and calumny. Since the money-making art begins from foreign exchange, the economic friendships between cities (and all political communities) are susceptible to ills that true friendship does not suffer. Calumny's threat to useful friendships defined by the exchange of some external good quietly indicates what is necessary for there to be true trust that economics and politics provide for what is good: *logos*.

Despite the proximate presentations of "complete" and "true" friendship, there is some ambiguity about virtue's place in friendship. Drawing on Book I's question of whether virtue belongs to *hexis* or activity, Aristotle wonders if those who form the authoritative friendship are good according to a *hexis* or an activity. As in Book I, at first it seems friendship belongs more to activity from seeing how those living-together delight in and provide good things to each other, while those who are sleeping or separated by place do not. Such friends, however, hold to be active (*energeō*), for place loosens the activity of friendship, but not friendship simply. With this door open for *hexis*, after reiterating the need for the pleasant in living-together and passing the days together with friends, Aristotle states that while "friendly-affection" (*philēsis*) looks like a passion because it occurs toward things without-soul, friendship is with choice and from a *hexis* because friends wish for the good things for each other out of love and according to a *hexis*. Each friend loves the good for oneself and they both come to be good for each other. In friendships between the good, the saying "friendship is equality (*isotēs*)" is present most of all since these friends give back "the equal" (*to ison*) in wish and the pleasant (1157b5–1158a1). For those concerned with economics and politics, the most important part of this argument is how Aristotle roots equality in friends' wishes, which derive from choice and *hexeis*. In Book I, the inquiry into happiness as the human work that is an activity of the soul according to the proper (*oikeia*) virtue begins by setting down that activity seems to be more authoritative than *hexis*. At the end of Book VI, from the perspective of the authoritative good, natural *hexeis* cannot become authoritative virtue without prudence informed by intellect.[24] Since politics and economics emanate from the *hexis* of prudence, the authoritative view of these practical pursuits and their equality requires accounting for the intellect's work in friendship's choice of the good.

With a return to complete friendship, readers catch a glimpse of what is naturally liberal in life. Complete friendship (like *erōs*) does not admit of being toward many because it is not easy to please or be good to many; rather, a complete friendship needs experience and habituation-together. But with useful and pleasant friendships, these things can please many with little time. Despite this similarity, the pleasant friendships are closer to complete friendships than the useful, for there is more of "the liberal" (*to eleutherion*) in the delight friends have in each other (as is the case with the young). Conversely, friendships through the useful belong to the "things of the marketplace" (*agoraiōn*). In support of this argument, Aristotle adds that while blessed persons do not need useful people, they wish to live-together with pleasant people, for people cannot remain holding-together (*sunechōs*) in what is painful, even if it contained the good itself. Aristotle then returns to equality and refines its character in the forms of friendship: while equality resides in wish for complete friendships, in useful and pleasant friendships, it resides in the exchange of something useful or pleasure for a benefit. Finally, although friendships according to virtue hold the useful and the pleasant, they do not listen to calumny, are stable, and are not subject to sudden-change and many differences like the useful and the pleasant (1158a10–b11). For contemporary readers, the notion that the marketplace lacks what is liberal might seem strange. But for Aristotle, to take pleasure in something is more liberal than exchange, and it is vital to people holding-together with the good. Because equality is different in complete friendships characterized by holding-together with the good than the equality characterized by exchange in useful and pleasant friendships, a similar difference must be present in economics and politics.

Looking back at Book VIII's initial comparison between useful, pleasant, and complete friendships along with earlier arguments about pleasure in the *Ethics* clarifies why the pleasant is closer to what is naturally liberal than the useful and exchange. The backdrop for these arguments is Book I's likening of virtue's *hexis* and activity to acquisition and use. Later in Book I, being unprovided (*diaporeō*) and without-provision (*aporia*) in questions about the need (*chreōn*) to see an end to proclaim (*chraō*) someone is happy witness to the *logos* that the activity of contemplating and acting according to virtue is a living that is most holding-together.[25] Though Book VIII suggests friendships according to virtue are holding-together with pleasure, Aristotle noticeably omits "happiness" from this account. Pleasure, however, is a constant in Book VIII's summaries of complete friendships according to virtue. A deficiency of useful and pleasant friendships is their dependence on some good that another person provides by way of exchange, while complete friendships according to virtue derive from the actions that are properly-one's-own (*oikeia*) and according to pleasure. In complete friendships, providing for the pleasant through exchange is unnecessary because pleasure is properly-one's-own. It is possible to hold-together in pleasure because human beings hold it within themselves and do not need to acquire it from others. In this respect, pleasures and *hexeis* (ways of holding oneself) are akin to one another. But how is a *hexis* an acquisition if a person holds it within oneself?

Book VIII's discovery of friendship as something with choice and from a *hexis* where equality resides in mutual wishes and pleasures suggests both the good and pleasure are properly-one's-own. In Book II, the use of pleasures and pains to become good is the common concern of virtue and the political art. What precedes this argument is the recognition that the pleasant is among three things of choosing, and while the good person is most correct about the pleasant, the bad person is most errant. This problem reappears in Book III where—between characterizing choice as "with *logos* and thought (*dianoia*)" and defining it as some "deliberate desire" (*bouleutikē orexis*) toward ends— Aristotle alerts readers to the problem of wish seeming to be for the apparent good as its end instead of the good by nature because the pleasant distorts one's ability to see and judge the truth of each *hexis* like the serious person. When Book VII turns to pleasure, the good is both an activity and a *hexis*, and pleasure emerges as "an activity of the *hexis* according to nature." Pleasure leads to the completion (*teleiōsis*) of nature, as is evident in the contemplative activity of the nature not in-need that is without pains and desires (*epithumia*). Such pleasure is distinct from the incidental pleasure that restores and sets-standing-accordingly one's own nature (like medicine).[26] Like incidental pleasures, the natural art of exchange produced between households only restores the self-sufficiency that is according to nature through the acquisition of useful things. But exchange cannot complete the nature of the household that uses these acquisitions. Just as *hexis* and activity must hold together in the soul, acquisition and use must hold together in economic life. In both the soul and the household, acquisition and use need the good to hold together, and only friendship provides a holistic view of how to choose the good and use pleasure to complete one's own nature.

Although virtue is a prominent theme in the *Ethics* and the apparent foundation of complete friendships, the centrality of love (*phileō*) to friendship challenges the authority of virtue in pursuit of the good. Looking at the love of honor (*philotimia*), Aristotle finds that the many seem to wish to be loved more than to love, choosing (*haireō*) honor incidentally in the hope that those in positions of authority (*tas exousias*) will allow them to hit upon what they need, treating the honor as a sign of "comfort" or "luxury" (*eupatheia*).[27] Opposed to the many are those who desire (*oregō*) and delight in honor from the decent to confirm "the opinion that is properly-one's-own" (*tēn oikeian doxan*), namely, to trust that they are good. But because those who desire honor delight in being loved, this seems stronger than honor, and friendship is choiceworthy according to itself. But it also seems friendship is more in loving than being loved, and from mothers' delight in loving their children, love looks like a virtue of friends (1159a12–35). In all its cases, the love of honor reveals how people seek the acquisition of some good for themselves, either in material possessions, or the opinion they hold about themselves. Through friendship and choice, however, the argument moves away from a passive acquisition of some good toward some active holding of it. A mother who loves her child seeks no sign of comfort or luxury, nor does she expect the child to help her trust that she is good. For the mother, it is sufficient to love her child. Here readers must wonder what love's natural source is and what sort of virtue this is. Whatever the case may be, it is clear that friendship is liberal in the sense that its love actively trusts the good proper to oneself.

With loving looking like the virtue of friendship, Aristotle turns to matters of worth (*axios*) that point to how understanding the nature of friendship is necessary for preserving what is liberal in economic and political life. Friendships are stable when love is according to worth, and this allows those who are equal and unequal to be friends. Even friendly-affection—which looks like passion and is neither with choice nor from a *hexis*—is equality and likeness. This likeness is most stable between those who are virtuous, and least stable among the wretched. As for useful and pleasant friends, their friendship lasts so long as they provide pleasures and benefits to each other. Useful friendships seem to come about most of all between opposites like poor and wealthy persons, or those who are unlearned and knowers, where the former are in need and the latter aim to give something back. Another example occurs among two lovers deeming themselves worthy (*axioō*) of being loved (*phileō*) more than they deserve. The only thing that would render them worthy of equal love is if they are similar; otherwise, they hold something laughable. This prompts Aristotle to wonder if the aim among opposites is a desire (*orexis*) for the middle term that is good (a question he leaves open) (1159a35–b21). Though the case of lovers is humorous, there is a troubling political implication to the proposed useful friendship of poor and wealthy persons. While the poor person is in need of wealth, if the wealthy person gives some of one's own wealth to the poor, what could the poor give in return? What does the wealthy person need? In terms of wealth, there is no equality between the two persons, and there is no other basis for equality in this example. If the only form of friendship possible between poor and wealthy people is the useful, then equality is impossible. Though beyond the scope of this chapter, this passing argument poses a serious challenge for economics and politics: If all political communities have the wealthy and the poor within them, then any equality between these two classes requires something other than wealth.

Though questions about worth and the just seem to be most pressing in economics and politics, they do not hold the same weight in Aristotle's political philosophy. Indeed, once Aristotle uncovers the natural foundation for friendship in Book IX, worth disappears from the inquiry. A hint of why this occurs appears in Book VIII's seventh chapter, which sits between introducing equality as part of the explanation for how friendship (like virtue) involves *hexis* and activity *and* seeing this equality bound to loving as the virtue of friends. With the friendship between husbands and wives, parents and children, it is possible for friendships involving persons holding-over (*huperochē*) others in the sense of preeminence to be stable and decent. These friendships are different than those between ruler and ruled because the equal in the just things does not hold the same as it does in friendship. With the just, the equal is first according to worth, and then "a certain quantity" (*poson*).[28] With friendship, the equal is first according to a certain quantity, then worth. Examples of these "certain quantities" include virtue, vice, and well-provision (*euporia*). But here Aristotle acknowledges that there is no precise "boundary-marking" (*horismos*) for how people stay friends, and leaves readers uprovided (*aporeō*) over what it means to wish for the greatest goods for friends despite taking away (*aphaireō*) many things (1158b11–1159a12). Careful readers should notice a significant omission from this first account of how the just and friendship hold distinct approaches to equality. In Book I of the *Politics*, parents and children—who are free persons—are the natural parts of the household (*oikia*), and their introduction coincides with declaring that one must contemplate how the money-making art holds in relation to the art of household management (*oikonomikē*).[29] Though parents and children form the household in the *Politics*, Book VIII of the *Ethics* omits the "household" from its first accounts of equality, which suggests that friendship holds the natural foundation for what is liberal in economics and politics, not community.

Although Aristotle returns to worth in the last chapters of Book VIII and the early chapters of Book IX after a brief consideration of friendship, the just, political community, and regimes, the fact that friendship holds the naturally liberal foundation for all communities necessitates discerning its true nature to understand what preserves freedom in ruling and acquisition, the respective concerns of politics and economics. In Book I of the *Politics*, worth's corrosive influence on politics and economics is first evident in an errant deeming-worthy in the just and law (*nomos*) of how nature produces and marks-the-boundary of free and slave that leads people to customarily-consider (*nomizō*) that they can acquire natural slaves through violent conquest in war (something they would never wish for themselves). Curiously, Aristotle ends this account of slavery by law with an allusion to some worthy friendship by nature between master and slave. Second, it is through the strangeness of someone being well-provided in legal-currency but unprovided in food due to a change in the legal-currency's worth that there is a difference between the art of household management and art of retail-trade as money-making arts: the former art acquires useful things and wealth according to nature, and the latter produces useful things and wealth contrary to nature.[30] Since Book VIII's early arguments about friendship, equality, and worth bring forth people's desire for the good, one must see how all judgments about worth in politics and economics grow from this natural desire.

The emergence of desire in Aristotle's outlines of the complete form of friendship according to virtue subtly signals why readers should not treat Book VIII as if it holds the *Ethics'* definitive teaching on friendship. In Book VI of the *Ethics*, Aristotle defines human beings through choice as a beginning or first-principle (*archē*) that is either desiring intellect or thinking desire. In Book III—where Aristotle characterizes choice as "with *logos* and thought" and deliberate desire toward ends—he distinguishes the money-making art and science from precise and self-sufficient sciences (like those concerned with letters) on the grounds that what concerns money-making does not always come to be in the same way. To make this argument, Aristotle observes the human intellect is a cause of things alongside nature, necessity, and chance. In Book VII, a pivotal step toward defining pleasure as "an activity of a *hexis* according to nature" is Aristotle defining what it means to hold science as a *hexis* as acquiring a *logos*, trusting and naturally-growing-together (*sumphuō*) with the *logos*, and holding and using the *logos* in contemplation.[31] Since human nature holds intellect and desire together, the intellect's absence from Book VIII means its account of friendship is incomplete. But what is the intellect's practical role in friendship? Recall that each person's desire for the good corresponds to seeking confirmation for "the opinion that this properly-one's-own": the trust that one is good. As practical arts and sciences, politics and economics aim to provide what is good in ruling and acquisition through *logos*, which no person will choose to use without trusting that it is good. This trust is impossible without knowing how to trust in one's own knowledge of the good. In Book IX, Aristotle shows through friendship how human beings naturally trust in the knowledge of the good through the intellect, and this knowledge is the true source of all that is liberal in life.

## FRIENDSHIP, THE DECENT, AND THE NATURAL BOUNDARIES OF POLITICAL AND ECONOMIC SELF-SUFFICIENCY (*ETHICS* 1123B14–21, 1124A1–20, 1129A23–B6, 1166A1–B2, 1168A28–1171A20, 1171B29–1172A15)

Another way to see the incompleteness of Book VIII's account of complete friendship is through the absence of two ideas essential to the *Ethics'* turn toward the practical and acquirable good in Book I that reappear in Book IX: happiness and self-sufficiency. When Aristotle introduces the complete form of friendship in Book VIII as bound to the actions that are properly-one's-own (and is therefore simply good and pleasant), he asserts that despite the quick wish to produce the proofs of friendship (*ta philika*), friends do not appear lovable and trusted until they know that they are lovable.[32] In

Book IX's fourth chapter, Aristotle uses the proofs of friendship to propose that it looks like friendships mark-the-boundaries (*horizō*) from "the things toward oneself" (*ek tōn pros heauton*), for a friend is set-down either as one who wishes and does the good or the apparent things for the sake of the friend, or "the one wishing for the friend to be and to live for the sake of the friend's self" (which is how "mothers are affected towards their children") (1166a1–10). There is a split between these two views of friendship from the things toward oneself: these things belong either in acting toward the friend, or in wishing for the friend's being and living for its own sake (and not acting toward the friend). For those reading the *Ethics* for the first time, it is not readily apparent how this argument marks the beginning of the text's revision of its definition of happiness in relation to virtue and self-sufficiency in Book X. This revision, however, has profound implications for understanding how Aristotle roots politics' and economics' provision of good things in his political philosophy's intellectual provision for the good necessary for one's own life.

How politics and economics find a common boundary in an intellectual sense of the good is evident from key arguments about boundaries in the *Ethics*. When Book I of the *Ethics* uses happiness as a complete end chosen (*haireō*) on account of itself to propose that self-sufficiency characterizes the complete good, Aristotle cautions readers against thinking either that the self-sufficient is for living life alone, or that connections to family, friends, and citizens stretch without-limit. Although human beings are by nature political, there is some boundary to this. Book VI of the *Ethics* begins by choosing to divide (*diaireō*) correct *logos* (the asserted basis for virtue in Book II) to mark-its-boundary for the soul's *hexeis*. Over the course of Book VI, readers learn that, as *hexeis*, science and prudence (and therefore politics and economics) need to trust in natural first-principles as "the unmoving (*akinētos*) first boundaries" of which there is no *logos* but sense-perception through the intellect. But this raises a question Book VI does not answer: How does intellect hold according to nature? In Book VII, the prudent person returns as someone seeking the good and pleasant in life without pain, with happiness holding a claim to the best thing as the most choiceworthy *hexis* with an unimpeded activity and pleasure. This allows happiness to be the boundary of good fortune, even if happiness needs the addition of bodily goods, external goods (which include wealth), and chance. Book VII then builds toward its final comparison between the god's single, simple, decent, and divine pleasure that rests in the activity characterized by the absence of motion (*akinēsia*), *and* the non-simple human nature that is laboriously-wicked (*ponēros*) when needing change. After this comparison, Aristotle turns the inquiry to friendship.[33] Books VI and VII leave readers with the theoretical mystery of how to hold their intellect toward unmoving first-principles so that their nature and pleasure rest in an activity without motion. With stability as a characteristic of complete friendship, there is a signpost that friendship shows how to rest pleasantly in the good.

In contrast to the *Ethics'* abundance of boundaries, the *Politics'* examination of the money-making art has only one in its assertion that the art of household management according to nature (as opposed to the unnecessary money-making art) holds a boundary concerning the acquisition of food. Though Aristotle does not define the art of household management's boundary as self-sufficiency, this idea appears twice in the first half of that inquiry. First, the pursuit of the self-sufficient as need necessitates governs human beings' pleasant mixing of the five acquisitive lives that hold their work in relation to what is natural. Second, to make the argument that a natural art of acquisition needs either to be present or provided to the art of household management, Aristotle defines "true wealth" as "a store of such useful things (*chrēmata*) that are necessary towards living, and useful to community in a city or a household"; to this he adds that self-sufficiency of true wealth's acquisition is not without-limit toward good living.[34] Throughout Aristotle's political philosophy, boundaries (particularly those related to self-sufficiency) necessarily turn readers' attention back to themselves. Although many wish to find tangible, external boundaries for politics and economics, for Aristotle, the true boundary for all practical choices and pursuits is the good, and Book IX's natural view of friendship provides readers a *logos* through which they can trust in their intellect's sense-perception of the good.

Book IX's first portrait of the decent person brings together intellect and desire toward the good. The decent person is "of one mind" (*homognōmoneō*) with oneself, desires (*oregō*) the same things for oneself with all the soul, wishes for the good things and the apparent things for oneself and labors at them for the sake of oneself. This labor is for the sake of "the thinking thing" (*to dianoētikon*)[35] through which the decent person is prudent (*phroneō*), and since each person seems to be this thinking thing most of all, the decent person wishes to live and be preserved. Seeming to shift his reference point, Aristotle states that it is good to the serious person to be, and because each person wishes for the good things for oneself, no one chooses (*haireō*) to become another to hold all things (for the god holds the good). From this it seems each person is most of all "the intellecting thing" (*to nooun*).[36] Whatever confusion there may be about the status of the decent versus the serious person is something Aristotle dismisses by noting that while virtue and the serious person look like they are the measure in each, all the remaining persons assume they are decent. Aristotle next describes how the decent person's "going through together" (*sundiagō*) with oneself produces the pleasant, for the decent person's thought is well-provided with contemplative things (*theōrēma*), and the same thing is always painful and pleasant to the decent person. Because the decent person holds toward the friend as oneself—"for the friend is another self (*allos autos*)"—friendship seems to be one of these things, and raises the question of whether there is friendship toward oneself "insofar as it is two or more,"[37] for such friendship is like an "excess" or "superiority" (*huperbolē*) (1166a10–b2). With the decent person, desire, wish, intellect, choosing, labor, and the pleasant all hold together in a well-provided contemplating of the good things. Yet this account is a setup for a question Book IX sets out to answer: How does one become decent?

Aristotle's passing comment that friendship toward oneself is like an "excess" or "superiority" provides a playful hint of how to approach the discordant *logoi* surrounding "love-of-self" (*philautos*) in Book IX's eighth chapter that provide for readers' need to trust in the good. In Book II, Aristotle introduces the teaching that the mean preserves *hexeis* and virtues while excess and deficiency ruin them. This teaching follows immediately from assuming the virtues are according to correct *logos* (whose boundary Book VI chooses to divide) since the inquiry seems to be for the sake of becoming good, not contemplation. Yet because the general *logos* concerning actions and advantageous things holds nothing stable, readers must-attempt (*peirateon*) to help the *logos*. In Book VII, while the good and pleasant things are not harmful in themselves, they are when someone is more serious about them than there is need to be by being affected (*paschō*), desiring (*epithumeō*), and loving (*phileō*) them to excess and contrary to *logos*. The good and pleasant things in this argument are useful things, gain, victory, and honor (things that are all relevant to economics and politics).[38] The dual meanings of *huperbolē* ("excess" or "superiority") anticipate love-of-self's ambiguity: there is on the one hand an excess (or several excesses) contrary to *logos*, and on the other hand a superiority that is good and pleasant because it is according to *logos*.

Book IX's inquiry into love-of-self begins by being unprovided (*aporeō*) over whether there is need to love (*phileō*) oneself most of all, or some other person. For example, people shamefully "censure" (*epitimaō*)[39] as "lovers-of-self" those who most of all love (*agapaō*) and do all things for the sake of oneself (like a base person), while the decent person acts through the noble and for the sake of a friend, leaving oneself to the side. Yet the works are discordant with the *logoi*, and not without-*logos* (*alogōs*). Some assert there is need to love the friend most of all, while others assert all the things through which friendship marks-its-boundary are present toward oneself. All the proverbs— "one soul," "the things of friends [are] common," and "friendship [is] equality"—are of one mind in suggesting one is a friend most of all to oneself. These *logoi* about love-of-self fairly leave one unprovided about which one needs (*chreōn*) to follow, for they hold trust (*to piston*). Consequently, there is need to divide (*diaireō*) the *logoi* to mark-the-boundary of how they are true (1168a28–b13). The possibility of discordant *logoi* holding trust leaves readers to wonder what the foundation for this trust is, and being unprovided in what is true suggests they have some sense of this.

How this experience of being unprovided about love-of-self ultimately points to readers' natural sense of the good is clear by remembering that (since Book I) they are coworkers with the *logos* in seeking the precision proper (*oikeion*) to the inquiry that attempts (*peirateon*) to go after first-principles as is natural and mark-the-boundaries nobly, for these—like knowledge of the good—hold great weight. Although knowledge of the good ensures choosing does not go without-limit (*apeiron*)—thus leaving desire (*orexis*) empty and vain—the *logos* providing this knowledge would be vain and without-benefit to those with an improper character, one without-experience (*apeiron*) in a life of producing desires according to *logos*. Readers should view this challenge in light of Plato being well-unprovided over whether *logos* concerning first-principles should proceed toward or away from them as a limit (*peras*), and Book VI's wondering how to trust the experience (*empeiria*) of natural first-principles rather than abstraction (*aphairesis*) that is literally "away-from-choosing." For those who doubt working back and forth through these theoretical arguments provides practical experience of the good, remember that from the first sentence of the *Ethics* there is an analogy between inquiry (*methodos*) and choice (*proairesis*) aiming themselves at some good that invites readers to wonder if all things aim themselves at the good.[40] In choosing to divide (*diaireō*) the *logoi* concerning love-of-self to mark-the-boundary of what is true about friendship, readers work with Aristotle's *logos* to contemplate and trust how the good is the first-principle and limit that they choose in all that is properly-one's-own.

The division in *logoi* about love-of-self concerns "reproach" (*oneidos*). Those who receive reproach as "lovers-of-self" are people who "distribute" (*aponemō*)[41] to themselves "what is more" (*to pleon*) in things one uses or needs (*chrēma*), honors, and bodily pleasures, for many desire (*oregō*) these things and are serious about them as if they are best (*arista*), and through this they are "fought-over things" (*perimachēta*). Such lovers-of-self are "those-holding-more" (*pleonektēs*) who delight in desires (*epithumia*) and wholly in passions and what is without-*logos* in the soul. For this, many receive the name of "base" and are justly reproached as "lovers-of-self" (1168b13–23). These reproachable lovers-of-self are examples of people who Aristotle blames in Book VII for being more serious about good and pleasant things by pursuing their excess contrary to *logos*. But since these things are truly good and pleasant, there must be a way to love and desire (*oregō*) them according to a true *logos* of the good.

Before taking up Book IX's account of the unreproachable love-of-self, a brief digression on an early argument from Book V's inquiry into justice is necessary for seeing how friendship's perspective on the good and the pleasant provides the authoritative lens for understanding the nature of politics and economics in Aristotle's political philosophy. When looking at the just (*to dikaion*) and the unjust (*to adikon*) *and* justice (*dikaiosunē*) and injustice (*adikaia*), Aristotle notes that people speak of these things "in-various-ways" (literally "in-more-ways," *pleonachōs*). Because these things are near to each other and "have the same-name" (*hōmonumian*), it escapes notice how they differ greatly in "form" (*idea*) (unlike the difference people notice in the necks of animals and door locks that share the name *kleis*). Accordingly, it seems the unjust person is the person "contrary to law" (*paranomos*), the one-holding-more, and "the unequal person" (*anisos*); the just person is therefore "the lawful" (*to nomimon*) and the equal person. Of the three unjust persons, Aristotle subjects the one-holding-more to further scrutiny, characterizing this person as unjust concerning the good things belonging to good fortune and bad fortune that are simply good, but not always for some person. While human beings "pray" (*euchomai*) for and pursue these things, perhaps there is need not to; rather there is need to pray that the simply good things are good for themselves and that they choose (*haireō*) the good things for themselves (1129a23–b6).[42] An odd feature of Book V's outline of just and unjust persons is that while there are parallel persons regarding law and equality, there is no parallel for the one-holding-more. That this derives from the *Ethics'* authoritative concern with the good is clear upon recalling that the just things in Book I hold difference and wandering so that they seem to be solely by law and not by nature, whereas the good things are by nature but hold some wandering on account of those who destroy themselves through them. Such an example appears in Book I of the *Politics* with King Midas, whose insatiably greedy prayer (*euchēs*) confirms the strangeness of someone being well-provided in wealth in the form of legal-currency but going unprovided in necessary food when there is a change in the law that sets-down legal-currency's worth.[43] Beneath the injustice of the one-holding-more that afflicts politics and economics is a reproachable love-of-self that has no remedy in law, but in a love-of-self through which a person loves the good according to nature and chooses the good things within its boundaries.

Returning to Book IX, Aristotle uses the city to outline how the intellect is the foundation for an unreproachable love-of-self. The argument starts by acknowledging no one would blame someone as a "lover-of-self" who is always serious about doing all that accords with the virtues and distributing to oneself the noblest things and most of all good things, delighting and in all things "trusting" (or "being persuaded by," *peithō*)[44] the most authoritative thing in oneself. Just as a city and every "whole set-standing-together" (*sustēma*)[45] seem most of all to be the most authoritative thing, so too is a human being. From the distinction between the persons with and without self-restraint deriving from whether or not the intellect is strong (*krateō*), it is clear that each person is most of all the intellect, and the decent person most of all loves (*agapaō*) and gratifies this. The decent person is a lover-of-self who differs in form from the reproachable lover-of-self as much as living according to *logos* differs from living according to passion, or the desire (*oregō*) of the noble differs from what is seemingly advantageous (1168b29–1169a6). Within Book IX, the difference between the one-holding-more's reproachable love-of-self and the decent person's unreproachable love-of-self clarifies how friendship toward oneself is two or more: the one-holding-more holds an excess of such friendship, while the decent person holds a superiority. Love-of-self's two forms also mark a growth in discernment since Book V where the just and the unjust things having the same name obscures their different forms. In Book IX, the *logos* reveals how love-of-self differs in form despite holding one name.

The comparison between human beings and wholes set-standing-together on the basis of the intellect's strength is something readers should see in light of Book I of the *Politics*, which begins by establishing every city and community is "set-standing-together (*sunistēmi*) for the sake of some good." In the inquiry into slavery, the rule of intellect and the part holding *logos* over desire and the passionate part of the soul is political rule, a form of rule fit (like the art of household management's rule) for free persons. This first hint about the free character of political rule and household management precedes a quiet suggestion that what is free is a matter of being. What initiates this line of argument is the inquiry into slavery by law ending with the *Politics'* first mention of "friendship."[46] Together, Book IX of the *Ethics'* introduction to unreproachable love-of-self and Book I of the *Politics'* sketches of the city, political rule, and household management indicate the free character of politics and economics begins with the authoritative love of the good.

Despite the clear division between reproachable and unreproachable love-of-self, within the latter there is an ambiguity regarding the noble and the serious that uncovers the natural need for friends and, through this, the natural boundaries of self-sufficiency and happiness. Aristotle begins by observing the praise given to those who are serious about noble actions on the condition that virtue involves everyone competing in common to do the noblest things so that "for all there would be the needful things (*ta deonta*) and for each person privately (*idios*)[47] the greatest of the good things" (for such a lover-of-self is good through doing the noble things that profit oneself and benefit others). Here the love-of-self characterizing the decent person and the serious person part ways. From observing that "every intellect chooses (*haireō*) the best thing for itself," the decent person is someone who "trusts-the-rule" (*peitharcheō*)[48] of the intellect. The serious person, in contrast, chooses many things to cause the noble to remain above oneself, including: giving up useful things, political offices, honors, and fought-over things for friends; choosing an intense pleasure to live nobly for a short time; choosing a great noble thing to die for others; and giving up a noble action to a friend to be that action's cause. According to Aristotle, this serious person "distributes the greater good to oneself" and, in all things, "distributes (*nēmo*) more (*pleon*) of the noble to oneself." While there is need to be a lover-of-self in this way, there is no use or need (*chrē*) to be a lover-of-self as the many say (1169a6–29). Readers should hesitate to put much stock in this conclusion about the superiority of the serious person. For one, when Aristotle first brings forth the decent person as a model for friendship toward oneself, he notes that even serious persons assume they are decent, which suggests decency is superior. Second, the serious person's distributing more of the noble and good-things to oneself indicates such a person is one-holding-more and therefore a reproachable lover-of-self.[49]

Some may find it puzzling for the serious person's pursuit of the noble things to be a reproachable love-of-self, especially when Aristotle declares the serious person's love-of-self is preferable to many's (though both concern the same things). To understand the nature of the serious person's error, recall from Book I that the noble things (and the just things) hold much difference and wandering that make them seem—unlike the good things—to be by law and not by nature. This difference and wandering is evident in the contrast between the serious person choosing many different things to distribute more of the noble to oneself, and the decent person holding a singular concern with gratifying and trusting-the-rule of the intellect. This serious person's pursuit of the noble may seem choiceworthy because these actions involve virtue, but notice that "virtue" never appears in this comparison between the serious and decent persons. While the potential for virtue to provide for what is needful for all and good for each person privately precedes this account of the decent and the serious person, Aristotle refrains from asserting that virtue is truly capable of providing what is good and needful in life in this way. Perhaps it is not possible to do the noble things to profit oneself and provide for the common benefit.[50] To see how this is true, readers must follow Book IX to the end to discover through the decent person how virtue rests on the foundation of choice and contemplation of the good.

Following the unprovided matters concerning love-of-self, Aristotle takes up disagreements about the happy person's need for friends with questions that merge themes from Book I with Book VIII's beginning for the inquiry into friendship. The argument against the happy person needing friends is those who are blessed and self-sufficient need the addition of nothing since the good things are present for them. If the friend is "another self" (*heteron auton*),[51] one would only need to provide a friend if one lacks this capacity. On the other side of the dispute, it looks strange to distribute all the good things to the happy person except friends, "which seem to be greatest of the external goods." If it belongs to a friend more to produce well-being than be affected by it, it belongs to the good person and virtue "to be a benefactor" (literally a "good-worker," *euergeteō*), and it is nobler for the serious person to produce well-being for friends. This need to be a benefactor suits times of good fortune, while bad fortune requires friends to be benefactors to oneself. One also sees a need for friends from the strangeness of producing the blessed person as solitary since "no one would choose (*haireō*) to hold all the good things according to oneself, for the human being [is] political and naturally living-together." And so friends are present to the happy person who holds all the good things by nature, and it is stronger to pass the days together with friends and decent people (1169b3–22). Like Book I, self-sufficiency in Book IX remains bound to choice, the good things, and human beings' political nature. Unlike Book I, Aristotle refrains from reminding readers that this political nature holds a boundary and that friends (along with parents and descendants) do not stretch without-limit.[52] Considering Book VIII begins with similar statements about no one choosing to live without friends while holding the other good things, readers must wonder why happiness does not appear in Book VIII and self-sufficiency's boundaries do not coincide with its return in Book IX. What does friendship teach about the good that happiness and self-sufficiency fail to deliver on their own terms?

The statement that friends "seem to be the greatest of the external goods" points back to Book IV's account of the "great-souled man" (*megalopsuchos*), whose central concern is his own worthiness for great things (on account of which he is among the noblest persons). People speak of worth in relation to external goods, and honor is set-down as the greatest of the external goods. The problem facing greatness of soul—which looks like "some adornment (*kosmos*) of the virtues"— is that even when the great-souled man receives honors proper (*oikeiōn*) to him from serious persons, there is no honor worthy of "all-complete virtue" (*pantelēs aretē*). Though this means the great-souled man is measured toward fortune, wealth, and dynasty (three things for which one chooses to live with friends in Book VIII),[53] the latter two things are choiceworthy to him because of honor (1123b14–21, 1124a1–20). While the great-souled man is worthy of careful examination in his own right,[54] his character raises a question relevant to politics and economics: Why is honor the greatest of external goods in Book IV, yet friends *seem* to be such goods in Book IX? Given honor's tie to worth, readers should also know that the only other moral virtue in the *Ethics* to receive a designation of "complete" (*teleia*) virtue is justice (1129b25–26). Like greatness of soul, justice concerns worth, and Book VIII reveals that when it comes to the equal, the just's primary concern is "worth," whereas friendship's is a certain quantity. In Book I, defining happiness with the serious person and proper virtue as an activity of the soul according to complete virtue sets the stage for a threefold distribution of good things (external, body, and soul).[55] Unlike earlier approaches to happiness and the good things in the *Ethics*, Books VIII and IX are reluctant to use this distribution, suggesting that friendship offers a view of the good things that is more complete than the apparent peaks of moral virtue.

Using the blessed person as a model, Aristotle challenges the idea that friends are external goods by reminding readers of pleasure's importance in life.[56] When good things are present to the blessed person, there is no need for useful friends. Though it initially seems the blessed person has no need for pleasant friends since this person's life is pleasant in itself, this assumes happiness is like some piece of acquisition, not an activity. In a heavily conditional argument, Aristotle wonders if the good person's activity is serious and pleasant (which is itself properly-one's-own), and if "we ourselves have the capacity to contemplate" those near to us and their actions better than those that are properly-one's-own, then the serious person's actions are pleasant to those who are good, for both hold the pleasant things by nature. Consequently, the blessed person will need such friends if one chooses (*proaireō*) to contemplate the actions of those who are decent and what is properly-one's-own, and such are the actions of the good person who is a friend. Similarly, given the need to live pleasantly, since it is not easy to hold-together in activity according to itself, if the serious person delights in actions according to virtue, there might be some practice according to virtue from living-together with those who are good, thus spurring a most holding-together activity that is pleasant according to itself (1169b22–1170a13). The common characteristic of these arguments is the pleasure that is properly-one's-own spurring activities, and this pleasure begins with what a person chooses to contemplate. The argument echoes many of the themes in Book VIII's later account of complete friendships where Aristotle relegates useful friendships to the marketplace while elevating pleasant friendships as more liberal, for no one can hold-together in what is painful, even if it contains the good itself.[57] With happiness, Aristotle uses friendship and pleasure to prepare readers for seeing what is naturally liberal in life is not acquisition, but choosing to contemplate the good.

Although the preceding argument aligns the need for friends with Book I's definition of happiness as an activity of the soul according to complete virtue, a "more natural" (*phusikōteron*) examination of friendship finds the choice of the good and pleasant in life is more authoritative than happiness and virtue. From the serious friend looking to be choiceworthy by nature (and thus good by nature and pleasant) to the serious person, Aristotle turns to how people mark-the-boundary of living for human beings as "sense-perception (*aisthēsis*) or intelligence (*noēsis*)." With a capacity, "the authoritative thing is in the activity," and living authoritatively looks like "perceiving or think-ing" (*to aisthanesthai ē noein*) because "living [is] among the good and pleasant things according to itself, for [it is] itself bounded (*hōrismenon*), and bounded belongs to the nature of the good. The good is by nature and for the decent person, on account of which it looks to be pleasant for all." Here Aristotle cautions against taking hold either of a wretched or ruined living, or one in pain. Though he declares a wretched or ruined living is unbounded (*aoristos*), what concerns pain awaits readers in the things holding ahead (*tois echomenois*) in the inquiry (1170a13–25). Within the *Ethics*' inquiry into friendship, Aristotle's appeal to a "more natural" perspective recalls Book VIII's opening chapter and its turn away from the unprovided matters regarding nature (including *erōs* and the advantageous) toward the proper (*oikeia*) and human concern with characters and passions. Since Book I, there is an implicit tension in the *Ethics* over whether what is naturally most pleasant belongs to friendship or *erōs*.[58] With this introduction to Book IX's more natural view of life, Aristotle suggests that friendship holds a naturally bounded sense of the good and the pleasant.[59]

Before proceeding with Book IX's natural account of friendship, it is necessary to outline how these arguments root economics and politics within political philosophy. In the *Politics*' inquiry into the money-making art, one cause of the art of retail-trade is people mistaking living well as excessive bodily enjoyments and making-an-attempt (*peiraō*) to provide this excess through producing all things as if money-making is their end by using their own capacities in ways that are not according to nature. This argument imme-diately sets up the conclusion that the art of household management holds a boundary, but the art of retail-trade does not. From the *Ethics*' perspective, this errant use of one's own capacities represents a failure to live according to sense-perception and intelligence bounded by the good, thus revealing a wretched and ruined nature. Aristotle's instruction in Book IX of the *Ethics* to avoid looking at wretched and ruined natures recurs in Book I of the *Politics*' inquiry into the slave by nature where the soul's rule over the body and the intellect's free political rule over desire by holding *logos* is according to nature. What holds together the *Politics*' inquiries into money-making art and slavery is not only how these things hold as part of household management, but the broader context of assuming that the work and capacity that marks-the-boundary of human nature and self-sufficiency comes to ruin if the city abolishes (*anaireō*) itself. Prior to the argument that justice is the political good that completes human nature is the observation that a person without the capacity to form-community is a beast, while the one who needs nothing through self-sufficiency and is not part of the city is a god.[60] In light of the *Ethics*, the *Politics*' early attempt to look at economics and politics as if the authoritative work of choosing the good belongs to communities instead of the persons who form them is not natural. And if the political philosopher's work is contemplating pleasures and pains as the architect of the end toward which all things are simply good or bad, the statement in Book IX of the *Ethics* that what concerns pain is forthcoming indicates readers will need Book X to complete their view of political philosophy.

Returning to the natural examination of friendship, Aristotle's *logos* next draws upon the practice of friendship to engage readers' own perception of the good. It looks like living is good and pleasant from everyone desiring (*oregō*) it (most of all the decent and the blessed, whose life is most choiceworthy). Just as everyone perceives their own sense-perceptions, every person perceives being active (*energeō*) in thinking (*noeō*), so that through perceiving or thinking:

> we are (for being is either perceiving or thinking), and the perceiving of living belongs to the things pleasant according to themselves (for by nature living [is] good), and perceiving the present good in oneself [is] pleasant), and living [is] choiceworthy and most of all for those who are good, so that being is good to them and pleasant (for they take pleasure in perceiving-together [*sunaistha-nomai*] the good according to itself), and as the serious person holds towards oneself, also [one holds] towards the friend (for the friend is another self). Therefore, just as being is itself choiceworthy for each person, so is the friend's being, or nearly such. (1170a25–b10)

The many steps to this argument all move toward the same conclusion: human beings hold a natural sense that living is good and pleasant according to itself. This sense does not depend on virtue or happiness, but in the perceiving of one's own sense-perception and thinking. Through such perception of one's own activity is a sense of how a person holds toward oneself, and how one holds toward oneself derives from a choice of how one holds toward the good. The friends one chooses are the most personal extension of one's own choice of the good to another. Friendship itself is the naturally pleasant activity of the intellect and desire holding together and perceiving-together the good.[61]

Lest readers think Aristotle's natural view of friendship is far more theoretical than their own experience with friends, he brings in *logos* to reveal the whole nature of friendship and, through this, gestures toward a complete view of economic and political life. Friends need to perceive-together their being through "living-together and forming-community in *logoi* and thought, for in this way seems what is said [to be] the living-together of human beings, and not as of fatted beasts grazing in the same place." If being is choiceworthy according to itself, good by nature, and pleasant for the blessed person, it is also choiceworthy for the friend. Since what is choiceworthy needs to be present to the blessed person to avoid being in need, the happy person will need serious friends (1170b10–19). Implicit in Aristotle's comparison between human beings and fatted beasts is the recognition that both are active in perceiving-together their being, but only human beings' living-together includes the activity of thinking and community in *logos* and thought. The bridge between human sense-perception and thinking that engages their pleasantly active sense of the good is *logos*. Yet there is a gap between the natural view of living-together for human beings and the happy person's need for friends: human beings' forming-community in *logoi* and thought is open to a wide variety of goods that they choose for their own being.

To consider the significance of this gap over the good for economics and politics, readers should follow the comparison between living-together for human beings versus fatted beasts back to Book I where the good and happiness look like pleasure because the many choose (*proaireō*) the life of enjoyment akin to that of fatted beasts. The other lives are the political life (through which the good first shows itself as what is properly-one's-own), the contemplative life (the nature and end of which is open), and the money-making life (which is something forced or violent, with wealth not being the sought-for good). In Book IX, the verb Aristotle uses in its passive voice for "grazing" (*nemō*) holds a different meaning in the active voice ("to distribute") that first appears in Book I with the threefold distribution of good things. The relevance of this difference between the passive and active senses of *nemō* for economics comes forth by remembering that in Book I of the *Politics* it is nature that produces, marks-the-boundaries, and sets-standing-apart animals' lives toward the choosing (*hairesis*) of food with the pleasant. The human lives, in contrast, hold their work and provide food either in relation to what is natural, or through exchange and retail-trade. Before Aristotle examines exchange and retail-trade (thus bringing community and *logos* into the mix), the attempt to view all natural things in terms of acquisition runs into the problematic hypothetical argument that war is by nature a just art of acquisition.[62] From the perspective of acquisition, Aristotle's pun on *nemō* in the *Ethics* regarding what it means to live-together suggests that animals' passive acquisition of food from nature cannot inform human acquisition, for this requires a necessary distribution of goods through exchange between communities that cannot exist without *logos*, thought, the choice of some good, and the pleasure bound to this choice.

Sown within Aristotle's more natural approach to friendship that seems to affirm the life of the serious person is a correction of this person's character through the decent that is important for the last set of arguments from Book IX that bound political and economic self-sufficiency with friendship's natural sense of the good. When Aristotle first wonders if there is friendship toward oneself, it seems the decent and serious persons both desire, choose, and labor at holding the good things for the sake of the intellect (which each person seems to be most of all). Yet only the decent person finds pleasure in being well-provided with contemplative things, and once the *logos* takes up the unprovided matters over love-of-self, the decent person who trusts-the-rule of the intellect that chooses the best thing for itself is set apart from the serious person who distributes more of the noble to oneself in all things. Once the natural account of friendship reaches its end, the decent and serious persons come back together with the understanding that life is choiceworthy through the pleasant activity of perceiving and thinking of the good present in oneself through *logos*. True love-of-self begins with love of the good. With the decent person, readers discover the good is not something one distributes to oneself, but something one holds within oneself. Through this argument, there is now an answer to what it means for the intellect to hold sense-perception of first-principles as unmoving boundaries "of which there is no *logos*," for friendship demonstrates how the *logos* in which friends choose to form-community and live-together grows from their unmoving sense of the good. Since true prudence needs the intellect, and because politics and economics are the same *hexis* as prudence, it follows that friendship discloses the true natural boundaries of political and economic life.[63]

After working through the *logos* that uses the happy person's need for friends to provide readers a demonstration from their own choices that they hold an intellectual sense-perception of the good, Aristotle takes up the arguments about the number of friends one should produce that first appear in this chapter's introduction. Knowing the decent person's naturally good and pleasant intellectual love-of-self fully corrects the reproachable love-of-self belonging to the person holding-more casts new light on the argument that having more friends than are adequate for the life that is properly-one's-own is an impediment to living nobly (as is most evident from the laborious work of serving friends toward use). The political and economic significance of this argument becomes apparent in the question that immediately follows it: Is there some measure to the number of people with whom one could be a serious friend just as there is some measure for a city? Aristotle answers, "The certain quantity (*to poson*) is not perhaps-equally (*isōs*) some one thing (*hen ti*), but anything between some bounds (*hōrismenōn*)," as is evident from someone not having the capacity to live-together and to distribute (*dianemō*) oneself to many. It is also "troublesome work" (*ergōdes*)[64] for all one's friends to pass the days together and befriend each other; further, the delighting and suffering together that is properly-one's-own (*oikeiōs*) is difficult among many (1170b20–1171a8). Through the experience of friendship and living-together, Aristotle teaches that there are boundaries to political and economic life. While there is no precise number for these boundaries, there is a sense that it is laborious and troublesome work to distribute oneself beyond what is properly-one's-own. Since the money-making art (*chrēmatistikē*) is toward use (*chrēsis*) and aims to distribute useful things (*chrēmata*), its provision for living nobly depends on its respect for the boundaries of what is properly-one's-own (*oikeia*). The same holds true for the city in relation to the household (*oikia*) as communities, and for political rule in relation to the art of household management's (*oikonomikē*) rule. In every case, friendship preserves the sense of what is properly-one's-own that holds people back from laborious work *and* toward a truly free and liberal life.

How friendship houses its freedom and liberality within its natural sense of boundaries is also apparent through *erōs*. Aristotle proposes it may not "hold well to seek to be as many-friended as possible," confining oneself instead to what is adequate for living-together since it seems one does not admit to be an "intense friend" to many just as there is not *erōs* for many, "for this wishes to be some excess or superiority (*huperbolē*) of friendship, and this [is] towards one, and intense [friendship] towards few." It looks like things hold this way in acts, in part because those who happen upon everyone as if they are properly-one's-own are obsequious,[65] while those who are like citizens (*politikōs*) and friends to many are "truly decent." Thus, those who are friends through virtue and themselves are not toward many, and it is either loved or something to be content with (*agapēton*) to discover few of such friends (1171a8–20). The appeal to *erōs* serves two purposes. First, it provides another experience of the natural boundary to the number of people with whom living-together is possible. Second, if *erōs* wishes to be intense friendship, then friendship is more of an end than *erōs*. Citizenship as a form of friendship is commensurate with the decent and love-of-self so long as one does not treat everyone as properly-one's-own (i.e., as if they belong to one's own household). Rounding out these seemingly disparate arguments is the first mention of friendships according to virtue since the more natural examination. What unites these arguments is the final statement about having few of these friends being "loved" or "something to be content with," a term Book I applies first to taking hold of and preserving the good for one person alone rather than cities and nations, and later to the precision of any *logos* of the noble, just, and good things.[66] The boundaries to the human good may not be precise in *logos*, but people sense their truth in the loves (*philia*, *erōs*, and *agapē*) necessary for forming communities in households, cities, *logos*, and thought.

In Book IX's final chapter, Aristotle gives more content to the broad scope of living-together in a community while echoing every person's need to hold sense-perception of the good by wondering if living-together is most choiceworthy for friends based on how seeing is the most loved (*agapētaton*) sense-perception that lovers choose more than the other senses. In response,

Aristotle says, "For friendship [is] a community, and as one holds towards oneself, in this way [one holds] towards a friend. And just as the sense-perception concerning oneself that one *is* [is] choiceworthy, so too [is the sense-perception] concerning the friend, and this activity comes to be in living-together, so that in all likelihood they aim themselves at this." For friends, being belongs to that for the sake of which they choose living, and so they pass the days together in whatever they love (*agapaō*) most of all in life. Some friends drink together, play dice together, exercise together, hunt together, or philosophize together, for from their wish to live-together, they produce and form-community in these things (1171b29–1172a8). Book IX's earlier description of friends engaged in the naturally good and pleasant activity of perceiving-together their being and forming-community in *logos* now appears in wholly human terms, with three forms of love all bound to what people choose as good and pleasant in their lives. The goods friends hold in common do not appear in a threefold distribution, but bound within the activity of friendship that necessarily involves the body and the soul, though perhaps not always external goods. The initial comparison between friends and lovers opens readers to friendship's wholeness by encouraging them to notice that just as their sense-perception holds more than seeing, their friendships hold paths to choosing many goods in life. Additionally, there is a broadening of what constitutes living-together, for if friends hold toward each other as they hold toward themselves, they do not need to live-together like lovers who rely solely on seeing each other. As Book VIII reveals, friendship is with choice and from a *hexis* because friends hold to be active even when not being in the same place loosens their activity.[67] When it comes to living-together in friendship, friends holding the good in common begins with them holding the good within themselves.[68]

The last argument in Book IX and all of the *Ethics'* inquiry into friendship contains an appeal to the decent that turns Aristotle's *logos* back toward pleasure much like the decent turns readers toward friendship at the end of Book VII. Contrary to the unsteady and wretched friendship of those who are base is the friendship of decent persons that increases-together with their association. Through being active, correcting one another, and taking an impression of the things satisfying to themselves, it seems decent persons become better. With this last look at the friendship between the decent, Aristotle proposes going through what concerns pleasure (1172a8–15). At first glance, this need to return to pleasure seems like a non-sequitur. While Book IX's last chapter draws on its natural account of friendship and the pleasant activity of perceiving-together the good according to itself, these concluding arguments about choice and decent friends omit any mention of pleasure within friendship. Although Books VIII and IX provide some separation between the good and pleasant as ends, Book X begins with an acknowledgment that there is more to learn about this choice. What economics and politics stand to learn from this choice is present in Aristotle's final characterizations of friendship as involving people producing and forming-community in good things through which their very own being increases-together in friendship. If production, increase, and community are all bound by the naturally pleasant choice of the good within friendship, then the production and increase of wealth within and between political communities are also bound to this choice.

## CONCLUSION: FRIENDSHIP, PHILOSOPHY, AND FREEDOM IN ECONOMICS AND POLITICS (*ETHICS* 1163B1–5)

In the *Politics'* inquiry into the money-making art, production and increase occur in relation to an idea that Aristotle omits from the natural account of friendship in the *Ethics*: gain. Following the provision of legal-currency for necessary exchange, with experience, retail-trade became more of an art concerning how to produce the most gain. And while both the arts of household management and retail-trade use legal-currency, some exchange the former art's work for the latter's and go through-to-the-end (*diateleō*) supposing they need to preserve or increase the substance (*ousia*) of legal-currency without-limit. Though "gain" emerges as a defining characteristic of the art of retail-trade, the term has no other appearances in Book I of the *Politics*. Similarly, "gain" appears only three times in the *Ethics'* inquiry into friendship (twice in Book VIII's final chapter, and once in Book IX's first chapter).[69] Two questions arise from these considerations. First, since both friendship and economics (which encompasses household management and all forms of exchange) naturally hold a common concern with producing, preserving, and increasing good things, why is gain rare in Aristotle's accounts of these things? Second, why is gain a corrosive idea in economics but not friendship?

The two appearances of gain in Book VIII of the *Ethics'* final chapter allude to its natural foundation. In a friendship between someone in-need (*endeēs*) and someone holding-over that person, it looks like each person correctly deems oneself worthy of something, and each should distribute more (*pleon*) of something to the other. To the person in-need, the one holding-over distributes gain; to the person holding-over, the person in-need distributes honor as a gift of virtue and a good-work (1163b1–5). This argument responds to the earlier problem of what to do in useful friendships between the poor and the wealthy where the problem of worth (partly displayed through laughable and unequal lovers) opens the question of whether or not desire (*orexis*) is for the middle term that is good. Two shifts occur with the present case: it is not a useful friendship, and the resolution to the problem of worth is not a middle term, but distributing more of disparate good things fit for each person. Although Aristotle does not describe it in this way, the argument about gain offers a more liberal perspective on worth than the poor and the wealthy. Both the person in-need and the one holding-over this person need something good, but these goods are bound to who they are, not how they are useful to each other. These persons also seem to embody an unreproachable love-of-self in the sense that they avoid being ones-holding-more who distribute to themselves more either of things used or needed (*chrēma*), or honors.[70] To liberate oneself from the problems of gain and worth, one must understand the comprehensive nature of human beings' need for the good.

By revealing that the pleasant is naturally bound to the choice to contemplate the good—a choice that is properly-one's-own—friendship provides readers a glimpse into why gain becomes corrosive in economic life. In Book VII of the *Ethics*, Aristotle places gain among the desires (*epithumia*), pleasures, and good things for which there is blame when one acts contrary to *logos* by going to excess and being more serious about them than there is need to be. After introducing the political philosopher and on his way to defining pleasure as "the activity of a *hexis* according to nature" that completes one's nature (thus making pleasure simply good), Aristotle describes "the contemplative activity belonging to the nature not being in-need" as a pleasure without pain and desire. This contemplative activity belongs to the intellect, the nature of which is not in-need like the body, hence why its contemplation of the good is naturally free and the source of what is truly liberal in life. Though the intellect is not present by name in the *Politics*' inquiry into the money-making art, its activity is present from the start when Aristotle invites readers to contemplate all of acquisition and introduces the money-maker as someone who contemplates sources of useful things, acquisition, and wealth. After the art of retail-trade enters the inquiry, the money-making art contemplates how to produce wealth and useful things. In the inquiry's last chapter, the use of the money-making art holds within itself both "free contemplation" and "necessary experience," a contemplation later set apart from those who find something beneficial in contemplating stories of those who succeed in money-making. With the *Ethics*' help, it now possible to see how contemplation in money-making admits of being free or unfree: either contemplation takes its bearings from the intellect's naturally pleasant sense of the good to ensure the use, production, increase, and gain of wealth corresponds with need, *or* the intellect's contemplation and all economic activity are subject to ruin by desires, enjoyments, and pleasures that are excessive and without-limit.[71]

Through uncovering how contemplation of the good is the necessary foundation for all that is free and liberal in economic life, the importance of friendship prioritizing a certain quantity (*poson*) over worth when it comes to the equal for Aristotle's political philosophy begins to become clear. Aside from its two appearances in Book VIII's comparison between friendship and the just, the only other time "a certain quantity" appears in the *Ethics'* examination of friendship is in Book IX's setting the measure of friends with whom one could live-together as "between some bounds" that are properly-one's-own (the argument also implies that the city's measure is between bounds). The path to this argument begins with Aristotle identifying the unreproachable love-of-self with the decent person who loves (*agapaō*) and gratifies the intellect as the most authoritative thing in oneself through an analogy with the city as a "whole set-standing-together" (*sustēma*). Despite the kinship between the city and the decent person being how they are set-standing toward what is authoritative, the natural love-of-self ultimately concerns holding (*echō*) toward and holding-together (*sunechō*) in contemplating the good, an activity and pleasure that is properly-one's-own. The difference between the most authoritative political community being "set-standing" and each person "holding" toward the good is not trivial. From the first sentence of the *Politics*, Aristotle declares "every community is set-standing-together (*sunistēmi*) for the sake of some good." In Book I's second chapter, the attempt to contemplate the city as if it naturally-grows concludes with praise for the first person who set-standing-together a community as a "cause of the greatest goods" because of the supposed completion of human nature through law and the just.[72] Since the *Ethics* teaches that the just puts worth ahead of a certain quantity, it seems that justice is deficient for completing human nature because how people are set-standing in community cannot provide them a truly trustworthy sense of how they hold toward the good.

To illustrate justice's deficiencies when compared to friendship in providing for the human need to trust in holding the good, consider how the external view of acquisition in Book I of the *Politics* that focuses solely on "standing" becomes hostile to human freedom. The account of natural acquisition that begins with how nature sets-standing-apart (*diistēmi*) animals' lives with their different pleasures bound to the choosing of food concludes with the specious argument that war might be a just art of acquisition when used against certain human beings. This argument hinges on the assumption that nature produces nothing incomplete or in vain. Though one could attempt to tie this argument to the prior examination of slavery, readers should remember that Aristotle twice denies in this inquiry that nature produces human beings who are set-standing-apart in body and soul as free or slave *and* are worthy of being such. A crucial challenge to this view of nature occurs earlier in Book I where the first statement in the *Politics* about nature producing nothing in vain leads to Aristotle defining human beings as political animals because they hold *logos*. Through *logos*, human beings hold sense-perception of what is pleasant and painful, advantageous and harmful, good and bad, just and unjust, and "community in these things produces a household and a city." The specious argument that there are human beings who naturally stand worthy of acquisition as slaves fails to account for what holding *logos* means for freedom in political community and acquisition. The economic consequences of this omission are evident when Book I's third chapter starts with the statement that the complete household is set-standing-together from slaves and free persons, but ends by declaring how the money-making art holds in relation to household management is something one must contemplate.[73] Both slavery and the money-making art raise questions about how the household holds toward acquisition. Since these are not questions of standing and worth, one can only answer them through a *logos* that concerns holding the good.

For Aristotle, political philosophy is the only practical pursuit that provides for true economic and political freedom. In Book VI of the *Ethics*, despite showing wisdom requires the intellectual sense-perception of natural first-principles, it still seems wisdom is incapable of providing for the human good based on the errant assumption that its concern is—in part from the example of Thales—the divine nature from which the cosmos is set-standing-together. But to latch on to this characterization of wisdom is to ignore his care since Book I to attempt to provide for the human need to hold knowledge of the good as the end that prevents choosing from going without-limit, thus leaving desire (*orexis*) empty and vain. In the *Politics*, the only two mentions of "wisdom" are in relation to Thales, whose success in money-making countered the reproach he received for philosophy not being beneficial. While the *Politics* leaves open the question of how wisdom is beneficial for the human good, the *Ethics'* analogy between acquisition and *hexis* suggests wisdom is beneficial through its active holding of the good, an activity that seems more within reach after discovering love-of-self as the natural foundation for friendship in Book IX. This discovery is remarkable given how clarity on love-of-self avoids the failure to see the different forms of the just things in Book V on account of them having the same name. Similar problems appear in Book I of the *Politics*: first in the *logoi* about slavery by law through conquest in war exchanging-upon some good, then in the exchange of the art of household management's work for the art of retail-trade's because they exchange-upon the use of legal-currency.[74] Whereas the confusion about the forms of just things and economic exchange cannot resolve itself on political and economic terms, there is little confusion on the forms of friendship, even if they all hold something good and pleasant. What first-time readers of the *Ethics* do not know as they head into Book X is that they are on the brink of discovering the intellectual foundations of freedom with philosophy—the love and friendship of wisdom—playing a decisive role in deepening their sense of what is properly-one's-own in political and economic life.

## Chapter 7

# Justice, Pleasure, and the Good

Although Aristotle's inquiry into friendship in Books VIII and IX of the *Ethics* provides an accessible account of how to choose what is naturally good in life and live pleasantly—thus allowing readers to uncover through love-of-self (*philautos*) the foundational choices of the good in political and economic life—his political philosophy is not yet done with pleasure, the subject to which he returns at the beginning of Book X (X.1–6) before completing his account of happiness (X.7–8) and contemplating *logos* and law to move into the *Politics* (X.9). The introduction to this book's third chapter claims that readers who seek Aristotle's economic teaching by supplementing *Politics* I.8–11 with *Ethics* V.5's account of the just and legal-currency's worth risk concealing the depths of Aristotle's political philosophy in their interpretation. After demonstrating how Books VI through IX of the *Ethics* unfold the nature of choice with a careful awareness of how pleasure affects human beings' pursuit of the good—the political philosopher's natural concern—readers can now begin moving toward understanding why justice offers an incomplete perspective on politics and economics. From the beginning of Book V, pleasure presents a problem justice cannot solve. The natural remedy to this problem is friendship, and through approaching Book X with this in mind, readers find a richer sense of *oikonomikē* ("the art of household management") depends on deepening their sense of what is "properly-one's-own" (*oikeion*) with political philosophy's provision of a trustworthy *logos* concerning what is naturally good and pleasant in life.

In the *Ethics*, the concerns of politics and economics intersect in Book V's inquiry into justice (*dikaiosunē*), and the examination of friendship in Books VIII and IX. Readers who approach the *Ethics* assuming economics' primary concerns are exchange and money-making may wish to focus most on Book V where three forms (*eidos*) of justice address these matters. The first concerns "distributions" (*dianomē*) of honor or useful things (*chrēmata*) for those forming-community in the regime, the second is in "the things exchanged-together" (*sunallagma*),[1] and the third regards the exchange of legal-currency that holds-together (*sunechō*) communities. Aristotle identifies the first two forms as justice "according to a part" (*kata meros*), while the third—which "seems . . . to be the just simply"—does not fit either of the first two forms (1130b30–1131a9, 1132b21–1133a25). Though these forms of justice relate to Aristotle's political and economic teaching, they hold only a partial view of these pursuits. Thus, before looking more closely at these partial forms of justice in the next chapter, it is necessary to see how Book V anticipates the *Ethics'* dialectic between pleasure (Books VII and X) and friendship (Books VIII and IX) that provides political philosophy's authoritative perspective on politics, economics, self-sufficiency, and the pursuit of happiness in Book X.

From the preceding chapter, one clear way Book V's inquiry into justice points beyond itself is through the introduction of the one-holding-more (*pleonektēs*), a person who Book IX reveals as holding a reproachable love-of-self (*philautos*) through which one distributes to oneself more of the things one uses or needs (*chrēma*), honors, and bodily pleasures, desiring (*oregō*) an excess of these good things and delighting in desires (*epithumia*), passions, and what is without-*logos* in the soul. Contrary to the one-holding-more is the decent person's (*epieikēs*) unreproachable love-of-self through which one loves (*agapaō*), gratifies, and trusts-the-rule (*peitharcheō*) of the intellect, choosing (*haireō*) what is best by living according to *logos* instead of passion and desiring something other than the seemingly advantageous things. With the discovery of the decent person's love-of-self, Aristotle criticizes producing more friends toward use than are adequate for the life that is properly-one's-own (*ton oikeion bion*) as laborious (*epiponos*) and toilsome work (*ergōdes*), for the certain quantity (*to poson*) of friendship is between bounds. The living-together that is properly-one's-own means people do not have the capacity to distribute themselves to many. A similar conclusion arises through *erōs* and its wish to be some excess or superiority (*huperbolē*) of friendship, which helps show it is truly decent to be friends to many like citizens, but not as if everyone is properly-one's-own.[2] Unlike the three partial forms of justice, friendship—through the decent love-of-self—provides boundaries to political and economic life through what is properly-one's-own.

Knowing friendship and the decent people's natural sense of what is properly-one's-own in life from the *Ethics* allows readers to see justice's insufficiency to account for how politics and economics hold toward each other in the *Politics'* inquiry into the money-making art. The first appearance of the "just" in this inquiry is the specious argument that war is by nature a just art of acquisition when used toward human beings whom nature supposedly produces neither incomplete nor in vain as fit for being ruled but unwilling. The second appearance occurs when Aristotle identifies the money-making art's name as "just" because it does not seem there is a limit to wealth and acquisition. This runs contrary to the natural art of acquisition that needs either to be present or provided to the art of household management "so that there is present a store of such useful things that are necessary towards living, and useful to community in a city or a household." This looks to be "true wealth" (*alēthinos ploutos*), "for the self-sufficiency of such acquisition is not without-limit towards good living (*agathēn zōēn*)." The final appearance of what is just comes at the end of being unprovided over how to subordinate money-making to the household manager and politician when Aristotle "justly" blames the art of usury and declares it is with most good-*logos* hated for producing more (*pleon*) legal-currency from itself through interest and contrary to its provision for exchange.[3] The problem with the first argument about the just is it approaches acquisition with complete disregard for community. The second argument suggests what is "just" can identify forms of wealth and acquisition contrary to what is according to nature for households, cities, self-sufficiency, and good living. Only in the third argument is the just according to nature and good-*logos*, but it does not provide for how household managers and politicians subordinate money-making to their communities' ends.

The reason why justice is deficient in providing a true sense of the natural boundaries to politics and economics is its incapacity to be—like friendship—a *hexis* with its pleasure bound to the activity of holding oneself toward the good. Within the *Ethics*, there are two textual justifications for judging justice in light of friendship. First, while "justice" and what is "just" (*dikaios, dikē*) appear in Books VIII and IX, aside from one mention of "friend" (*philos*), neither "friendship" (*philia*) nor its "love" (*phileō*) ever appear in Book V.[4] Second, at the beginning of Book VIII, Aristotle observes how it looks like friendship holds-together cities and is the remedy legislators seek in the form of like-mindedness (*homonoia*) to drive out standing-faction (*stasis*); later, he characterizes useful friendships as things of the marketplace (*agoraiōn*) in opposition to more liberal (*eleutherion*) pleasant friendships by alluding to people's need to hold-together pleasantly with the good. In Book IX, happiness briefly appears not as an acquisition, but the most holding-together activity of choosing (*proaireō*) to contemplate what is decent and properly-one's-own. This argument precedes the more natural perspective on friendship as living-together and forming-community in *logos* and thought (*dianoia*) because being is choiceworthy, good, and pleasant according to itself. Because the path toward this natural view of friendship begins with questions about self-sufficiency and the need for friends, it should be set against Book I of the *Politics* and its attempt to define the end of the human work as self-sufficiency based strictly on how the city is set-standing-together, not each person's choice of the good.[5] If political communities and the economic exchanges within them all reflect how human beings hold toward the good, then friendship's insight into the nature of *hexis* and pleasure must take precedence over justice and its concern with standing (*histēmi*) for those who seek a true understanding of politics and economics within Aristotle's political philosophy.

Because friendship holds happiness and self-sufficiency toward the good through a truly natural sense of what is pleasant and properly-one's-own with the example of the decent person's natural love-of-self, it is best to approach Book X of the *Ethics'* teaching on happiness and self-sufficiency by first working through how Book V reveals that only decency (*epieikeia*) is a *hexis*, not justice. This approach is necessary because Book X's examination of happiness and self-sufficiency does not occur until Aristotle makes a second inquiry into pleasure, one that begins with the search for a trustworthy *logos* about the good and pleasure. Perhaps the most important argument for bridging Books V and X is Book VII's revelation that human nature is not simple, holding some divine nature not in-need that pleasure completes as the contemplative "activity of the *hexis* according to nature." The subsequent recognition that the god's simple pleasure resides in an activity without-motion (*akinēsia*) provides an opening for readers to wonder how their nature can become decent, and this is how the *Ethics* turns toward friendship. This move is not possible without Aristotle's introduction of the political philosopher, the person who contemplates pleasures and pains as the architect of the end toward which all things are simply good or bad.[6] Because true love-of-self requires contemplation of the good that does not ruin itself through a false understanding of pleasure, it belongs solely to political philosophy to provide a *logos* about the good that frees human beings to use politics and economics in pursuit of happiness and self-sufficiency, all the while caring for what is properly-one's-own.

## JUSTICE, GAIN, PLEASURE, AND THE DECENT (*ETHICS* 1109A20–35, 1129A3–21, 1130A5–B5, 1134B18–1135A5, 1137A31–1138A3)

At the beginning of Book V, Aristotle subtly questions the hopes people have for justice *and* a key assumption about the moral virtues. Searching for what actions fit the middle term and mean that is justice, Aristotle observes that "we see" everyone wishes to say justice and injustice are *hexeis* from which people respectively wish for and do the practically just and unjust things. But it seems what holds in sciences (*epistēmē*) and capacities (*dunamis*) does not hold in *hexeis*. Although the first two things can be of contraries and a "good-*hexis*" (*euexia*) makes apparent both "the things conducive to the good-*hexis*" (*ta euektika*) and the "bad-*hexis*" (*kakexia*), the process of knowing or becoming familiar (*gnōrizō*) with these things does not work in reverse (i.e., one does not know or become familiar with a good-*hexis* through a bad-*hexis*). In Book III's account of the moral virtues, the mean, excess, and deficiency are all contrary to each other, and Aristotle associates moral virtue with "aiming" or "guessing" (*stochazomai*, like the cities and communities at the beginning of the *Politics*)[7] at the middle term since it is difficult to hit precisely, hence one must take hold of the least bad things (1129a3–21, 1109a20–35).[8] Compared to Book III, Book V's opening with good-*hexis* and bad-*hexis* no longer admits of approaching the good indirectly. To hold a good-*hexis*, one cannot mistake the good by nature for the apparent good because of pleasure (which is consistent with the serious person's judgment in Book III). Readers must also remain cognizant of Book III's distinction between wish (which is for an end) and choice (which is deliberate desire with *logos* and thought concerning things toward an end).[9] People may wish for justice to be a *hexis*, but that does not mean it is one, nor that others would choose to hold it.

The lone appearance of "friends" occurs near the one mention of "pleasure" in Book V with a closer look at the one-holding-more. The worst person who embodies the injustice that is the whole of vice is one who uses wretchedness toward oneself and one's friends, while the best person who embodies the justice that is the whole of virtue does the difficult work of using virtue toward another. The difference between justice and virtue is the former is toward another (*heteros*), while the latter is a *hexis* simply (and implicitly toward oneself). Further support for thinking there is a justice and injustice that are parts of the whole of virtue and vice comes from how a person who is active (*energeō*) as one-holding-more receives blame for some laborious-wickedness (*ponēria*) and according to injustice. Specifically, one-holding-more's "gaining" (*kerdainō*) holds its capacity toward another concerning honor, useful things, or preservation, "and we might hold some one name to take hold of all these things, and through pleasure from gain." Though this partial injustice has the same name as the whole of injustice because it marks-its-boundaries in the same class of things, the whole of injustice concerns all things that belong to the serious person (1130a5–b5). Aristotle refuses to name "justice" as the whole of virtue and *hexis* toward oneself. Readers must wait until Book IX for the happy and self-sufficient person as a model for someone who holds toward the friend as another self (*heteros autos*). Decent people are among those with whom such a person passes one's days, and through their example, Aristotle turns the serious person away from distributing more of the noble things to oneself, and toward holding a friend as another self in the naturally good and pleasant activity of contemplating the good by forming-community in *logos* and thought.[10] Although the one-holding-more commits injustice through the pleasure from gain, the only *hexis* fit to remedy this is not justice, but friendship and true love-of-self.[11]

An opening for the intellectual character of the decent to emerge in Book V appears in its seventh chapter's overview of the politically just (*to politikon dikaion*), which is on the one hand natural, and on the other hand lawful (*nomikon*). While the natural "holds the same capacity everywhere," it does not matter what the lawful is from the beginning (*archē*) until it is set-down (*tithēmi*). To some, it seems all the just things are lawful, since what is by nature is unmoving (*akinētos*) and holds the same capacity everywhere (such as fire burning the same in all places), yet people see the just things moving (*kineō*). But this is not how it holds, for there is something altogether moving (*kinētos*) that is by nature and not by nature (1134b18–30). In its immediate context, this abstract argument distinguishing the natural from the lawful in the politically just opens readers to the possibility that what is by nature is both moving and unmoving. Books VI and VII illuminate what justice itself cannot uncover about nature. In Book VI, recognizing that thought for the sake of an end moves what is practical and productive helps readers learn that choice is the first-principle or beginning (*archē*) of action, and the nature of choice—of human beings—is either desiring intellect (*orektikos nous*) or thinking desire (*orexis dianoētikē*). As the inquiry into prudence unfolds, readers learn this practical *hexis* needs the intellect's sense-perception of unmoving boundaries and first-principles. At the end of Book VII, the pleasure and activity of the god that rests in the absence of motion (*akinēsia*) is implicitly set within human nature alongside pleasures and activities of motion (*kinēsia*).[12] Since there is no way for the politically just to exist apart from human beings and choice, what is moving and unmoving by nature corresponds to human beings' sense of unmoving first-principles as ends and the choices that move toward and away from them.

The three examples Aristotle provides in support of what is just by nature being both moving and unmoving bring together human nature, economics, and politics in a way that alludes to their intellectual character. Among the things that admit to hold otherwise, if both are similarly moving, then it is clear what sort of things are not by nature, but lawful and "set-down-together by compact" (*sunthēkē*). For most human beings, by nature, the right hand is stronger, yet all admit of becoming ambidextrous. As for the things set-down-together by compact and the just things' advantage, in economics, they are like measures that are not equal everywhere: the measures are greater where buying occurs, but lesser where selling occurs. Finally, in politics, the just things that are not natural but human are not the same everywhere (as is evident by regimes not being the same), though there is one regime according to nature that is the same everywhere: the best regime (1134b30–1135a5). In these arguments, Aristotle broadens readers' sense of what is "by nature." The ambidexterity argument teaches that some things are given by nature (like the predominance of one hand over the other), but one could move this toward equal or greater strength in the other hand. With economics, the inequality of measures for buying or selling shows these movable things may obscure a need for exchange given by nature, for Book I of the *Politics* teaches that the provision of legal-currency set-down-together in agreement according to *logos* that produces the money-making art responds to an unequal distribution of things necessary according to nature. Finally, with regimes, although they have a human beginning that sets-down the lawful, there is no reason why regimes cannot move toward the best regime by nature, which Book VII of the *Politics* approaches by seeking the most choiceworthy life. As productive and practical *hexeis*, economics and politics concern things that admit to hold otherwise (exchange and regimes), and their provision for well-being requires choice and *logos* to trust in a truly complete discernment of what is good by nature.[13]

In the second to last chapter of Book V, Aristotle turns to decency (*epie-ikeia*) and the decent (*epieikēs*), stating in what way decency holds toward justice and the decent holds toward the just is what holds next for the inquiry to address. How these things are neither simply the same nor belong to a different class of things is evident in the way the praise for the decent person metaphorically leads to other things receiving praise as "decent" instead of "good" (which makes clear that more decent things are better). Still, from following the *logos*, it is strange for the decent to be more praiseworthy than the just, for if the two differ, either the just is not serious, or the decent is not just. But, if both are serious, they are the same thing (1137a31–b5). Aristotle's introduction to how decency and justice hold toward each other echoes the earlier inquiry seeking a distinction between partial justice and injustice *and* the whole of virtue and vice. This inquiry concludes that the partial injustice of the one-holding-more in seeking pleasure from gain marks-the-boundaries in the same class of things as the whole of injustice that concerns all things belonging to the serious person. While this inquiry is unclear about the nature of the *hexis* and virtue that holds toward oneself, the present inquiry is unclear on how the just and the decent hold toward the good.

Seeing readers are without-provision (*aporia*) about the decent and the just, Aristotle observes that it holds that these things are in some way correct and not contrary to each other. Although the decent and the just are the same thing and serious, the decent is stronger. What produces the matter without-provision is that the decent is not the just according to the law, but a "correction" (*epanorthōma*) of the lawfully just. The law needs correction because it necessarily speaks generally, taking hold of what is more (*to pleon*) when the nature of the practical things does not permit the legislator to speak to all of them when setting-down the law. Law is therefore deficient, and there is need for a decree to be the standard to "move-with" (*metakineō*) what is unbounded (*aoristos*) in the practical things. From these considerations, the decent person is one who chooses and is practical with the decent things, is not "precise to the just" (*akribodikaios*) and strains the law, but "one who takes less" (*allattōtikos*) even when holding the helpful law. This *hexis* is itself decency, and it is some justice (1137b5–1138a3). The strength of decency as a *hexis* over the just is that it can move with the nature of the practical things because it is naturally bound to choice in a way that law is not. Why this is true is not fully evident in Book V, though by the end of Book IX, the decent person's unreproachable love-of-self and the natural view of friendship shows how it is possible to live a naturally pleasant life bounded by choosing to hold oneself toward the good and contemplate the actions that are properly-one's-own. Because the one-holding-more commits injustice by seeking pleasure from gain through a reproachable love-of-self—an injustice that plagues economics and politics—one must seek the proper remedy for this errant love. Since gain is a choiceworthy pleasure and good thing that one needs to pursue according to *logos, and* because friendship binds gain to need, friendship must prove decisive in providing a true *logos* of pleasure that sets economics and politics firmly within the bounds of each person's choice and love of the good.[14]

## PLEASURE AND *LOGOS* (*ETHICS* 1172A19–1173A5)

Book X and the *Ethics'* second inquiry into pleasure begins by reiterating familiar arguments about pleasure that push readers toward the question of the good. After noting pleasures and pains are important for the young's education, Aristotle claims the greatest thing related to the virtue of character is delighting and hating what there is need to since these extend throughout all life, holding weight and capacity toward virtue and the happy life, for people choose (*proaireō*) the pleasant things and flee the painful things (1172a19–26). Though the first part of this summary echoes Book II's statement that all the matter of concern for virtue and the political art is pleasures and pains, it is conspicuously silent about the political art. This introduction also reminds readers of Book I's argument that knowledge (*gnōsis*) of the good holds great weight since it could allow people to hit upon what is needful by preventing their choosing (*haireō*) from going without-limit, thus leaving desire (*orexis*) empty and vain.[15]

Setting the stage to think more seriously about the good, Aristotle provides two competing arguments about pleasure: either pleasure is the good, or it is base. Within the latter opinion, some hold it because they trust (*peithō*) it, and others hold it supposing that it is better for life to lead the many (who are slaves to pleasures) to its contrary to come to the middle term. This, however, may not be nobly said (1172a26–34). Unlike Book VII which provides three competing views of pleasure (i.e., either it is not good, some are good, or, even if all are good, they do not admit to be the best thing),[16] Book X explicitly presents the opinion that pleasure is the good. At the same time, Book X reduces the number of arguments about pleasure to two, setting up the possibility that pleasure is some middle term between the good and the base. But if this not a nobly stated argument, resolving the question of whether pleasure is the good cannot come down to balancing between contraries like the moral virtues in the first half of the *Ethics*. As the previous section shows with the decent in Book V anticipating the movement in the *Ethics'* second half of intellect, desire, and pleasure toward the good through friendship, understanding pleasure's natural place in life depends on trusting in knowledge of the good.

From the ignobly stated views of pleasure, Aristotle turns to the question of how one trusts *logos*. The difficulty facing *logoi* of passions and actions is the trust (*pistoi*) in them is less than works, for whenever they are dissonant according to sense-perception, they despise and abolish (*prosanaireō*) the truth (1172a34–b1). As the verb for "abolish" implies, the dissonance between *logos* and works threatens choosing (*haireō*) because it abolishes the truth that these two things belong together. As an example of this dissonance, if there is someone who blames pleasure that others see at some time aiming toward this, it seems this person inclines toward pleasure as if all things are pleasures, for marking-the-boundary does not belong to the many (1172b1–3). This adds a wrinkle to the problem posed by dissonance between *logos* and works, bringing in the pressure of the many's opinion with the caution that they are not discerning about others' actions. To avoid these errors, Aristotle proposes that the true things of *logoi* look like they are most useful (*chrēsimos*) not only toward knowing, but life, for they are themselves trusted when they sing together with the works, and through this, they urge those persons who understand toward living according to them (1172b3–8). A line of argument that starts with the lesser trust in *logos* thus concludes by raising the possibility that trust in *logos* is stronger when it holds truth. The truth within *logos* is useful for life because it is naturally comprehensive, for Aristotle does not partition it into the political, economic, practical, or contemplative.

What, then, is this truth that one can trust to harmonize *logos* and works? Readers should look back to Book I where, after sketching the good as happiness and considering how it is complete and self-sufficient, Aristotle turns to how to contemplate first-principles, saying one-must-attempt (*peirateon*) to go after each in a way that is natural and be serious about nobly marking-the-boundaries, for they—just like knowledge of the good—hold great weight in what follows from them. After declaring "the beginning or first-principle is more than half of the whole," Aristotle urges readers to consider what concerns this is not only from the conclusions of the *logos*, but other things said about it, for while all things belonging to the truth sing together, the false is quickly dissonant with the truth.[17] Though the good is ever-present in the *Ethics*, Aristotle's consideration of how the truth makes *logos* trustworthy at the beginning of Book X reiterates that this naturally comprehensive truth is the good.

To take on the argument that pleasure is the good, Aristotle turns to the philosopher Eudoxus (whose name means "good-opinion," *eu-doxa*), who supposed pleasure to be the good through seeing how all things aim themselves at it, both those with and without-*logos*. In all things, he supposed the choice-worthy to be the decent, and the most choiceworthy thing to be the strongest. Furthermore, since all things bear themselves toward the same thing as the best thing—"for each thing discovers the good for itself, just as food"—the good is the good for all things, and that at which all things aim themselves (1172b9–15).[18] Eudoxus' argument that all things aim themselves at the good recalls the first sentence of the *Ethics* where various human pursuits seeming to aim themselves at some good nobly display from themselves the good as that at which all things aim.[19] While the good is of the same character in both arguments (i.e., that at which all things aim), it is not clear if the good is pleasure. It is in this regard that Eudoxus' argument falls short, for it does not declare what pleasure is. But this does not prevent people from trusting Eudoxus' *logoi*, a trust attributed to the virtue of his character, for he seemed moderate (*sōphrōn*). Yet Aristotle does not suspect Eudoxus' motives for this *logos*, adding he seemed to say them not as a friend of pleasure, but to hold according to the truth (1172b15–18). Although Aristotle acknowledges one could examine Eudoxus' character to detract from the trust in his *logos*, the far more important matter is if it holds true that pleasure is the good.

With Aristotle's observation that Eudoxus' *logos* that the good is pleasure seems to come from him holding it according to the truth and not as a friend of pleasure, readers should return to the first appearance of "friends" in the *Ethics*. In this passage, Aristotle wonders if it is better and needed for philosophers to abolish (*anaireō*) the things that are properly-one's-own (*ta oikeia*)—namely, the truth and friends—for the truth's preservation.[20] In this regard, Aristotle's statement that Eudoxus is not a friend of pleasure suggests that he may, as a philosopher, be a friend to the truth. For this to be true, however, pleasure must be the good. But if this is not true, how does a philosopher show it? A path that is not viable is in the *logos* that the good is not that at which all things aim, for such people speak nothing. In support of this argument, Aristotle first notes that what seems to be for all is what "we assert" to be, and the person who abolishes this trust does not say anything more trusted (1172b35–1173a2). While tempting to read the first part of Aristotle's argument as suggesting the good will forever remain what "seems" to be good, his point about *logos* is more profound and definite: everyone speaks of what seems to be good, and there is no way to speak around this truth, especially when it comes to choice. If one attempts to deny the truth that people always assert what seems to be good in *logos*, then one abolishes the possibility of trust in any *logos*. The basis of trust in *logos* is that it speaks of what seems to be good, which begs the question of whether what seems to be is truly good.

Further probing the *logos* that all things do not aim at the good, Aristotle considers the one condition that might support this *logos* before further proving its error. If only things without intelligence (*ta anoēta*) desire (*oregō*) pleasures, there might be something to what those who deny the good is that at which all things aim say. But if "things with presence of mind" (*ta phronima*, which could mean "the prudent things") desire pleasures too, in what way will those who deny the good speak? Perhaps there is some natural good in the base things that is stronger than they are according to themselves, and it aims itself at the good that is properly-one's-own (*to oikeion agathon*) (1173a2–5). In the first part of this argument, Aristotle suggests the only possible way to deal away with the good as that at which all things aim and to assert that they aim only at pleasure is to assume nothing has intelligence. But this is obviously false because intelligent things pursue pleasure too, and the unstated implication of the argument is no one pursues pleasure without thinking it is good. Though the last argument about the natural good points to questions about nature's order, in the context of countering the *logos* that all things do not aim at the good, it suggests there is something in all persons capable of aiming at the good that is properly-one's-own: the intellect.

From Eudoxus' *logos* that pleasure is the good and the problematic *logos* of those who hold all things do not aim at the good, Aristotle's own *logos* must reveal the nature of pleasure while preserving the truth that the good is that at which all things aim. Implicit in Aristotle's exploration of how to trust the truth in *logos* is the need for contemplating the good as a first-principle. With his observation that those who are prudent desire pleasure, Aristotle recalls an important problem facing prudence in Book VI that has implications for political and economic life. From the example of politicians and household managers as prudent people, Aristotle discusses how pleasures and pains not only ruin practical assumptions, but become ruinous of the first-principle through vice, a *hexis*. Not long after this argument, Aristotle posits the well-being of oneself may not be possible without household management or a regime, prompting him to wonder why the young do not trust in the experience of natural first-principles. The source of the problem is prudence's dependence on the intellect and its sense-perception of the unmoving boundaries and natural first-principles (of which there is no *logos*) that are not abstractions (*aphairesis*) away from choosing. As Aristotle shows in Book VII, vice can always ruin choice and the intellect because *logos* and sense-perception impel desire (*epithumia*) toward enjoyment with the pleasant.[21] What distinguishes Book VII's account of pleasure from Book X's is the latter follows the inquiry into friendship in Books VIII and IX, and the nature of friendship helps readers understand the nature of pleasure so that Aristotle's own *logos* preserves the truth that the good is that at which all things aim.

## PLEASURE AND THE CONTEMPLATIVE LIFE'S SELF-SUFFICIENCY (*ETHICS* 1173B31–1174A12, 1174B14–23, 1175A3–1179A35)

Although the first five chapters of Book X focus on pleasure, Aristotle's turn back toward happiness in the subsequent three chapters features pleasure as a prominent theme before the final chapter of the *Ethics* explores the relationship between *logos* and law to prepare the way for the *Politics*. The blending of all these themes in Book X initially seems to be a departure from the way the *Ethics* unfolds, but it is truly a fulfillment of Aristotle's aim to think comprehensively about human beings' need for the good. How Aristotle brings these themes together is evident in the way he turns to happiness in Book X's sixth chapter, and the turn to *logos* and law in the ninth chapter. In Book X's sixth chapter, after noting what concerns the virtues, friendship, and pleasures has been said, Aristotle says it remains to go through an outline concerning happiness since "we set-down this as an end of the human things" (1176a30–32). By reminding readers that happiness is an end they set-down, Aristotle likens it to law in a way that also teaches both belong to the broader category of the human things, not just politics. In Book X's ninth chapter, following the outline of the things concerning happiness, Aristotle wonders if the outlines concerning these things, virtues, friendship, and pleasures are all adequately stated, asking, "Must one suppose the choice to hold an end?" (1179a33–35). If the *Ethics* is a "choice," then it is akin to the first-principle that is a human being: a combination of intellect and desire. If desire is empty and vain without knowledge of the good, the one must suppose the *Ethics* holds the good as its end and that this truth becomes clear through some final interplay between virtue, pleasure, friendship, and happiness in Book X.

Starting with pleasure, its first characteristic that builds Book X's case for the good is what makes it complete (*teleios*). Not long after establishing that the difference between the friend and the flatterer seems to show that how people choose (*haireō*) the good is different from choosing pleasure and that not all pleasures are choiceworthy, Aristotle considers how every sense-perception is active toward "the perceptible thing" (*to aisthēton*). This activity is best, most complete, and most pleasant when it belongs to the best disposition (*tou arista diakeimenou*) toward the strongest of the things under itself. Whether it is every sense-perception, thought, or contemplation, there is a pleasure, but the most pleasant thing is most complete when it belongs to the thing holding well toward the most serious things (1173b31–1174a12, 1174b14–23). The language of this account draws heavily on Book IX's inquiry into love-of-self where the decent person—whose thought is well-provided with contemplative things and always finds the same thing painful and pleasant—holds toward a friend just as one holds toward oneself. Aristotle later says the same of the serious person, whose sense-perception of oneself being good and pleasant is how one chooses to hold toward a friend, leading these friends to perceive-together (*sunaisthanomai*) the good itself.[22] The comparison between pleasure and friendship on this point invites readers to wonder toward what things should they hold themselves so that pleasure is most complete. From love-of-self, people should hold themselves toward the contemplative things and sense-perception of the good itself, both of which are conspicuously absent from this first characterization of pleasure.

The next characteristic of pleasure raises the question of what holds human beings together. Pleasure completes activities not as a *hexis* that is present, but some end that comes upon it. Whether it is sense-perception or contemplation, as long as the productive and the passive (or "passionate," *to pathētikon*) things are holding the same way toward each other, pleasure naturally comes to be. Recognizing some may think this argument provides the possibility for perpetual pleasure, Aristotle raises the question of why no one feels pleasure in a way that is holding-together, prompting the sober observation that all human things lack the capacity to be active in a way that is holding-together (as is evident from the slackening activity of sight and thought toward something new) (1175a3–10). Here is the first hint of why pleasure cannot be the good, for pleasure holds human beings together only so far as they can be in activity, and one cannot rely on an activity for an extended time.

Aristotle considers another reason why pleasure seems to be the good, observing that some could suppose all things desire pleasure because they aim themselves at living, which is some activity that each person directs toward the things they most of all love (*agapaō*). For example, the activity of a musical person's hearing is towards songs, and the lover of learning's (*philomathēs*) thought is in activity toward contemplative things. Because pleasure completes both activities and living (which people desire), it is with good-*logos* that people aim themselves at pleasure since it completes living for each person and is choiceworthy. But here one finds some ambiguity over whether people choose pleasure through living or living through pleasure, for activities do not come without pleasure, and pleasure completes every activity (1175a10–21). Though Aristotle leaves this ambiguity about living and pleasure unresolved, its solution resides in the last chapter of the inquiry into friendship. Elaborating on how friendship is community (*koinōnia*), Aristotle discusses how the choiceworthy sense-perception of how friends hold toward themselves leads to them aiming themselves at living-together in the activity of this sense-perception, thus passing the days in the things they most of all love (*agapaō*) in life (which could range from drinking, playing dice, exercising, hunting, or philosophizing together). In every friendship, friends produce and form community in these things.[23] In light of Book X's argument about pleasure, all the things friends most of all love hold a pleasure belonging to their activity, yet Aristotle refrains from speaking of pleasure in Book IX's argument. Consequently, each friend's fundamental choice is for living, though pleasure closely accompanies this.

From the two preceding arguments about pleasure revealing it resides in many activities, Aristotle further refines his inquiry to demonstrate how human life needs something more fundamental than pleasure to be choice-worthy. Pleasures seem to differ in form, as is evident from how the pleasures that complete the activity of thought differ from those of sense-perception. The proper (*oikeia*) pleasure increases-together with the activity, for through the delight in the activity, people become more precise and better judge the things belonging to it. In support of the idea that each activity holds a proper pleasure, Aristotle notes how pleasures from other activities become impediments to each other. For example, lovers of the aulos (*philoauloi*) lack the capacity to hold-toward *logoi* if they hear someone playing the aulos because they take more delight in this music. In this way, the activity of the pleasure according to the aulos playing ruins the pleasure concerning *logos*. Proper pleasures, then, produce the activities so that they last a longer time and are better, while "foreign" (*allotrios*, literally "other") pleasures ruin them, from which it is clear that there is much that is set-standing-apart in pleasures. Indeed, these foreign pleasures are similar to the activities' proper pains, with the only difference being pain is contrary to the pleasure, while the foreign pleasure displaces the proper pleasure (1175a21–b24). The sense of proper pleasures increasing-together with their activities points back to Book IX's concluding argument that the friendship of the decent increases-together with their association, and they come to be better through being in activity together and correcting one another, taking an impression of satisfying things from each other.[24] Before turning to how Aristotle deploys the decent in his account of pleasure, readers should notice how foreign pleasures ruining proper ones adds depth to Book VI's problem of pleasures and pains ruining the intellect, its sense-perception of natural first-principles, and therefore human nature itself. Since the first-principle of human nature is choice—a combination of intellect and desire—one must understand how pleasure relates to these two things.

Beginning the sequence of arguments that eventually bring the intellect and desire together, Aristotle uses decency to think about how desire relates to activities and pleasures. After establishing that the proper pleasure for the serious activity is decent while a base activity's pleasure is wretched, Aristotle states pleasures are more proper in activities than desires, for desires are themselves bounded from these things by time and by nature, while pleasures and activities are unbounded in the same way because they are near to each other. On account of this, it looks like pleasure is neither thought nor sense-perception, but since they are not separated, they appear to be the same (1175b24–1176a3). Desire, then, is always at some remove from pleasure. While desire can be for the sake of some pleasure, since Book I, desire needs knowledge (*gnōsis*) of the good so that it is not empty and vain. What makes dealing with desire difficult is Aristotle's acknowledgment in Book I that "every knowledge and choice itself desires (*oregō*) some good," which prompts the *Ethics'* turn toward happiness as the political art's end.[25] But desire is not alone in human nature, for it exists along with intellect, the presence of which is implicit in Book X's account of pleasure, but does not explicitly come forth until the turn to happiness. A hint of its emergence appears in Aristotle's appeal to decency, and his choice to conclude Book X's inquiry into pleasure by wondering which of the decent pleasures should belong to a human being (1176a24–25). Since Book IX, the decent person embodies the unreproachable, intellectual love-of-self. Thus, in raising a question about decent pleasures, Aristotle creates an opening for readers to consider the intellect's role in their own happiness.

The first characteristic of happiness Aristotle considers in Book X is what makes it self-sufficient. One must set-down happiness as self-sufficient because it is an activity that is choiceworthy according to itself, not for the sake of something else, and in-need (*endeēs*) of nothing. The actions according to virtue seem to be of this character, for doing the noble and serious things seems choiceworthy through themselves (1176a35–b9). Being self-sufficient and in-need of nothing is something that characterizes happiness in Book I,[26] but in Book X, Aristotle refrains from saying "life" is in-need of nothing. Aristotle's hesitance to bring life back into the picture for the self-sufficient is evident from the way he challenges the reliability of things being choiceworthy through themselves as a standard, for the same could be said about the pleasures of "play" (*paidiē*, which can also mean "childish play" given its root of *pais*, "child"). Such pleasures can be more harmful than beneficial when people are careless about their bodies and acquisition (1176b9–11). This is a striking argument considering it follows the supposedly choiceworthy noble and serious things and quietly suggests these are just as choiceworthy as the pleasures of play. As in Book I, there must be more to the self-sufficient than being choiceworthy, and it must point people toward caring for their bodies and acquisition in economic and political life in ways fit for a complete human being.

Moving readers toward the self-sufficient pleasures, after chastising the many and tyrants for thinking happiness resides in the pleasures of play, Aristotle declares neither virtue nor intellect (the source of serious activities) belongs to dynasty, and one should not take such people as a sign of anything because they are without taste of pure and liberal (*eleutherios*) pleasure. With the possibility of such pleasures in the inquiry, Aristotle concedes that it seems correct to play so one might be serious, for "relaxation" (*anapausis*) looks like play, and because people lack the capacity of holding-together in labor, they need relaxation. As a result, relaxation is not an end, for it comes to be for the sake of the activity (1176b11–1177a1). In the first part of this argument, Aristotle liberates virtue and intellect from politics through his own *logos* without causing it to conflict with any works. Then, with *logos*, he presents readers the idea of pure and liberal pleasures that allows his *logos* to find a place for play that conflicts neither with virtue and intellect, nor the care for the body and acquisition.

In Book X's seventh chapter, Aristotle brings together many of the preceding arguments to show the intellect is the natural foundation for happiness. The account, however, begins with a significant change to the definition of happiness that holds throughout most of the *Ethics*. While Book I defines happiness "as some activity of the soul according to complete virtue (*aretēn teleian*),"[27] in Book X Aristotle declares that it is with good-*logos* for this activity to be according to the strongest (*kratistē*) virtue. And whether it is intellect or some other thing, this seems according to nature to rule, to lead (*hēgeomai*), to hold in-thought (*ennoia*) concerning noble things and divine things, and its contemplative activity according to the proper (*oikeia*) virtue would be complete happiness (1177a12–18). Book X's definition of happiness thus begins with a paradox: Why is happiness complete if the proper virtue that defines it is not?

To answer the preceding question about the proper virtue of happiness, readers must push forward in Aristotle's account. After stating the preceding summary view of happiness seems to agree in *logos* (*homologeō*) with the things previously said and the truth, Aristotle says the intellect is the strongest thing in human beings, and its activity is the most holding-together, for people have the capacity to contemplate in a way that is holding-together more than they can do anything. And people suppose there is need to mix pleasure with happiness, and there is agreement that the most pleasant of the activities according to virtue are according to wisdom. Philosophy, at least, seems to hold wondrous pleasures according to their purity and steadiness, and it is with good-*logos* that those who know pass the time with greater pleasure than those who seek (1177a18–27). Lest readers mistake this last statement as a mere sales-pitch for philosophy, there is a helpful discrepancy between the first two parts of the argument. With respect to the intellect, Aristotle does not qualify anything he says about it being strongest or how it holds-together with a "seems." Philosophy, however, only enters the picture because people "suppose" happiness needs pleasure, and it "seems" the pleasures of philosophy are wondrous because those who know have greater pleasure than those who seek. The question that philosophy invites is if the intellect's activity of contemplation needs philosophy—or anything else, for that matter—to feel pleasure. If this is true, then the intellect is not self-sufficient.

Since being choiceworthy is an insufficient standard for determining the nature of what is self-sufficient, Aristotle provides further clarity on how he understands this idea through contemplation. The "so-called self-sufficiency (*hē legōmenē autarkeia*)[28] would most of all concern the contemplative (*tēn theōrētikē*),"[29] for while the wise person, just person, and all the remaining persons need the necessary things for living, when the necessary things are adequately "resourced" (*chorēgeō*),[30] those who are just, moderate, and courageous will still need others toward whom they can act, but the wise person has the capacity to contemplate according to oneself, and more so if wiser. Even if it may be better to hold coworkers, the wise person is most self-sufficient, and the contemplative activity seems loved (*agapaō*) through itself, for nothing comes to be besides the contemplating, while the practical things themselves "produce concern to obtain" (*peripoieō*)[31] the more (*pleiōn*) or the lesser besides the action (1177a27–b4). Through the contemplative activity, the self-sufficient applies to an activity loved according to itself that one can work in through oneself, though it is possible for one to work with others in it. The contrast between the contemplative activity and actions belonging to the practical things suggests this activity is free from a need to produce concern with what is more or less, thus opening one's own life to true love-of-self.

Adding depth to the contemplative life's self-sufficiency, Aristotle turns to politics and offers a glimpse into the moral core of his political teaching. Happiness seems to be in "leisure" (*scholē*), and people "are without leisure" (*ascholeō*) in order "to be in leisure" (*scholazō*).[32] But the activity of the practical virtues is either in the things of war or politics, both of which seem to be "without leisure" (*ascholos*). The politician's activity is also without leisure, though even through this the politicians seek happiness either for themselves or their citizens as something different from the activity. The intellect's contemplative activity is more serious, seems not to aim at an end besides itself, and it holds a proper (*oikeia*) pleasure that increases-together with the activity, so that the self-sufficient is as leisured and unwearied as could be for a human being. This all characterizes the life of the blessed person whose happiness would be complete if it is a complete life, for nothing incomplete (or "without-end," *ateles*) belongs to happiness (1177b4–26). To arrive at the conclusion that leisure characterizes the self-sufficient, Aristotle answers the question of whether the contemplative activity needs anything besides itself to feel pleasure, for the contemplative activity holds a proper pleasure even when directed solely at itself. The activity of this proper pleasure defines its leisure. Politics, however, is by its nature without leisure, and even though the people who engage in its practical activities are without leisure, the fact that they still seek happiness suggests they want this leisure too. Since this leisure is proper to the contemplative activity, one must never forget that the self-sufficiency of politics seeks something only the intellect offers.

The complete life and complete happiness of the blessed person receives an immediate revision that solidifies the intellect's place as the natural foundation for happiness. Aristotle begins by declaring this complete life and complete happiness is stronger than a human being, though the intellect is something divine within oneself that differs from the set-down-together thing (*to sunthēton*, "compounded"). Though some would say there is no use or need (*chrē*) to think or be prudent about anything besides the human things, the strongest thing within human beings holds-over all things in capacity and honor, and it seems each person is this strongest thing *if* it is the authoritative and better thing. After commenting that it would be strange for someone to choose (*haireō*) the life of another and not of oneself, Aristotle concludes that "the proper (*to oikeion*) thing for each person is by nature strongest and most pleasant for each person, and thus for a human being [is] the life according to the intellect, if this most of all [is] a human being, and therefore this is the happiest" (1177b26–1178a8). Though there are important qualifications to this line of argument, one should understand them in relation to its last phase: the life that is most properly-one's-own is the life one *chooses* to live according to the intellect. No human being lives according to the intellect by necessity, but by choice. To the extent this life is divine, it is not (as some arguments in Book I suggest) the gift of the gods,[33] but a choice to set the intellect as the most authoritative thing for oneself. But notice Aristotle does not say this choice is for happiness. How, then, does one choose to live according to the intellect?

From the definition of happiness Aristotle sets at the beginning of the *Ethics*, it seems the way one chooses to live according to the intellect is to choose the life of virtue. But in Book X, not only does the "strongest virtue" supplant "complete virtue" as part of happiness, but virtue itself comes into question. Opposed to the life according to the intellect that one chooses so that it is most properly-one's-own, the life according to "the other virtue" (*tēn allēn aretē*) is second. Such activities (like the just and the courageous things) are human in the sense that the virtues are toward others, acting toward things-exchanged-together, needs or uses (*chreia*), and actions in all the passions where they watch closely what fits each. These virtues have close ties to prudence *if* its first-principles are in the moral virtues *and* the correct thing (*ton orthon*) in the moral virtues is according to prudence. Because these virtues are knit together with the passions, they concern the set-down-together thing and are human; so too is the life and happiness according to these. Nevertheless, the life and happiness belonging to the intellect is separate from these, though one cannot be precise about it (1178a9–23). Thus, at the end of the *Ethics*, Aristotle introduces ambiguity over whether virtue is the intellect, or the moral virtues he examines in the first half of the work. Awareness of this ambiguity is crucial to understanding Aristotle's political philosophy. If one reads the *Ethics* and thinks its fundamental teaching is that politics and economics should promote virtue and happiness, is this the virtue and happiness associated with the contemplative life, or the life of moral virtue?

Although Book X marks the first point where Aristotle directly questions with what virtue the activity of the soul that is happiness accords, careful readers should follow his qualified statement about the first-principles of moral virtue back to Book VI to see this ambiguity is nothing new. At the end of the *Ethics*' inquiry into prudence, Aristotle turns to the authoritative good to suggest that prudence can lead a person's *hexis* to be authoritative virtue instead of natural virtue by taking hold of intellect.[34] Considering Aristotle qualifies his statement that the moral virtues have close ties to prudence *if* these are its first principles, the mention of "the authoritative good" in Book VI—combined with his acknowledgment in Book X that the life with the intellect as the authoritative thing is a choice—suggests there is room for another first-principle to guide prudence.

How prudence being caught between different first-principles is central to Aristotle's teaching about the relationship between politics and economics becomes clearer by looking a little further back in Book VI, before the authoritative good emerges. After suggesting the legislative art is architectonic prudence and household management (*oikonomia*) is a kind of prudence—which allows him to consider why the young do not trust in natural first-principles in thinking about their own being—Aristotle makes the ambiguous statement that prudence itself either "poses against" or "corresponds with" (*antikeimai*) the intellect. The discrepancy comes from the fact that prudence is a sense-perception of the last thing (*eschatos*) in something practical (like doing the just thing in exchange), while intellect is sense-perception of what is last in practical things *and* of the unmoving boundaries and first-principles of which there is no *logos*. All these arguments tend toward the same question: Will prudence pursuing one's own well-being correspond with the intellect's sense-perception of the natural first-principle of the good, or will prudence pose itself against this natural first-principle in favor of a less authoritative good and first-principle? If politics and economics are forms of prudence, a related question emerges: What distinguishes forms of politics and economics directed toward the naturally authoritative good from forms directed toward a less authoritative good?

To get some sense of where prudence relates to authoritative and less authoritative goods, Aristotle compares the life according to the intellect to the life according to moral virtue on the basis of external resources (*tēs ektos chorēgias*), for it seems the former life either needs little of these, or less than the latter life. Supposing the need for the necessary things is equal between the two lives (yet conceding the politician labors more for the things of the body), the difference between the two lives is small. But from the perspective of activities, the difference is greater, for both the liberal and the just person will need useful things (*chrēmata*) to do just and liberal things. Moving back toward the intellect's lack of need for external resources, Aristotle addresses the question of whether the more authoritative thing in virtues belongs to choice or actions, though it is clear that the complete thing (*to teleion*) is in both. While actions need more things (and the nobler the actions are, the more things needed), the person who contemplates has no need (*chreia*) for such things, which may actually be an impediment to the activity of contemplation. Nevertheless, there will be need for such things for choosing to do the actions according to virtue because one is a human being who lives-together with others (1178a23–b7). Aristotle's account of need in this passage is twofold. On the one hand, from the perspective of the need for the necessary things, both the life according to the intellect and the life according to moral virtue are in need. But from the perspective of the activities, the contemplative life of the intellect does not need external resources like the life of moral virtue. This does not mean the contemplative life and the life of moral virtue are mutually exclusive; after all, Aristotle adds that if the person contemplating chooses to live according to moral virtue, then one will need the things toward this. Aristotle seems to confirm this by insisting the more authoritative thing resides in the complete thing that comes to be from bringing choice and action together. But if choice and action must come together, and if choice is the first-principle that is human nature defined as a combination of intellect and desire, then how can one provide for this nature's need?

Before turning to how Aristotle suggests one can provide for human nature's intellectual need, it is necessary to account for a final nuance in his treatment of self-sufficiency. After settling on the conclusion that happiness extends along with contemplation (thereby making happiness *some* contemplation), Aristotle says there will be need for external good days (*euēmeria*) for a human being, for one's nature is not self-sufficient toward contemplating since there is need for the body to be healthy, food, and remaining attendances to be present. At the same time, one must not suppose being happy needs many and great things, for neither the self-sufficient nor action are in excess. This is evident from private persons seeming to do more of the decent things than persons in political dynasties. As a result, measured means are adequate for a happy life to be in activity according to virtue (1178b28–1179a9). At first glance, readers whose interest in Aristotle is primarily economic may find his emphasis on bodily needs shows economics must provide for these needs before human beings can be happy. In support of this view, readers could point to Aristotle's observation above that politicians labor more for the things of the body as a demonstration of the primacy of economic concerns in his political philosophy. While it is impossible to deny the necessity of providing for bodily things, this economic reading ignores the preceding arguments' teaching that the contemplative life is self-sufficient because it comes to be through oneself in the activity of one's own intellect. Though the intellect is inseparable from the body and its needs, its activity is free from these needs, for one can contemplate anything. It is only after discovering this freedom of the intellect that Aristotle turns toward human beings' lack of self-sufficiency in bodily things. In this way, the self-sufficiency of the intellect governs Aristotle's approach to self-sufficiency in external resources, allowing him to acknowledge that while there is a need for such resources, one should not provide for this need with excess.

To move toward thinking of what provides for the intellect's need (and desire along with it), readers should look back to Book VII where Aristotle speaks of the good (as well as *hexeis* and natures) as being twofold: the good simply, and the good for some person. Speaking to the relationship between *hexis*, activity, and pleasure, Aristotle distinguishes the good that is an incidental pleasure by settling a natural *hexis* from the good that is the contemplative activity of the desires in the *hexeis* that belong to the nature not in-need, an activity that holds pleasures without pains.[35] In light of Book X's arguments, the intellect emerges as the *hexis* that is not in-need in the sense that its activity requires no external resources, though one needs to provide for the body to be alive. Barring some natural defect or horrible accident, contemplation is inseparable from living. But what does Aristotle mean when he says the pleasures of the nature not in-need are painless? The answer seems to be that because the intellect does not need external resources to be in activity, the pleasure proper to contemplation has no pain. To make Aristotle's argument more concrete, contrast the intellect's painless pleasure through it being a nature not in-need with the beginning of his account of natural acquisition in the *Politics*, where there is a natural pleasure in human beings' and animals' acquisition of food that marks-the-boundaries of their lives, with human beings also being able to add to each way of life that is most in-need whatever it happens to lack in what is self-sufficient. If pleasure accompanies the natural acquisition of food, the pain of hunger is the natural result of failing in the pursuit of acquisition. To carry acquisition further, the pleasure from gain associated with the injustice and the one-holding more bears with it the pain of loss.[36] Contemplation does not bear a similar pain in itself, though one should not take this to mean it is impossible to contemplate painful things (more on this momentarily). For now, the intellect's self-sufficiency seems to belong to its activity found in a *hexis* holding the good, thus providing a pleasure with no corresponding pain.

As further evidence of Aristotle not losing sight of the ties between the intellect's self-sufficiency and the self-sufficient in political and economic life, consider the appearance of these ideas from his inquiry into the money-making art from Book I of the *Politics*. To start, after defining "true wealth" as "a store of such useful things that are necessary towards living, and useful to community in a household or a city," Aristotle contends the self-sufficiency of this acquisition is not without-limit toward good living. Later in the inquiry, to prove the art of retail-trade that pursues the gain of legal-currency without-limit does not by nature belong to the money-making art, Aristotle describes the art of exchange (*hē metablētikē*) through which households exchange more or less useful things as is necessary according to people's needs as a restoration of the self-sufficiency that is according to nature. Shortly after this argument, in searching for why some turn the art of household management toward the pursuit of legal-currency without-limit, Aristotle finds the turn rests on mistakes about living and living well. The first occasion where these ideas appear concurrently in the *Politics* is in Book I's second chapter, where the city—supposedly a result of communities naturally-growing—arises "holding every limit of self-sufficiency so to speak, coming-into-being itself on the one hand for the sake of living, and on the other hand being for the sake of living well." It is on this basis that Aristotle describes self-sufficiency as an end and best.[37] In every case where self-sufficiency appears as a limit in politics and economics, what constitutes living in relation to such things is inseparable from the question of what makes living "well" and "good." As the final treatment of self-sufficiency in the *Ethics* shows, one must address the practical concerns of politics and economics without losing sight of the contemplative life's authoritative nature.

Though some readers may see Aristotle's case for the authoritative place of the contemplative life in natural self-sufficiency as a philosopher's prejudice, it is in truth a response to an inescapable need. At the end of Book VII, before Aristotle turns his inquiry toward friendship, he makes what seems to be a very impractical argument about pleasure. After observing "the nature of ourselves [is not] simple," Aristotle contrasts the single and simple pleasure of the god's activity that belongs to the absence of motion and rest with the nature needing change that is laboriously-wicked (*ponēria*) since it is neither simple nor decent.[38] In Book X, Aristotle contrasts the divine thing within human nature that is the intellect with the set-down-together thing that is knit with the passions and is the concern of the moral virtues, whose life provides a second-ranked happiness. Together, these two passages portray human nature as a setting-together of the intellect that is somehow capable of the absence of motion, and the passions that tend to be more full of motion.

The body is also part of this set-down-together thing with its need for food and care so that one's own intellect and passions can be in activity. In human nature, there is a tension between the intellect that has some capacity to be without motion, and the passions and body that need motion. Aristotle's account of self-sufficiency points to the intellect being the authoritative thing because its capacity to be without motion can order the motions of the passions and the body. But people rarely understand their own lives in the terms of this abstraction, and Aristotle recognizes this, hence why he puts it more practically. In Book X, for example, Aristotle contrasts the absence of leisure in political life with the leisure of the contemplative life whose proper pleasure increases-together with its activity. The precedent for this argument appears in Book IX's teaching that living is good and pleasant according to itself because it is bounded (which is the nature of the good), but a ruined living is in pain because it is unbounded. From here, Aristotle uses the decent person's love-of-self to reveal the natural foundation of friendship is the intellectual perceiving-together of the good itself through friends living-together and forming-community in *logos* and thought; later, he describes the friendship of the decent as increasing-together with their association. Both politics and economics aspire to forming community in some way and having people's friendship (in a very loose sense) increasing-together with their association in citizenship and exchange. But to divide politics and economics on this point is misleading, for in all human things people seek what the decent friends seek: what is good and pleasant according to itself as the boundary for their own lives.

To the extent that friendship depends on a natural sense-perception of the good through living-together and forming-community in *logos* and thought, it provides a helpful context for interpreting Aristotle's last arguments in Book X about the happy person and external resources. Aristotle cites the opinions of Solon and Anaxagoras that what characterizes the happy person is a measured quantity of external resources and not being wealthy, noting the latter opinion is strange to the many who judge by the external things because their sense-perception is only of these. From the *logoi*, Aristotle concludes these things hold some trust, for one judges the truth in practical things from works and life, for the authoritative thing is in these. From the things previously said, there is use or need (*chrē*) to see how they bear upon works and life, and one must either admit them if they sing together with the works, or if they are dissonant, one must regard them as mere *logos* (1179a9–22).

Recall that when Aristotle begins Book X with a similar argument, he adds that dissonance between *logoi* and works through sense-perception abolishes (*prosanaireō*) the truth.[39] Aristotle thus leaves it to readers to choose (*haireō*) how to judge if his own *logos* about self-sufficiency in the contemplative life providing a boundary to external resources is true. While this admits the possibility of error, readers should not take Aristotle's emphasis on sense-perception in these arguments lightly, especially since friendship provides a practical image for how people hold an intellectual sense of the good. Everything Aristotle addresses in his political philosophy points readers back to their own need for the good, the fundamental lens through which they engage in all activities (including politics and economics). The question facing readers is if they will choose to seek out the good and live according to it.

## THE NATURAL LIMITS OF *LOGOS* AND
## LAW (*ETHICS* 1179A33–1180B7)

As Aristotle prepares readers for the *Politics* in the final chapter of the *Ethics*, he dwells more on the effectiveness of *logos* and its relationship to law in ways that leave open the need for understanding politics (and to a lesser extent economics) in light of human nature's need to befriend the good. Following his question of whether the choice (*proairesis*) that is the *Ethics* holds an end, Aristotle wonders if the end in practical things is more in doing these things instead of contemplating and knowing them. If it is not adequate to know the virtues, one-must-attempt (*peirateon*) to hold and use them, "unless we ourselves come to be good in some other way" (1179a33-b4). This question refers back to Book II, where Aristotle sets becoming good against contemplation and approaches the *hexeis* that are the moral virtues from the common understanding that they are according to correct *logos*, something the inquiry takes up later.[40] A notable difference between Books II and X on this question about contemplating and the good is Book X presents readers a choice about how to approach virtue.

By now, careful readers know the necessity of their own choice about how to approach Aristotle's *logos* is ever-present in the *Ethics*. In Book I, Aristotle informs readers of a need (*chrē*) to seek the precision proper (*oikeios*) to the inquiry, prompting a comparison between how the carpenter and geometer examine the right angle (*hē orthē*): the carpenter because it is useful (*chrēsimē*) to the work, and the geometer who seeks what it is as one who contemplates the truth. Like Book X, Aristotle preserves readers' choice of how to approach his *logos*, though he merely hints in Book I at a lack of tension between the useful and the contemplation of the truth. In Book VI, Aristotle begins the inquiry into prudence by proposing to divide (*diaireō*) correct (*orthos*) *logos* and uncover its boundary.[41] The common term between Books II and VI in these arguments is *orthos*, taking the form of the "right angle" in Book II and "correct" *logos* in Book VI. One could read the inquiry into the moral virtues in the first half of the *Ethics* as the carpenter's seeking out what is useful to the work, and the second half of the text as the geometer's contemplation of the truth about virtue. While this is a reasonable way to think of *Ethics'* two halves, one should not draw a sharp division between the two inquiries because Aristotle sets them together as one whole work. The useful does not exist apart from contemplation, but to see this, readers must accept Aristotle's invitation to choose (*haireō*) to divide (*diaireō*) the correct *logos* behind the moral virtues to discover the boundary of which their intellects hold sense-perception. The search for that boundary is "proper" (*oikeios*) to the *Ethics*, and through this search, readers uncover what is properly-one's-own (*oikeios*), the true natural basis of political and economic life.

From the question of how people become good, Aristotle considers how *logos* is not self-sufficient, beginning with the observation that if it were toward producing decent people, it would bear wages and there might be need to provide these. But it is apparent that *logos* has the strength only to exhort those who are liberal among the young, whereas the many naturally trust-the-rule of fear, holding themselves back from base things through fear of retribution. This is because many live according to passion and do not seek the proper (*oikeia*) pleasures through themselves and flee the corresponding pains. Since it is difficult to "change the standing" (*methistēmi*)[42] of these things in their characters with *logos*, it is something to be content with or loved (*agapēton*) if all the things that seem decent come to be present, and through this "we ourselves might take hold of a share of virtue" (1179b4–20). After spending most of the *Ethics* thinking of the self-sufficient in relation to oneself, now even *logos* lacks the self-sufficient. Just as human beings need the good, *logos* needs liberal people to be strong. From the preceding arguments in Book X, people are not truly liberal unless they (like the decent person) love (*agapaō*), gratify, and trust-the-rule of the intellect through which they find the self-sufficient activity and pleasure of contemplation. The last part of Aristotle's argument is crucial since he still upholds the decent in the face of many people's tendency to trust fear more. Aristotle also defends the decent by hearkening back to Book I's observation that even if the political art's taking and preserving the human good for cities and nations is nobler and more divine, doing so for one alone is something to be content with or loved (*agapēton*). From this statement, Aristotle concludes the inquiry into the human good is "something political" or "some political art" (*politikē tis*).[43] In keeping with Aristotle's description of his own inquiry as a choice, Book I's two views of the human good from the political art's perspective provide readers a choice of how to think about this art's end. Book X adds nuance to the choice, opposing the many to those who are liberal and questioning if it is more natural to trust-the-rule of *logos*, or fear.

To resolve whether the more natural foundation for the political art's pursuit of the human good resides in fear or *logos*, Aristotle draws his readers into a probing account of what is necessary in law. From the supposition that people come to be good either by nature, habit, or teaching, Aristotle wonders what "changes trust" (*metapeithō*) of a person holding according to passion, for such a person does not listen to *logos*, and passion does not seem to give way to *logos*, but to force or violence (1179b20–29). The problem of passion recalls Aristotle's observation in Book I that the proper (*oikeios*) listeners to the political art's *logoi* are not those whose characters pursue the passions, especially when the end is not knowledge (*gnōsis*) but action. For *logos* to be of great benefit, one must produce desires according to *logos* and act in this way. In Book I, Aristotle does not point to a need for force or violence to produce people according to *logos*, keeping the focus squarely on oneself. But in Book X, force or violence is a possibility, and the actions needed for becoming good displace (at least for the moment) the need for knowledge of the good that—in keeping choosing from going on without-limit so that desire is not empty and vain—allows people to hit on what is needful in life.[44]

To provide what *logos* lacks in the self-sufficient and by way of force or violence, Aristotle turns to the need for law, saying it wholly concerns all life, for the many trust-the-rule by necessity (*anankē*) more than *logos*. Indeed, while the decent person living toward the noble will trust-the-rule of *logos*, one checks the base person desiring (*oregō*) pleasure by pain just as one would with a beast. Through this, it is said that there is need for the pains that are most of all contrary to the loved (*agapaō*) pleasures so that decent pursuits and living according to some intellect and correct ordering comes to be *if* they hold strength (1179b29–1180a18). Setting aside this important qualification for the moment, notice the return of the ignoble *logos* from the beginning of Book X that proposes pleasure is base for the sake of leading the many (who are slaves to pleasure) to the middle term.[45] With the inclusion of the decent, Aristotle allows the life according to the intellect to come in as an explanation for what those who hold this *logos* attempt to approximate with law's use of force of violence. Given this opening, Aristotle states the command of a father or one man does not hold strength or necessity unless they are kings, but the law holds a necessitating capacity (*anankastikēn dunamin*) since it is a *logos* from some prudence and intellect. And while human beings detest things contrary to their impulses—even if it is correct (*orthōs*) to do so—the law is not heavy when it orders the decent (1180a18–24). Where necessity in law seems to belong solely to force or violence, Aristotle reveals that law is nothing other than *logos*, and its own necessitating capacity resides in prudence and intellect corresponding with each other by ordering the decent, thus drawing the naturally good and pleasant foundation for friend-ship into political life.

The importance of friendship for revealing the necessitating capacity of *logos* becomes apparent in Aristotle's subsequent examination of where there is care for the things through which people come to be good. With the excep-tion of Sparta (which seems to care for these things), most cities are careless toward such things, with each person living as one wishes. While the stron-gest thing is for the common care (*koinēn epimeleian*) to become correct, when cities are careless for the common, it seems it would belong to each person to contribute to caring for virtue for their own children and friends, or to choose (*proaireō*) to do this (1180a24–32). The choice to care for virtue is ever-present in political life. Either the legislator makes it the common care, or each person does. But care alone is not enough, for it must be correct, and the boundary for this is not the noble or the just, but the good.

How this care for the good is properly-one's-own appears in Aristotle's next argument. Although it seems this care for virtue would require one to become a legislator, Aristotle finds a kinship between laws and customs (or "characters," *ēthē*) being strong in cities, and the *logoi* and habits (*ethē*) of fathers in households (*oikias*). The latter are stronger through kinship and good-works, for from the beginning those in the household love (*stergō*) and are "well-ready-to-trust" (*eupeithō*) by nature (1180a32–b7). Though a faint sketch of political things, the strength of *logos* diminishes the further community moves away from the household. Within the context of Book X of the *Ethics*, this is because each person in the household is far closer to the prudence and intellect of the father ruling it both in terms of proximity and natural affection. While the art of household management (*oikonomikē*) is not part of this inquiry, readers should at the very least see that whatever this art entails is more than the acquisition of useful and necessary things that they encounter in the inquiry into the money-making art from Book I of the *Politics*. From Book X of the *Ethics*, it is clear that one cannot understand the art of household management independently of the intellectual care for the good that is properly-one's-own.[46]

## CONCLUSION: THE INTELLECT, JUSTICE, AND THE SEARCH FOR THE GOOD (*ETHICS* 1180B28–1181A12, 1181B1–15)

Aristotle refrains from exploring what the more natural care for the good within the household means for political life in the remainder of the *Ethics*, choosing instead to consider how one might come to be a legislator. Within this inquiry, Aristotle raises questions about the importance of thought versus experience for such a work, and further, considers contemplating regimes as if they are akin to the body's *hexeis*. These questions lead into Aristotle calling for an inquiry into legislation to complete "the philosophy concerning the human things" (*hē peri ta anthrōpeia philosophia*) (1180b28–1181a12, 1181b1–15). Aside from the obvious conclusion that Aristotle's own *logos* is not yet complete, readers must also notice that political and economic matters all fall under Aristotle's more comprehensive "philosophy concerning the human things." In this respect, the *Ethics* and *Politics* form a whole inquiry. While readers can think of Aristotle's inquiry as having different parts, they should remember his passing remark in Book I of the *Ethics* that one can mark-the-boundaries of things as if they are parts in *logos* even though they are naturally inseparable.[47] Some readers may wish to look for the strictly political or economic in Aristotle's philosophy, but doing this requires them to mark boundaries that are contrary to his comprehensive view of the human things. All of Aristotle's inquiries related to politics and economics in his philosophy find their way back to the question of how each person chooses the good that is properly-one's-own.

With the comprehensive nature of Aristotle's philosophy in mind, one can now return to the virtue of justice with a firmer grasp of why its view of politics, economics, and the human things is always partial. One place to start is Book X, where "justice" only makes one passing appearance in the inquiry into pleasure,[48] and is entirely absent from the final chapter's comparison between *logos* and law. At least one opening for the just to appear in Book X is in Aristotle's statement about law and its necessitating capacity not being heavy when it orders the decent, presumably because this is not contrary to people's impulses. In Book I of the *Politics*, after observing that all human beings by nature have an impulse toward community, the person who first set-standing-together one is a cause of the greatest goods because human beings are best of all animals when completed, but worst of all when separated from law and the just. Though Aristotle does not attribute the greatest goods to the decent in the *Ethics*, why does he not invoke the just? Recall that Aristotle's praise for the just in the *Politics* comes only after he says human beings have sense-perception of the good and bad, just and unjust, pleasant and painful, advantageous and harmful through *logos*, and adds that "community in these things produces a household and a city."[49] Like the *Ethics*, *logos* connects the household (the first community) and the city. But because Book I of the *Politics* emphasizes the perspective of community, it omits the *Ethics*' more natural view of community exemplified by decent friends' shared intellectual sense-perception of the good through which they form-community in *logos* and thought. Both the decent and friendship are closer to the natural foundation for community, something to which Aristotle seems to nod in Book I of the *Politics* by mentioning sense-perception. Nevertheless, Aristotle's choice to mention what is good and bad in this sense-perception points attentive readers to the natural and authoritative basis for community.

Book X revealing the intellect as the strongest virtue (if chosen) and necessitating capacity in law also provides an answer to the question from Book V of what is natural in the politically just. In that part of the inquiry, Aristotle declares the natural holds the same capacity everywhere, though there is something moving (*kinētos*) among the things that admit to hold otherwise. Insofar as *logos* holds a necessitating capacity when it is from some prudence and intellect, intellect is the source of what is natural in the politically just. Here one must clarify that intellect is ultimately more authoritative than prudence, for according to Book X, prudence's first-principles could either be in the moral virtues, or something else.[50] If readers follow this argument back to Book VI's insight that prudence either "poses against" or "corresponds" with intellect, and further, that prudence can lead a person's *hexis* to be authoritative virtue instead of natural virtue by taking hold of intellect, then only through the intellect does prudence find its first-principle in the authoritative good. In this case, one finds another demonstration that intellect can be by nature by elevating *hexis* above what nature gives.

The preceding accounts of what is natural are not contradictory when readers remember Aristotle's presentation through a matter without-provision (*aporia*) of the decent as better and stronger than the just because decency—as a *hexis* bound to choice—is a correction of the lawfully just that moves-with what is unbounded in the law.[51] The decent shows the space in which intellect operates as what is natural in the politically just. And since the intellect's nature is simple, decent, and experiences pleasure through an activity characterized by the absence of motion, it provides something akin to rest among the practical things that are moving and admit to hold otherwise. If intellect moves virtue and *hexis* from the natural to the authoritative, it is because its own unique capacity to be in activity without motion holds strength over the practical things. But here readers should notice that the intellect is not capable of exercising this authority according to itself, for it needs the authoritative good.

With the intellect's authority over prudence settled, readers should remember how in Book VI Aristotle declares prudence and the political art are the same *hexis*, and goes on to name household management and legislation as forms of prudence, which prompts the question of whether one's own well-being is possible without household management or a regime. This all leads to the question of how to trust in the experience of natural first-principles. The question of the good as the authoritative first-principle is inescapable, though readers may rightly ask if Aristotle "proves" what it is. If readers hope to find a single sentence where Aristotle defines "the good," it does not exist. But readers should not take the lack of provision for such a sentence in Aristotle's philosophy as a sign that it is an empty, ever-changing, formless idea. In the midst of being unprovided about the good, readers should remember Aristotle's assertion that those who claim in *logos* that the good is not that at which all things aim speak nothing, thereby abolishing (*anaireō*) the trust in *logos*.[52] From the beginning of the *Ethics*, Aristotle keeps the possibility that the good is that at which all things aim open. But how do readers discover that the good is a true, natural first-principle and not just a rhetorical device?

As a path toward answering this question, recall how Aristotle begins Book V by acknowledging people's wish to speak of justice as a *hexis*, leading to the argument that one can only know a good-*hexis* through the good, not the bad.[53] In the inquiry into friendship, the choice for the good becomes clearest, and through the decent friends' unreproachable love-of-self that allows them to choose the good and find what is pleasant bound in that choice, Aristotle provides the *Ethics* with the image that clarifies how pleasure is the activity of a *hexis* according to nature. This leads to the discovery of the intellect's pleasure and, through it, the authoritative place of the intellect in the contemplative life that governs self-sufficiency. Justice aspires to be the *hexis* that is friendship, but never reaches it. Thus, by turning to the just in political and economic life while keeping in mind how justice always falls short of friendship, readers can consider how Aristotle's *logos* continually offers them the choice to contemplate how to bring the care for what is properly-one's-own under the authority of the good.

*Chapter 8*

# Justice, Economic Exchange, and Friendship

After seeing how the problem of pleasure from gain in the *Ethics'* inquiry into justice (*dikaiosunē*) (V.3) contrasts with Book X's discovery of happiness holding a pure, liberal, and proper (*oikeia*) pleasure in the intellect's contemplative activity (X.7-8)—a discovery made possible by Book IX's inquiry into friendship (*philia*) and the natural love-of-self (*philautos*) (IX.8-9)—the deeper sense of what is properly-one's-own (*oikeion*) to emerge from these arguments affords readers the opportunity to reassess the nature of the relationship between justice, the art of household management (*oikonomikē*), and the money-making art (*chrēmatistikē*). Between Books V, VIII, IX, there are common themes regarding the good things, worth, exchange, legal-currency, community, and household management (*oikonomia*). Whereas justice in Book V holds some deficient understanding of these things, friendship in Books VIII and IX proves to hold a more comprehensive view of them, one more amenable to the preservation of freedom in politics and economics. Remembering that the political philosopher's perspective is one that carefully attends to the persistence of human beings' need for knowledge of the good to choose what is naturally pleasant in life, readers can work through these arguments from Books V, VIII, and IX of the *Ethics* to discover how Aristotle demonstrates in Book III of the *Politics* that only political philosophy can provide the *logos* of the good necessary for a truly free politics and economics.[1]

Given the *Ethics'* conclusion that happiness (*eudaimonia*) is—to the extent possible for a human being—complete (*teleios*) through the intellect's activity in the contemplative life, it may be helpful to revisit Aristotle's outline in Book I of the lives in which happiness may reside to see the anticipation of this life's authoritative place in all human things. Before Aristotle introduces these lives, he notes it would be vain to examine all the opinions about

happiness, choosing instead to focus readers' attention on those opinions that
are either most prevalent, or seem to hold some *logos*. Next, he praises Plato
for being well-unprovided (*eu aporeō*) about how to seek out or examine
first-principles (*archai*) in *logos*, likening the path toward or away from them
to athletes running toward or away from the limit (*peras*) of a racecourse.
With this contemplative question in mind, Aristotle then turns to the three
lives that are candidates for the good and happiness (one of enjoyment, the
political, and the contemplative), but surprises readers with the addition of
the money-making life. While the life of enjoyment, the political life, and
money-making life each receive scrutiny concerning their ends—pleasure
understood solely as the life of fatted beasts, the deficiencies of honor and
virtue, and wealth being useful for the sake of something else—Aristotle says
nothing of the contemplative life's end, merely stating that "we ourselves will
produce the investigation in what follows."[2]

Although from Book I it is a mystery where the contemplative life shows
up in the remainder of the *Ethics*, after readers run the race of Aristotle's
work to the limit in Book X, the ever-present nature of the contemplative
life in his philosophy and all human things is self-evident. Indeed, in running
back to Aristotle's inquiry into the lives in which the good and happiness
reside, the movement toward and away from the limit of first-principles is
clear: from the life of enjoyment, the political life, and the money-making
life, Aristotle brings readers to these lives' ends (pleasure, honor or virtue,
and wealth, respectively), all of which are deficient in relation to the good.
The contemplative life does not receive a specific end in Book I because the
good is already known or familiar (*gnōrimos*) to readers, and as Aristotle says
of being unprovided about first-principles, "one must begin" (*arkteon*) from
what is known or familiar to oneself to discover what is known or familiar
simply (*haplōs*).[3] Through the contemplative life, readers can run the other
three lives Aristotle presents up to their limits and discover their ends are
incomplete when compared to the good.

The comprehensive view of the contemplative life allows readers to return
to Book V's inquiry into justice and see its partial view of the good in politics
and economics. One place to start is in the connection between the lawful
things (*nomima*) and justice, for all the lawful things are in some way just
since they are bounded by the legislative art (*nomothētikē*). The laws "proclaim" (*agoreō*) concerning all things, "aiming themselves" or "guessing"
either at "what is common belonging to the advantage for all" (*tou koinē
sumpherontos pasin*), or the best, or the authoritative (*kurios*) according to
virtue, or some other such way. From this, "we say" the just things are productive and guarding of the political community's happiness and its parts
(1129b11–19). After going through Book X's final chapter where "justice"
does not appear even though Aristotle turns to the legislative art and declares

it holds a necessitating capacity as *logos* from prudence and intellect, readers should see more clearly how much Aristotle qualifies his account of the just in Book V. Particularly revealing is the final observation about how the just things approach happiness *and* its parts, suggesting a more fractured view of happiness than what the contemplative life offers. Aristotle also suggests some ambiguity over how the advantage at which the just things aim is common, showing it holds many possible directions. The verb Aristotle uses for "aim" (*stochazomai*) in this passage prefigures the ambiguity, for it is distinct from the verb in the *Ethics'* opening sentence for all things "aiming themselves" (*ephiēmi*) at the good, a verb that also means "to desire." Aristotle's use of an ambiguous verb for the just things' "aim" is likely intentional, especially since he begins the *Politics* with the same verb to say all communities "aim themselves" or "guess at" some good, building to the conclusion that all things aim not at the good simply, but the city as the authoritative good.[4] Whether it is the just things or the city, those who take Aristotle's invitation to the contemplative life seriously must sense that the authoritative good in his philosophy is not political.

A further glimpse of justice's incompleteness appears in Aristotle's account of how justice is a specific use (*chrēsis*) of virtue. To frame this argument, readers should consider it in light of the verb Aristotle uses to say the laws "proclaim" (*agoreō*) concerning all things, for its root is *agora*, the place in the city for both public assembly and the market. The laws have an explicit public concern for political assembly and exchange. After pointing to how the laws order works related to virtue and defining justice as virtue that is complete, Aristotle mentions how justice seems to be the strongest (*kratistē*) virtue. Justice is also complete most of all because it is the use of complete virtue toward another and not according to oneself, for while many have the capacity to use virtue in the things that are properly-one's-own (*tois oikeiois*), they lack the capacity to do so toward another. Here Aristotle suggests a saying of Bias holds well, namely, "*Archē* ['first-principle,' 'beginning,' 'rule,' or 'ruling office'] points out the man," for this person is toward another as a ruler in community, and so only justice among the virtues seems to be another's good (1129b19–1130a5). Since Book X reveals intellect is the strongest virtue, justice ultimately fails to live up to its superlative status. One way Book V anticipates this conclusion is through directing justice toward another, thus allowing the intellect to emerge in Book X as the virtue one uses toward oneself *and* another. There is also the question of why people are more likely to use virtue toward what is properly-one's-own than another. Insofar as the laws "proclaim" in both political assembly and exchange, since exchange occurs between households (*oikia*)—the first community where there is no work for the art of exchange (*hē metablētikē*) because all things are common[5] to those living within it—readers should think of what gaps there are between the just things and the care for what is properly-one's-own that the contemplative life can fill with the good as its first-principle.

A hint of how friendship (*philia*) fills in this gap regarding what is properly-one's-own among the just things with the contemplative life appears at the beginning of Book VIII, with Aristotle noting that while friends have no need of justice, those who are just need the addition of friendship, and further, the most just *seems* to be what befits a friend. Justice's need for friendship suggests justice is not self-sufficient (*autarchēs*), but friendship is. Friendship holds a much stronger connection to the contemplative life, as is evident in how the decent (*epieikēs*) (which is stronger than the just) is crucial to discovering the unreproachable love-of-self (*philautos*) in Book IX that proves decisive in separating pleasure from the good in Book X to reveal the contemplative life's strength.[6]

Approaching justice's lack of self-sufficiency in relation to friendship is helpful for thinking through the relationship between politics and economics in Aristotle's political philosophy since justice concerns the use of virtue, and the money-making art (*chrēmatistikē*) that provides for exchange between households and communities is literally "the art of the useful things." As Book VIII's inquiry into friendship reveals, though what is useful (*chrēsimon*) is among the loveable things (*to philēton*) along with what is pleasant (*hēdus*) and what is good (*agathos*), since it seems something good or pleasant comes through the useful, the good and pleasant are loveable as ends.[7] Since Book V's inquiry into justice and the inquiry into friendship from Books VIII and IX contain examinations of community, exchange, and what is properly-one's-own in the household, readers can see how the inquiry into friendship provides for politics' and economics' perpetual need for contemplation of the good. Through this need, readers can better understand why justice explicitly comes under the authority of political philosophy in Book III of the *Politics*.

## THE PARTIAL FORMS OF JUSTICE IN POLITICAL AND ECONOMIC LIFE (*ETHICS* 1129B11–1131A33, 1131B25– 1132A22, 1132B11–1133B23, 1134A23–B18, 1136A34–B14)

Following Aristotle's account of the justice that is part of virtue through which he uncovers the one-holding-more's (*pleonektēs*) pursuit of the pleasure from gain (*kerdos*) in honor, useful things, and preservation (an inquiry he follows by raising but then setting aside the distinction between a good citizen and a good human being), he turns to two parts of justice. One form concerns distributions (*dianomē*) of honor, useful things, and other divisible things for those forming-community in the regime, for in such things each person holds what is equal and unequal. The other form is "the corrective" (*to diorthōtikon*) in things-exchanged-together (*sunallagma*), of which there are two parts: the "voluntary" (*ekousia*) and the "involuntary" (*akousia*). Among the voluntary things-exchanged-together are "sale (*prasis*), buying (*ōnē*), money-lending (*daneismos*), security (*eggun*), use or lending-loan (*chrēsis*), deposit (*parakatathēkē*), or letting for hire (*misthōsis*)." Among the involuntary things-exchanged-together are secret crimes (which include theft), violent acts, and slander (1130a14–1131a9). The "economic" concerns in the contemporary sense appear most in the corrective form of justice that focuses on various exchanges. While it seems as if exchanges are somewhat independent of forming-community in regimes, the useful things in these exchanges necessarily connect them to the distribution of useful things in the regime. Considering distributive justice's concerns are the same as the one-holding-more who (as a reproachable lover-of-self) does not understand how to choose the good things,[8] it is clear that—from the perspective of the good—political and economic concerns do not admit of easy separation.

Further refining his inquiry into the partial forms of justice, Aristotle begins from the understanding that the just is the equal through being the middle term between the unequal: the more (*to pleon*) and the less (*to elatton*). To anyone who doubts the association of the just and the unjust with the equal and unequal, Aristotle adds this is how it seems to all, even without *logos*. It is necessary, then, for the just to be the middle term between four things, namely, two persons and two practical matters (*pragmata*) between them. While mathematically simple, fights and accusations arise in these matters either when equal people hold unequal distributions of things, or unequal people hold equal distributions of things, as is clear from distributions according to worth (*axios*). Though all agree in *logos* (*homologeō*) that distributions need to be according to worth, they do not say worth is the same: democrats say it is "freedom" (*eleutheria*), oligarchs that it is wealth, some that it is good-birth, and aristocrats that it is virtue. The just is therefore some "proportion" (*analogos*) (for the proportion belongs not only to abstract number on its own, but the whole of number), and proportion is the equality of *logoi* (1131a10–33).[9] Notice that an argument that appeals to the equal because this is how it seems to all even without *logos* concludes with proportion belonging to *logos* (as its own name of *analogos* attests). Here readers should recall Book VI's observation that the young do not trust (*pisteuō*) the experience of natural first-principles, but they do trust the abstractions (*aphairesis*) of mathematical ones that are literally "away-from (*apo*) choosing (*hairesis*)."[10] The movement in Book V to see the just and the equal with a fuller sense of *logos* indicates that one way to address the fights and accusations among democrats, oligarchs, the well-born, and aristocrats about how they choose to judge worth is through *logos*. Though Aristotle does not demonstrate this in the *Ethics*, his return to these fights in Book III of the

*Politics* suggests readers need to gain philosophic experience before working through this *logos*.

With the distributive form of the just settled as always being from common useful things according to a proportion of *logos*, the corrective form of the just in things-exchanged-together is equality according to an arithmetical (i.e., a strictly numerical) proportion. Without considering worth, the law uses people as equals and looks at the harm done, and the judge attempts (*peiraō*) to make things equal with a penalty or "loss" (*zēmia*) that takes away (*aphaireō*) the gain. This prompts Aristotle to note that in speaking this way (thus drawing readers' attention back to *logos*), "gain" is not the proper (*oikeios*) name. Restoring depth to this deficient *logos*, Aristotle appeals to the equal as a middle term between the more and the less, with gain being more of the good, and loss less of the bad. Pointing to what the corrective form of justice aspires to, Aristotle states the judge wishes to be like the just ensouled (1131b25–1132a22). The corrective form of the just approaches things-exchanged-together as if the reckoning of gains and losses is their sole concern. Yet when the judge "takes away" (*aphaireō*) a gain, one also takes away a loss that person caused by "choosing" (*haireō*) a gain as a good. The true understanding of what meets the judge as a question of corrective justice is a person's choice of what is good and bad, a choice that is inseparable from the ensouled nature that is most properly-one's-own.

How one needs to move beyond thinking in terms of gain and loss to what is good and bad appears at the end of Aristotle's account of corrective justice, noting the names "loss" and "gain" are from the voluntary exchange, for to hold more of "the things of oneself" (*ta autou*) is to gain, and to hold less of things from the beginning (*archē*) is "to cause loss" (*zēmiō*). "But whenever there is neither more nor less of the things through themselves (*ta di'autōn*), they assert to hold the things of themselves, and neither to cause loss nor to gain," thus leaving the just as the equal middle term that designates holding what is equal both before and after the exchange (1132b11–20). According to this last argument, while "gain" and "loss" are part of exchanges, the terms cannot account fully for holding the equal. Instead, the equal in exchanges belongs to oneself (*autos*), something one can only account for through *logos* that approaches the exchange from the perspective of what is properly-one's-own (*oikeios*): the love-of-self (*philautos*) bound to how one chooses to hold towards the good.

The insufficiencies of distributive and corrective justice from the perspective of *logos* of the good lead to Aristotle introducing a form of the just readers could not anticipate at the beginning of the Book V, one that reveals the just requires accounting for the equal and the unequal together. From the idea of "reciprocity" (*antipeponthos*),[11] Aristotle observes how this sort of the just holds-together the exchanging communities (*tais koinōniais allaktikais*), with the reciprocity being according to proportion, not equality. The city "remains-together" (*summenō*) by "producing-in-turn" (*antipoieō*)[12] proportion, and people seek either to produce-in-turn bad for bad (for it seems slavish if they do not), or well-being (*to eu*). If they do not, no mutual-giving comes to be, and it is by mutual-giving that they remain-together (1132b21–1133a2).[13] Before proceeding, notice how Aristotle stretches mutual-giving (which Book I of the *Politics* characterizes as the mutual-giving of useful things between households as is necessary according to their needs)[14] beyond acquisition to what is bad and well-being (i.e., good). Thoughtful readers should wonder if the mutual-giving of the bad for the bad is ultimately good for a community. Are good and bad merely matters of exchange?

Aristotle next focuses on the need to produce giving according to proportion by observing how community arises out of a need to make equal those who are wholly another (*holōs heterōn*) and unequal. As an example, he considers the disparate works of the housebuilder and the shoemaker, and generally all those whose works need "compared" (*sumblētos*) for there to be community. This is why legal-currency (*nomisma*) came into being as a measure and a middle term *in a way* (*pōs*), for it measures both excess and deficiency, and serves as means for comparing houses, foods, shoes, and all other works. Without legal-currency, there is neither exchange nor community, for the community's works are not equal *in a way* (1133a5–25). Through legal-currency, exchange in community comes to be (implicitly through *logos*) according to a qualified equality that begins from the recognition that all the works are unequal. Though Aristotle confines this insight to the "economic" exchange of works within the community, a necessary consequence of this argument is political community requires *logos* to compare and make equal in some way those persons within it who are equal and unequal.

Through legal-currency and exchange, Aristotle reveals a broader natural foundation for all community. In light of the preceding arguments, there is need for all things to be measured themselves by "some one thing" (*heni tini*), and, in truth, this is need (*chreia*), which holds-together all things. If people do not need anything or do not need it in the same way, there will either be no exchange or not the same exchange. Legal-currency came through being set-down-together by compact as the "exchangeable representative" (*hupallagma*) of need, and through this holds its name since it is not by nature but by law (*nomos*), and is "up to ourselves to change and produce [as] useless" (1133a25–31). Here it is helpful to consider how features of this account of need holding-together all things in Book V of the *Ethics* appears in the inquiry into the money-making art from Book I of the *Politics*. To start, the art of exchange (*hē metablētikē*) to which all things belong begins according to nature from human beings holding more or less than what is adequate. This argument follows immediately after Aristotle distinguishes between the proper (*oikeia*) and improper (*ouk oikeia*) uses of pieces of acquisition: the proper use is according to what something is, and the improper use is its exchange.[15] In both the *Ethics* and the *Politics*, exchange is necessary and according to nature, but using pieces of acquisition for exchange is never proper to their nature (which suggests nature itself is not capable of exchange).

A nuanced difference between the *Ethics* and *Politics* regarding legal-currency's place in exchange is how the latter work describes the money-making art as coming into being according to *logos* once exchange turned to more foreign sources, with legal-currency finding its place in the exchange of useful things because it held a manageable use or need (*chreia*). With experience (*empeiria*) and time, the art of retail-trade (*kapēlikē*) used legal-currency to become more of an art concerning from where and how to produce the most gain. Whereas the *Ethics* emphasizes legal-currency being something set-down-together by compact, the *Politics* speaks of legal-currency coming into being through *logos*. While the role of *logos* is certainly implicit in Book V of the *Ethics*, readers should remember that it not until Book X of this work that Aristotle reveals law is *logos* that holds a necessitating capacity from some prudence and intellect.[16] The need for *logos* is thus present in Book V's account of legal-currency, but Aristotle does not think it is proper at this point in the *Ethics* to highlight it.

Pushing forward in his account of legal-currency and need, Aristotle hints at the political and economic challenges facing community. For the sake of reciprocity, there is need for the proportions between the work exchanged to be set before the exchange when the people hold the things belonging to themselves so that they are equals and "community partners" (*koinōnoi*). In this way, need holds-together just as they are "some one thing" (*hen ti*), for while people do not exchange when they do not need each other, they do exchange when one person needs what another holds. Yet despite presenting need as a key to exchange, Aristotle then presents legal-currency as a "security" (*eggunētēs*) for exchange in the future. But legal-currency does not always have the capacity to be equal, though it wishes to stay more equal. On account of this wish, there is need to honor (*timaō*) all things so there will always be exchange and, through this, community. Equality in community is possible if things are commensurable, which admits to be done adequately toward need. There is need, then, for "some one thing" from hypothesis, and this "calls itself" (*kaleō*) legal-currency that produces all things as commensurable by measuring them (1133a31–b23). This sequence of arguments holds competing claims about what makes community "some one thing": need (*chreia*) (1133b6), or legal-currency (1133b20).[17]

The path to legal-currency's claim is much more tenuous than need's, which is not surprising considering Aristotle's observation that people can change legal-currency and produce it as useless (cf. 1133a28–31). Compared to the need that always defines human things and ensures a place for exchange in life (though it may not be equal at all times and in all places), legal-currency can only "wish" to stay equal to the things it helps people exchange. But instead of drawing legal-currency back to need, Aristotle turns to how people honor all things, thereby changing how legal-currency holds toward these things. With honor in the picture, legal-currency's purpose changes from producing exchange according to need, to becoming the measure of all things' honor (which Book I teaches is not properly-one's-own when compared to the good). This seems to be why Aristotle draws attention to how legal-currency "calls itself" this name, thus mimicking the city in the opening of the *Politics* that claims for itself the most authoritative of all goods and, through this, encompasses all other communities.[18]

Although Aristotle holds back from showing readers the absurdity of legal-currency's claim to measuring all things and—through this—community, in the inquiry into the money-making art from the *Politics*, recall that a change in the setting-down (*metatithēmi*) of legal-currency so that it has no worth (*axios*) makes it possible for someone well-provided (*euporeō*) in this to be unprovided (*aporeō*) in necessary things, for the legal-currency is no longer useful. As Aristotle indicates in Book V of the *Ethics*, legal-currency is the exchangeable representative of need by being set-down-together by compact (*sunthēkē*), and the lawful is something set-down as part of the politically just.[19] The great matter without-provision regarding legal-currency, exchange, and community is one could set-down these things so that they are either according to need and nature, or contrary to need and nature. All these things admit to hold otherwise and could be done through *logos*, yet the possibility that one way leads to legal-currency being useless for necessary things suggests that not all *logos* is toward the good.

After his account of the partial forms of the just and leaving behind reciprocity, Aristotle reminds readers that the sought-for thing (*to zētoumenon*) is both the simply just and the politically just (1134a23–26). This is an ambiguous statement, and Aristotle does not decide for readers if the sought-for thing is the simply just or the politically just (though in the next chapter the politically just appears as on the one hand natural, and on the other hand lawful). But "the sought-for thing" points to a broader horizon. If readers go back to the inquiry into the lives to which happiness belongs in Book I, they find Aristotle rejects honor as the sought-for thing because "we divine ourselves" that the good is something properly-one's-own (*oikeios*) and hard-to-take-away (*dusaphaireton*). Similarly, in the money-making life, Aristotle rejects wealth as the sought-for good because it is useful and for the sake of another thing.[20] While both honor and wealth are parts of Aristotle's inquiry into the just, they also fall short of the good one chooses for life. Thus, in Aristotle's short outline that puts the simply just and the politically just in relation to the sought-for thing, he directs them to the good that is properly-one's-own.

Like "some one thing" making community in Aristotle's discussion of reciprocity bringing forth competing claims between need and legal-currency, there are competing claims within the context of the just. On the one hand, the just is among those forming-community in life toward self-sufficiency (*autarkeia*) who are free (*eleutheros*) and equal (either according to proportion or number), otherwise there is not the politically just toward each other. On the other hand, there is the just when people have law toward themselves, and where there is law, there is injustice, understood primarily as distributing more of the simply good things and less of the simply bad things to oneself (1134a26–34). Aristotle's turn toward forming community in life supports reading "the sought-for thing" in relation to the simply just and the politically just as a clue that one should think more explicitly about the good in this part of Book V. Also, this passage marks the sole appearance of "self-sufficiency" in Book V, though readers have yet to discover Book X's account of the intellect and contemplative life's authoritative place in providing an activity and pleasure that is properly-one's-own and therefore self-sufficient, even if human nature is not self-sufficient on account of the body's needs.[21]

With these connections in mind, one can attend to Aristotle's present inquiry and the competing claims of self-sufficiency and law to the just with greater care. A clear sign within Book V that these competing claims point to a broader horizon is how they blur the lines between the three ways people speak of the unjust person from the beginning of the inquiry into justice: the one contrary to law, the one-holding-more, and the unequal person.[22] Despite injustice in the present context appearing as both contrary to law and being one-holding-more in the distributions of good and bad things, Aristotle does not appeal to the labels he puts forth at the beginning of Book V. And while he associates the equal with the just in relation to self-sufficiency, he does not associate injustice with being unequal (which quietly suggests being unequal is not necessarily unjust). Taken together, Aristotle's arguments suggest Book V's preoccupation with the just as it relates to the equal and unequal must give way to the more complete perspective afforded by life, the good things, and the bad things.

Though first-time readers of the *Ethics* do not know it when they encounter injustice as distributing more of the simply good things and less of the simply bad things to oneself, Aristotle offers them a glimpse into the thinking of a figure whose sole appearance in the entire work is in Book VII: the political philosopher, who contemplates pleasures and pains as the architect of the end in relation to which "we speak" of each thing as simply bad and simply good.[23] Considering how the pleasure from gain drives the one-holding-more, it would seem fitting for Aristotle to introduce the political philosopher in

Book V. Indeed, why does Aristotle fail to provide the political philosopher in an inquiry into justice?

The reasons why Aristotle withholds the political philosopher in Book V become apparent in the next part of the inquiry with yet another ambiguity. From the just either toward self-sufficiency or law, on account of the injustice in the distributions of the simply good and simply bad things to oneself, Aristotle declares this is why "we allow" or "permit" or "suffer" (all possible meanings of *eaō*) not a human being to rule, but *logos* (or law),[24] for a human being who distributes these things to oneself in this way comes to be a tyrant. A ruler, in contrast, guards the just and the equal, and does not distribute more of the simply good to oneself unless it is a proportion toward oneself. On account of this, the ruler labors for another, and through this justice is said to be another's good. As a result, there is some wage of honor and privilege for the ruler, while those to whom this is not adequate become tyrants (1134a34–b8). Now the ambiguity in the just shifts to whether the rule immune to injustice in distributions of the simply good and simply bad things is *logos*, or the ruler. But if one of the injustices plaguing distributions is the one-holding-more, and the pleasures from gain for this person hold their capacity toward useful things and honor, then neither wages nor honor adequately guard against tyranny. This problem leaves readers with two related questions. First, how does *logos* rule in place of a human being? Second, how can *logos* guard rulers from becoming tyrants?

Although Aristotle does not answer in Book V how *logos* rules in place of a human being and can guard against tyranny, he points to the grounds on which his own *logos* meets this challenge in Book X. Before taking up Book V's allusion, it may be helpful to begin with Book X's arguments at the end of the *Ethics*, where Aristotle brings the many and tyrants together in thinking happiness resides in pleasures of play, likely because their lack of taste for pure and liberal pleasure prevents them from taking hold of virtue and intellect. Gesturing toward this pleasure, Aristotle notes human beings lack the capacity for holding-together in labor, so they need relaxation. Through this argument, Aristotle leads readers to discover the contemplative life's leisure that opposes the labor of war and politics. In this respect, Aristotle first provides an answer to the question of how to guard rulers from becoming tyrants: the contemplative life's self-sufficiency and proper (*oikeios*) pleasure can provide for the ruler's happiness that is properly-one's-own in a way that the politician's activity never could. Through recognizing the politicians' activity does not aim at the happiness that is properly-one's-own, Aristotle puts forth a way to help rulers liberate themselves from the pursuit of gain in ruling (whether in wages or honor) that destroys their political communities. As to how *logos* rules instead of a human being, in Book X's final chapter, Aristotle turns to the argument that the many trust-the-rule by necessity rather than by *logos*, especially on account of how they desire (*oregō*) pleasure. In opposition to this argument, Aristotle notes law holds a necessitating capacity that is not heavy when it is *logos* from some prudence and intellect.[25] With the decent playing such a central role in discovering the unreproachable love-of-self that serves as the basis for discovering the contemplative life's self-sufficiency through community in *logos* and thought, readers should notice the opening Aristotle creates for friendship in response to the problem posed by the understanding that justice in ruling is another's good.

Following the unresolved problem of ruling and the risk of injustice through gain in the distribution of the simply good and simply bad things, Aristotle turns to the household to uncover grounds to which justice does not appeal. Whether it is the just in the sense of a master or a father, these are like the simply just and the politically just, but not the same. This is because there is not injustice simply toward the things of oneself (*ta autou*), for both the piece of acquisition and the child are like a part of oneself, and no one chooses (*proaireō*) to harm oneself. After reiterating there is neither what is unjust nor the politically just toward oneself, Aristotle observes law is natural where there is equality in ruling and being ruled, on account of which what is just is more toward a wife than toward children and pieces of acquisition, for this is the just in the sense of household management (which differs from the politically just) (1134b8–18). Within the *Ethics*, Aristotle does not consider what the just might look like in household management in Book V, deferring such an inquiry until Book VIII (the first half of the inquiry into friendship). Since the arguments from Books VIII and IX bearing on the just in both economic exchange and the household appear shortly, it is sufficient first to focus on Aristotle's argument that no choice is to harm oneself, which hearkens back to three important arguments about the good from Books I through III.

In Book I, Aristotle draws readers' attention to the difference and wandering of the just things (along with the noble things) that make it seem they are by law and not by nature, whereas the good things hold wandering (but no difference) through the harm that comes to some people through them (like people who destroy themselves through wealth). In Book II, the bad person misses the mark in choice because of pleasure, which leads to the assertion that all the matter of concern for virtue and the political art is pleasures and pains. In Book III, on the question of whether wish is for the good or the apparent good, the many choose the apparent good because pleasure deceives them, leading them to choose the pleasant as good and flee pain as bad, rather than judging the good according to the truth.[26] Though all these arguments concern one's own choice of the good, Aristotle's use of the household in Book V brings his own *logos* home. If some readers struggle to see how their confusion about the pleasant and the good in their own choices is harmful to themselves, their own aversion to choosing to harm and commit injustice toward members of the household (whether it is the spouses, children, and slaves who all seem to belong among what is properly-one's-own) suggests justice's insufficiency in confronting the most confounding problem in one's own choices.

Two further appearances of this question about justice and injustice toward oneself within Book V compel thoughtful readers to seek something more than justice. The first is in the chapter preceding Aristotle's examination of decency and the decent, where he places among the unprovided things the question of whether one admits to do injustice toward oneself, setting the argument on a path to the conclusion that the just things are among those having a share in the simply good things with no set amount (i.e. excess, defect, but no mean) proving beneficial, which is a human thing (1136a34–b1). The failure of "the mean" to show up in such a crucial argument about justice is a subtly damning indictment of how much weight one can put on the authority of the account of the moral virtues. To understand the just things, one must understand the good things, but not in the sense of a mean between excess and defect. This argument anticipates Book VI's choice to divide (*diaireō*) correct *logos* (which says there is need to choose the middle term and not excess or defect) to mark its boundary (*horos*). Readers should also remember how Aristotle initially defines prudence as "a true practical *hexis* with *logos* concerning the good things and bad things for a human being," only to redefine it as "a true practical *hexis* with *logos* concerning the good things for human beings." After Aristotle introduces the political philosopher in Book VII, he presents the good as twofold (either simply, or for some person), leading to the mystery of pleasures without pains and the contemplative activity belonging to the nature not in-need. As first-time readers make their way through Book V of the *Ethics*, they do not know what these arguments mean. But to readers who complete the *Ethics*, racing back to Book V from the limit of Book X's call to complete "the philosophy concerning the human things" allows them to see how Aristotle finds a need for philosophy within justice's failure to provide for the question of how to hold oneself toward the good things.[27]

The second appearance of the question concerning justice and injustice toward oneself contains a refinement to the idea that points readers both to friendship and the inquiry into natural slavery from the *Politics*. In the final chapter of Book V (which immediately follows the inquiry into decency and the decent person), Aristotle states that according to metaphor and similarity there is not what is just toward oneself, but of some of the things of oneself that is not every sense of what is just, but is either in the sense of the master or the household manager. These *logoi* set-standing-apart (*diestēmi*) the part of the soul holding *logos* from the part without *logos*, from which it seems there is injustice toward oneself through people being affected in some way contrary to the desires of themselves (*tas heautōn orexeis*), so that there is something just in these as there is for ruler and ruled (1138b5–14). Within Book V, Aristotle refers to the argument that no one chooses (*proaireō*) to harm oneself, with desire coming in to offer some account for why there is harm. But choice drops from this latest argument, which invites the question of why Aristotle chooses this approach. A clue resides in Aristotle's important qualification for this line of argument as not concerning what is toward oneself, and further, allowing *logoi* that "set-standing-apart" the soul. Insofar as choice and a human being are a first-principle that is either desiring intellect (*orektikos nous*) or thinking desire (*orexis dianoētikē*), it would not be true to speak of human beings as if they are set-standing-apart. While it is perfectly plausible to do this in *logos*, one must remember that it is possible to mark-the-boundaries (*diorizō*) of naturally inseparable things as parts in *logos*.[28] Consequently, one could find the just in some "parts" of oneself, but risk missing the whole of choice and human nature.

Aristotle's nod to a metaphorical *logos* about the just residing in the relationship between the parts of oneself is a clear allusion to Book IV of Plato's *Republic* and Socrates' account of justice among the classes of the soul. In Socrates' *logos*, justice truly concerns the things within oneself, setting-down (*tithēmi*) well the things that are properly-one's-own, ruling oneself, adorning (*kosmeō*) oneself, and coming to be a friend to oneself. In whatever the just person does—which includes the acquisition of useful things (*hē chrēmatōn ktēsin*)—one names a just and noble action one that preserves this *hexis*, with wisdom (*sophia*) as the science (*epistēmē*) overseeing actions (443c–444a). Even though Socrates' *logos* divides the soul into classes resembling the city, he bookends the many ways of speaking of this work as a whole with setting-down the things that are properly-one's-own *and* befriending oneself. Though Aristotle does not find anything supporting the idea of justice toward oneself, in Book IX, he discovers friendships mark-the-boundaries (*horizō*) from the things toward oneself, thus setting up the inquiry into love-of-self. In the *Ethics*, friendship fills justice's void in accounting for what is properly-one's-own, which seems to explain why he begins Book V by drawing attention to people's wish to speak about justice as if it is a *hexis* and preparing readers to think of *hexis* as a choice for the good, not an approximation of the good as a mean between contrary bad things.[29] With respect to what this means for politics and economics, just as Socrates argues that what governs the just person's acquisition of useful things is the preservation of this *hexis* that is friendship, Aristotle's allusion to this Socratic *logos* anticipates his return to the just, community, and the exchange of useful things in Books VIII and IX that fully situates these matters in terms of how to choose and preserve the good that is properly-one's-own through friendship.

## FRIENDSHIP, JUSTICE, AND COMMUNITY (*POLITICS* 1259A37–1260B24, *ETHICS* 1159B20–1160A30, 1161A32– 1162B31, 1163A21–1165B20, 1167B17–1168A29)

Before turning to Books VIII and IX of the *Ethics*, it should not escape readers' notice that Aristotle's two mentions of the just in the sense of a master gesture toward the *Politics*, where the inquiry into slavery (I.4–7) sits between Book I's inquiry into the natural growth of political community (I.1–2) and the inquiry into the money-making art (I.8–11). One reason why Aristotle undertakes the inquiry into slavery is because the "complete household" is set-standing-together from slaves and free persons, and the three parts of the household are master and slave, husband and wife, and father and children. But by the end of the inquiry into slavery, no human being meets the standard for natural master and natural slave (which means only free persons naturally belong to the household), and for the first time in the *Politics*, friendship appears as a possibility for even master and slave.[30] Through finding slavery is an unnatural part of the community that is properly-one's-own, Aristotle frees readers to think more liberally about the first community and acquisition through friendship.

One key argument Aristotle uses to prove no human being meets the definition of a natural master and slave comes from contemplating the living animal whose soul rules its body despotically, while intellect rules desire in a political or kingly way. Aristotle then puts the matter somewhat differently, saying the intellect and the part holding *logos* rule the passionate part, and from this proposes one definition of a natural slave is someone who has the capacity to belong to another by forming-community in *logos* by having sense-perception of it but not holding it oneself.[31] The latter account about "parts" of the soul in relation to *logos* should remind readers of Aristotle's allusion to Plato's *Republic*. In treating human nature's relationship to *logos* as master and slave in the *Politics*, Aristotle seems to do something similar to Socrates: he sets-standing-apart things within oneself in search of mastery and slavery knowing this *logos* may not be an accurate reflection of the whole. If intellect rules desire with political or kingly rule, and if both choice and human nature are a combination of intellect and desire, then the only natural approach to acquisition—and, through this, all economic concerns— is a political or kingly one. And if the political and kingly rule in this sense opposes the master, only the former forms of rule are free.

Though the question of political rule drops from Aristotle's inquiry into the money-making art from Book I of the *Politics*, it returns immediately after this inquiry in Book I's final two chapters where he considers the arts related to the free parts of the art of household management (*oikonomikē*), namely, wives and children. While a man rules his wife with political rule, he rules his children with kingly rule (1259a37–b1). As Aristotle suggests with monarchy in the household before alluding to friendship between master and slave, the presence of free persons within the household allows the art of household management to include different forms of rule. In this respect, the household and its ruling art are more comprehensive than the political things, and this seems to be because its natural parts are free persons. The significance of this insight is not obvious in Book I of the *Politics*, and it might even seem that the structure of that inquiry obscures it. After all, despite naming free persons as parts of the household in Book I's third chapter, they do not return to Aristotle's inquiry for eight chapters, even after the examination of the slavery suggests human beings are naturally free. Why, then, does Aristotle withhold the return of free persons to Book I of the *Politics* until after he concludes his inquiry into the money-making art?

At the beginning of the final chapter in Book I of the *Politics*, Aristotle states it is apparent that household management (*oikonomia*) is more serious about human beings than soulless acquisitions, and further, is more serious about the virtue of free persons than the virtue of acquisition (which is wealth) and slaves. These observations prompt several questions about virtue and the soul that culminate with Aristotle suggesting there is need to look at the relationship between virtue in the household to virtue in the city since the former community is part of the latter. After mentioning how women and children are community-partners and stating what concerns these things has marked-its-boundaries, Aristotle concludes Book I by proposing to leave off these *logoi* as holding an end (*telos*) and asks readers to produce another beginning (*archē*) concerning the best regime (1259b18–1260b24).[32] Considering a major theme in Aristotle's inquiry into the money-making art is liberating the art of household management from seeking the gain of legal-currency without-limit, going through this inquiry is necessary for the community that is properly-one's-own to find what makes it free in virtue. But the household is only a free community if its members are free, something Aristotle purposely leaves behind to examine regimes. Thus, at the end of Book I of the *Politics*, neither the political nor the economic understood in relation to community, acquisition, and rule provide a full account of what makes human beings free. Readers must search for freedom in a more natural context, one intimately bound to their choices of the good: friendship.[33]

## Friendship, the Just, and the Household (*Ethics* 1159b20–1160a30, 1161a32–1162a29)

The just and community enter Aristotle's inquiry into friendship after his examination of the useful, pleasant, and complete forms of friendship. In the chapter immediately before Aristotle turns to the relationship between friendship and the just, he reveals that underneath the desire (*oregō*) for honor is an aim to confirm an opinion that is properly-one's-own (*tēn oikeian doxan*), seeking to trust that one is good. After suggesting love (*phileō*) looks like the virtue of a friend, Aristotle uses equality and likeness to bring forth the problem of worth. Useful friendships seem to arise between opposites most of all, with the poor and wealthy person as one example, for the poor person needs what the wealthy person has, and what the poor person gives back is an open question. But rather than suggesting a solution, Aristotle appeals to the case of lovers (*erastēs*) to show they hold something laughable when they deem themselves worthy (*axioō*) of more love than they deserve. From this example, Aristotle wonders if desire (*orexis*) in these cases is for the middle term that is good. Like Book V's inquiry into the just, Aristotle presents competing arguments, for one can understand the useful friendship between the poor and the wealthy either in terms of need and worth, or one could see them as a desire for the good. The former perspective leads to a major challenge for all regimes, while the latter perspective is freer. To understand this, readers must see how the household is a community more naturally aligned with the good in Aristotle's political philosophy, for the good is the "certain quantity" (*poson*) that friendship (unlike the just) puts ahead of worth.[34]

Aristotle's approach to the just in Book VIII's ninth chapter begins on familiar ground, noting friendship and the just concern the same things, for it seems that in every community there is something just, and friendship. Supporting the idea that friendship is in community, Aristotle cites the proverb "the things of friends are common" (*koina ta philōn*). Both the just things and friendship admit of more or less, and both increase with friendship. But whereas the unjust things are more terrible when the friendship is closer, the just things naturally increase themselves in friendship (1159b25–1160a8). There is a natural affinity between friendship and the just, but there is nothing natural about the unjust in relation to friendship, even if it is more terrible. Aristotle does not yet give a reason for this, though it becomes clearer as he pushes ahead. For now, Aristotle turns his attention to the communities, which all look like parts of the political community that comes together for some advantage, providing some of the things in life. Legislators aim (*stochazomai*) the political community at this, and they say that the common advantage is just. As for all the other communities, they aim themselves at the advantage according to a part, such as sailors working for useful things (*chrēmata*). But just as Aristotle hints at the comprehensive nature of political community in terms of advantage, he mentions the existence of communities through pleasure, though he quickly subsumes these under the political community that aims itself at the advantage of life altogether (1160a8–30). The challenge for political community in the remainder of Book VIII of the

*Ethics* is if it can naturally justify its claim to subsume all things in life to the common advantage. But if the standard is life itself, readers know from Book X that the life that is proper (*oikeios*) to human beings is the contemplative one according to the intellect's activity, one to which Aristotle's *Ethics* leads readers by showing the political life is without leisure.

In Book VIII's tenth and eleventh chapters, Aristotle outlines the different forms of regimes and explores how they have models within the household. For the purposes of thinking about politics and economics, the conclusion of this part of the inquiry into friendship is helpful for seeing how Aristotle thinks human beings are naturally free. In both tyranny and slavery, there is either no friendship or a little friendship because there is nothing common between ruler and ruled. The connection between tyranny and slavery is both the tyrant and the master benefit themselves by using human beings as if they are soulless things, and there is neither friendship nor the just toward these things.[35] But this is not quite right, for there is friendship insofar as a slave is a human being, and through this, there is a small amount of friendship and the just in tyranny, and more so in democracy since people are equals in many of the common things (1161a32–b10). Even in conditions most hostile to freedom, Aristotle finds human nature itself holds open the possibility for friendship. No matter how much authority one human being claims over another, no one can treat other human beings as if they are soulless. Though Aristotle does not draw the connection, one reason for this conclusion is Book VI's description of human beings as a combination of intellect and desire. No set of external conditions can fully deprive human beings of their nature that makes choice possible. The most one can do is constrain people's choices (as in tyranny or slavery). Alternatively, one could expand the areas where they can make choices (like democracy). But these political conditions rest on human nature, which is free in the sense that people can engage in more than political life.

With the turn to parents and children—to the free persons of the household—in Book VIII's twelfth chapter, Aristotle finds through friendship of "kinsfolk" (*sungennikos*) the natural foundations for community liberated from the problem of worth. For one, both parents and children feel-affection (*stergō*) for each other: parents because the children are of themselves, and children because they are from their parents. Parents love (*phileō*) their children as themselves, for children are other selves (*heteroi autoi*). After accounting for the friendship between siblings and noting the friendship between parents and children has more of the useful and the pleasant within it, Aristotle says the friendship between husband and wife seems to be present according to nature, for a human being is by nature more "coupling" (*sunduastikon*) than political, seeing that a household is before and more necessary than a city. This is because human beings "dwell-together-in-households" (*sunoikeō*) not only for the sake of having children, but for all the things in life. Through this, the useful and pleasant seem to be in the friendship of a husband and wife, and virtue too if they are decent. Finally, children seem to be a "bond" (*sundesmos*), for they are a common good (*koinon agathon*)[36] to both parents, and the common holds-together (1161b11–1162a29). Whereas Aristotle's examination of the just, community, and friendship begins in Book V with all communities providing parts of the things toward life in service of the political community, the friendship between husband and wife now cares for all things in life. Unlike the political community that finds the just in the common advantage, friendship between parents holds a common good through children. The friendship between husband and wife seems to be the complete form of friendship that encompasses the useful and the pleasant and has virtue as its foundation and culminates with a consideration of how friendship is equality.[37] But Aristotle never refers to the friendship between parents as "complete," nor does he mention equality and inequality. Within the friendship between parents and children, love (*phileō*) and feeling-affection (*stergō*) take the place of equality and inequality, and disputes about these things are not present in the household because its members are friends through themselves. All of this emerges through Aristotle describing human beings as more "coupling" than "political," a distinction that rests in part on the discovery of a common good not in the city, but the household, the community that is properly-one's-own. If the good is to become a common part of political and economic life, its only natural way in is through friendship, which is more naturally suited to the household than the city.

## Friendship, Exchange, and the Problem of Worth (*Ethics* 1162a35–b31, 1163a21–1165b20, 1167b17–1168a29)

Following the natural friendship between free persons in the household, Aristotle returns to the three forms of friendship with careful attention to the problems facing equality in useful friendships, especially since accusations and blame come to be either in this friendship only, or this friendship most of all, and with good-*logos*. In using each other for a beneficial thing, such friends always need more and suppose they hold less of what seems "befitting" (*prosēkō*), and so they blame each other because they do not hit or happen upon (*tunchanō*) what they need and what they deem themselves worthy to have (1162a35–b21). In stating this problem with useful friendships in general terms, Aristotle shows how the useful left to itself opens up questions about a multitude of needs that are inseparable from worth. The inquiry thus enters the familiar territory of the just in distributions according to proportion (*analogos*)—which is equality of *logoi*[38]—but now from the perspective of friendship.

Aristotle, however, does not focus on distribution in the present inquiry, turning instead to a division within useful friendships into the moral (*ēthikē*) and the lawful (*nomikē*), with only the latter bearing directly on economic exchange. The lawful is on the one hand upon "stated terms" (*rētos*) and is wholly from the hand-to-hand things in the marketplace, and on the other hand more liberal in time but according to an agreement (*homologia*) of something for something else. The latter form of the lawfully useful friendship has a clear debt that is undisputed, but holds what befits a friend (*philikon*) in the delay. Consequently, there are no arbitrations (*dikai*) of these things, supposing there is need for those exchanging together (*sunallassō*) according to trust to feel-affection for each other (1162b21–31). Notice that in separating useful friendships into the moral and the lawful, the latter form omits the problem of worth. At first glance, it seems possible to arrange things in the marketplace so that the stated terms of hand-to-hand exchanges prevent accusations about worth. It also seems desirable to arrange things regarding debts so that the person who loans something and the person who receives it feel-affection for one another, an affection of the same kind as the one felt by the free members of the household. In either case, economic exchange seeks a trust liberated from worth that is not possible in any other context besides friendship.

What is liberal about friendship in comparison to economic exchange emerges in two small arguments at the end of Book VIII that provide a helpful context for a new approach to the problem of worth in Book IX's opening chapter. The first argument in Book VIII marks a conclusion to Aristotle's division of useful friendships into the moral and the lawful. In this argument, there are no accusations in friendships according to virtue because it looks like the choice (*proairesis*) is the measure of doing some great things, for in virtue and character, the choice is the authoritative thing (1163a21–23). Although this argument appears as an aside, it significantly sets friendships according to virtue (the model throughout Book VIII) outside the bounds of the lawful and moral friendships. The appeal to choice as the authoritative thing in these friendships should instantly remind readers of the first-principle that is a human being, a combination of intellect and desire. To friends who know each other's choices, accusations do not arise because they know and are familiar with the "measure" of the thing done. Or, to put it another way, these friends know or are familiar with what they contemplate and desire.

But perhaps measure is not the right way to think about friendships, as is evident in Book VIII's final chapter in the arguments surrounding Aristotle's account of a friendship between someone in-need and someone holding-over that person. In such friendships, each person correctly deems worthy, and so one distributes to the person holding-over more of honor, while to the person in-need one distributes more of gain. Leading into this argument, Aristotle points to how those in a community of useful things suppose those who throw in more take hold of more, so that there is need for friendship to be this way too. But those who are in-need say the reverse, that it belongs to a good friend to assist those in-need. Following his account of the worthy distribution between the person holding-over and the person in-need, Aristotle says the honor is a reward of virtue and a good-work, while gain is an aid to the person in-need. It appears to hold in this way in regimes, where there is no honor for those providing nothing good, for honor is the common thing given to the person doing good work. Money-making, however, is not honored, for people distribute honor to those losing useful things. From this consideration, although Aristotle initially says that what is according to worth makes equal and preserves friendship, he follows this up by saying friendship seeks to give back the possible (*to dunaton*, related to "capacity," *dunamis*), not what is according to worth (1163a30–b18). This whole sequence of arguments begins with the implicit assumption that community in useful things (in economic exchange) should inform how people view friendships, and this in turn is how one should view regimes. All things become questions of worth, yet friendship is not primarily about worth. One way Aristotle offers out of this predicament implicitly involves the household, for he concludes Book VIII by discussing how neither a father nor a son who have a natural friendship (*tēs phusikēs philias*) can renounce each other (1163b18–28). The love (*phileō*) and feeling-affection (*stergō*) of the free members of the household provides a natural basis for community that does not care about worth. The challenge for political community is its liberation from this concern, especially since it is not as natural a community as the household.

The supposedly authoritative place of economic exchange serves as readers' point of entry into Book IX, the second half of the *Ethics'* inquiry into friendship. Aristotle begins by observing that in all "friendships without-like-form" (*tais anomoioeidesi philiais*) the proportion (*analogos*) makes equal and preserves the friendship, as was said in the political (*hē politikē*) where legal-currency provides a common measure for all things (1163b32–1164a2). As in Book V, legal-currency is a measure for all things, but unlike Book V, Aristotle neither speaks of legal-currency in relation to the just as representing need (*chreia*) that holds-together all things, nor does he mention "community" despite implying that friendships involving the exchange of legal-currency belong to "the political."[39] The perspective on what readers wish to call an "economic" concern is again one of friendship, which is naturally broader than both the "economic" and the "political."

From the example those who have *erōs* for each other quarreling over the pleasant and the useful because they do not have the same character, Aristotle turns to the more general problem of how people differ whenever that which they desire (*oregō*) does not come to be for themselves, for it is like nothing coming to be when they do not hit or happen upon that at which they aim themselves. All of this prompts a question about how to arrange things regarding worth, leading to the idea that in matters where there is no agreement (*homologia*, "same-*logos*") about "services rendered" (*hupourgia*), one must produce (*poiēton*) the "compensation" (*amoibē*) according to the choice, for this is something of friendship and virtue. This is what it looks like for those who form-community in philosophy, whose worth is not measured according to useful things (*chrēmata*) and honor could not come to be "equally balanced" (*isorropos*) with it, perhaps leaving only what is adequate, as with gods and parents (1164a2–b6). A problem that begins with desire and aims culminates with a resolution that finds worth unsatisfactory from the perspective of philosophy. Though some readers may again wish to reject Aristotle's appeal to philosophy, notice that the way philosophers deem worth insufficient is similar to how children hold toward their parents in the household. The latter example perhaps holds even more weight than philosophy since it carries with it an implicit growth on the part of children who did not choose to become part of the household, but nevertheless choose to compensate their parents as adequately as they can, and parents choose to accept this because of the love and affection in the household. In either case, choice transcends worth. Insofar as knowledge of the good since Book I has the potential to prevent choosing from going on without-limit so that desire is not left empty and vain,[40] both the household and philosophy (which are friendships) are far closer to this good than political and economic community.

The possibility of community in philosophy transcending worth allows Aristotle to return to economic exchange with a clearer hint of where what is properly-one's-own fits in these things. Unlike forming-community in philosophy, whenever there is a giving back of one thing for another, either both people involved seem to form an opinion according to worth, or it would seem necessary and just for the person "first-to-hold" (*to proechonta*) something to give an opinion of its worth. This is how it comes to appear in things bought and "for sale" (*hōnios*). After covering the familiar territory of trust in the more liberal exchanges that are not subject to arbitration (though this time they appear not in the context of useful lawful friendships, but forming-community),[41] Aristotle draws attention to how many things are not honored equally by those holding them as those who wish to take hold of them, for the things that are properly-one's-own (*oikeia*) and that which they give to each person show themselves to have much worth. From this, Aristotle tentatively concludes that perhaps there is need to honor something's worth according to how much one honored it before holding it (1164b6–21). Unlike Book V's account of how legal-currency provides a common measure for things, this account of the things bought and sold shows that things' worth ultimately comes back to the honor each person bestows on the things that are properly-one's-own, thus leading to difficulties in determining the worth of things exchanged. At best, Aristotle can only suggest that *perhaps* the person who takes hold of what someone gives of the things that are properly-one's-own can resolve the difficulty. But this resolution is not complete since the person who wishes to take hold of something aims to bring that into what is properly-one's-own as well. In this respect, if one wishes to grasp how economic exchange fits into political community, one must recognize questions of worth exist on top each person's understanding of what is properly-one's-own.

With worth from the perspective of forming-community in philosophy pointing to the need to know what is properly-one's-own, it is not surprising that the next two chapters of Book IX preceding its introduction to the possibility of friendship toward oneself[42] hold without-provision (*aporia*) in "economic" things that become fruitful ground for the *Ethics'* turn toward love-of-self in light of what is properly-one's-own. In Book IX's second chapter, the matters without-provision concern what one distributes or pays back in various contexts, including debts (*opheilēma*) and lending. This inquiry culminates with Aristotle observing that whether it is families, fellow tribesmen, citizens, and all the remaining people with whom there is community, one must attempt (*peirateon*) always to distribute (*aponemō*) what is properly-one's-own (*to oikeion*), and to compare the means presently belonging to each according to being-properly-one's-own (*oikeiotēma*) and virtue, *or* use. While it is easier to compare families in this regard, it is a troublesome-work among those who differ. But one cannot give up doing this, and one must bound (*dioristeon*) this as it might admit (1164b22–1165a35). The preceding inquiry is akin to the just in distributions from Book V, yet Aristotle refrains from bringing the just and its concern with what is equal and unequal into this portion of Book IX.[43] The inclusion of what is properly-one's-own complicates the question of how to address distributions in community, for not only is distribution a troublesome-work outside of families, but one could compare the things belonging to what is properly-one's-own according to either virtue or use. Despite raising this difficulty, Aristotle does not resolve it immediately, leaving readers to wonder what happens if one directs what is properly-one's-own in one direction rather than the other.

Though Aristotle explores this more in Book IX of the *Ethics*, readers should recall how he shows in Book I of the *Politics* that while the art of household management's work makes a limit to all wealth appear necessary, all those engaging in money-making who increase legal-currency without-limit through the art of retail-trade cause an "exchange-upon" (*epallassō*) one art for the other. The source of confusion between the two arts is their use of the same acquisition (i.e., legal-currency), but for different ends. While the art of retail-trade's end is the increase of legal-currency, Aristotle does not say what the art of household management's end is within the inquiry into the money-making art.[44] The most readers see in Book I of the *Politics* regarding household management's (*oikonomia*) end is Aristotle's statement in the final chapter that it is more serious about human beings than soulless acquisitions, and further, the virtue of free persons rather than wealth and slaves. As for the end through which people are free, Aristotle does not take it up, proposing to leave off these *logoi* as holding an end to turn toward the best regime (presumably because what concerns virtue in the household and the city has marked-its-boundaries through households being part of the city).

All of this connects to the first matter without-provision in Book IX of the *Ethics* where Aristotle bookends the inquiry with two remarks on the difficulty in precisely bounding what one pays back or distributes in different contexts (cf. 1164b27–28 and 1165a33–35). In between these bookends, when Aristotle speaks of debts and lending, he observes these things hold similar bounding (*to hōrismenon*) as *logoi* concerning the passions and actions (1165a2–14). Aristotle's observation implies these matters lack precision in a way that brings together two arguments about *logos* from Book I. The first argument concerns the proper (*oikeios*) listener to the political art's *logoi*. Though Aristotle initially says the young are not proper listeners because they are without experience (*apeiron*), he revises this to say *logoi* are vain and without benefit to those who follow the passions and do not produce their desires (*orexeis*) according to *logos* because their end is action, not knowledge. In the second argument, Aristotle's caution that precision is not the same in all *logoi* leads to observing how the wandering that the noble, just, and good things each hold makes it seem these things are only by law and not by nature.[45] If one seeks to understand what is natural and properly-one's-own in economics and politics, then one must attempt (*peirateon*) to bound these things within the limit (*peras*) of the good through the experience (*empeiria*) of moving toward or away from it as a first-principle (*archē*).

Book IX's second matter without-provision concerns the loosening of friendships. While it does not seem strange for friendships through the useful or the pleasant to loosen when friends no longer hold these things, Aristotle wonders about cases where someone who is a friend through the useful or the pleasant "pretends to produce-towards" (*prospoieō*) loving (*agapaō*) the friend through character. When the error is the result of someone assuming to be loved (*phileō*) through character, the "cause for censure" (*aitiaomai*) is oneself. But when the other person pretends to produce-toward oneself the deception, the accusation is just, and more than adulterating the legal-currency since the malice concerns what is more honorable (1165a35-b12). Insofar as the money-making art is the art of useful things, it is reasonable that any and all exchanges it facilitates endure only so long as people who hold these things are useful to themselves. If the use corresponds with need, it is possible for exchanges in the money-making art to remain more enduring. Aristotle's appeal to adulterating legal-currency seems to acknowledge this, and its ties to honor hearken back to Book V's competing claims between need (*chreia*) as "some one thing" (*hen ti*) that holds-together community through exchange because need holds-together all things, *and* legal-currency as "some one thing" as a hypothesis that produces all things as commensurable by measuring them (though it is "up to ourselves" to change this and produce it as useless).[46] The adulterating of legal-currency deprives the person who receives it in exchange for useful things of the exchangeable representative of need that is not by nature but by law. If this is akin to the person who adulterates character in friendship, even if one grants that character is more honorable than legal-currency, two questions arise. First, of what need does the deceiver deprive someone? Is this need by nature and not by law?

The answer to the two preceding questions arrives when Aristotle considers whether one should still love (*phileō*) a friend who one initially admits as good, but comes to be wicked. This leads Aristotle to ask, "Or is this not possible, if indeed not all things are lovable but the good?" (1165b13–15). Aristotle's question about what is lovable points readers back to the beginning of Book VIII's second chapter where he proposes there are three forms of friendship in line with what is lovable: what is good, what is pleasant, or what is useful. After suggesting only the good and pleasant are lovable as ends since people seek these through the useful, Aristotle asks if people's love is for the good, or the good for themselves.[47] Within short order, Aristotle's three lovable things in Book VIII come down to a question about the good, one that recurs in Book IX's question of whether one can love a friend who was good but becomes wicked.

In weighing the options of what to do when a friend comes to be wicked, Aristotle proposes one must help those who hold "correcting" (*epanorthōsis*) more in their character than their substance or property (*ousia*), for character is better and what is more properly-one's-own in friendship (1165b19–20). Much like the preceding argument about deception in friendship, an "economic" idea (i.e., substance or property) comes into this argument about correcting friends and comes up lacking. Character is the more honorable thing that the deceiver adulterates, and it is more honorable than legal-currency because it is more properly-one's-own than anything outside of oneself. The question of whether one friend should correct a good friend who becomes wicked adds depth to the problem, for it is perfectly plausible that one decides to loosen the friendship and be done with it. Why bother, then, with correcting the friend? One would do so because the friend was good, and through being good, was good for oneself. The good is more properly-one's-own in friendship because character is something of oneself, whereas legal-currency and substance or property are external things that belong to oneself. To use these things well, one must know what is good for oneself. But legal-currency and substance or property do not choose to be friends, hence why there is not friendship with these soulless things.[48] This is what makes someone who deceives another about friendship wicked, for the deception deprives a person of one's own need for the good.

A final argument that downplays the importance of useful things and legal-currency appears in Book IX's seventh chapter, which immediately precedes the third unprovided matter in the Book's eighth chapter: love-of-self. From the question of why those who do a good-work (*euergetēs*) seem to love those benefited more than those benefited love them, Aristotle sees a discrepancy between this and what occurs with debts and lending that seems to have a more natural cause. Because being is lovable and choiceworthy for all and "we are by activity (*energeia*)" (and living and doing are in activity), in activity the producer is the work in some way, thus feeling-affection (*stergō*) for the work on account of feeling-affection for being. While the activity is pleasant and lovable, to the person who receives the benefit, there is only an advantage. Through this insight, Aristotle observes all feel-affection for the things that come to be from labor (*epiponos*), like those who acquire useful things as opposed to those who take hold of them from another. Similarly, mothers love children more than fathers because the children are of themselves, and this would seem to be properly-one's-own to those who do good-works (1167b17–1168a27). Like Book IX's two earlier arguments involving legal-currency and substance or property, Aristotle's contrast between lending and those who do good-works uses a more "economic" concern to move toward a more natural foundation for these concerns in friendship. In this case, the works that people produce bring forth the activity underlying all works that people choose and through which they live and do all things.

The language of this idea prefigures the more natural perspective on friendship and love-of-self in Book IX's ninth chapter that culminates in describing friends as living-together (*suzaō*) and forming-community (*koinōneō*) in *logos* and thought. What is different about the present account is the way Aristotle speaks of "feeling-affection" (*stergō*) through activity, thus using a verb from Book VIII's description of friendship between the free or liberal persons of the household (i.e., parents and children) through which he says human beings are more coupling than political by nature since they dwell-together-in-households (*sunoikeō*) for all the things in life, for the household is both before and more necessary than the city.[49] If the person who acquires useful things (presumably through the money-making art) feels-affection for them through toilsome labor, and this feeling-affection finds its natural beginning in the friendship and community of the household, then only friendship can draw "economic" concerns in community toward a natural care for what is properly-one's-own.

The need for friendship to provide for the natural care for what is properly-one's-own in political and economic life becomes clear when one contrasts its comprehensive view of the good things with the divided view of the just. In Book V's inquiry into justice, Aristotle introduces both the simply just and the politically just as "the sought-for thing," thus recalling "the sought-for good" that he uses in Book I to reject the money-making life and its end of wealth as the life in which happiness resides. On top of the ambiguity over whether the simply just and the politically just are the same, Aristotle presents competing accounts of the just: it is either among those who are free and equal forming-community in life toward self-sufficiency, or when people have law toward themselves that addresses the injustice of distributing more of the simply good things and less of the simply bad things to oneself. These competing accounts give way to whether it is *logos* or a ruler who guards people from the injustice of one-holding-more who makes the preceding distribution of the simply good and simply bad things to oneself. Notice how Aristotle does not speak of self-sufficiency in relation to the simply good and simply bad things, as if these things are only relevant to law and not what makes people free. In Book X, however, the self-sufficiency of the contemplative life and its proper (*oikeia*) pleasure belonging to the intellect's activity provide a way for Aristotle to show law holds a necessitating capacity when it is *logos* from some prudence and intellect. A key foundation for these arguments is the unreproachable love-of-self in Book IX that opposes the one-holding-more's love-of-self. But the love-of-self does not emerge in Aristotle's inquiry without the turn to friendship in Book VIII, which begins with the statement that no one would choose living without friends, even when holding all the remaining good things.[50] As opposed to the just, friendship brings self-sufficiency and the good things together, for there is no care that is more naturally and properly-one's-own than the good for the sake of which one chooses to live.[51]

## CONCLUSION: JUSTICE AND POLITICAL PHILOSOPHY (*POLITICS* 1279B11–1280A21, 1280B29–39, 1282B14–30)

The questions without-provision (*aporia*) about worth, what is properly-one's-own, and friendship from Book IX of the *Ethics* account for what justice cannot: one's own need for the good. To provide for this need, Aristotle notes the discord between works and *logoi* about love-of-self, then takes up the conflicting *logoi* about this, a question that fairly leaves one unprovided (*aporeō*) about which position one needs (*chreōn*) to follow since they both hold trust. Accordingly, Aristotle proposes there might be need to divide (*diaireō*) the *logoi* and mark-the-boundary of the extent to which and in what ways they are true. In Aristotle's political philosophy, whenever one faces a matter without-provision, the only way to provide for it is *logos*. A practical example of this provision occurs with legal-currency, for its use (*chrēsis*) was provided (*porizō*) out of necessity to produce a manageable foreign exchange of the things that are necessary according to nature. It is in this way that the money-making art came into being according to *logos*.[52] From a natural lack of provision for the exchange of naturally necessary things, *logos* provides a means for this exchange. If *logos* provides for human beings' natural need for necessary exchange, why could it not provide for their natural need for the good?

One of the great difficulties facing *logos* is not only its potential discordance with works, but the possibility for conflict in how it provides for the good. Although the money-making art came into being according to *logos* in a way that provided for natural and necessary exchange, through retail-trade and with experience and time it became more of an art concerning from where and how to produce the most gain. Through this development, wealth is set-down as a quantity of legal-currency, which is indeed without-limit. This understanding of wealth is contrary to "true wealth"—"a store of such useful things that are necessary with a view towards living, and useful to community in a city or a household"—for the self-sufficiency of such acquisition toward good living is not without-limit. The kinship between the "true" and the "good" in this teaching on wealth draws on Aristotle's argument at the beginning of Book X of the *Ethics* that the true things of *logoi* are most useful toward knowing and life because they are trusted when they sing together with the works. The foundation for this trust is in saying the good is that at which all things aim, for to say otherwise is to speak nothing. The trouble facing a true understanding of wealth comes from the ambiguous nature of art. In Book VI of the *Ethics*, although Aristotle defines "art" (*technē*) as a productive *hexis* with true *logos* and artlessness as a productive *hexis* with false *logos*, in the end he does not allow art to remain alongside science, prudence, wisdom, and intellect as ways of arriving at truth.[53] Though Aristotle defines "art" only in relation to true *logos*, art admits of following a false *logos*. With the money-making art, its *logos* could either provide for a natural and necessary exchange and a true understanding of wealth toward good living, or for the gain of legal-currency without-limit. For a *logos* of the money-making art to be true and trustworthy, it must speak of the good.

Although a true *logos* of the good in the money-making art is necessary for understanding Aristotle's economic teaching, this *logos* is inseparable from his political teaching. On the one hand, this is not surprising since Aristotle's "philosophy concerning the human things" begins in the *Ethics* by raising the question of the good at which all things aim.[54] On the other hand, first-time readers of the *Ethics* and *Politics* may not notice how Aristotle's arguments about wealth and the good in both works bear on a pivotal inquiry into the just in Book III of the *Politics*, which focuses on the nature of a regime.

The arguments most relevant to the present question about wealth and the good start in Book III's seventh chapter, which Aristotle begins by saying there is need to speak more of regimes, for these hold some things without-provision (*aporia*) and it is properly-one's-own (*oikeion*) for a person who philosophizes not only looking to doing things to make clear the truth concerning each thing. A notable conflict concerning what is authoritative in regimes is between oligarchy and democracy. In oligarchy, those who are authoritative are the people holding property or substance (*ousia*). Democracy is contrary to oligarchy, for those who are authoritative are not those who acquired a quantity of property or substance, but those who are unprovided (*aporoi*). The first matter without-provision (*aporia*) concerns marking-the-boundary for these regimes, which leads to Aristotle settling on the *logos* that the difference between democracy and oligarchy resides in poverty (*penia*) and wealth, respectively. Wherever people rule (*archō*) through wealth, there is necessarily oligarchy; wherever they rule through being unprovided, there is necessarily democracy. While the wealthy are few, the unprovided are many. Nevertheless, although few are well-provided (*euporeō*), all hold-a-share (*metechō*) of freedom (*eleutheria*), which causes disputes (1279b11–1280a6). Insofar as oligarchy and democracy base their claims to rule on wealth, it is tempting to approach political disputes solely from an economic perspective, perhaps by focusing on the distribution of wealth within a regime. But Aristotle does not take his inquiry in this direction, for the philosopher's concern that is properly-one's-own is the truth of the dispute between democracy and oligarchy. The dispute is itself a matter without-provision, and the philosopher must mark-the-boundary to provide what democracy and oligarchy cannot. With respect to regimes, neither democrats nor oligarchs can fully provide for freedom, though the reasons why are not yet clear.

After outlining the dispute between democracy and oligarchy, Aristotle turns to the boundaries (*horos*) of oligarchy and democracy and whatever the just is in the oligarchic and democratic contexts. While Aristotle concedes both speak of something just, they do not speak of all the authoritatively just. The reason why democracy and oligarchy hold partial views of the just is because it *seems* to each that the just is either equality or inequality for all, whereas the just is equality for equal persons and inequality for unequal persons, and the democrats and oligarchs take away (*aphaireō*) what concerns persons and therefore judge badly (1280a7–14). Before proceeding, notice how Aristotle holds a connection between regimes and the people within them that acknowledges the need to account for what it means to choose (*haireō*) a regime, something the democrats and oligarchs take away from their boundaries for the just by focusing solely on equality and inequality. The cause of this taking away is people are base in judging the things that are properly-one's-own (*tōn oikeiōn*), and they do not divide (*diaireō*) equality regarding matters and persons in the same way as said in the *Ethics*. Accordingly, oligarchs suppose themselves to be wholly unequal because they are unequal in useful things (*chrēma*), while democrats suppose themselves to be wholly equal if they are equal in freedom (1280a11–25). The reference to the *Ethics* is Book V's inquiry into distributions according to worth, where the same dispute between democrats and oligarchs helps develop the idea that distributions according to proportion (*analogos*) are not simply the search for a mathematical number that is the middle term between the unequal in the form of the more or the less, but the equality of *logoi*.[55] Although Aristotle does not provide for what this *logos* might be in the *Ethics*, he takes this inquiry back up in the *Politics* to show that this *logos* is of the good.

Providing a fuller account for why democrats and oligarchs are bad judges concerning the things that are properly-one's-own and take away persons (and their choices) from their regimes' boundaries for the just, Aristotle charges both groups with failing to speak of the most authoritative thing (*to kuriōtaton*). Though initially vague, Aristotle concedes that if it were for the sake of acquisition that people form-community and come together, people would hold-a-share of the city to the extent they did in acquisition, in which case the oligarchs' *logos* would seem strong (*ischuō*) and it would not be just for someone who does not contribute equally to the city to hold-a-share equally (1280a25–31). While not explicit, "the most authoritative thing" is the city's end (*telos*), and both the oligarchs and democrats take this for granted. Embedded within Aristotle's concession to the oligarchs is the recognition that their claim to the just rests on a *logos* that seems strong *if* the city's end is acquisition. Curiously, Aristotle does not subject democrats to the same scrutiny, which suggests they may be closer to the truth about the city's end in their pursuit of freedom. The most Aristotle does within Book III's ninth chapter to point to a truer *logos* of the city's end is to say the city is a community of living well in households and families for the sake of complete and self-sufficient living that is the work of friendship, the choice (*proairesis*) to live-together (1280b29–39). If the natural basis for friendship in the *Ethics* is the unreproachable love-of-self through which each friend chooses the good, then the good must break through in Book III of the *Politics* to provide a true *logos* of the city's end.

In Book IX's twelfth chapter, the good emerges along with a matter without-provision about the just:

> Since in every science and art a good is the end, a greatest ['good' or 'end'] is most certainly in the most authoritative of all these [sciences and arts]; this is the

political capacity, and a political good is the just, and this is the common advantage, so it seems to all the just is something equal, and up to some point they agree with philosophic *logoi*, in which boundaries-were-marked concerning the ethical things (for they assert the just [is] something for some persons, and there is need for these to be equal for equal persons), but of what sort of things there is equality and of what sort of things there is inequality, there is need not to escape notice. For this holds without-provision and political philosophy. (1282b14–23)

Aristotle's presentation of the just as a political good concludes with the only use of the phrase "political philosophy" in the *Ethics* and *Politics*. Unsurprisingly, "political philosophy" coincides with something without-provision in political life: the basis for equality and inequality. This provision—like all political disputes—falls to *logos*, but only philosophy can fully provide for it. Before seeing how Aristotle outlines the work of political philosophy in the *Politics*, readers should recall his presentation of the political philosopher in Book VII of the *Ethics* as the person who contemplates pleasures and pains as the architect of the end toward which "we speak" of each thing as simply bad and simply good.[56] For political philosophy to provide *logos* on the basis for equality and inequality, it needs to bring pleasures and pains toward the good, their true end.[57]

With political philosophy and its need to provide for the matter without-provision concerning equality and inequality in political life now clear, Aristotle returns to the problem of worth and the implicit need to liberate political life from it with a true understanding of what is properly-one's-own through friendship. A difficulty emerges when someone asserts there is need to distribute ruling offices unequally according to holding-over in any good (even among those who happen to be similar) because the just and what is according to worth is different for people who differ. But if this is true, there will be holding-more in the politically just things for those holding-over in complexion, height, or any of the good things (1282b23–30). This problem recalls Aristotle's competing arguments in Book V of the *Ethics* concerning whether it is *logos* or rulers that guard people from the injustice of the one-holding-more in distributions of the simply good and simply bad things. In this example from the *Politics*, it is possible that people bring their holding-more of the good things into the distributions of ruling offices, in which case the rulers do not guard the ruled from the injustice of holding-more but perpetuate it upon them. Here readers should remember how Aristotle shows in Book V of the *Ethics* that what underlies the laborious-wickedness of the one-holding-more is the pleasure from gain. Through Book IX's presentation of the one-holding-more as a reproachable lover-of-self in contrast to the unreproachable love-of-self where friends choose the good with their intellects, Aristotle prepares the way to show in Book X that only the contemplative life

holds a liberal pleasure that is properly-one's-own and at home in a life of leisure, not political life.[58] In sum, its falls to friendship within Aristotle's *logos*
to ensure the care for what is properly-one's-own in political and economic
life is according to each person's choice of the good.[59]

By using the dramatic tension between the democrats and the oligarchs to
discover disputes about the politically just things are truly disputes about the
good things, Aristotle invites readers look at these disputes from a more natural perspective. In Book X of the *Ethics*, Aristotle shows that self-sufficiency
requires living according to the liberal pleasure of the intellect's activity that
is properly-one's-own, all the while recognizing that one's nature is not self-
sufficient toward contemplating on account of a need for external good-days
that provide for the body and its health.[60] The democrats and the oligarchs
represent these two halves of self-sufficiency in isolation from each other.
The democrats rightly recognize self-sufficiency requires freedom, but they
are unprovided because they do not see their freedom needs the good. The
oligarchs rightly recognize that self-sufficiency requires being well-provided
with external prosperity in the form of wealth, but they do not see that they
are without-provision in freedom from thinking wealth is the good. So long as
both democrats and oligarchs understand themselves solely in terms of how
they stand in the regime, they will not be self-sufficient human beings. But if
a political philosopher liberates them to think of self-sufficiency in terms of
what is properly-one's-own, the democrats and oligarchs will see that both
freedom *and* external prosperity and wealth are good things that receive their
best provision not in relation to the ruling offices (*archas*) in the regime, but
the natural first-principle (*archē*) that is the good.[61]

*Chapter 9*

# Economics' Need for Political Philosophy

Although this book begins where most books on Aristotle's economic teaching concentrate their efforts (*Politics* I.8–11), the careful reading of these arguments compels readers to see the common threads running through the *Politics* and the *Ethics* to contemplate what politics and economics look like from political philosophy's perspective. For a political philosopher like Aristotle, the heart of political and economic life is not community, acquisition, and exchange, but the personal desire for the good and the choice of how to pursue and acquire it. Of all the human things, friendship (*philia*) most allows people to understand this desire and how it affects community, acquisition, and exchange. With the deficiencies of justice now fully apparent, one last way to demonstrate the need for political philosophy's authoritative view of politics and economics is to show how Aristotle's inquiries into matters concerning property in regimes attest to the persistence of desire's need to hold the good as its proper and natural end.

Because friendship (*philia*) is a natural community in Aristotle's political philosophy that begins and finds its preservation in each person's choice (*proairesis*) of the good that is properly-one's-own (*oikeios*), careful readers must attend to how he ensures political community (of which economic exchange is a part) does not destroy friendship. Everything Aristotle does toward this end begins with his care to ensure all things in his political philosophy emerge in light of the good. Bearing this in mind, one should return to the opening sentence of the *Politics*, where Aristotle begins with what is known or familiar to his readers about cities—for "we see every city is some community"—and turns to the good in two ways. First, Aristotle brings cities and communities in relation to the good, for "every community is set-standing-together for the sake of some good." Next, Aristotle shows that cities and communities are set-standing-together for the sake of some good because every human being pursues the good, for "all do all things for the sake of what seems to be good." Of course, saying cities and communities are set-standing-together for the sake of "some good" and everyone does things for the sake of "what seems to be good" does not necessarily mean these things all pursue *the* good, but it does suggest they all pursue something they think is good even though it might not be. Yet this is only the beginning of the *Politics*, and it reflects Aristotle's approach to first-principles (*archē*) in *logos* from Book I of the *Ethics* where "one-must-begin" (*arkteon*) from what is known or familiar (*gnōrimos*) to oneself to discover what is known or familiar simply (*haplōs*). In moving from what is known or familiar to oneself toward the limit (*peras*) of what is known or familiar simply, one runs the unprovided (*aporeō*) race that provides knowledge (*gnōsis*) of the good.[1]

Since Aristotle's approach to the good in *logos* endures throughout the whole of his political philosophy, readers need to run between the different limits in the *Ethics* and the *Politics* to discover the good. With cities and communities, one should approach what it means for them to be "set-standing-together" in the *Politics* from the perspective of the inquiry into friendship in Books VIII and IX of the *Ethics*. At the beginning of Book VIII, Aristotle elevates friendship over justice (*dikaiosunē*), observing that it looks like friendship holds-together (*sunechō*) cities since legislators are more serious about this than justice, for like-mindedness (*homonoia*) looks to be some friendship, and they aim themselves at this most of all to drive out standing-faction (*stasis*) from the city because it is hated.[2] Both "standing-faction" and "set-standing-together" (*sunistēmi*) hold the same root verb: "to stand" (*histēmi*). "Standing-faction" is part of the city "standing" apart from the rest, and it is not hard to see how the democrats and oligarchs attempt to stand in opposition to one another within the city because of wealth.

While the factions of the democrats and oligarchs may be most obvious in their attempts at holding-more (*pleonexia*) in the politically just things, standing-faction is an implicit part of economic exchange. In the last chapter of the inquiry into the money-making art (*chrēmatistikē*) from Book I of the *Politics*, when Aristotle shifts from the free contemplation (*theōrian eleutheran*) to the necessary experience (*empeirian anankaian*) in the use (*chrēsis*) of this art, he introduces commerce (*emporia*) as the greatest part of the art of exchange (*hē metablētikē*), with the three parts of commerce being ship-owning, carrying cargo, and selling (*parastasis*). The art of exchange also includes the practice of usury (*tokismos*) and wage-earning.[3] By its very name, "selling" is a "standing (*stasis*)-beside (*para*),"[4] and (barring a monopoly) a factious competition between different sellers. Consequently, whether it is wealth or economic exchange, the potential for people standing in some sort of faction is ever-present in political life, and it would seem legislators need to provide a remedy for this malady with laws that promote some friendship in the form of like-mindedness.

In Book IX of the *Ethics'* sixth chapter—which immediately precedes the inquiry into those who do good-works through which readers discover how people feel-affection (*stergō*) toward legal-currency (*nomisma*) through activity (*energeia*) in a way that is akin to the natural feeling-affection within the friendship between the free members of the household (*oikia*) in the community that is properly-one's-own (*oikeios*)—Aristotle returns to the idea of like-mindedness. After dismissing like-mindedness as "sameness-of-opinion" (*homodoxia*), Aristotle says people assert like-mindedness in the city is whenever people have the same judgment of the advantageous things (*tōn sumpherontōn*), choose (*proaireō*) the same things, and do "the things resolved, decreed, or seeming in common" (*ta koinē doxanta*) (1167a22–28).[5] Notice the way Aristotle plays with the verb for "to seem" (*dokeō*) to discuss how cities approach the common things, thus anticipating the opening of the *Politics* where he says all do all things for the sake of what "seems good." Since like-mindedness concerns the advantageous things and what is common, it on the one hand invokes Book V of the *Ethics'* presentation of the laws proclaiming (*agoreō*) what concerns all things and "aiming themselves" or "guessing at" (*stochazomai*) what is "common belonging to the advantage for all" (*tou koinē sumpherontos pasin*), and on the other hand Book III of the *Politics'* presentation of the just as the common advantage (*to koinē sumpheron*) and a political good.[6] The ambiguous sense of the verb Aristotle uses in Book V of the *Ethics* to suggest laws either "aim" or "guess at" what is common in the advantage for all carries into his introduction to the city being like-minded in Book IX, with what "seems" in common being what the city does. This ambiguous sense finds its way into the beginning of the *Politics*, where Aristotle immediately follows up his statement that everyone does things for the sake of what "seems good" by saying "all communities aim themselves or guess at some good." In every case where Aristotle speaks about the city, its aiming at the good holds an ambiguity that he does not use when speaking of how each person aims at the good.

Continuing his inquiry into like-mindedness, Aristotle brings in those who are decent (*epieikēs*), thus preparing the way to look at community with a mind to love-of-self (*philautos*). To be "standing in faction" (*stasiazō*) is the result of each person wishing oneself to rule. Accordingly, to be like-minded is not for each person to-have-in-intellect (*ennoeō*) the same thing (for in this way even those who stand in faction are like-minded because they wish to rule), but each person having-in-intellect the same thing in the same way, like whenever the *dēmos* and those who are decent have-in-intellect for the best persons to rule so that at which they aim themselves (*ephiēmi*) comes to be for all (1167a28–b1). The natural and intellectual foundations for community begin to peak through at this point in Aristotle's inquiry into friendship, though for now he confines his inquiry to the question of who should rule. Nevertheless, since his approach to like-mindedness includes persons (i.e., the *dēmos* and the decent), the "aiming" in question shifts away from the "guessing" that characterizes laws and communities and takes the form of an "aiming" that could also mean "to long after" or "desire" (*ephiēmi*)—the "aiming" that marks the beginning of the *Ethics* with the question of the good at which all things aim.[7]

Aristotle's final remarks on like-mindedness in the *Ethics* use those who are decent to make a brief introduction to the problem of holding-more as it relates to the just before taking this up again in Book IX's ninth chapter in terms of desiring (*oregō*) good things—namely, things one uses or needs (*chrēma*), honors (*timē*), and bodily pleasures—as if they are the best things and delighting in desires (*epithumia*), passions, and what is without *logos* in the soul.[8] In light of the like-mindedness between the *dēmos* and the decent about rule by the best persons, Aristotle says like-mindedness shows itself to be political friendship concerning the advantageous things and the things toward life. This like-mindedness is in the decent, who themselves wish for the just things and the advantageous things, and aim themselves in common at such things. Those who are base, in contrast, are not like-minded, nor are they friends since they aim themselves at holding-more in the beneficial things (*ōphelimos*), and by not laboring for or protecting the common, it destroys itself. From this, people stand in faction among themselves, necessitating each other (*epanankazō*) and not wishing to produce the just things themselves (1167b1–16). Political friendship in this argument confines itself to like-mindedness concerning the advantageous things and the things toward life, and the just things seem tied solely to the advantageous things through the decent. Nevertheless, the problem of holding-more in Book V is clearly in relation to the good things, which Aristotle first introduces by saying there is need for people to pray that the simply good things are good for themselves and that they choose (*haireō*) the good things for themselves.[9]

While legislators and cities may wish to produce like-mindedness to drive out standing-faction, the truth is that all standing-faction begins with each person's reproachable love-of-self that does not understand how one should hold toward the good things. As Aristotle shows in Book IX, the decent person embodies the unreproachable love-of-self that loves (*agapaō*), gratifies, and trusts-the-rule (*peitharcheō*) of the intellect through its naturally pleasant sense-perception of the good present in oneself, a sense-perception through which the friendships of those who are decent form-community in *logos* and thought. It is through this intellectual friendship of the good that Aristotle can show in Book X the necessitating capacity of *logos* derives from some prudence and intellect.[10] However reasonable it is to think about dealing with standing-faction from the perspective of political community, Aristotle's political philosophy compels readers to see all human things depend on how each person holds toward the good.

In Book IV of the *Politics*, Aristotle begins his case for the middle (*meson*) polity as the best regime and best life for most human beings by observing that there are three parts of *all* cities: the well-provided (*euporoi*), the unprovided (*aporoi*), and the middle persons (*mesoi*). Since people agree in *logos* (*homologeō*) that what is measured and middling is best, it is apparent that with the things of good-fortune the middling acquisition (*ktēsis*) most easily trusts-the-rule of *logos* (1295b1–6). While the nature of polity and its case for a regime with a large middle-class is interesting in its own right,[11] for the purposes of contemplating the relationship between politics and economics in Aristotle's political philosophy, it is necessary to confine one's focus to how acquisition and wealth affect regimes. In this regard, polity merits attention because Aristotle holds the boundary (*horos*) of polity is the mixing well of democracy and oligarchy so that one admits to speak of the same regime as a democracy and an oligarchy (1294b13–16). Aristotle refuses to do away with the distinction between the well-provided and unprovided in regimes, which suggests that when it comes to the relationship between acquisition, wealth, and political community, inequality is inevitable. At the same time, careful readers should wonder what is the significance of Aristotle singling out those who are middling as being more ready to trust-the-rule of *logos*.

To gain a full appreciation for why Aristotle does not propose the eradication of inequalities in wealth and acquisition from political life, readers should first look in Book II of the *Politics* to see Aristotle's criticisms of Socrates' city in *logos* from Plato's *Republic* and the regime of Phaleas of Chalcedon. With the former regime, Aristotle explores how it is hostile to friendship and mistaken in its aim to produce all acquisition and substance or property (*ousia*) common. With the latter regime, he shows the errors in thinking equality in acquisition and substance or property will rid the city of standing-faction. Together, these criticisms show the need to preserve the space in political and economic life to care for what is properly-one's-own through friendship and its free choice to pursue the good. Throughout his contemplation of these regimes, Aristotle holds true to his work as a political philosopher, providing readers a way to see their own need to limit their desires through the experience of contemplating the good.[12]

## PROPERTY AND POLITICAL COMMUNITY (*ETHICS* 1167A22–B16, *POLITICS* 1260B27–1261B40, 1262B7–24, 1263A21–1264A1, 1264B24–25, 1266A31–1267B21)

Aristotle begins Book II of the *Politics* by reminding readers that "we ourselves choose to contemplate the political community," and there is need to examine both the ones in use and those one prays for. The natural beginning (*archē*) for this examination is whether all citizens form-community in all things, nothing, or some things but not in others. Since it is impossible to form-community in nothing because every community has a place where citizens are community-partners (*koinōnoi*), Aristotle asks if it holds better for a city nobly (*kalōs*) "managed-like-a-household" (*oikeō*) to form community in all things, or in some things. The latter approach is how things are at present, whereas the former is like the regime Socrates proposes in Plato's *Republic* that asserts there is need for children, women, and acquisitions to be common (1260b27–1261a9).[13] Though Aristotle spends the next three chapters in Book II looking at the regime from Plato's *Republic*, his question more broadly concerns whether forming-community in the city is the same as managing a household. A similar question appears in Book VI of the *Ethics* where, after observing how people seek or examine the good for themselves and suppose there is need to do this, Aristotle first asks if the well-being of oneself (*to autou eu*) is possible without household management (*oikonomia*) or a regime, then in what way there is need to manage a household (*dioikeō*).[14] In both inquiries, the implicit question is if a person's seeking of the good that is properly-one's-own and forming-community in the household is akin to seeking the good and forming-community in the city.

### Friendship and the Failings of Common Property (*Politics* 1261a10–1261b40, 1262b7–24, 1263a21–1264a1, 1264b24–25)

Aristotle uses Socrates' regime from the *Republic* to examine the flaws in thinking the city's end (*telos*) is to be one (*to mian*), in part through making all substance or property common. Starting with the end of the city being one, it is apparent that as a city comes to be one, it is no longer a city. For the nature of the city is some multitude, but as it comes to be one, it comes to be a household instead of a city, and a human being instead of a household. Even if it were possible to produce this, there is need not to, for it will abolish (*anaireō*) the city (1261a10–22). Aristotle's argument reverses the course of Book I of the *Politics*, working back from the city, down to the household, and then a single human being. But it is a not a one-for-one comparison since Aristotle omits the village (*kōmē*). This may be by design, for in Book I the household is the community set-standing-together according to nature for every day, while the village (which consists of a multitude of households) is for the sake of non-daily use. This has some bearing on Book I's subsequent inquiry into the money-making art when Aristotle states there is no work for the art of exchange (*hē metablētikē*) in the household, finding this art occurs among many households where there is a mutual-giving (*metadosis*) as is necessary according to their needs, yet refraining from referring to the households engaged in this exchange as being in community with each other.

Exchange necessarily exists between communities, and the attempt to make the city one eliminates a way to provide for each person's need to restore the self-sufficiency (*autarkeia*) that is according to nature through the art of exchange.[15] The pursuit of self-sufficiency needs exchange, and exchange is something each person and household chooses (*haireō*). In abolishing (*anaireō*) the differences between the city, household, and a human being, the attempt to make the city one abolishes the work of choice in community.

The need to preserve choice and self-sufficiency in community becomes further evident after Aristotle reminds readers that it is necessary for those who are free and equal to have the equal that is reciprocal (*to ison to anti-peponthos*) as the *Ethics* shows. But unlike his presentation of this idea in the *Ethics*, Aristotle confines reciprocity solely to ruling and being ruled, omitting the role of legal-currency that facilitates the exchange of works within the community that are not equal.[16] From these arguments, Aristotle concludes the city is not naturally one, and this idea that some say is the greatest good (*to megiston agathon*) for cities abolishes them, while the good of each preserves each. Related to this last point, Aristotle notes that just as a household is more self-sufficient (*autarchēs*) than one person, a city is more self-sufficient than a household, and a city wishes to come to be whenever the community of the multitude is self-sufficient. As a result, since what is more self-sufficient is more choiceworthy, then what is less one regarding the city is also more choiceworthy (1261a32–b15). What constitutes self-sufficiency in the preceding arguments is not clear, though it retains the sense from Book I of the *Politics* that the city as a community holds within it every limit of self-sufficiency through the households and villages under its authority.[17] At the same time, Aristotle refrains from bringing in living and living well to define the self-sufficiency that is supposedly the city's natural end. Thus, at this point in Aristotle's criticism of Socrates' regime from Plato's *Republic*, while he establishes the need for each person and household within the city to be self-sufficient, he has yet to show how the good could preserve each thing.

Aristotle approaches the need to preserve the care for the good in relation to each person and community from two angles. First, Aristotle takes up Socrates' *logos* that the city will be completely (*teleōs*) one through each person saying "mine" and "not mine" in relation to all others. Whether it is in relation to wives and children (the naturally free persons of the household) or substance or property, if one wishes to speak of "all" these things in common, the closest one could come to speaking realistically is through recognizing in "all" how each person cares for the things that are of themselves. But the error is not merely a linguistic one, for it holds another harm because people give the least care to the common, instead most of all "thinking" (*phrontizō*, so perhaps with prudence, *phronēsis*) about one's own private things (*tōn idiōn*) (1261b16–40). Though Aristotle's argument begins rhetorically, it ends by drawing attention to the practical effects of using the *logos* of "all" toward what is in common in a way that abolishes (*anaireō*) the care of each for one's own private things that preserves their good. The disastrous effect is twofold, for it abolishes both the standing of the free persons within the household *and* the place of substance or property in the community, things necessary to provide for one's own good. If readers follow Aristotle's standard from the *Ethics* that trusting (*pisteuō*) the true things of *logos* requires them to sing together with the works,[18] Socrates' *logos* of "all" does not provide a true way to care for the good in political community.

Though Aristotle's arguments continue to circle around the importance of providing for the care for the good of each person and community, it may surprise readers to find the natural basis for his argument is the distinction between friendship and *erōs*. From the supposition that friendship is the greatest of good things for cities since it would prevent it from standing in faction (thus recalling the *Ethics*' discussion of friendship and like-mindedness),[19] Aristotle comments on how Socrates praises this city being one since this seems to be the work of friendship. In support of Socrates' argument, Aristotle makes what must be to first-time readers of the *Politics* an obscure reference to the erotic *logoi* of Plato's *Symposium*, drawing attention to the *logos* of Aristophanes that speaks of lovers who from intense love (*to sphodra philein*) desire (*epithumeō*) to naturally-grow-together (*sumphuō*) and from two come to be one (1262b7–13).[20] This intense friendship shows up in the tenth chapter of Book IX of the *Ethics* right before Aristotle observes that *erōs* "wishes to be some excess or superiority (*huperbolē*) of friendship." This argument appears within Aristotle's search for the bounds to the quantity of friends one should hold toward the life that is properly-one's-own (*oikeios*), all leading to the conclusion that the number of such friends is few.[21] In light of these arguments, it is not surprising that Aristotle rejects *erōs* as the foundation for friendship within the city, for not only does Aristophanes' *logos* require each person to ruin oneself through coming to be one, but the friendship in one's-own-proper-relationships (*oikeiotēs*) becomes watered down and no one thinks for another. The reason for this is because two things produce concern (*kēdo*) and love (*phileō*) in human beings—what is one's own private thing (*to idion*) and what is loved (*agapēton*)—and neither of these is present to those who are citizens as Socrates proposes (1262b14–24). Now the natural human flaw in attempting to produce a regime where the free persons of the household and the substance or property belonging to this first community are all in common comes into fuller view, for the eradication of choice and the distinct standing of each household and person in the political community reveals a confusion about *erōs* and friendship. Whereas friendship (both between parents and children *and* those who are decent) understands it is good and pleasant to love a friend as another self,[22] *erōs* wants to ruin the necessarily separate standing sown into the nature of friendship. Though Aristotle directs this criticism at Socrates' regime from Plato's *Republic*, the broader implication of his argument is any attempt to make each person and the property or substance that is properly-one's-own common to all and one is a form of political *erōs* that can only wish to be the friendship that it ruins. As for the source of this problem, Aristotle points to a familiar culprit: desire (*epithumeō*).

With friendship and its preservation of the good that is properly-one's-own in community now clear, Aristotle takes up the question of whether acquisition and uses in the best regime should be common. Here Aristotle proposes it holds good to balance between acquisitions being both common and wholly private (*idias*) and common if adorned (*epikosmeō*) with character or habits[23] and correct laws. By dividing (*diaireō*) the care of acquisition, people will not produce accusations against each other, and they will use things through virtue according to the proverb that "the things of friends are common." From this, Aristotle concludes it is better for acquisitions to be one's own private things (*idias*), but to produce these acquisitions common in use (1263a21–40). Consistent with his criticism of Socrates' regime, Aristotle allows acquisitions to belong to each person, and the use of these acquisitions in common begins with each person bringing them forth. This teaching also holds true to Book I's inquiry into the money-making art where Aristotle states the more natural form of the art of acquisition (*ktētikē*) is "according to nature part of the art of household management, insofar as there is need [for this] either to be present or to provide this so that there is present a store of such useful things that are necessary towards living, and useful to community in a city or a household."[24] Each household needs the natural art of acquisition to provide for itself, and this need to provide for itself (so that it is self-sufficient) leads households to use their acquisitions for the sake of exchange. This is the natural space in which the money-making art (the art of the useful things, *chrēmatistikē*) enters the community, with either character or habits *and* correct laws adorning this natural exchange rather than eliminating exchange altogether through making all acquisitions common.

In support of the idea that allowing acquisitions to be one's own private things and put to use in common fulfills the proverb that "the things of friends are common," Aristotle returns to an argument from the *Ethics*, noting the importance toward pleasure (*hēdonē*) in customarily-considering (*nomizō*) something is one's own private thing, for it is not vain that each person holds friendship toward oneself since it is something natural. While love-of-self (*philautos*) is blamed justly, to love oneself (*to philein heauton*) does not deserve the same reproach, for the blame falls to loving more than there is need like with the lover-of-money (*philochrēmaton*), for nearly everyone loves these things (1263a40–b5). Here Aristotle echoes the distinction in

Book IX of the *Ethics* between the reproachable lover-of-self as one-holding-more who delights in desires (*epithumia*) and passion *and* the unreproachable decent person as a lover-of-self who gratifies and trusts the most authoritative (*kurios*) thing in oneself (the intellect). At the same time, the criticism of the lover-of-money or lover-of-useful-things loving this good thing more than needed recalls the argument in Book VII that with desires and pleasures, there is no blame for being affected by, desiring, or loving (*phileō*) them, but in going to excess, which is contrary to *logos*. The role of *logos* in this argument is important since Book VII begins by exploring how one can only hold *logos* as a *hexis* and use it through contemplation *if* one's trust is not slight, a trust one builds by naturally-growing-together with *logos* over time. If one wishes to adorn the use of acquisitions in community, one cannot follow the *erōs* to make the city one out of a desire to naturally-grow-together that ruins each person and community. Instead, one must ensure the way is always open for each person within the community to naturally-grow-together in friendship with a *logos* holding knowledge of the good through which choosing does not go on without-limit, thus leaving one's own desires (*orexeis*) empty and vain.[25]

As Aristotle concludes his criticism of the *erōs* to make all things and persons in community one, it becomes clear that this form of *erōs* ultimately destroys the opportunity for each person to make the free and liberal choice to befriend the good. For one, in terms of moral virtues, producing all persons and things as common abolishes the work of moderation (*sōphrosunē*) regarding wives (and other spouses, for that matter) and liberality (*eleutheriotēs*) regarding acquisitions, for there are no families or acquisitions that are properly-one's-own (1263b7–14). Because no one can choose other people or acquisitions for oneself, there is no way to pursue one's own good, for the community must necessarily abolish what is one's own to be one. Strengthening his criticism, Aristotle observes that while legislation from this *erōs* seems fair-faced and philanthropic[26] (leading people to customarily-consider "some wondrous friendship" in all for all will come from it by eliminating all the bad things they mistakenly think arise solely because substance or property is not common), the true source of these problems is wretchedness (*mochthēria*). While there are bad things the community must handle (presumably stemming from reproachable love-of-self), one must think of the good things of which this *erōs* "deprives" (*stereō*) the community. Indeed, the life to emerge from this *erōs* is impossible, and after reiterating the need to preserve the household and the city, Aristotle suggests the only ways to correct the difficulties facing the city are habits, philosophy, and laws (1263b15–1264a1). Of these three things, only philosophy holds a constant relationship to the good things in Aristotle's *Ethics* and *Politics*, for philosophy alone is free to speak fully to choice, the first-principle (*archē*) that is either desiring intellect (*orektikos nous*) or thinking desire (*orexis dianoiētikē*) and, more importantly, a human being. And however harsh Aristotle is toward Socrates' regime in Book II of the *Politics*, the criticism ultimately is in service of philosophy, for he concludes with a remark about all matters without-provision (*aporia*) that Socrates' regime holds (1264b24–25). In going through each question without-provision with *logos*, Aristotle provides readers much needed experience to come to know and be familiar with the good so that they may preserve it in their lives and communities that are properly-one's-own through friendship.

## Phaleas and the Limits of Equal Property for Political Community (*Politics* 1266a31–1267b21)

In the seventh chapter of Book II of the *Politics*, Aristotle leaves behind the best regimes of Plato's *Republic* and *Laws* to examine those who begin their approach to regimes from the necessary things on the grounds that the greatest thing is to arrange the things concerning property or substance nobly since these produce standing-factions. Phaleas of Chalcedon represents this argument, for he asserts there is need for cities' acquisitions to be equal (1266a31–40). Whereas Socrates' regime eliminates private property as part of an *erōs* for the city to be one, Phaleas' regime has a more "economic" approach, hoping to rid the city of standing-faction through equality in property. The one advantage Phaleas' regime holds over Socrates' is it does not aim to eliminate what is properly-one's-own from the city, but its great failure is its narrow concern with acquisition and the necessary things leads it to misunderstand that the causes of standing-faction within human nature run deeper than anything acquisition can address.

Aristotle's initial criticisms of Phaleas' regime are gentle, appearing primarily as a search for clarity. To start, Aristotle contends that if one legislates about the quantity of substance or property within the city, one needs to legislate about the quantity of children. Because of population growth, the law setting the quantity of substance or property will loosen, for the distribution of substance or property within the regime will change. When this happens, those who are wealthy could become poor, and it will require work for these people not to become "revolutionaries" (*neōteropoios*). On account of this problem, Aristotle concedes the leveling of substance or property holds some capacity in political community (1266b8–16). The tension between democrats and oligarchs to which Aristotle hints in Book V of the *Ethics* has yet to emerge in full at this point in the *Politics*, but readers should take this concession to Phaleas as a sign that Aristotle recognizes the distribution of property could threaten the regime's stability.

While Phaleas is on to something about property being equal, it is not enough to say substance or property should be equal, for then people could live either luxuriously or in penury, so that one must aim or guess at (*sto-chasteon*) the middle term. But even this is not adequate, for there is need more to level desires (*epithumia*) through education under the laws than to level substance or property. While Phaleas mentions the need for the city's equality to be in acquisition and education, he does not say what this education should be, thus making it possible for people to choose (*proairetikos*) to hold-more in useful things, honor, or both (1266b16–38). While Socrates' regime seeks to abolish choice out of a desire belonging to an *erōs* for the city to be one, Phaleas does not take choice and desire seriously enough, leaving them unprovided through his exclusive focus on substance or property. The problem of one-holding-more once again rears its ugly head, and Phaleas has no plan for educating love-of-self toward preserving the good that is properly-one's-own.

Phaleas' ignorance of desire is the foundation for Aristotle's most damning criticisms of his regime. Phaleas focuses on the necessary things in his regime because he customarily-considers most people stand in faction on account of being unequal in such acquisitions. Similarly, Phaleas customarily-considers most people commit injustice through the necessary things, for some people steal because they are hungry or cold. To these arguments, Aristotle responds that people stand in faction not only through inequality in acquisition, but inequality in honors. As for committing injustice, people do this not only through the necessary things, but for enjoyment and desire (*epithumeō*). If people hold a desire greater than the necessary things, they will commit injustice as a cure. And the problem goes even further, for people may delight in pleasures without pains (1266b38–1267a9). Again, Aristotle does not deny that Phaleas is correct in identifying necessary things as sources for standing-factions and injustice, but he does blame Phaleas for failing to see that standing-faction and injustice have more extensive causes.

Given this omission, Aristotle provides remedies to the three ills Phaleas fails to treat through equality in property. For those who commit injustice on account of the necessary things, the remedies are a little substance or property and work. For those who commit injustice through enjoyment and desire beyond the necessary things, there is need for moderation. And for those who seek pleasures without pains, the only remedy Aristotle offers is philosophy, for the others need human beings. This prompts Aristotle to conclude that Phaleas' regime is helpful only for small injustices, for the greatest injustices are not things people commit through the necessary things, but excess. As proof, Aristotle humorously quips that a tyrant is not a person who tries to escape the cold (1267a9–16). Of the three ills and their remedies, the third is likely the strangest to readers who confine their reading of Aristotle's political philosophy solely to the *Politics*. But the connection between his comment about pleasures without pains and his joke about tyrants goes back to Book X of the *Ethics* and his criticism of tyrants and the many as people who are without taste in liberal pleasure, an observation that sets the stage for understanding the self-sufficiency of contemplation in not needing other people to contemplate, though human beings' bodily nature is still in need of being healthy and food, but not in excess. These arguments fill in the gaps in Book VII of the *Ethics'* vague conclusion that the contemplative activity holds pleasures without pains because it belongs to a *hexis* of a nature not in-need, namely, the intellect. Between these two sets of arguments sits Aristotle's inquiry into friendship, with those who form-community in philosophy—the love or friendship of wisdom—showing themselves as liberated from a concern with worth in useful things (*chrēmata*) and honor.[27] This need for philosophy is compelling in Aristotle's interrogation of Phaleas' regime because while it is important to notice how inequality in property and honor drive standing-faction in political community, there is still something within human nature that forms-community in more than what is political and economic, and there must always be a way to draw this toward the good to guard both oneself and the community from the greatest of injustices.

The final part of Aristotle's criticism of Phaleas' regime lays bare the problem of desire and its need for the good. After reiterating that there is something of the advantageous things toward not standing in faction through substance or property being equal and reminding readers that people stand in faction over worth and not wanting to be equals—thus "setting-down an attack upon" (*epitithēmi*) others—Aristotle declares the laborious-wickedness (*ponēria*) of human beings is insatiable (*aplēstos*), for people always need more. And so they go on without-limit because "the nature of desire (*epithumia*) is without-limit," and the many live toward the restoration of this (1267a37–b5). The many present a paradox for those who wish to deal with standing-faction in political life, for how does one show them that they cannot restore the desires within their own nature that are naturally without-limit? But the terms of the argument point thoughtful readers back to King Midas in Book I's inquiry into the money-making art, for the insatiable greed (*aplēstia*) of his prayer led all things set-down-before (*paratithēmi*) him to turn into gold, leaving him well-provided in wealth but unprovided in the necessary food that (like the natural art of exchange) could restore the self-sufficiency that is according to nature. In the account of Phaleas' regime, people's insatiably laborious-wickedness leads them to set-down an attack upon others in standing-faction. In both cases, what people set-down in their lives begins from a desire without-limit. But Midas points to the way out, for instead of following desire without-limit and attempting to provide for it with economic acquisitions, he could have followed Aristotle's prayer in response

to the one-holding-more from Book V of the *Ethics* that teaches people to
ask that the simply good things are good for themselves and that they choose
(*haireō*) the good things for themselves.[28] In short, the most natural and truest
way out of the paradox of trying to restore the nature that is without-limit is
to hold knowledge of the good so that one's choosing and desire do not go
on without-limit.

At the same time as Aristotle's inquiry points to philosophy and seeking
knowledge of the good as the best remedy for standing-factions in community, he offers a political solution by saying that the rule (*archē*) of the many
whose desire is without-limit requires not the leveling of substance or property, but preparing those who are decent by nature not to wish to hold-more
while ensuring the base will not have the capacity to hold-more, which will
be the case if kept inferior and they do not have injustice committed against
them (1267b5–9). While the natural, underlying problem is holding-more
and its errant love-of-self, Aristotle rebukes Phaleas by suggesting rule is not
so much a question of managing property as it is managing persons within
the community. This provides an opening for polity, which appears in the
examination of regimes in Books III and IV of the *Politics*. Before turning to
this regime, however, readers should take note of the conclusion to the criticism of Phaleas' regime, for despite the strong judgment against it, Aristotle
ends his inquiry by saying whether what concerns this regime has been nobly
said is something to contemplate (1267b19–21). Like his choice to end the
examination of Socrates' regime with the mention of matters without-provision (*aporia*), Aristotle leaves readers with a subtle acknowledgment of the
contemplative life's inherent freedom, allowing them to decide if they trust
the *logos* he provides.

## THE MIDDLE POLITY AND MANAGING
## ECONOMIC INEQUALITY (*POLITICS* 1279A17–B10,
## 1288B33–39, 1294B13–16, 1295A25–1296A12)

The case for the middle polity appears in Book IV of Aristotle's *Politics*, the
first chapter of which begins with the different types of regimes a political
science could contemplate. Most relevant to Aristotle's inquiry into polity
are the last types of regime, those that fit all cities. Aristotle turns to these
regimes because people who speak of regimes miss the mark entirely on the
useful things (*tōn chrēsimōn*), even if they speak nobly on other things. For
there is need to contemplate not only the best regime, but the possible regime,
and similarly the regime that is easier and more common to all (1288b33–39).
Aristotle's introduction to these last regimes reads in two ways. First, those

who contemplate the best regime miss the mark entirely of the useful because they do not contemplate if their regimes are possible, easy, or common (the dismissal of Socrates' regime, for example, is partly on the basis that neither it nor its life is possible).[29] Second, applying a narrower reading, missing the mark entirely of the useful things suggests people do not understand where these things fit into the regime. What unites both Socrates and Phaleas is their misunderstanding of the useful things' (i.e., property and acquisitions) place in regimes: the former by abolishing what is properly-one's-own, and the latter by thinking equality in these useful things is all that should concern a legislator. In either case, Aristotle prepares the middle polity to address the useful things from a perspective that is possible, easier, and more common than other regimes.

What makes polity an interesting case in Aristotle's political philosophy is the peculiar way he introduces it in Book III. Before naming this regime, Aristotle defines all regimes by two standards: the manner of rule, and the number of people who rule (one, few, or many). The manner of rule is either correct (*orthōs*) through being for the sake of the common advantage and thus for free persons, or erring (*hamartanō*) through being only for the rulers' advantage (and therefore despotic). Polity is correct "governing of the regime" (*politeuō*) by the multitude toward the common advantage, but its name is nothing special, for it calls itself by the name common to all regimes, *politea*. As for the erring counterpart to polity, it is democracy, and it seeks the advantage of those who are unprovided (*aporos*) (1279a17–b10). Prior to Book IV's case for the middle polity, Aristotle states the boundary of a well-mixed polity is the same regime admits to be spoken of as a democracy and an oligarchy (which is erring rule of the well-provided, *euporoi*) (1294b13–16, 1279b7–8). Polity, then, paradoxically uses two erring regimes contrary to each other in their provision of wealth to produce correct governing of the regime.

The case for the middle polity begins with Aristotle appealing to the happy life according the mean in the *Ethics* to suggest that since the middle life is necessarily the best life, then the boundaries for regimes and cities are necessarily the same as those for virtue and vice, for the regime is some life of a city. Through this Aristotle defines the three parts of all cities as the well-provided, the unprovided, and the middle persons (who most easily trust-the-rule of *logos*). Without the middle persons, the polity is in a tenuous position, for the well-provided know only how to rule as masters and not how to be ruled, while the unprovided know only how to be ruled as slaves and not how to rule. Through this, the city has no free persons, but only slaves and masters, and nothing holds-back (*apechō*) friendship and political community more than this. This poses a problem for all cities, for the city itself wishes to be from those who are equal and similar most of all, and this is present most of all with the middle persons, on account of which the city necessarily governs the regime best if it is standing-together (*sustasis*) from what "we assert" is by nature for the city (1295a25–b28). At first glance, Aristotle's argument appears to be a straightforward case for a middle class that is neither rich nor poor, so readers looking for a strictly "economic" teaching could take his argument as an indication that regimes should craft economic policies that produce a large middle class. Aristotle's appeal to the happy life and virtue also lends itself to the desirable conclusion that a large middle class promotes public happiness through virtue. It is appealing that Aristotle finds in a large middle class the free character necessary for political friendship. But perhaps caution is necessary in approaching Aristotle's argument for the middle class, in part because while he concedes in his criticism of Phaleas' regime that the quantity of property affects community, the deeper problem is desire.

Since Aristotle points directly back to the *Ethics* in his case for the middle polity, readers should think about the movement of that work as a whole to see that the case for this polity is not nearly as straightforward as it appears. Rather than going back to the association between virtue, the mean, and happiness, one should perhaps start from the statement that the city "wishes" to be from those who are equal and similar. The case for the middle persons rests on them being the largest group in the city, but without them, the city is stuck with the opposition between the well-provided and unprovided (i.e., the oligarchs and the democrats). In Book VIII's inquiry into friendship, Aristotle considers how useful friendships seem most of all to come about between opposites, like a poor and a wealthy person. The example prompts Aristotle to wonder if such friends aim not at the opposite according to itself, but incidentally out of a desire (*orexis*) for the middle term, for this is good. To make this argument, Aristotle appeals to the humorous case of two lovers (in the sense of *erōs*) deeming themselves worthy of being loved more than they deserve. In this instance, the only way to render both persons worthy of equal love is if they are similar.[30] The middle persons in Aristotle's polity are literal stand-ins for a good that the well-provided and the unprovided should desire, but their presence begs an important question: How do the middle persons come to be this way in the first place? The same question applies to the well-provided and the unprovided. It is self-evident that these groups exist in all regimes, but the limits of approaching them from the perspective of political and economic community become apparent when one realizes neither politics nor economics can account for why people choose to be wealthy, poor, or middling. The city can only wish for citizens who are equal and similar because it cannot make their choices about what good they desire.

Another curious feature of Aristotle's case for the middle persons in the polity is his defense of it in terms of friendship and political community, not justice. Indeed, at no point in Book IV's eleventh chapter does Aristotle mention the just, the unjust, justice, or injustice. The reason why may appear in the beginning of the inquiry into justice in Book V of the *Ethics*, which begins with Aristotle noting how everyone wishes to speak of justice and injustice as *hexeis*. Through this appeal to *hexis*, Aristotle suggests that when it comes to a good-*hexis*, one can only know it according to itself and not (like the mean that defines the moral virtues) through its contraries.[31] If virtues are *hexeis*, then they require each person to know the good. While justice is ultimately not such a *hexis*, friendship is, and every friendship begins with one's own choice of the good, not the least of the bad things. It is friendship's affinity for the good that ultimately allows Aristotle in Book X to show that virtue and happiness are not merely the middle life that pursues the mean, but the intellect and its self-sufficient activity that holds within itself a liberal pleasure that is properly-one's-own (*oikeios*) from living according to a *logos* of the good. In light of this conclusion, Aristotle's entire case for the middle persons in the polity is a reiteration of each person's need to befriend the good, the true foundation for happiness that the middle polity can only approximate in a secondary way.

One last way in which Aristotle's account of the middle polity brings home desire's own need for the good is in its treatment of standing-faction. The middle citizens preserve themselves in cities most of all because they do not desire (*epithumeō*) others' things like the poor do of the wealthy. The middle persons balance themselves between the poor and the wealthy, thus preventing standing-factions because they keep the city from being stuck between the contraries of the well-provided and the unprovided. It is on account of this that Aristotle says it is the "greatest good-fortune" (*megistē eutuchia*) for the governing of regimes to hold middle and adequate substance or property (1295b28–1296a12). Insofar as the distribution of property in the regime is something Aristotle attributes to good-fortune, it is not the work of good legislation or economic policy. For all the praise Aristotle gives the middle polity for what must "necessarily" come about, he offers no direct teaching on how to produce the city with middling citizens and property.[32] This is because Aristotle never allows his readers to forget that the foundation of all political and economic community is each person's choices about the good that require using the intellect's sense-perception of the good to provide a limit to one's desires. While politics and economics could contemplate the ways of arranging external things like regimes and means of economic exchange, only political philosophy can address the nature of the choices each person makes that affect their own lives and, through these, the life of the community.

## CONCLUSION: FRIENDSHIP AND POLITICAL
## PHILOSOPHY'S NECESSARY PROVISION OF
## THE GOOD TO POLITICS AND ECONOMICS

In Book VI of the *Ethics*, Aristotle says prudence and the political art (*hē politikē*) are the same *hexis*, with household management (*oikonomia*) appearing as a form of prudence as well. As forms of prudence, they all contribute to the well-being of oneself, which may not be possible without household management or a regime. Aristotle's introduction to politics and economics as forms of prudence appears eminently practical, especially since it follows his observation that philosophers like Anaxagoras and Thales are said to be wise but not prudent because they are ignorant of the advantageous things for themselves, knowing instead useless things and not seeking out or examining the human goods.[33] But after going through Aristotle's political philosophy in search of his understanding of the relationship between politics and economics, it may be prudent to reconsider what wisdom provides to political and economic life, especially since the philosopher's relationship to wisdom is one of friendship, and friendship offers the most complete perspective on politics and economics in the *Ethics* and the *Politics*.

Aristotle presents wisdom in Book VI of the *Ethics* in relation to a need to know not only the things from first-principles (*archē*), but to arrive at the truth concerning first-principles. The language of first-principles reminds readers of Book I's beautiful image of the unprovided (*aporeō*) movement toward and away from the limit of first-principles in *logos* that provides knowledge (*gnōsis*) of the good. From the perspective of wisdom, Aristotle says, "For it would be strange if someone himself supposes the political art or prudence to be the most serious thing, if a human being is not the best of the things in the cosmos," and from this goes on to say that there are things more divine than human beings most displayed by the things from which the cosmos is set-standing-together. In light of this, Aristotle defines wisdom as "science and intellect of the most honorable (*tōn timiōtaton*) things by nature," a grand definition that he seems to undercut by drawing attention to how neither Anaxagoras nor Thales could provide the good things for themselves through wisdom. For readers who wish to enter Aristotle's political philosophy solely through the *Politics*, they will never know there is a kinship in his philosophy between community and the cosmos, "for every community is set-standing-together for the sake of some good (for all do all things for the sake of what seems to be good)."[34] A reasonable temptation for those who study politics and economics is to focus (like Anaxagoras and Thales) on the *things* from which regimes and communities are set-standing-together, and so one could look at households, political institutions, legal-currency, and all the other elements of exchange, yet miss the most essential question driving all these things: What is the good for the sake of which people are set-standing-together in political and economic community?

Though it may seem appropriate to approach the question of the good in politics and economics by attempting to separate each thing into its own distinct realm, the political philosopher realizes all human things lead back to one's own choice of the good. A good example of this approach relevant to discerning Aristotle's teaching on the relationship between politics and economics is how his inquiry into the money-making art from Book I of the *Politics* seeks to understand why some people think the art of household management and the money-making art share the same end, especially since people turn both arts to the gain of legal-currency without-limit through errors about living and living well.[35] Both errors are mistakes about the good that is properly-one's-own (*oikeios*), and they begin with failing to provide for desire (*orexis, epithumia*), which is naturally without-limit. While politics and economics might try either to coopt this characteristic of human nature for the sake of prosperity or mitigate its potentially negative effects on political and economic community, the political philosopher sees a need for the good that holds no provision outside of the love or friendship of wisdom.

The way Aristotle brings political philosophy to bear on the relationship between politics and economics is through his recognition that the money-making art is, by its very name, "the art of the useful things (*chrēmata*)." Within his inquiry into this art from Book I of the *Politics*, Aristotle seems to divide his inquiry into what concerns knowledge and use, and further seems to act as if there is a firm distinction between free contemplation (*theōrian eleutheran*) and necessary experience (*empeirian anankaian*). From the perspective of politics and economics, experience is practical, but philosophy is not. Yet in Book VII of the *Ethics*, it turns out that when it comes to how human beings hold themselves through a *hexis* toward *logos*, contemplation *is* use.[36] Thus, when readers arrive at the beginning of the inquiry into friendship in Book VIII and discover the useful (*chrēsimon*) as a form of friendship through which one loves (*phileō*) either the pleasant or the good as an end, what they know or are familiar with from their own friendships becomes the course they run to its limit (*peras*) to gain experience (*empeiria*) contemplating whether they live their lives in the limit (*en-peras*) of pleasure or the good. This experience is of the utmost necessity given how easy it is for human beings to mistake pleasure for the good, and the difficulty to provide a trustworthy *logos* of the good is evident from how careful Aristotle is with pleasure throughout the whole of the *Ethics*.

Friendship is the authoritative basis for providing for human beings' need for the good in Aristotle's political philosophy because every friendship forms and either falls apart or endures according to whether friends think the good that holds them together is still present. In this way, friendship provides

the clearest possible demonstration for the truth of the good as a first-principle, though Aristotle constructs his political philosophy in such a way as to
provide readers a persistent choice about whether the search for some good in
each stage of the inquiry discloses the truth about the matters at hand. With
respect to politics and economics, friendship's dependence on a choice for the
good and its natural limits derived from the fact that it is through one's own
self means the bonds of political community and the boundaries of acquisition do not go on without-limit. Every person desires a good and pleasant life,
and it is through forming-community in *logos* and thought with friends that
people provide for this need. Aristotle's political philosophy recognizes this
is the foundation for freedom, and it does so without dismissing politics' and
economics' contributions in providing the necessary community that fosters
the exchange of the external and bodily goods necessary for supporting the
free and liberal self-sufficiency of the contemplative life. While the needs for
which politics and economics provide are persistent, they ebb and flow. But
what Aristotle sees is that regardless of whether someone is well-provided or
unprovided in political and economic community, one always needs the good,
and its only natural provision is in *logos* and thought, things which one's own
nature of intellect and desire always stand ready to befriend.

# Conclusion

With the search for Aristotle's economic teaching in his political philosophy now at its end, readers can better appreciate the wisdom of his statement in Book I of the *Ethics* that it is possible to mark-the-boundaries of things so that they are "two in *logos* but naturally inseparable" (1102a26–31). The academic tendency in approaching Aristotle's works is to set the boundaries between philosophy, politics, and economics, when in truth all of these belong to "the philosophy concerning the human things" and are inseparable from human beings whose nature is synonymous with choice, an intellectual desire and need for the good. Aristotle's political philosophy demonstrates his constant awareness of this natural inseparability, and it is only readers' choices to separate his *logos* into the economic and political that prevents them from seeing his care to provide them a trustworthy *logos* through which they can gain the practical and contemplative experience of living within the limit of the good.

Whether it is acquisition, exchange, or community, Aristotle's *logos* always leads readers to see the natural needs and choices vital to each thing. *Logos* holds the freedom to show readers the nature of the choices that form economic and political life, and readers hold the freedom to form their own judgments of these choices' goodness. Aristotle cannot make readers' choices for them, but he can produce a *logos* that makes clear what choices are naturally good and bad. This is why one must interpret Aristotle's work in the *Ethics* and *Politics* as that of a political philosopher, not an economist or political scientist. The common shortcoming of academic philosophers, economists, and political scientists is that even though they notice the importance of choice and friendship for economics in Aristotle's political philosophy, none of them notice how the nature of the choice behind the money-making art (*chrēmatistikē*) is visible in the useful (*chrēsimon*) friendship's unveiling of the competition between the good and the pleasant as ends, a competition present throughout the whole of the *Ethics*.

Lost in the academic debate over what is economic and political *or* practical and theoretical in Aristotle's works is a view of what his texts teach on his own terms. Aristotle's *logos* is free to contemplate a wide range of human pursuits because the only limit he sets to it is the pursuit of the good. In being open to this pursuit, consider some of the questions this book could explore. What is the relationship between economics and politics? Are there natural limits to economics and politics? Are economics and politics arts or sciences? What is happiness? Can economics and politics provide for happiness? In their provision for happiness, how do economics and politics balance the good of the community with the good of each person? How does each person's pursuit of the good affect economics and politics? What is the relationship between economics, politics, and justice? The answers to all these questions require readers to reckon with Aristotle's teaching on friendship, the part of his political philosophy where his *logos* provides a clear view of choices between the useful, the pleasant, and the good, and he uses friendship to begin accounting for how these choices bear upon forming community in households and cities. Through friendship, readers discover a deeper sense of what is properly-one's-own (*oikeios*), one that allows them to know that the natural and enduring foundation of economic and political life is not community, but their own choice of the good. Aristotle's *logos* is simultaneously theoretical, practical, and empirical because it provides readers the contemplative experience of coming to know their need for the good. This knowledge frees readers by providing them with a sense of the natural limits to their desires *and* the boundaries of economic and political life. Regardless of the time or place, readers who engage Aristotle's political philosophy on his own terms will confront their enduring need to choose the good.

In writing this book, one of the most wonderful and humbling revelations came in the form of gradually unfolding how comprehensively Aristotle uses *logos* to remind readers of their own desire for the good and provide them a path toward choosing it with the wish that they come to live good and pleasant lives. This is the heart of Aristotle's political philosophy, though it is easy to miss if readers choose to approach his work with the demand that he answers only the economic and political questions that interest them. But for readers who choose to wonder their way through Aristotle's *logos*, they will find that they can come to know far more about economics and politics than they thought at the beginning of their inquiries. Indeed, it will likely surprise these readers just how much they can learn about life if they trust Aristotle's *logos*. In all their pursuits, human beings need to befriend the good, and with Aristotle's political philosophy, they can come to know the truth of the Ancient Greek proverb that "The things of friends are common" (*koina ta tōn philōn*).

# Glossary

## A

Abolish (verb) *anaireō*; *prosanaireō* ("abolish besides")
Abstraction *aphairesis* ("away from [*apo*] choosing [*hairesis*]")
Acquisition *ktēsis*
Acquirable *ktēton*
Activity *energeia* ("in" [*en*] "work" [*ergon*])
Active (verb) *energeō*
Adequate *ikanos*
Adornment *kosmos*
Advantage (verb) *sumpherō* ("bear" [*pherō*] "together" [*sum*])
Affect (verb) *paschō*
Agree-in-*logos* (verb) *homologeō*
Agreement (or "same-*logos*") *homologia*
Aim (verb) *ephiēmi* (or "to long after, desire"); *stochazomai* (or "guess")
Alternating-exchange (verb) *parallassō*
Animal *zōon*
Architect *architektōn*
Architectonic *architektonikos*
Arrive at truth (verb) *alētheuō*
Art *technē*
Artfully contrive (verb) *technizō*
Artisan *technitēs*
Artistic *technikos*
Artlessness *atechnia*
Art of acquisition *ktētikē*
Art of exchange *metablētikē*

Art of housebuilding  *oikodomikē*
Art of household management  *oikonomikē*
Art of hunting  *thēreutikē*
Art of retail-trade  *kapēlikē*
Art of usury  *obolostatikē*
Art of war  *polemikē*
Assumption  *hupolēpsis*
Authoritative  *kurios*
Authority (or "political power")  *exousia*

# B

Badly-suffer (verb)  *kakopatheō*
Base  *phaulōs*
Beastliness  *theriotēs*
Beautifully (or "nobly")  *kalōs*
Befitting (verb)  *prosēkō*
Being-master (verb)  *despozō*
Beginning (or "rule," or "first-principle," noun)  *archē*
Believe (verb)  *hēgeomai*
Beloved  *erōmenos*
Benefactor (verb)  *euergeteō*
Beneficial  *ōphelimos*
Boundary  *horos*
Boundary-marking  *horismos*
Bring (or "come") to completion (or "end")  *apoteleō*
Bear-together (or "advantage," verb)  *sumpherō*

# C

Calculate (or "reason," verb)  *logizomai*
Calculation (or "reasoning")  *logismon*
Call (verb)  *prosagoureuō*
Capacity (noun)  *dunamis*
Care-upon  *epimeleia*
Cause for censure (verb)  *aitiaomai*
Caution-money  *arrabōn*
Censure  *epitimaō* ("honor" [*timaō*] "upon" [*epi*])
Certain-quantity  *poson*
Chance  *tuchē*

Change (or "exchange") *metabolē*
Change-the-setting-down (in the sense of changing something established) *metatithēmi*
Change trust (verb) *metapeithō*
Character *ēthos*
Choice (noun) *proairesis*
Choose (verb) *haireō, proaireō*
Choosing (noun) *hairesis*
Choiceworthy *hairetos*
Citizen (noun) *polite*; *politikōs* (adj.)
City *polis*
Commerce *emporia*
Come (or "bring") to completion *apoteleō*
Comfort (or "luxury") *eupatheia* (literally "good" [*eu*] "passion" [*patheia*])
Common *koinon*
Community *koinōnia*
Community partners *koinōnoi*
Compared *sumblētos*
Complete (adj.) *teleios*
Concern *kēdo*
Concerns superfluous work *periergon*
Contrary to law *paranomos*
Correct *orthos* (noun); *orthōs* (adj.)
Correction *epanorthōma*
Correspond (or "to pose against," verb) *antikeimai*
Couple (verb) *sunduazō*
Coupling (adj.) *sunduastikon*
Coworker *sunergos*
Customarily-consider (verb) *nomizō*

# D

Deem-worthy (verb) *axioō*
Decency *epieikeia*
Decent *epieikēs*
Defect *elleipsis*
Deficiency *endeia*
Deliberation *boulē*
Delight (verb) *chairō*
Deprive (verb) *stereō*
Desire *epithumia, orexis* (nouns); *epithumeō, oregō* (verbs)

Destroy (verb) *apollumi*
Differ (verb) *diapherō* ("bear" [*pherō*] "across" [*dia*])
Differences *diaphora*
Divisible-into-parts *meriston*
Disadvantageous *asumphoros*
Display (verb) *phainō*
Display-from (verb) *apophainō*
Dispose-through (verb) *diakeimai*
Distribute (verb) *nemō, aponemō*
Distribution (noun) *dianomē*
Divide (verb) *diaireō* ("through" [*dia*] "choosing" [*haireō*])
Does not listen to calumny *adiablētos*
Doing and faring well *eu prattein*
Dwell-together-in-households *sunoikeō*

# E

Easily-dissolved *eudialutos*
Enjoyment *apolausis*
Equal *isos*
Equality *isotēs*
Equally balanced *isorropos*
Errant *hamartētikos*
Examine (or "look," verb) *skopeō*; *zēteō* (or "seek")
Excess (or "superiority") *huperbolē*
Exchange *allagē, metablētikē, metabolē, sunallagma* ("things exchanged-together") (nouns); *allassō, katallassō, epallassō* ("exchange-upon") (verbs)
Exchangeable representative *hupallagma*
Exhort (verb) *keleuō*
Experience *empeiria* ("in" [*en*] "limit" [*peras*] or "attempt" [*peiraō*])

# F

False *pseudos*
Fleeing *phugē*
Feel-affection (with a sense of familial "love) *stergō*
Free *eleutheron*
Freedom *eleutheria*
Force (or "violence," verb) *biazō*

Fought-over things  *perimachēta*
First-principle (or "beginning," or "rule," noun)  *archē*
For sale  *hōnios*
Form (noun)  *eidos*
Form-community (verb)  *koinōneō*
Friend  *philos*; *philika* ("proofs of friendship"); *philikos* ("for a friend"); *philophilos* ("love-friends"); *poluphilia* ("many-friends")
Friendly-affection  *philēsis*
Friendship  *philia*


# G


Gain  *kerdainō* (verb); *kerdos* (noun)
General  *katholou*
Good  *agathos*
Good-action  *eupraxia*
Good days  *euēmeria*
Goodwill (or "good-thought")  *eunoia*
Go through together (verb)  *sundiagō*
Governing-the-regime  *politeuō*


# H


Habit (as in "a thing from habit")  *ethiston*
Habituated-together  *sunēthēs*; *sunētheia* ("habituation-together")
Happiness  *eudaimonia*
Hard-to-take-away  *dusaphaireton*
Have the capacity (verb)  *dunamai*
Have the same name (noun)  *hōmonumian*
Have the same passions (verb)  *homoiopatheō*
*Hexis*  holding (derived from *echō*)
Hit or happen-upon  *tunchanō*
Hit the mark (or "succeed")  *epitunchanō*
Hold (verb)  *echō*
Hold-a-share  *metechō*
Hold-against (verb)  *antechō*
Hold-back (verb)  *apechō*
Hold-before (verb)  *proechō*
Hold-concern-around  *periechō*
Hold-forth (verb)  *parechō*

Hold-over (or "preeminent")   *huperochē* (noun); *huperechō* (verb)
Hold-together (verb)   *sunechō*; *sunechēs* (adj.)
Holding-more   *pleonektēs* (person); *pleonexia* (*hexis*)
Hold-towards (verb)   *prosechō*
Honor *timaō* (verb); *timē* (noun)
Household   *oikia*
Household management   *oikonomia*


# I

Impulse   *hormē*
Inheritance   *klēronomia*
Injustice   *adikaia* (noun), *adikeō* (verb)
In-need   *endeēs*
Inseparable   *achōrista*
Intelligence   *noēsis*
Intellect   *nous*; *to nooun* ("intellecting thing")
Interest   *tokos*
In-various-ways (literally, "in-more-ways")   *pleonachōs*


# J

Judge (noun)   *kritēs*
Judge (verb)   *krinō*
Just (noun)   *dikaios*; *dikē*
Justice   *dikaiosunē*


# K

Kinsfolk   *sungennikos*
Know (or "be familiar," verb)   *gnōrizō*
Know-scientifically (verb)   *epistamai*
Knowledge (noun)   *gnōsis*


# L

Laborious   *epiponos*

Lasting  *monimos*
Last thing  *eschaton*
Law (or "convention")  *nomos*; *nomimon* or *nomikon* ("lawful")
Lead  *hēgeomai*
Learned thing  *mathēton*
Legal-currency  *nomisma*
Legislate (verb)  *nomtheteō*
Legislative-art  *nomothetikē*
Legislator  *nomothetēs*
Leisure *scholazō* (verb); *scholē* (noun)
Liberal  *eleutherios*
Liberality  *eleutheriotēs*
Life  *bios*
Like-mindedness  *homonoia*
Limit  *peras*
Live (verb)  *zaō*
Live-together (verb)  *suzaō*
Living (noun)  *zōē*
*Logos*  argument, rational account, reason, and speech
Look (or "examine," verb)  *skopeō*
Loss  *zēmia* (noun); *zēmiō* (verb)
Lovable (noun)  *philēton*
Love  *agapaō, eraō, phileō, stergō* (verbs); *agapē, erōs, philia, storgē* (nouns)
Loved (or "something to be content with")  *agapēton*
Lover  *erastēs*
Lovers  *erotikoi*
Love-of-self  *philautos*
Low-born  *agennēs*

# M

Make-an-attempt (verb)  *peiraō*
Manage-like-a-household (verb)  *oikeō*
Market  *emporion*
Marketplace  *agora*; *agoraiōn*
Mark-the-boundary (verb)  *horizō*
Master  *despotēs*; as a "ruler," *despotikos*
Mastery (as a science)  *despoteia*
Mean  *mesotēs*
Mechanical (or "vulgar")  *banausos*

Merchant   *emporos*
Middle term   *meson*
Mishaps   *sumphora*
Moderation   *sōphrosunē*
Monarchically-rule (verb)   *monarcheō*
Monarchy (noun)   *monarchia*
Money-maker   *chrēmatistikos*
Money-making *chrēmatismos* (noun); *chrēmatizō* (verb)
Money-making art   *chrēmatistikē* ("art" [*technē*] of "useful things" [*chrēmata*])
More   *pleon, pleōn*
Motion   *kinēsis*
Move (verb)   *kineō*; *metakineō* ("move-with")
Moving (adj.)   *kinētos*
Mutual-giving   *metadosis*


# N


Nation   *ethnos*
Naturally-grow (verb)   *phuō*; *sumphuō* ("naturally-grow-together")
Nature   *phusis*
Necessary things   *tōn anankaiōn*
Not-beneficial (or "without-benefit)   *anōphelēs*
Not-set-down-together (substantive)   *asuntheton*
Need (or "use")   *chreia*
Needful things   *ta deonta*
Need the addition (verb)   *prosdeō*
Noble (or "beautiful")   *kalon*
Nobly (or "beautifully")   *kalōs*


# O


Of one mind   *homgnōmoneō*
One-must-attempt   *peirateon*
One-must-begin   *arkteon*
One-must-divide   *diaireteon*
One-must-set-down   *theteon*
One-must-use   *chrēsteon*
Opinion   *doxa*
Outline   *tupos*

# P

Painful  *lupēros*
Pass the days together (verb)  *sunēmereuō*
Passion  *pathos*
Perceive (verb)  *aisthanomai*; *sunaisthanomai* ("perceive-together")
Perceptible thing (noun)  *to aisthēton*
Persuade (or "trust," verb)  *peithō*
Persuasive (or "trustworthy")  *pithanos*
Philosophize (verb)  *philosopheō*
Philosophy  *philosophia*
Pleasant  *hēdus*
Pleasure  *hēdonē*
Piece of acquisition  *ktēma*
Political Art  *hē politikē*
Pose against (or "to correspond," verb)  *antikeimai*
Practice-politics (verb)  *politeuō*
Pray (verb)  *euchomai*
Prayer  *euchēs*
Precise-in-*logos* (verb)  *akribologeomai*
Precision  *akribēs*
Preservation  *sōteria*
Preserve (verb)  *sōzō*
Pretend to produce-toward  *prospoieō*
Price (or "honor")  *timē*
Private  *idios*
Proclaim  *agoreō*
Produce (verb)  *poieō*
Produced-thing  *poiēton*
Produce-in-turn  *antipoieō*
Production  *poiēsis*
Profit  *epikarpia*; *lusitelēs* ("profitable")
Proofs of friendship  *philika*
Proper, properly-one's-own  *oikeia*
Property (or "substance")  *ousia*
Proportion  *analogos*
Proportionate  *summetra*
Propose (verb)  *hupokeimai*
Prosperity  *euetēria*
Prudence  *phronesis*; *phronimos* ("prudent person")

# R

Reason (or "calculate," verb)  *logizomai*
Reasoning (or "calculation")  *logismon*
Reciprocity  *antipeponthos*
Regime  *politea*
Relaxation (noun)  *anapausis*
Remain (verb)  *diamenō*; *summenō* ("remain-together")
Reproach  *oneidos*
Requisite (or "longed-after")  *potheō*
Resources (noun)  *chorēgia*
Retail-trade  *kapēleia*; *kapēlikos*
Returned friendly-affection  *antiphilēsis*
Revenue  *poros*
Revolutionaries  *neōteropoios*
Ruin (verb)  *diaphtheirō*
Rule (or "beginning," or "first-principle")  *archē* (noun); *archō* (verb)

# S

Same-character  *homoēthēs*
Sameness-of-opinion  *homodoxia*
Science  *epistēmē*
Security  *eggun, eggunētēs*
Seek (or "examine," verb)  *zēteō*
Seem (verb)  *dokeō*
Self-restraint  *enkrateia*
Self-sufficiency  *autarkeia*
Self-sufficient  *autarchēs*
Selling  *parastasis* (noun); *pōleō* (verb)
Sense-perception  *aisthēsis*; *aisthētikē* ("sense-perceptible")
Serious  *spoudaios* (noun); *spoudazō* (verb)
Services rendered  *hupourgia*
Set-down (or "establish," verb)  *tithēmi*
Set-down-against  *antitithēmi*
Set-down an attack  *epitithēmi*
Set-down-before  *paratithēmi*
Set-down-in-addition (verb)  *prostithēmi*
Set-down-through  *diatithēmi* (verb); *diathesis* (noun)

Set-down-together (sometimes with the sense of a "covenant" or "agreement," verb) *suntithēmi*; "by compact," *sunthēkē*; as a substantive, *to suntheton* ("compounded", opposite of *asuntheton*, "uncompounded")

Set-standing-apart (verb) *diistēmi*

Set-standing-out (verb) *existēmi*

Set-standing-together (verb) *sunistēmi*

Set-standing-upon or over (verb) *ephistēmi*

Simply (adj.) *haplōs*

Skillful in aiming or guessing *stochastikos*

Slavish (adj.) *doulikos*

Something to be content with (or "loved") *agapēton*

Sought-for-thing *to zētoumenon*

Spend-time-in (verb) *endiatribō*

Stand (verb) *histēmi*

Standard *kanōn*

Standing-faction *stasis* (noun); *stasiazō* (verb)

Stated terms *rētos*

Strong *ischuros, kratos* (nouns); *ischuō, krateō* (verbs); *kreitton* ("stronger"); *kratistē* ("strongest," "most excellent")

Substance (or "property") *ousia*

Sudden-change *metapiptō*

# T

Take away (verb) *aphaireō*

Take hold of (verb) *lambanō*

Take pleasure (verb) *hēdomai*

That for the sake of which *to hou heneka*

Think (verb) *noeō*; *phrontizō*

Thinking thing *to dianoētikon*

Those in positions of authority *tas exousias*

Those working in a trade *dēmiourgoumenoi*

Through-to-the-end (verb) *diateleō*

Thought *dianoia*

True *alēthēs*

Trust *pistis* (noun); *peithō, pisteuō* (verbs)

Trusts-the-rule (verb) *peitharcheō*

Trust-upon *epipeithēs*

# U

Unequal  *anisos*
Unfruitful  *akarpōn*
Unmoving (adj.)  *akinētos*
Use  *chraō* (verb); *chrēsis* (noun); *chreia*, which also has the sense of "need"
Useful things  *chrēmata*, which can also mean "property" or "money"; *chrēsima*
Unprovided (or "perplexed")  *aporia* (noun); *aporeō, diaporeō* (verbs); *aporos* ("unprovided person")
Usury (practice, as opposed to art)  *tokismos*

# V

Vainly (adj.)  *mataiōs*
Vice  *kakia*
Village  *kōmē*
Violence (or "force")  *biaion* (noun); *biazō* (verb)
Virtue  *aretē*
Vulgar (or "mechanical")  *banausos*

# W

Wage-earning  *mistharnia*
Wandering  *planē*
Way-of-spending-time  *diatribē*
Wealth  *ploutos*
Wealthy (verb)  *plouteō*
Well-provided  *euporia* (noun); *euporeō* (verb); *euporos* ("well-provided person")
Whole set-standing-together  *sustēma*
Wickedness (or "laborious-wickedness")  *ponēria*
Wisdom  *sophia*
Wise  *sophos*
Wish  *boulēsis* (noun); *boulomai* (verb)
Without-art  *atechnōs*
Without-benefit (or "not beneficial)  *anōphelēs*
Without-experience  *apeiron*
Without leisure (noun)  *ascholeō* (verb); *ascholos* (noun)
Without-like-form  *anomoieidēs*

Without-limit  *apeiron*
Without-provision  *aporia*
Without-resources  *achorēgēton*
Without self-restraint  *akratēs*
Without-thought  *anoia*
Wonder (verb)  *thaumazō*
Work  *ergon*; *ergasia*
Worth  *axios* (noun); *axioō* (verb, "deem worthy")
Wretched  *mochthēros*; *mochthēria* ("wretchedness")

# Notes

## INTRODUCTION

1. M. I. Finley provides a similar etymology for *chrēmatistikē* in "Aristotle and Economic Analysis" (1970, 15), but neither he nor any of the other prominent interpreters of Aristotle's economic teaching connect *chrēmatistikē* to the useful form of friendship in *Ethics* VIII.

2. Although Booth brings together choice, friendship, the household, and the city in his book *Households: On the Moral Architecture of the Economy*, unlike Nichols, he does not catch Aristotle's argument that the human beings who are masters and slaves are better suited to the free character of friendship (1993, 38–39). Instead, Booth commits to the interpretation that the ruler of the household in Aristotle's *Politics* is synonymous with being a "master" (1993, 36). This is the result of an errant interpretation of *Politics* I, and chapter 4 of this book demonstrates the nature of this error.

3. The basis for reading Aristotle's inquiry into friendship as vital for disentangling pleasure and the good as ends is my dissertation, "Friendship, Politics, and The Good in Aristotle's *Nicomachean Ethics*" (Pascarella 2015). Prior scholarship that points to the importance of friendship for understanding pleasure in the *Ethics* is Aristide Tessitore's *Reading Aristotle's* Ethics: *Virtue, Rhetoric, and Political Philosophy* (1996, 73) and Lorraine Smith Pangle's *Aristotle and the Philosophy of Friendship* (2003, 180–181, 196).

## CHAPTER 1

1. While translators render *ktēsis* as "possessions" (Lord 2013) or "property" (Simpson 1997), I use "acquisition" to keep open the scope of things one may acquire beyond property.

2. Both Meikle (1995) and Crespo (2014, 16) omit Aristotle's inquiry into slavery from their interpretations of his economic teaching. As this book's first two chapters demonstrate, readers must understand how *Politics* I.4–11 work together to help them contemplate "all of acquisition," Aristotle's explicit context for examining slavery, household management, and the money-making art.

3. In Aristotle's political philosophy, the verb *aporeō* and its corresponding noun *aporia* usually mean "being at a loss" and "perplexity," respectively (Liddell and Scott 1889, 105). Since both terms derive from *porizō* ("to provide"), it is helpful in the search for Aristotle's economic teaching to use the terms' senses of being "unprovided" and "without-provision" to see how philosophy truly illuminates the nature of economics.

4. The primary definition for *parechō* is "to hold in readiness, to furnish, provide, or supply"; it also means "to afford . . . grant, give" and "to present or offer" (Liddell and Scott 1889, 608). To bring out these meanings while retaining the appearance of the root "to hold" (*echō*), here and throughout the translation for *parechō* is "to hold-forth."

5. The idea of "bringing to completion" derives from Aristotle's use of the verb *apoteleō*, something not reflected in the translations of Lord (2013, 12) and Simpson (1997, 20). Given one of the roots of the verb is *telos* (end), it is worth drawing attention to passages where this idea appears in Aristotle's works.

6. The phrase "in themselves" conveys the middle voice of the verbs for "provide" (*porisasthai*) and "use" (*chrēsasthai*). In Greek, the middle voice indicates subjects acting on themselves.

7. In its singular form, *chrēma* means "a thing one uses or needs," while in its plural form (*chrēmata*) it means "property, money" (hence why *chrēmatistikē* is the "money-making art") (Liddell and Scott 1889, 894). Aristotle's political philosophy demonstrates a careful awareness that *chrēmata* points to a broader horizon than money and property. Consequently, the term's translation here and throughout this book is "useful things."

8. "Choosing" is the primary meaning of *hairesis* (Liddell and Scott 1889, 22), which both Lord (2013, 13) and Simpson (1997, 21) obscure by translating it as "predilection" and "getting," respectively. From surveying the literature on Aristotle's economic teaching, I could not find an interpretation that considers the significance of *hairesis* in this context. Given the importance of "choice" (*proairesis*) in Aristotle's *Nicomachean Ethics*, it is important to catch the appearance of its root in Aristotle's inquiry into the money-making art, even if it is in relation to nature rather than human beings. For the sake of consistency, *hairesis* always appears as "choosing," and *proairesis* as "choice."

9. For a more thorough look at the questions surrounding Aristotle's use of "nature" in his inquiry into acquisition, see Wayne Ambler's "Aristotle on Acquisition" (1984).

10. How this argument is not Aristotle's own is clearer in the Greek through the combined use of the adverb *hōs* with the participle of the verb "to be" (*onta*). The combination of *hōs* with any participle "indicate[s] that the writer is giving the

presumed reason or purpose of the subject, but does not himself assume responsibility for the correctness of the fact" (Chase and Phillips 1961, 74).

11. A difficulty with the original Greek is lack of clarity over what the pronoun *autēn* refers to following the verbs "to be present" (*huparchein*) or "to provide" (*porizein*). Given the feminine ending of the pronoun, it corresponds either to the "art of acquisition" or the "art of household management." Simpson changes the subject to "property" (which is how he renders *ktēsis*, "acquisition"), but this seems wrong given the sentence is about "arts" (1997, 22). Lord reads the sentence as suggesting the art of household management must "supply" the art of acquisition (2013, 14), but since "to provide" is an infinitive, it does not appear to act in service of the art of household management. In light of the textual difficulties and the variance among translations, I render the Greek as literally as possible to bring out the original text's ambiguity.

12. Contrary to Simpson (1997, 22) and in line with Lord (2013, 14), I read *oikonomikōn* and *politikōn* as referring to "household managers" and "politicians," not the arts of household management and politics (1997, 22). The genitive declensions of both terms leave some ambiguity since they are the same in the masculine, feminine, and neuter genders. This makes it difficult to determine if the terms refer to practitioners of arts (whose names usually have masculine endings) or the arts themselves (which usually have feminine endings). Though the preceding clauses speak of arts, the sentence immediately following this one speaks of practitioners. Additionally, one of the other manuscripts indicates the same line could say "a household manager and a politician" (Ross 1964, 14). Finally, given Aristotle normally treats the art of household management and the political art in the singular, it would not seem correct to read him as suggesting each art has multiple forms.

13. Linguistic support for how Aristotle avoids asserting there is a limit to the natural art of acquisition comes through his choice not to use the term for "limit" (*peras*) in this argument, relying on its negative ("without-limit," *apeiron*) at 1256b32 and 1256b35. "Limit" first appears at 1257a1. As for Solon's term for "limit" (*terma*), 1256b33 marks the only appearance of this word in Aristotle's *Politics*.

14. Not all interpretations of Aristotle's economic teaching catch his distinction between "true wealth" and "wealth" (cf. Finley 1971, 16 and Chan 2006, 28).

15. This translation combines the first two definitions of *nomizō*—"to hold or own as custom or usage" and "to consider"—to bring out the term's derivation from *nomos* ("law" or "custom") (Liddell and Scott 1889, 534).

16. Here and in the next paragraph, there are many terms with initial meanings of "exchange." Rather than trying to provide different translations for each word that distort their meaning, I adhere to their main definition but parenthetically include the different terms Aristotle uses.

17. Here I read the pronoun *autēs* as referring back to the art of exchange (*hē metablētikē*) in 1257a14–15. The pronoun could also refer back to "the exchange" (*tēn allagēn*) at 1257a19, which appears in a brief digression concerning "the money-making art" (*chrēmatistikē*) and "the art of retail-trade" (*kapēlikē*) that helps clarify

the art of exchange's nature. Despite lack of clarity on the pronoun's object, the argument remains the same: exchange is not the household's work.

18.  One can also translate *metadosis* as "exchange," but I add "mutual-giving" to emphasize the literal reading of the conjunction of *meta* and *dosis*. Polanyi argues for a similar reading (1968, 111–112).

19.  Unlike Lord (2013, 3) and Simpson (1997, 10), I do not read "use" or "needs" as following the household's natural "every day" concerns at 1252b12–14 since Aristotle only uses *chrēsis* when talking about the village at 1252b16.

20.  Though both Meikle (1995, 54–55) and Crespo (2014, 17) acknowledge Aristotle's passage about "proper" and "improper" use in their interpretations, neither considers the potential puns on *oikeia, oikia, oikos, oikonomia,* and *oikonomikē*.

21.  Cf. 1256a10–13.

22.  Because *logos* has many related meanings that tie together reason and speech, and further, its centrality to Aristotle's understanding of what makes human beings political animals, I choose to transliterate the term throughout the book.

23.  "Set-down-together an agreement" combines two meanings of the verb *suntithēmi*: "set-down-together" and "to agree" or "to make a covenant" (Liddell and Scott 1889, 780). The root verb (*tithēmi*) means "to set down" or "to establish" (Liddell and Scott 1889, 806). To keep track of this verb's variants in Aristotle's *Ethics* and *Politics*, their translations throughout this book consistently tie them to their root by always using the phrase "set-down".

24.  As indicated in this passage, *chreia* means either "use" or "need." The context indicates "use" may be the more proper reading, one that builds on the arguments' mentions of "use" (*chrēsis*) and "useful things" (*chrēsima*). At the same time, noting the term's association with "need" complements the appearances of "necessity" (*anankē*) and being "in-need" (*endeō*) in the arguments.

25.  The weight placed on the phrase *kata logon* ("according to *logos*") is, as far as I could see in the literature, unique to my interpretation. For example, Shulsky (1991, 84) and Chan (2006, 29–31) follow Lord's translation as "reasonably enough" (2013, 15), but do not push their interpretations to dwell upon how *logos* affects acquisition and money-making. Finley, by contrast, misses the argument completely (1970, 17).

26.  Cf. 1256a29–b7.

27.  Scott Meikle's *Aristotle's Economic Thought* (1995) focuses on the problem of worth and commensurability in Aristotle's philosophy and economists' difficulty in reckoning with it.

28.  The inclusion of "may" and "equal" in this passage reflects the ambiguity of Aristotle's use of the word *isōs*, which means either "may" or "perhaps," or "equal." While Lord (2013, 16) and Simpson (1997, 24) only translate *isōs* according to the former sense, I include both senses of the term.

29.  Polanyi provides a history of the development of the art of retail-trade in his interpretation to outline the nascent Greek market (1968, 101–106), though Finley challenges this account's accuracy (1970, Note 45, 14). Also, contrast Aristotle's suspicion of gain with Robert L. Heilbroner's praise for gain in his book *The Worldly Philosophers* (1986, 18, 22, 35–36).

30. Cf. 1256b40–1257a13.

31. Polanyi (1968, 113), Finley (1970, 15), and Meikle (1995, 50–51) all note the importance of catching the ambiguity of "the money-making art" (*chrēmatistikē*) in the *Politics*, with Meikle adding a helpful survey of translators and scholars who either catch or miss this ambiguity.

32. Cf. 1257a13–30.

33. Cf. 1256a14–19 and 1256b7–10.

34. Cf. 1256b28–34.

35. Cf. 1257a21–28.

36. Cf. 1256b26–30 and 1257a13–38.

37. Cf. 1256a19–b7.

38. Here I read *stoicheon* ("element") and *peras* ("limit") as indefinite parts of exchange. By contrast, Lord (2013, 16) and Simpson (1997, 25) translate these terms as if there are definite articles attached to them, which cuts against Aristotle's argument that the art of retail-trade could be about either necessary exchange, or the gain of legal-currency.

39. For other appearances of *allagē*, cf. 1256a40–b2, 1257a5–13, 19–37.

40. Cf.1256b34–37.

41. Contrast this interpretation that questions the validity of the tool size argument with Chan's (2006, 28).

42. This translation is mostly in line with Lord (2013, 16–17) and Simpson's (1997, 25), with the key difference being the choice to render the last clause of the sentence as "an end" instead of "the end" since a definite article does not precede *telos* in the original Greek.

43. The verb *sunkeimai* ("to compose," literally "to compose-together") is a passive form of the verb *suntithēmi* ("to set-down-together"), a kinship derived from their root verbs *keimai* ("to be laid," "to set up, propose") and *tithēmi* ("to set-down" or "establish") (Liddell and Scott 1889, 754, 780, 425, 806). Though related, throughout this book, all verbs derived from *keimai* appear with "pose" in their translation, and all verbs derived from *tithēmi* appear with "set-down" in their translation.

44. A precedent for blending Aristotle's inquiry into the money-making art with the inquiry into slavery is in Mary Nichols's "The Good Life, Slavery, and Acquisition: Aristotle's Introduction to Politics" (1983).

45. The translation of this passage is difficult for several reasons. To start, the first subject of the sentence is *ktetikē*, which I translate as "the art of acquisition." Because Aristotle draws the distinction between *ktetikē* and the sciences of mastery and slavery (referred to by the genitive pronoun *toutōn*), one could read *ktetikē* as "the science of acquisition" (cf. Simpson 1997, 20; Lord 2013, 12). But given Aristotle's inquiry into the money-making art describes how it turned to gain as it became more of an art (1257b1–4), and further, his naming of "household management" (*oikonomia*) as a possible "science" (1253b18–20) while "the art of household management" (*oikonomikē*) does not appear as a science, it is reasonable to treat the art of acquisition as more of an art than a science (how an art differs from a science receives explicit attention in later chapters). Second, like Simpson

(1997, 20) I read the "art of acquisition" in this passage as its own art, not as "the acquisition of slaves" like Lord (2013, 12).

46. Cf. 1256b20–26.

47. Cf. 1256b40–1257a5.

48. The inclusion of "the stronger" in this passage brings out the root of the verb *krateō* ("to be strong"), which Aristotle uses here as participles (Liddell and Scott 1889, 448).

49. A "writ of illegality" is a "technical term of Athenian jurisprudence for a suit brought against anyone proposing in the public assembly a measure contravening the fundamental laws of the city." (Lord 2013, Note 28, 9)

50. This translation reflects the ties between the term Aristotle uses here (*huperochē*) and the verb from which it derives, *huperechō*, "to hold-over," which could also indicate being "preeminent" or "superior" (Liddell and Scott 1889, 837, 835–836).

51. While Ross's manuscript has *anoia* ("without-thought") at 1255a17, his footnote indicates another manuscript has *eunoia* ("good-will") in its place (1957, 9). Both Lord (2013, 9) and Simpson (1997, 18) follow the latter reading, though Lord notes the ambiguity in the passage and the difficulties in interpreting it (2013, Note 29, 10).

52. Cf. 1257a30–b11.

53. Lord (2013, 10) and Simpson (1997, 18) translate *axioō* as "claim," which is in line with one of the verb's definitions provided by Liddell and Scott (1889, 85). But since the root word *axios* means "worth," and further, Aristotle mentions the opinion that those who are "unworthy" (*anaxion*) to be enslaved should not be slaves (1255a25), it is fitting to try to bring out the pun in English. Further reason for this interpretation resides in Aristotle's use of *nomizō*— "to hold," "acknowledge," or "consider" (Liddell and Scott 1889, 534), rendered in this passage as "customarily-consider"—when discussing what others think of barbarians (cf. 1255a34).

54. For a similar conclusion that Aristotle's inquiry into the slave by law raises doubts on this practice, see Wayne Ambler's "Aristotle on Nature and Politics: The Case of Slavery" (1987, 401–405).

55. Cf. 1257b1–17.

56. Cf. 1256a19–b7.

57. Cf. 1257b25–31 and 1255a3–19.

58. Chan misses this argument about the arts of household management and retail-trade exchanging-upon the use of legal-currency in his interpretation (2006, 31–32), an oversight possibly attributed to overlooking the role of *logos* in Aristotle's inquiry.

59. This is a difficult passage to translate, and there is some variance between translations on a couple key points. To start, both Lord (2013, 17) and Simpson (1997, 25) depart from the Ross manuscript's inclusion of *ktēseōs chrēsis* ("use of acquisition") at 1257b37 and read the phrase as *chrēseōs ktēsis* ("acquisition of use") in accordance with another manuscript (1957, 17), whereas I follow the Ross

manuscript. Outside of the manuscripts, the argument at 1257a6–9 that every piece of acquisition has a proper and improper use indicates that it is use that leads to a difference between the arts of money-making and household management. Second, my reading of the passage follows Lord (2013, 17) in his reading of *hekateras tēs chrēmatistikēs* at 1257b36 as "the two forms of the money-making art"; Simpson renders the phrase as "the two uses of business" based on another manuscript's declension of the first word of the phrase as *hekatera* (1997, 25). Finally, though my translation of the second part of the passage leads to the same reading as the translations by Lord and Simpson, the Greek in this section is ambiguous. Accordingly, I try to adhere to the syntax of the manuscript and infer what the subjects of the pronouns might be based on the context. To clarify, *tauton* (the crasis of *to auton*) at 1257b37 can only refer to one other neuter subject in the sentence, namely, *telos* at 1257b38. As for the repetitions of the definite article *tēs* at 1257b37–38, these could refer either to "use" (*chrēsis*) at 1257b37, or "each money-making art" at 1257b36, since the passage aims to clarify why there is some exchange of meaning between the arts of money-making and household management. Though both readings are possible, they do not change the meaning of the clause since arts make use of their tools.

60. Cf. 1256b34–37.

61. This translation of *diateleō* uses a couple senses of *dia* in composition offered by Liddell and Scott—"through," "right through," "to the end, utterly" (1889, 184–185)—to bring out the verb's use of the root for *telos*. *Diateleō* can also mean "to bring quite to an end, accomplish," though with a participle (*oiomenoi* in this passage) it means "to continue being or doing" (Liddell and Scott 1889, 195).

62. Cf. 1256b26–1257b31.

63. Both Polanyi (1957, 101) and Finley (1971, 16) argue that the term for the "art of retail-trade" (*kapēlikē*) is a pejorative, one that refers to "hucksters." Regardless of whether or not Aristotle intends to be derogatory in the naming of this art, the more salient argument seems to be the distinction he draws between the arts of retail-trade, money-making, and household management.

64. Cf. 1257a5–13 and 1252b12–16.

65. The primary meaning of *diathesis* is "disposition," but because the term derives from the verb *diatithēmi* ("to place separately, arrange . . . dispose," literally "set-down-through" or "establish-through"), it is important to capture its association with all the verbs derived from *tithēmi* (Liddell and Scott 1889, 187, 189).

66. Cf. 1253b23–26 and 1252b29–30.

67. Cf. 1257a30–b17.

68. Cf. 1256a19–b7.

69. Cf. *Nicomachean Ethics*, Book III, Chapters 6–9.

70. Cf. 1257b5–8.

71. Cf. 1257a30–b4 and 1256b26–34.

72. Cf. 1255a3–19, 32–b4.

# CHAPTER 2

1. Cf. 1256a1–19 and 1257b32–1258a19.

2. Here I read *huparchein* at 1258a21 as "to be present," which is in line with Lord's translation (2013, 18). Simpson translates the verb as "property" (1997, 26), but this seems incorrect since *huparchō* has that meaning only as a participle.

3. The last part of this passage is difficult to translate (*hōs dei tauta diatheinai prosēkei ton oikonomon*), though my translation aligns with Simpson's (1997, 26–27). Lord, in contrast, translates the last clause in this way: "while it befits the household manager to have what comes from those things in the state it should be in" (2013, 18). The reason for variance seems to follow from lack of clarity over how to read *dei* since combining it with accusative subjects means "there is need," and both *tauta* ("these things") and *ton oikonomon* ("the household manager") are in the accusative case. However, because *dei* carries the sense of "there is need of" when combined with an accusative subject and a verb in its infinitive form (Liddell and Scott 1889, 175), the appearance of *diatithēmi* in its aorist infinitive suggests it bookends everything that relates to *dei* in the sentence. It follows, then, that the accusative case of *oikonomikos* is a result of its relation to the verb *prosēkō* ("befits").

4. Cf. 1256a19–b7.

5. Cf. 1256a3–10.

6. Cf. 1256b28–37.

7. Chan reads Aristotle as suggesting how technology could end slavery (2006, 15–21).

8. Cf. 1256a19–b7 and 1257a5–b4.

9. Cf. 1256a3–10 and 1258a19–25.

10. Cf. 1253b33–1254a8 and 1257b25–1258a14.

11. Cf. 1252a7–13.

12. Though Ross does not include this second "by nature" in the body of his manuscript, he notes it appears in other manuscripts (1957, 2). The lack of this second "by nature" in Ross's manuscript is consistent with its non-appearance at 1252a33. In either case, ambiguity surrounding what is "ruled by nature" is a feature of this passage.

13. Ross's manuscript has *ponein* ("to labor") as the verb at 1252a33, though other manuscripts have *poiein* ("to produce") in its place (1957, 2). Given Aristotle later defines the slave in relation to action instead of production (cf. 1254a1–8), I choose to include both readings to show the inquiry's gradual refinement of what constitutes mastery and slavery.

14. For this argument about Aristotle's use of the neuter gender, see Wayne Ambler's "Aristotle on Nature and Politics: The Case of Slavery" (1987, 392).

15. Booth overlooks Aristotle's distinction between "ruler by nature and mastering by nature" and "ruled and by nature slave," speaking simply of "master and natural slave" (1993, 36). This oversight is deliberate since he asserts Aristotle's arguments about slavery are "strictly cultural artifacts with no residual philosophic value" (1993, 68). In addition to my own interpretation, the work of Nichols (1983,

1992), Ambler (1984, 1987), and Shulsky (1991, 89–94) strongly attest to the true philosophic value of Aristotle's inquiry into slavery.

16. Cf. 1253b33–1254a1 and 1258a21–25.

17. 1256b40–1257a5.

18. Cf. 1282b14–23 and 1253a7–19, 29–39.

19. Cf. 1256a19–b7, 1257a1–5, and 1257b1–4, 11–17, 30–38.

20. Cf. 1253b1–14.

21. The verb for "to take hold" (*lambanō*) is the root of the verb Aristotle uses in its middle participle for "assumptions" (*hupolambanō*). In this light, Aristotle suggests readers can "take hold of" what they know about master and slave from "the current assumptions," or some other way of knowing these things.

22. The literal translation of this phrase that means ruler and ruled are "in turn" is "according to part ruler and ruled" (*kata meros achōn kai archomenos*). Mary Nichols also notes the significance of this alternate reading in *Citizens and Statesmen* (1992, 6).

23. Cf. 1254a8–17.

24. Also see Ambler (1987, 396).

25. Polanyi simply asserts that slavery is natural to Aristotle (1957, 98), and thus ignores this crucial statement that the *logos* allows readers to contemplate if slavery is truly natural. Polanyi's error is not without precedent, for Finley quotes part of Marx's *On Capital* where he says, "Greek society was founded upon slavery, and had, therefore, for its natural basis, the inequality of men and their labour power" (1971, 13). For a more thorough look at Marx's misunderstandings of Aristotle, see Mansfield (1980).

26. The adjective *sunechēs* ("holding-together") derives from the verb *sunechō* ("to hold-together") (Liddell and Scott 1889, 775). The translation of these terms throughout this book reflects this connection.

27. Cf. 1253b23–1254a1.

28. The verb *diakeimai* ("disposed-through") is a passive form of the verb *diatithēmi* ("to set-down-through"). See Chapter 1, Note 43 above.

29. *Orexis* means "desire, appetite" or "longing," and relates closely to *epithumia*, "desire, yearning, longing" (Liddell and Scott 1889, 566, 292). In Book I of the *Nicomachean Ethics*, Aristotle states *epithumia* is a subset of *orexis* (1102b28-31). Throughout this book, I translate both terms as "desire," noting parenthetically which term Aristotle uses in each passage.

30. This is what Harry Jaffa suggests in his interpretation of the passage, though Aristotle's language is vague on where intellect and desire reside (1963, 75).

31. In his interpretation of this passage, Ambler writes, "The evident progression here is from the problem of rule between parts of the same being, to the problem of rule between different species, to the problem of rule between different members of the same species. This progression illustrates two different aspects of the general problem of rule: Is there truly a common good between ruler and ruled (as Aristotle is at pains to assert in the case of man/beast)? Is there truly a natural (and sufficient, or appropriate) superiority of ruler over ruled (as Aristotle is at

pains to assert in the case of male/female)? Both of these problems become more acute as we approach the case of despotic rule as actually practiced among men" (1987, 398).

32. I owe this observation to Ambler, who writes, "[Aristotle] strengthens these doubts [about natural precedents for slavery] by dropping the paradigm for natural rule within a species, the rule of male over female, from his conclusion. Whatever the natural differences here, they do not justify despotic rule (1252a34–1252b5). This encourages us to doubt that the human species is so divided that it is, in effect, two species, of which one deserves to rule the other despotically" (1987, 399).

33. For different reasons, Nichols finds this characterization of the natural slave "[makes] the concept . . . all the more problematic," for "If the master has a body as well as a soul and the slave has a soul as well as a body, how could the master differ from the slave as much as the soul from the body?" (1983, 175).

34. Cf. 1252a24–1253a1.

35. The verb *hupēreteō* means "to serve," but given its kinship with "subordinate" (*hupēretikos*), I translate it as "to subordinate" (Liddell and Scott 1889, 839).

36. Strictly defined, *parallassō* means "to make things alternate, to transpose" or "to change or alter a little" (Liddell and Scott 1889, 599). My translation of "alternating-exchange" aims to capture the presence of the root verb *allassō* ("to change, alter" or "to give in exchange for"), which is one of the verbs Aristotle uses for "exchange" in his inquiry into the money-making art (Liddell and Scott 1889, 37).

37. For other arguments that Aristotle's inquiry into natural slaves ultimately undermines the case for their existence, see Harry Jaffa's chapter on Aristotle in the first edition of Leo Strauss and Joseph Cropsey's *History of Political Philosophy* (1963, 74–76, 78–80), Mary Nichols's "The Good Life, Slavery, and Acquisition" (1983), Wayne Ambler's "Aristotle on Nature and Politics: The Case of Slavery" (1987), and John Antonio Pascarella's "War and Peace in Aristotle's Political Philosophy" (2017, 43–48).

38. Cf. 1256a29–b7.

39. For a similar conclusion, see Ambler (1987, 406–407).

40. Cf. 1255a3–b4.

41. Nichols also raises this question, saying, "But since the master needs the slave . . . could the master be simply independent or free?" (1983, 174).

42. Normally *oikonomikē* appears as "the art of household management," but since it follows in the context of a passage about "the rules" (*hai archai*), its translation reflects Aristotle speaking of it here as a form of rule.

43. Cf. 1257a13–30.

44. The proper definition for the verb *kakopatheō* is "to suffer ill . . . be in distress" (Liddell and Scott 1889, 393). The translation of "badly-suffer" aims to bring out the term's two roots: "bad" (*kakos*) and "passion" or "suffering" (*pathos*).

45. Cf. 1255a19–32.

46. Cf. 1254b2–9, 1252a24–33, and 1257b32–1258a14.

47. This conclusion aligns with the core thesis of Mary Nichols's "The Good Life, Slavery, and Acquisition: Aristotle's Introduction to Politics," where she

writes, "By satisfying some of man's basic needs, commerce removes the necessity of slavery, and therewith its justification. Commerce thus makes possible political life, which is characterized by political rule, the rule of free men over free men. Commerce, however, also inhibits political life to the extent that politics is characterized by freedom from rule by the bodily pleasures which commerce and wealth provide" (1983, 171).

48. Cf. 1258a19–21, 1254b27–34, 1255a32–b4, and 1257b17–30.

49. Cf. 1258a21–34 and 1253b23–1254a17.

50. Cf. 1258a27–34.

51. Cf. 1256a29–b26.

52. Cf. 1256b26–39.

53. A similar ambiguity occurs back at 1257a9, 14–15, where Aristotle speaks of "exchange" in the first passage, and the "art of exchange" in the second. Though the current context suggests Aristotle's discussion is of the "art of exchange," I choose to leave both meanings on the table.

54. Cf. 1257a30–b4.

55. Cf. 1257a5-28.

56. The literal meaning for "the art of usury" (*hē obolostatikē*) is the "weigh[ing] of obols" (i.e., coins) (Liddell and Scott 1889, 542).

57. Cf. 1257a30–38.

58. Cf. 1253a9–18.

59. Together, these conclusions tie together Nichols's assessment that Aristotle's criticism of usury is it "has no origin in nature . . . [and] even more radically than money removes man from the limits imposed by nature's heterogeneity" to part of her main thesis that claims "[commerce] also inhibits [man's] actualizing his distinctive natural capacity—his capacity for politics, or for sharing in speech about the advantageous and the just" (1983, 179–180, 171).

60. Cf. 1253b33–1254a17 and 1254b16–23.

61. Cf. 1258a2–14.

62. Cf. 1256a19–b2, 1257a37–b4, and 1258a14–19.

63. Cf. 1253b11–14, 1257a1–3, 14–19, 1257b5–8, and 1258a19–b8.

64. Nichols also argues that Aristotle does not "[abandon] his theoretical perspective" in *Politics* I.11, but "actually broadens his knowledge" by considering "how nature and art complement each other" (1992, Note 33, 187).

65. Though Ross has *ktēmata* in his manuscript at 1258b12, he notes another manuscript has *ktēnē*, "flocks and herds" in its place (1957, 19). Lord (2013, 19) and Simpson (1997, 28) follow this alternate manuscript. Though the examples Aristotle offers in subsequent lines adhere to the theme of livestock, following Ross's manuscript allows readers to think of the money-making art's broad concern with pieces of acquisition (including but not limited to livestock).

66. Ross's manuscript has *prōtēs* ("first thing" in the singular) at 1258b21, though he notes another manuscript has *prōta* ("first things" in the plural), which matches the case of "parts" (*moria*) (1957, 20).

67. Cf. 1258a34–b2.

68. While Ross has *technitōn* ("artisans") at 1258b26, he notes another manuscript has "arts" (1957, 20). As for *banausos* ("vulgar" or "mechanical"), Lord writes in his translation, "The reference is to a class of artisans who work indoors and with their hands at repetitive tasks, as in modern factory work" (2013, Note 48, 19). Similarly, Simpson notes *banausos* "literally means someone who works by fire, but it has a general reference, along with a derogatory connotation, to all artisans or craftsmen engaged in bodily work" (1997, Note 47, 28).

69. Cf. 1257a37–41, 1256a3–10, and 1258a34–38.

70. Cf. 1258a2–6.

71. Cf. 1255a32–b4.

72. Cf. 1252a24–33, 1255a19–21, and 1254b2–9.

73. Cf. 1255b9–37.

74. Cf. 1257b40-1258a2.

75. Cf. 1252a1–13.

76. "To deposit" is one of the many meanings of *tithēmi*, but for the sake of continuity with the verb's meanings of "to set-down," I translate it in this passage as "to-set-down-in-deposit" (Liddell and Scott 1889, 806). See Chapter 1, Notes 23 and 65 above.

77. The clunky nature of this translation is necessary to bring out Aristotle's two uses of the verb *politeuō* in the phrase *politeuontai tōn politeuomenōn*. *Politeuō* assumes its active, middle form in the first part of the phrase, which suggests a subject (the participle "of-those-practicing-politics") "practicing-politics" itself or in its own interest in the second part of the phrase. Because Aristotle uses "politicians" (*politikoi*) at 1259a33–34, it seems deliberate that he does not repeat the term at the end of the thought.

78. Both Lord (2013, Note 55, 20) and Simpson (1997, Note 51, 29) note it is unclear if Aristotle refers to Dionysius I or II, though both rulers were tyrants.

79. Cf. 1252a1–13 for the four forms of rule, and 1255b16–20 for household-management's rule as monarchy.

80. Cf. 1253b33–1254a1 and 1258a19–34.

81. Cf. 1254a21–24, 1254b6–9, and 1255a3–b9.

82. Cf. 1253a9–18 and 1254b16–23.

83. Cf. 1255b20–37.

84. Cf. 1256b20–26, 34–1257a1, and 1258a38–b2.

85. Cf. 1256a19–29.

86. Cf. 1252b12–16, 1253b1–14, ,1254a24–33, and 1255b16–20.

87. The syntax of this sentence is difficult. Contrary to Lord (2013, 81) and Simpson (1997, 99), I do not translate *agathon* without its definite article at 1282b15 as "some good" since that makes it appear as if the phrasing is analogous to *agathou tinos* ("some good") in *Nicomachean Ethics* 1097a2. To account for the lack of a definite article, I translate *agathon* and *politikon agathon* as "a good" and "a political good," respectively. Furthermore, I include "good" or "end" in brackets at 1282b15 because "greatest" (*megiston*) appears in the neuter, which could refer back to both *agathon* or *to telon*. "Good" is most likely the subject since it recurs at 1282b17 as

"political good," but it seems reasonable to note both possibilities since the good is an end. Additionally (and once again contrary to Lord and Simpson), I translate *kai malista* at 1282b15 as "most certainly" in accord with one of Liddell and Scott's definitions of the phrase (1889, 486) since the *men . . . de* sentence construction suggests the phrase functions as a response. A more detailed examination of how this passage from the *Politics* compares to the opening of the *Nicomachean Ethics* appears in the next chapter.

88. Cf. 1257b8–17.

89. Cf. 1258a19–34 and 1255b9–15.

# CHAPTER 3

1. In his chapter "On Aristotle's *Politics*" in *The City and Man*, Leo Strauss points to the connection between prudence, the political art, and the money-making art (1964, 23–24, 28–29). Following Strauss and Shulsky (1991, 77–78), Chan describes prudence within his analysis of *Politics* I.8-11 as "the hallmark of Aristotle's political science" because it "concerns itself with the whole rather than the partial human good," yet does not wade into the depths of the *Ethics'* inquiry into the good (2006, 12, 17).

2. Meikle's *Aristotle's Economic Thought* concentrates on *Politics* I.8–11 and *Ethics* V.5, but neglects a thorough engagement with prudence, justice, and political philosophy in Aristotle's works (1995).

3. Cf. 1259a33–36 and 1257a13–30.

4. Cf. 1259a23–28 and 1282b14–23.

5. Cf. 1256a1–19 and 1258a19–34.

6. Cf. 1255b20–39.

7. Cf. 1256b37–1257a5 and 1257b1–4.

8. Cf. 1257a30–38 and 1258a38–b5.

9. Cf. 1253a9–18.

10. The sole appearance of "choice" (*proairesis*) in Book I of the *Politics* is negative, with Aristotle describing the necessary coupling of male and female for the sake of generation as *not* being from choice (1252a26–30). This receives more attention in the next chapter.

11. Cf. 1257b25–30 and 1258a10–14.

12. The use of "itself" and "themselves" in this translation reflects the appearance of the verbs *ephiēmi* ("to aim") and *apophainō* ("to display-from" or "declare-from") in the middle person. The middle person suggests the subjects of these verbs (art, inquiry, action, and choice) act on themselves, as if they have their own agency. Aristotle does not use the first person until he says "we ourselves wish" for there to be some end of actions at 1094a19. The former passage presents arts, inquiries, actions, and choices as somehow detached from human beings. The contrast between the two passages invites readers to wonder if these pursuits are truly independent of the people who engage in them.

13. In *Aristotle's Dialogue with Socrates*, Ronna Burger describes the opening passage of the *Nicomachean Ethics* as "preposterous" since "the reference to that at which all things aim appears to be a more grand claim about a single end: from the opinion that there is some particular good for particular types of human endeavors, a conclusion is drawn about *the* good as a comprehensive end" (2008, 13–14).

14. Burger, with good reason, describes this passage about ends as "what may well be the most abstract and obscure statement in the *Ethics*," and she goes on to note how "activity" and "work" come together is not apparent until Book VI at 1144a5–7 (2008, 14–15).

15. Cf. 1256b26–37 and 1257b8–31.

16. The verb *haireō* means "to choose," and is at the root of *proaireō* (literally, "to choose-first"), the verb related to "choice" (*proairesis*) (Liddell and Scott 1889, 670). "Choose" translates both verbs throughout this book, though parenthetical notes indicate which verb appears in the relevant passages.

17. Cf. 1257b17–1258a14.

18. Cf. 1256a29–b7, 26–34.

19. As Lord notes in his translation, "[*Politics*] I.8–11 is the most important discussion of what we today call economics not only in Aristotle's works but in all of ancient literature" (2013, Note 33, 12). Though Lord points this out not to discourage reading the rest of the *Politics*, his note illustrates how approaching Aristotle's works from the perspective of a certain discipline narrows down his philosophy in ways that close interpretations of his works do not permit.

20. The lines for the appearances of *peras* and *apeiron* (which is the most-used of the two terms) are as follows: 1257b23, 23–24, 25, 26, 27–28, 29, 31, 32, 34, 40, 1258a1, 2, 9, and 18.

21. Cf. 1258a21–25, 1257b25–30, 1254b27–34, and 1255a3–b4.

22. Because *kuriotatēs* and *architektonikēs* have feminine endings, the two closest subjects to which they refer are either *epistēmē* (science) or *dunamis* (capacity). But as noted elsewhere, the *-ikē* ending in Greek tends to denote an art (*technē*), and at 1094a7, Aristotle sets the inquiry to look into arts and sciences. Unless otherwise noted, the translation of *hē politikē* is "the political art." For a similar precedent, see Robert Bartlett and Susan Collins's translation (2011, 2–3).

23. Cf. *Politics* 1255b16–20.

24. Bywater's manuscript inserts *praktikais* ("practical") before "sciences" at 1094b4–5, but notes the term does not appear in other manuscripts (1894, 2).

25. Though the primary meaning of *lambanō* is "to take hold of," it is distinct from *echo*, which primarily means "to hold." The translation of these terms throughout adheres to their primary meaning, but will note which verb is at work to prevent confusion.

26. Given *methodos* ("inquiry") is a feminine term, in the context of the sentence, it is likely that *politikē* modifies *methodos*. However, since *politikē* can also mean "political art," it could be helpful to consider how Aristotle approaches the political art not only as one of the subjects of his inquiry in the *Ethics*, but as a form of inquiry in itself.

27. Cf. 1257a35–b11, 1256b34–1257a1, and 1258a38–b2.

28. Cf. 1257b11–17 and 1258a6–14.

29. Cf. 1256b40–1257a5 and 1257b1–4.

30. The word for "unprofitable" (*anonētos*) in this passage is distinct from the term for "profitable" (*lusitelēs*) in the *Politics* at 1258b16.

31. Aristotle does not take up the problem of lacking self-restraint until Book VII of the *Ethics*.

32. Cf. 1258b9–35.

33. The primary meaning of *oregō* is "to reach out," but given its kinship with *orexis* (desire) and its metaphorical meaning "to yearn for," I translate it as "desire."

34. I owe this insight to Burger's observation that "the good seems to erode in stages" in Book I of the *Ethics* (2008, 14). The final "stage" does not appear until the examination of happiness in a later chapter.

35. Cf. 1254b2–9 and 1255b16–20.

36. I owe this emphasis to Bartlett and Collins's note in their translation (2011, Note 18, 5).

37. Cf. 1259a6–21.

38. Cf. *Politics* 1259a21–23 and 1258b39–1259a6; *Ethics* 1094a18–24.

39. Cf. 1258a21–25.

40. Cf. 1094b7–10 and 1095a14–25.

41. Cf. 1256a29–b7.

42. Cf. 1094a1–3 and 1094b10–11.

43. The primary definition of *meristos* is "divisible," but to bring out its root in "part" (*merē*) and avoid confusion with "divided" (*diaireō*), I translate it as "divisible-into-parts" (Liddell and Scott 1889, 499).

44. The primary meaning of *oikeiotēs* is "kindred," but also conveys "the proper sense of words" (Liddell and Scott 1889, 545). Translating this term as "proper-kinship" brings out both of these senses while reminding readers of its connections to *oikeia* ("proper") and the "household" (*oikia, oikos*).

45. Cf. 1254a8–b9.

46. Here and throughout this book, I transliterate *hexis*, which has as its root *echō*, "to hold." In this way, I depart from many translations of the term: for example, "characteristic" by both Bartlett and Collins (2011, 15) *and* Ostwald (1962, 308–309), "active condition" by Sachs (2002, 201), and "characteristic disposition" by Burger (2008, 56). Though all these translators note the kinship between *hexis* and *echō*, there is no easy way to bring it out in the term's translation. The closest one could come is "a holding," which is not the most elegant translation and confuses *hexis* with *echō* as a participle. The prevalence throughout the *Ethics* of the idea of what it means "to hold" something—especially *logos*—should strengthen the case for putting heavy emphasis on the role of *hexis* in Aristotle's political philosophy. The basis for this approach is my dissertation (Pascarella 2015, esp. 104). Among the interpretations of Aristotle's economic teaching, only Crespo's takes time to define *hexis*, and while he notes the term can mean "having," he translates it as "habit," which confuses *hexis* with *ethos* (2014, 31).

47. *Archē* means both "beginning" and "first-principle" (Liddell and Scott 1889, 121). Throughout this book, *archē* appears as one or both of these potential translations, depending on the context.

48. Cf. 1257a30–38.

49. Cf. 1256a14–b7, 1257b1–8, and 1258a21–38.

50. Contrast Aristotle's characterizations of "deliberation" and "choice" with Thomas Hobbes's definitions of "deliberation" and "will" in *Leviathan* as the alternation of appetites and aversions, and "the last appetite and aversion immediately adhering to the action," respectively (VI.49–50, 53).

51. Cf. 1254a1–8, 1254b2–9, 27–34, 1255a3–b4, 1257b40–1258a2, 1259a6–23, and 1257b25–30.

52. I owe emphasis on this phrase to Burger's interpretation, who notes the curiosity (and perhaps irony) of Aristotle appealing to supposition at 1139b20 after dismissing supposition as a way to arrive at truth at 1139b17–18 (2008, 116). Also, to avoid confusion with the verb for "to suppose" (*oiomai*), here and throughout, the translation of *hupolambanō* is "to assume," though it also means "to suppose" (Liddell and Scott 1889, 844).

53. Cf. 1252a7–16, 1253b18–23, 1255b20–40, and 1282b14–23.

54. Cf. 1256a1–3.

55. Cf. 1094a18–24, 1094b23–1095a11, and 1102a26–31.

56. Cf. 1256a19–29, 1256b26–30, 37–39, 1257a13–19, 28–30, 1257b17–22, 1258a6–10, 14–19, 34–38, and 1258b27–31. Cf. 1257b17–22 and 1258a6–10, 14–19.

57. The verb *stergō* means "to love" in reference to "the mutual love of parents and children," though it could extend to countries as well (Liddell and Scott 1889, 744–745). The other verbs for "love" in Greek are *phileō*, *eraō*, and *agapaō*, which respectively relate to *philia* (friendship), *erōs*, and *agapē*. Here and throughout, the preferred translation for these verbs is "love," but always includes parenthetical notes about which verb Aristotle uses. As for the differences in these forms of love, this book examines them as far as is necessary for understanding Aristotle's political and economic teaching.

58. Cf. *Ethics* 1112a30–b12, and *Politics* 1257a13–19, 1258b21–27, 35–39.

59. Cf. 1256b26–34 and 1257b11–17.

60. Cf. 1095a17–25.

61. Cf. 1094b11–19.

62. The verb *hēgeomai* (translated here and throughout as "believe") also means "to lead," "to hold," "to suppose," or "to think" (Liddell and Scott 1889, 347). Translating the verb as "believe" helps distinguish it from *echō* ("to hold"), *oiomai* ("to suppose"), *nomizō* ("to customarily-consider"), and *hupolambanō* ("to assume").

63. In his famous funeral oration from Thucydides' *The Peloponnesian War*, Pericles describes Athens as a "city worthy of wonder," saying, "We love-the-noble (*philokaleō*) with thrift (*euteleia*) and love-wisdom [or philosophize (*philosopheō*)] without softness. We ourselves use wealth more for critical work than boasting *logos*, and do not agree (*homologeō*) that being poor is shameful, but that not to flee by work is shameful. Moreover, the same persons care-upon things of households

(*oikeiōn*) at the same time as things of cities (*politikōn*)" (II.40.1–2). The extent to which Aristotle knew of Thucydides' work is unknown, but there is an undeniable parallel between the passage about Pericles in the *Ethics* and the preceding quotation from *The Peloponnesian War*. For the mixed results of Pericles' rule of the Athenian Empire, consider Thucydides' eulogy of the statesman in *The Peloponnesian War* (III.65).

64. Cf. 1094b7–10.

65. At the root of the verb for "to call" (*prosagoureuō*) is an implicit public element related to the *agora*, the "marketplace."

66. While the primary meaning of *phthartikos* is "destructive," translating it as "ruinous" brings out its kinship with the verb *diaphtheirō* ("to ruin") (Liddell and Scott 1889, 860).

67. Crespo does not catch art's fall from a way of arriving at truth in his interpretation (2014, 55).

68. Cf. 1094a28–b7 and 1140b6–11.

69. Cf. 1095a14–17.

70. The substantive *to eu* means "the right, the good cause" (Liddell and Scott 1889, 321–322). To avoid confusion with "the good" (*to agathon*) and adhere to the term's primary meaning of "well," the translation of *to eu* is "the well-being."

71. Cf. 1252a1–6 and 1253b1–14.

72. The dual translation of *stochastikos* as a person "skillful in aiming" or "guessing" aligns with the term's first two meanings; it relates to the verb *stochazomai*, the first two meanings of which are "to aim" and "to guess" (Liddell and Scott 1889, 748). As the next chapter demonstrates, the need to apply both these meanings becomes evident when one compares the different verbs Aristotle uses for "aiming" in the opening sentences of the *Ethics* and *Politics*.

73. Cf. 1094a9–28.

74. Cf. 1256a19–b7, 1259a6–21, and 1258a2–14.

75. The Greek in this passage is vague, with the inference that *toutous* at 1141b28 refers to "those who make decrees" lining up with the translations from Ostwald (1962, 159), Sachs (2002, 110), and Bartlett and Collins (2011, 124).

76. Cf. 1258a2–6.

77. Cf. 1094b23–1095a11.

78. Here the translation of *antikeimai* emphasizes the verb's paradoxical meanings: "to be set over against, lie opposite" on the one hand, and "to correspond with" on the other (Liddell and Scott 1889, 78). This seems appropriate since Aristotle brings the concerns of intellect together with sense-perception at 1143a32-1143b17. Also, on *keimai*, see chapter 1, Note 43 above.

79. This translation of *tōn idiōn* according to its primary meaning of "one's own, pertaining to oneself" differs somewhat from how other translators render the phrase (Liddell and Scott 1889, 375). Ostwald parenthetically adds "each of our five senses" (1962, 160); Sachs adds "of the separate senses" (2002, 111), and Bartlett and Collins use the phrase "things peculiar to one of the senses" (2011, 126). While this translation runs the risk of reading very close to how Aristotle discusses "the good for

themselves" (*to autois agathon*) at 1142a7 and "the well-being of oneself" (*to autou eu*) at 1142a9, the translation also retains the sense that what Aristotle says about prudence, science, and sense-perception bears on the question of how one comes to know one's own good.

80.  Cf. 1257b40–1258a19.

81.  Aristotle's use of the genitive participle *endechomenou* ("what admits to be possible") is only part of the phrase that he uses for "what admits to hold otherwise," *endechethai allōs echein* (cf. 1139b20–21, 1140b2–3).

82.  Bywater notes this passage seems to be inappropriately placed (1894, Note 9, 123), and would seem to follow after 1143b5.

83.  Cf. *Politics* 1256a19–b7, 26–34, and *Ethics* 1104b13–21, 30–1105a1, and 1113a15–b2.

84.  Cf. *Ethics* 1140b35–1141a8 and 1142a23–30; *Politics* 1252a26–31, 1252b12–16, 1253b1–14, and 1254a21–33.

85.  Cf. *Ethics* 1094b11–1095a28, 1105a7–13, 1139a31–35, and 1140b6–21; *Politics* 1254b2–9.

86.  Cf. 1143b9–11.

87.  Cf. 1094a18–26 and 1142a10–20.

88.  In Greek, the prefix *en-* becomes *em-* when placed in front of a labial letter, which in this case is *pi*.

89.  Cf. *Ethics* 1139a35–b5 and *Politics* 1254a1–8.

90.  Cf. 1139a9–b8 and 1143a35–b5.

91.  Cf. 1257b22–1258a14 and 1252b27–1253a1.


## CHAPTER 4

1.  In *Aristotle's Economic Thought*, Scott Meikle ironically argues that "Aristotle did not do any economics," for his "inquiries are … ethical and metaphysical" (1995, 196–198).

2.  In his interpretation, Meikle disagrees with respectively translating *autarchēs* and *autarkeia* as "self-sufficient" and "self-sufficiency" in all contexts, arguing that the term should mean "having enough" and "independent of others" in *Politics* I, yet he points to self-sufficiency's association with what is choiceworthy in *Ethics* I (1995, 44–45). Even if these terms hold different meanings in these contexts, the character of Aristotle's political philosophy compels readers to consider what they might learn from comparing their uses in the *Ethics* and *Politics*.

3.  Cf. 1256b26–34.

4.  "Self-sufficiency" (*autarkeia*) only appears eight times in the *Politics* (1252b29, 1253a1, 28, 1256b32, 1257a30, 1275b21, 1321b17, and 1326b24), and three times in the *Ethics* (1097b7, 1134a27, 1177a27).

5.  Cf. 1256a19–b7.

6.  Cf. 1253b23–26 and 1257b40–1258a19.

7.  Ross's manuscript has "without-choosing" (*anairesis*) at 1332a17, but notes other manuscripts have "choosing" (*hairesis*) (1957, 236). The argument is the same

either way: retributions and punishments either require choosing how to address bad things, or address bad things people would not choose.

8. Cf. 1094b11–19.

9. Cf. 1141a20–1142a20 and 1140a31–b30.

10. Cf. 1094a18–24.

11. Cf. 1139a17–b5.

12. Cf. 1258a19–b8.

13. Cf. *Politics* 1257a30–b22; Ethics 1139b11–17 and 1140b21–1141a8.

14. Cf. 1256b2–7, 30–34, 1257a28–30, and 1257b40–1258a14.

15. The term here for "lawless" is *athemistos*, and therefore does not derive from *nomos*. Similarly, the term for "without-hearth and home" is *anestios*, and does not derive from *oikos*.

16. Cf. 1252a24–33 and 1256b20–26.

17. For a link between war and the departure from the necessary boundary of self-sufficiency through acquisition of useful things (*chrēmata*) without-limit, see Book IV of Plato's *Republic*, 373d–e. That such a desire may have something to do with disregarding the natural importance of the household, compare Aristotle's argument in *Politics* 1253a1–6 with Thomas Hobbes's *Leviathan* and his account of the "state of war" in chapter 13, "Of the Natural Condition of Mankind, as Concerning Their Felicity and Misery."

18. Cf. 1140b11–16, 1141b23–29, and 1143a35–b5.

19. Though both Lord (2013, 4) and Simpson (1997, 11) translate the middle participle of *anaireō* as "destroyed," in the middle voice, the verb does not have this meaning (cf. Liddell and Scott 1889, 55). Because none of the middle voice meanings of the verb fit this context, it makes sense to adhere to "destroy" as the primary meaning. Still, because the Greek word for "body" (*sōma*) does not appear in the argument (though one could, like Lord and Simpson, reasonably infer it), it may be helpful to bring in an alternate meaning of *anaireō* ("to abolish," though the term also means "to confute") since the subject of the sentence is "the whole" (*ton holon*) (1253a21). This alternate meaning invites readers to contemplate what it means to "abolish" the whole and how it bears on choice since *anaireō* has at its root *haireō* ("to choose").

20. This passage is very difficult to translate, though its general sense adheres to that of Lord (2013, 5) and Simpson's (1997, 12). One of the difficulties in the passage concerns the verb *phuetai*, which sits between "the human being holding weapons" and "prudence and virtue" (*ho de anthrōpos hopla echōn phuetai phronēsei kai aretē* at 1253a34–35). Lord translates the passage as "man is born naturally possessing arms [for the use of] prudence and virtue," while Simpson renders it as "the weapons a human being has are meant by nature to go along with prudence and virtue." Lord infers "for the use of" from the verb *chrēsthai* at 1253a35, which has that meaning when associated with dative nouns (which is the case with *phronēsis* and *aretē*). Simpson, however, does not infer the presence of this verb, and instead draws on the meaning of *phuetai* when combined with dative subjects as "meant by nature." Given *hopla* ("weapons") is in the accusative, it seems to belong to *echōn* ("holding"); this leaves *phronēsis*

and *aretē* in their dative forms to belong to *phuetai*, "to fall to one by nature, be one's natural lot" (Liddell and Scott 1889, 877. By this reading, Aristotle invites readers to wonder how prudence and virtue are natural if human beings need law and the just to bring them about.

21. Cf. 1331b24–1332b11.

22. Nichols comes to a similar conclusion about Book I of the *Politics*, and interprets Aristotle as providing "the dual origins of the city," treating politics as natural on the one hand "because it calls forth the exercise of humanity's highest natural capacity" (i.e., *logos*), and on the other hand by treating "the city as a natural growth" to show the role of necessity in human life. The purpose is to see how the human "need for survival" relates to "the possibility that they establish cities based on deliberation, choice, and political rule" (1992, 13). Nichols's reading exposes a weakness in Booth's interpretation, who contends that Aristotle's focus on the art of household management in Book I poses an "exegetical difficulty" to placing weight on the "human capacity for speech and ... the uniquely human ability to distinguish the good from the bad, the just from the unjust" (1993, 35). Based on Nichols's interpretation and my own, the text indicates Aristotle's approach in Book I of the *Politics* is not an "either/or" account of the city, but a *logos* that uses both accounts to encourage readers to contemplate the nature of political life.

23. Cf. 1259b18–21 and 1257b32–40.

24. For a similar reading of this implication, see Burger (2008, 17–18) and Pangle (2011, 89).

25. Cf. 1094a6–1095a25.

26. Cf. 1257a5–28 and 1258a2–10.

27. Cf. *Politics* 1252a24–31 and *Ethics* 1139a21–27.

28. Cf. 1142a10–20, 1094b23–1095a11, and 1094a18–22.

29. Cf. 1258a6–14.

30. The appearance of *logos* in the phrase *tunchanousi de logou* in this passage does not come through in the translations of Bartlett and Collins (2011, 6), Sachs (2002, 5), and Ostwald (1967, 8), who respectively translate the phrase as "attain a hearing," "get listened to," and "views seem plausible." While understandable given the multiple meanings of *logos*, it is important to track this idea since Aristotle confines his inquiry into the lives in which happiness resides to the opinions that hold some *logos* (cf. 1095a29–30).

31. In their translation, Bartlett and Collins provide the following note on Sardanapallus: "An Assyrian king (ruled ca. 669–627) renowned for, and apparently boastful of, his extravagant way of life and sensual indulgences Aristotle mentions him also in the *Eudemian Ethics* (1216a16)" (2011, Note 23, 6). Sachs notes Sardanapallus receives credit for saying, "Eat, drink, and be merry, since the other things are not worth this snap of the fingers" (2002, Note 4, 4).

32. Burger offers a similar interpretation, saying, "Behind this disdain lies the unexamined assumption that all pleasure is of one sort—the sort humans share with other animals—with no consideration of the various activities that can be a source of

pleasure for human beings, or of the difficult problem of how pleasure is related to those sources" (2008, 22).

33. Cf. 1142a7–10.

34. Cf. 1256a14–19 and 1257b1–8.

35. For this line of argument, see the following passages from *Politics* I.8–11: 1256a19–b7, 1258a2–14, 1257b32–40, 1257a5–13, 30-38, 1258b35–39, 1258b10–11, 1255b37–40, 1253b20–23, and 1255a3–b4.

36. Cf. 1094a26–b11.

37. One can translate *philos* as both "friends" and "loved." *Philos* is distinct from *erōs* and *agapē* in the sense that it consistently relates to the love of friends. Throughout this book, I translate *philos* either as "friend" or "loved" depending on the context. To avoid confusion with other Greek terms for love, I note parenthetically when the term is not *philos*.

38. Cf. *Ethics* 1141b2–8 and *Politics* 1259a6–18.

39. See 1096a5–10 for "the sought-for good" in the money-making life. Also, according to Burger, this is the last stage in the erosion of the good in Book I of the *Ethics*. The "eroding" moves from "*the* good (1094a22) to the human good (1094b7), then to the practical good (1095a16–17), and finally to the sought-for good (1097a15)" (2008, 14).

40. Cf. 1094a3–5.

41. Cf. 1256a3–10 and 1256b34–37.

42. Cf. 1252b12–1253a1, 18–28.

43. This insertion reflects Bywater's note that some manuscripts have "sufficient (*arkion*) and choiceworthy (*haireton*)" or "choiceworthy and sufficient" at 1097b15, though his manuscript only has "choiceworthy" (1894, 10).

44. Cf. 1256b26–34 and 1257b36–1258a2, 14–19.

45. Cf. 1255a3–19, 1257b32–36, and 1323a14–1324a4.

46. *Epipeithēs* is unique to Aristotle's *Ethics*, and derives from the verb *epi-peithomai* ("to be persuaded," "to trust"), the root of which is *peithō* ("to persuade" in its active sense, and "to be persuaded" and "to trust" in its passive sense) (Liddell and Scott 1889, 298, 615–616). A term related to *peithō* is *pistos* (a thing "to be trusted"), which derives from *pistis* ("trust") (Liddell and Scott 1889, 641–642). Since Aristotle wonders in Book VI why the young do not trust (*pisteuō*) in natural first-principles (1142a10–20), it is helpful to see how holding and trusting-upon *logos* might provide this trust.

47. This bracketed insertion of "living" reflects an inference from the feminine ending of the pronoun *tautēs* at 1098a5 back to the previous feminine subject of *praktikē* at 1098a3. This differs from Bartlett and Collins, who insert "of that which possesses *logos*" in place of this pronoun, though they note the ambiguity of the phrase (2011, Note 42, 13).

48. Cf. *Politics* 1253a7–18 and *Ethics* 1094a18–22, 1095a3–11, 1095a17–b4, and 1096b14–1097a14.

49. Burger offers an excellent account of this argument's heavily conditional nature (2008, 32–36). In line with this book's interpretation of Aristotle's approach

to the human work, Burger notes how the significance of these arguments about the human work does not emerge until Books VI and X (2008, Note 54, 237).

50. Cf. 1113a15–b2, 1139a21–27, 1141a20–22, 1142a10–30, 1143a35–b21, 1144a3–6, and 1144b6–16.

51. Cf. 1094a18–26 and 1095a17–b4.

52. Burger makes a similar argument, though she does not bring out the pun on "experience" (*empeiria*) in her interpretation (2008, 36).

53. Cf. *Politics* 1252a24–31, 1257b32–40, and 1258a14–19; *Ethics* 1094a26–b10.

54. This is the term translators tend to render as "deficiency" throughout the *Ethics*, but its more proper meaning is "defect," and it is distinct from the term Aristotle uses to introduce "deficiency" (*endeia*) at 1104a12. Some translators consistently render both *endeia* and *elleipsis* as "deficiency" (cf. Sachs 2002, 23–24; Bartlett and Collins 2011, 28–29), whereas Ostwald reverses their meanings (i.e., *endeia* as "defect" and *elleipsis* as "deficiency) (1962, 35–36).

55. Bartlett and Collins emphasize the musical connotation in a note to their translation (2011, Note 2, 115), whereas Burger draws the comparison to a bow (2008, 112). Interestingly, in chapter VI of the *The Prince*, when advising the "prudent man" to imitate the actions of great men, Machiavelli says, "He should do as prudent archers do when the place they plan to hit appears too distant, and knowing how far the strength [or 'virtue'] of the bow carries, they set their aim much higher than the place intended, not to reach such height with their arrow, but to be able with the aid of so high an aim to achieve their design" (1985, 22). Machiavelli puts virtue in the weapon, whereas Aristotle puts virtue more in the archer's hands.

56. Cf. 1142a10–30 and 1143a35–b5.

57. Cf. *Ethics* 1097b22–24 and *Politics* 1252b12–1253a1.

58. Cf. 1094b11–1095a11.

59. Cf. 1140b13–21.

60. A shadow of this argument appears in Aristotle's examination and dismissal of the political life's claim to happiness, though without any hint that the issue comes down to the difference between *hexis* and activity (cf. 1095b30–1096a1).

61. Cf. 1257a5–13.

62. Cf. 1095b14–22.

63. Cf. 1095a17–b4.

64. Cf. 1104b30–1105a13, 1113a15–b2, and 1140b11–21.

65. The translation of the verb *eraō* as "to have *erōs*" instead of "to love" aims to bring out the first appearance of this form of love in the *Ethics*.

66. For *erōs* in the *Ethics*, see 1116a13 and 1171b29, 31. For *eraō*, see 1099a28, 1155b3, 1157a6, 1158a11, 1159b16, 1164a5, 1167a4, 1171a11, and 1171b29.

67. For an earlier iteration of this argument, see Pascarella (2015, 109–111).

68. Cf. 1112a30–b8.

69. Cf. 1139a31–b5, 1140a1–20, 1095a14–b4, and especially 1095a26–28 for the good as a cause.

70. Cf. 1095b22–25, 1096a4–10, and 1098a20–b8.

71. Cf. 1097a25–b21.

72. Cf. *Ethics* 1098b30–1099a16, 1099a31–b2, and 1100b7–22, and *Politics* 1256a29–b7, 1256b30–34, and 1257a28–30.

73. Cf. 1094a6–18, 26–b14, and 1100a4–b22.

74. Cf. *Ethics* 1141b23–1142a20 and *Politics* 1323a14–1324a4, 1331b24–1332b11.

75. Cf. *Politics* 1252a24–b16, 1257a5–28, and *Ethics* 1099a31–b2.

76. Cf. 1254a17–1255a3 and 1255b16–37.

77. Cf. *Politics* 1255a3–b19 and *Ethics* 1099a31–b2.

78. Cf. *Politics* 1256a19–29, 1259a23–28, and *Ethics* 1104b30–1105a13.

79. Cf. *Politics* 1253a7–39, 1282b14–23; *Ethics* 1094b11–19 and 1098b12–1099a16.

## CHAPTER 5

1. Cf. *Ethics* 1094a1–3 and 1094b7–10; *Politics* 1252a1–7 and 1252b27–1253a1.

2. Glaucon makes a similar argument for avoiding injustice in Book II of Plato's *Republic* (358e–359b). This argument also appears in Hobbes' *Leviathan* (chapter XIII) and Locke's *Second Treatise* (chapters VIII–IX).

3. Cf. 1257a19–28.

4. Though Crespo briefly alludes to the importance of friendship in Aristotle's economic teaching, when he quotes from this part of *Politics* III, he omits the definition of "friendship" as "the choice of living-together" (2014, 59, 63). In light of my interpretation's emphasis on choice, Crespo makes a significant omission in his reading of Aristotle.

5. Cf. 1139a31–b5, 1113a15–b2, 1104b32–34, and 1105a7–13.

6. Cf. 1141b23–1142a2, 1140a31–b21, and 1142a10–20.

7. Cf. 1098a20–1099b9.

8. Cf. 1145a6–11.

9. These readings of *tou tēn politkēn philosophountos* as "the one who philosophizes about the political art" and "the political philosopher" follow Burger's interpretation (2008, 153) and Bartlett and Collins's translation (2011, 155).

10. For the political art's seemingly authoritative claim to the good, see 1094a9–18, 26–b7. For the personal need for the good, see 1094a18–26.

11. Cf. 1141b2–8 and 1096a11–17.

12. Cf. 1144b6–16 and 1094b23–1095a11.

13. Cf. 1256a14–19, 1257b1–8, 1257b40–1258a10, 1258b9–11, and 1259a6–21.

14. Cf. 1098b30–1099a7.

15. The translation of *phusiologōn* as "those who study nature" follows that of Bartlett and Collins (2011, 142).

16. Cf. 1139b18–36, 1140b31–35, 1142a23–30, and 1143a35–b5.

17. Cf. 1142a7–20, 1095a17–b4, 1140b11–12, 1104b30–1105a1, and 1113a15–b2.

18. Cf. 1253a33–39.

19. Cf. *Politics* 1252a24–31 and 1256a19–b7, and *Ethics* 1094a5–18, 26–b11.

20. Cf. 1252a31–33, 1252b4–9, and 1258a2–6.

21. For a similar connection between money-making, the necessary pleasures and desires, and gain, see Books VIII and IX of Plato's *Republic*, especially 558d–559c and 580d–581b.

22. Cf. 1257b40–1258a2

23. Cf. 1099a7–16

24. Cf. 1253a18–39 and 1256b20–26.

25. Cf. 1144b6–16.

26. Cf. 1140b11–21.

27. Cf. 1094b11–19, 1095a17–b4, and 1098a7–b8.

28. Cf. 1152b1–13, 1103b26–1104a11, 1105a7–13, 1146b24–35, and 1147a10–24.

29. Cf. *Politics* 1256b26–34 and *Ethics* 1097b16–1098a7.

30. Cf. 1094a5–6, 1096b26–1097a3, 1097a15–b16, and 1098b30–1099a16.

31. Cf. *Ethics* 1095a17–25, 1095b14–1096a10; *Politics* 1257a19–30, 1252b12–1253a1, and 1253a18–28.

32. Cf. 1258a2–14.

33. Cf. 1099a7–b9.

34. Cf. 1099b25–1100b22.                                    ʻ

35. Cf. 1094a1–3. Burger also reads this part of Book VII as a return to the *Ethics'* "search for *the* good" (2008, 157).

36. Cf. 1095a17–b4.

37. The adverb *sphodra* means "very, very much, exceedingly, violently" (Liddell and Scott 1889, 786). Here and throughout, this term's translation as "intense" or "intensely" aligns with how Bartlett and Collins render the term in a passage about *erōs* and friendship in Book IX (1171a4–13), though in this passage from Book VII, they translate it as "highly" (2011, 206, 160).

38. Cf. 1142a10–20.

39. Meanings of *sunēthēs* are "dwelling or living together," "like each other in habits," and "habituated, accustomed" (Liddell and Scott 1889, 776). Since the term relates to "habit" (*ethos*), it is helpful to translate it as "habituated-together."

40. Cf. *Ethics* 1147a10–b19 and *Politics* 1331b24–1332b11.

41. An intervening argument for this conclusion is in the comparison between spiritedness (*thumos*) and desire (*epithumia*) in Book VII's sixth chapter, where Aristotle describes spiritedness as "more natural" than desires for excess, for such desires are unnecessary (1149b6–8). Aristotle's likening of spiritedness to a dog in this chapter is the same account Socrates gives to introduce spiritedness in Book II of Plato's *Republic* (375a–376c). In Book IV, Socrates speaks of spiritedness listening to *logos* to restrain desires on his way to presenting justice in the soul as a *hexis* through which a person cares for the things that are properly-one's-own (*ta oikeia*)

and befriends oneself through wisdom (439d–444a). In Books VIII and IX, Socrates distinguishes between necessary and unnecessary desires to set the stage for a closer examination of pleasures in the soul that roots the love (*phileō*) of gain and money or useful things (*chrēmata*) in the desires. This inquiry concludes with Socrates arguing that only the philosopher holds true judgment about pleasures and pains in the soul through experience, prudence, and, most importantly, *logos* (558d–559d, 571a–572b, 580a–587a). Together, these arguments suggest Plato and Aristotle are in agreement about the nature of political philosophy, and hold similar views on economics' need to know how to choose the good among pleasures and pains.

42. Cf. 1147b20–31 and 1152b25–1153a14.

43. The definition of *phthartos* is "perishable," but since it derives from the verb *phtheirō* ("to ruin"), its translation here and throughout is "subject to ruin" (Liddell and Scott 1889, 860).

44. Cf. 1140b6–30 and 1149b27–1150a8.

45. For this teaching on the God's simple nature, intellect, activity, and pleasure, see also Aristotle's *Metaphysics* (Book XII, chapter 7). According to Burger, this argument about the God challenges those who wish to isolate Aristotle's *Ethics* from the rest of his philosophy (2008, 154). In this respect, Meikle's *Aristotle's Economic Thought* is correct to consider the questions of exchange value in Book V of the *Ethics* in relation to the *Metaphysics* (1995).

46. Bartlett and Collins attribute this quotation to Euripides' *Orestes*, 234 (2011, Note 64, 162).

47. Cf. 1150b29–36.

48. Cf. 1137a31–1138a3 in Book V, and 1168a28–1170b19 in Book IX.

49. Cf. 1252a24–33.

50. Cf. 1257a5–28.

51. Cf. 1257a30–b14.

52. Cf. *Politics* 1256a3–10, 1258a19–b8, and 1257b32–1258a14, and *Ethics* 1153b25–1154b21.

53. Cf. 1252a24–31, 1253a7–18, and 1256a19–b7.

54. Cf. 1147a10–b19 and 1154a26–b14.

55. Cf. 1332a39–b11, 1331b24–1332a18, 1253b1–14, and 1254a17–1255a2.

56. Cf. 1154b32–34, 1095a3–11, 1145a6–11, 1141b2–8, 1142a10–30, 1143a35–b5, and 1144b6–16.

57. Cf. *Politics* 1259a6–21; *Ethics* 1098b30–1099a16 and 1155b17–21.

## CHAPTER 6

1. In some economic interpretations of Aristotle, there is a hesitance to translate *philia* as "friendship." Polanyi prefers "good will" (which confuses *philia* with *eunoia*) (1968, 96), while Finley (1971, 8) and Booth choose "mutuality" (1993, 1). Whereas these interpretations alter the meaning of *philia* to speak from an economic

perspective, this chapter demonstrates why it is necessary to retain this term's personal sense of "friendship" in Aristotle's political philosophy.

2. Cf. 1139a31–b5.

3. Cf. 1147b20–31, 1154a1–b34, and 1152b1–3.

4. All the references to "friends" in Book VII are passing. In the first, Aristotle talks about dogs barking at guests knocking on the door before knowing if those guests are friends to illustrate the nature of spiritedness (*thumos*) (1149a29). In the second, Aristotle quotes Evenus giving a friend a lesson about care (1152a32). The final mention of friendship in Book VII occurs in the conclusion, when Aristotle states it is the subject of Book VIII (1154b34).

5. Cf. 1098b9–29 and 1099a31–b9.

6. Cf. *Politics* 1253b1–14 and *Ethics* 1099a7–16.

7. Crespo briefly alludes to this passage about friendship's superiority to justice in his interpretation (2014, 59), but does not consider what friendship could add to Aristotle's economic teaching.

8. While *poluphilia* means "abundance of friends," rendering it as "many (*polu*)-friends (*philia*)" brings out its literal roots (Liddell and Scott 1889, 659).

9. Cf. 1094b11–1095a11.

10. Though *periergon* could mean "superfluous," rendering it as "concerning (*peri*)-superfluous-work (*ergon*)" brings forth its literal meaning (Liddell and Scott 1889, 626).

11. Cf. 1095b14–1096a10.

12. Cf. *Ethics* 1099a17–31, 1137a31–1138a3 and 1168a28–1170b19; *Politics* 1323a14–1324a4, 1331b24–1332b11, and 1282b14–23.

13. Cf. 1095a17–b4 and 1113a15–b2.

14. Cf. 1256a3–10 and 1258a19–b8.

15. Cf. 1257a5–19 and 1258b9–11.

16. Cf. 1098a7–b8, 1142a7–20, and 1155b13–16.

17. Cf. 1253b23–33 and 1257b36–1258a14.

18. Following the translation of Bartlett and Collins, the translation of *stergō* when it appears alongside other forms of love is "feel-affection" (2011, Note 16, 166).

19. Cf. *Ethics* 1148b15–24, 1149a34–b1, and 1154b20–31; *Politics* 1259a19–b7 and 1257a30–1257b4.

20. Cf. 1280b29–39, 1252a24–1253a1, 1256a3–13, and 1257a19–30.

21. Cf. 1095b22–31 and 1141b23–1142a20.

22. Cf. 1258b12–21.

23. According to Finley, "The first principle of a market economy is . . . indifference to the *persons* of the buyer and seller: that is what troubles most commentators on Aristotle" (1970, 10).

24. Cf. 1098b30-1099a7, 1097b22-1098a20, and 1144b6-16.

25. Cf. 1098b30-1099a7 and 1100a4-b22.

26. Cf.1104b30-1105a13,1112a13-17,b11-12,1113a9-b2,and1152b28-1153a14.

27. The term *eupatheia* means "the enjoyment of good things," and in the plural carries the sense of "luxuries" (Liddell and Scott 1889, 330). The inclusion of

"luxury" alongside "comfort" aims to clarify the term's nature while avoiding confusion with "the good things" (*ta agatha*).

28. The primarily translation of *poson* is "a certain quantity," and unfortunately does not have more specific content to its definition (Liddell and Scott 1889, 663).

29. Cf. 1253b3-14.

30. Cf. 1255a3-b15 and 1257b8-22.

31. Cf. 1139a35-b5, 1112a30-b8, 1146b24-35, and 1147a10-24.

32. Cf. 1096a24-1097a14 and 1156b7-32.

33. Cf. 1097a15-b13, 1103b26-1104a11, 1138b18-34, 1139b25-36, 1140b35-1141a8, 1142a7-30, 1143a35-b14, and 1153a27-1154b34.

34. Cf. 1258a14-19 and 1256b2-7, 26-34.

35. While "the thinking thing" is an awkward translation of *to dianoētikon*, it purposely departs from other translators' inference of "part" (cf. Ostwald 1962, 253; Sachs 2002, 168; Bartlett and Collins 2011, 194). Given Aristotle's argument in Book I that one may divide (*diaireō*) things in *logos* that are naturally inseparable (1102a26-31), it may be helpful to use the language of "part" (*merē, moira*) only when he explicitly uses it.

36. Though the proper translation of the verb *noeō* is "to think," this makes *to nooun* at 1166a22 look the same as *tou dianoētikou* at 1166a17-18 (Liddell and Scott 1889, 533-534). The parenthetical suggestion to treat the verb as "intellecting" stems from the kinship between *to nooun* and the term for "intellect," *nous*.

37. Whether the verb for "it is" (*esti*) refers to "friendship" (*philia*) or "self" (*autos*) is uncertain. Both Sachs (2002, 168) and Bartlett and Collins (2011, 194) insert "each person" into the passage; Ostwald inserts "a man" into the passage (1962, 254). Bartlett and Collins note "some commentators think that the sentence is an interpolation," while others "argue that the phrase refers to the conditions of friendship that have just been discussed" (2011, Note 10, 195).

38. Cf. 1103b26-1104a27 and 1148a22-32.

39. There is an untranslatable pun at work in Aristotle's use of the verb for "censure." While the verb *epitimaō* carries the meaning of "censure" in this context, it literally means "to honor-upon" (Liddell and Scott 1889, 305), which suggests a couple things: some people honor what is shameful, others honor a lover-of-self. Such ambiguity seems intentional given Aristotle's designation of friendship toward oneself as an "excess" or "superiority."

40. Cf. 1098a20-b8, 1094a18-24, 1094b23-1095a3, 1142a10-20, and 1094a1-3.

41. While the primary meaning of the verb *aponemō* is "to assign," its translation here and throughout is the same as its root verb *nemō*, "to distribute" (Liddell and Scott 1889, 103, 528).

42. Socrates offers a similar prayer in Plato's *Phaedrus* at 279b-c.

43. Cf. *Ethics* 1094b11-19 and *Politics* 1257b11-17.

44. The verb *peithō* actively means "to persuade," and has a passive sense of "trust" and "obey" (Liddell and Scott 1889, 615–616). Though different than the verb for "trust" (*pisteuō*), there is kinship between these verbs, and throughout their

translations convey this common sense of trust with parenthetical notes for which verb appears in the passage. Cf. chapter 4, Note 46 above.

45. Though the definition of *sustēma* is "a whole compounded of parts," translating the term as "a whole set-standing-together" brings out the root verb *histēmi*, "to stand" and "to set" (Liddell and Scott 1889, 783, 384–385).

46. Cf. 1252a1-7, 1254b2-9, and 1255b9-37.

47. While the primary meaning of *idios* is "one's own," its translation here and throughout brings out its "private" sense to avoid confusion with *oikeion*, "properly-one's-own" (Liddell and Scott 1889, 375).

48. The definitions of *peitharcheō* are "to obey one in authority" and "to be obedient" (Liddell and Scott 1889, 615). Translating the verb as "to trust-the-rule" brings forth the meaning of its two root verbs: *peithō* ("to persuade" or "to trust") and *archō* ("to rule").

49. Burger comes to a similar conclusion about the serious person being one-holding-more in pursuit of the noble, and she later notes that the only time "the noble" appears in Book V's inquiry into justice is with an unresolved hypothetical that perhaps the decent person could attempt to hold-more of the noble for oneself at 1136b21–23 (2008, 175–176; Note 40, 274).

50. Aristotle's citing of the opinion that everyone competing to do noble actions for oneself produces a common benefit is the closest analogue in his philosophy to Adam Smith's "invisible hand." In *Wealth of Nations*, it is one's own security and gain that leads to a preference for domestic industry, so that "in this, as in many other cases, [one is] led by an invisible hand to promote an end which was no part of his intention" (IV.2). The connection to Smith's *Theory of Moral Sentiments* is even stronger since that work includes the "noble" and "beautiful," two possible translations of *kalos*. According to Smith, nature provides a "deception" through which "pleasures of wealth and greatness . . . strike the imagination as something grand and beautiful and noble," a deception that "rouses and keeps in continual motion the industry of mankind . . . which first prompted them to cultivate the ground, to build houses, to found cities and commonwealths, and to invent and improve all the sciences and arts, which embellish human life." Smith points to the "proud and unfeeling landlord" for whom the "capacity of his stomach bears no proportion to the immensity of his desires" as an example of someone who spurs the continual motion of industry by thinking of consuming the entirety of his harvest "to no purpose." Because the rich consume little more than the poor and provide for the poor not out of "humanity" or "justice" (the latter is a virtue for Aristotle, but not the former), "the rich are led by an invisible hand to make nearly the same distribution of the necessaries of life, which would have been made, had the earth been divided into equal portions among all its inhabitants, and thus without intending it, without knowing it, advance the interest of the society, and afford means to the multiplication of the species" (IV.1.9–10). In both passages about the "invisible hand" from Smith, there is—like Aristotle's account of people competing for the noble—no choosing to

promote the common good. Smith and Aristotle also agree that there is something deceptive about the "noble" or the "beautiful," but where Smith roots the deception in nature, Aristotle roots it in public opinion. Smith's argument is also more radical because he admits the possibility that those who are corrupt can advance the common good, but Aristotle denies this. Finally, Smith speaks of "the multiplication of the species" unmoored from the generation and preservation of human beings that Aristotle roots in necessary couplings that form the household in Book I of the *Politics'* attempt to look at communities from choice (*proairesis*) (cf. 1252a24–31). The *Ethics*, however, looks at families in the context of friendship within the household, proposing that human beings are more coupling animals than political animals (VIII.11–12, especially 1162a16–19 compared with *Politics* 1253a1–18). For Aristotle, friendship and the household put firmer limits on the ability to provide for the good than Smith's "invisible hand."

51. The phrase here for "another self" (*heteron auton*) differs from *allos autos* at 1166a31–32, though the significance of this change in language is unclear. Burger renders the former as "an other self," and the latter as "another self" (2008, 176, 173).

52. Cf. 1097b6–21.

53. Cf. 1155a3–12.

54. Cf. Burger (2008, 82–87), or Jacob Howland's "Aristotle's Great-Souled Man" (2002).

55. Cf. 1158b11–1159a12, 1097b22–1098a20, and 1098b9–16.

56. Burger also doubts the characterization of friends as external goods in her interpretation, citing the work of Thomas Smith in *Revaluing Ethics* (2001, 185) and Harry Jaffa in *Thomism and Aristotelianism* (1952, 126) in support of her arguments (2008, 177, Note 43, 274–275).

57. Cf. 1158a10–b11.

58. Cf. 1155a28–b16 and 1099a11–b9.

59. Booth suggests *erōs* explains the pursuit of money-making without-limit, something opposed to *philia* and *Ethics* V.5's account of need in community (1993, 53–54). Booth, however, does not provide the same level of textual analysis as this chapter. For a first attempt at this argument about *erōs, philia*, the good, and the pleasant, see Pascarella (2015, 349–359).

60. Cf. 1258a2–19, 1254a34–b9, and 1253a18–b18.

61. For an interpretation of Aristotle's political philosophy that focuses on shared sense-perception (*sunaisthēsis*) and friendship, consider John Von Heyking's *The Form of Politics: Aristotle and Plato on Friendship* (2016).

62. Cf. *Ethics* 1095b14–1096a10, and *Politics* 1256a19–b26.

63. Cf. 1166a10–b2, 1168a28–b13, and 1169a6–29, 1142a23–30, and 1143a35–b5.

64. Though the definition for *ergōdēs* is "irksome, troublesome" (Liddell and Scott 1889, 312), it seems fitting to add "work" to the translation of the term to bring out its shared root with *ergon*.

65. Being obsequious is an excess of a nameless moral virtue that looks like friendship that concerns causing pleasures and pains to others in *logos* (*Ethics* IV.6).

66. Cf. 1094b7–22.

67. Cf. 1157b5–1158a1.

68. Though Booth rightly sees the household is like friendship in the sense that it forms through a choice to live-together and permits leisure in different ways of life, his own choice to exclude the importance of *logos* from his interpretation keeps him from seeing the connection between this passage and true love-of-self (1993, 35, 38–39, 45–47).

69. Cf. *Politics* 1257b1–4, 36–40, *Ethics* 1163b3–5 and 1164a19.

70. Cf. 1159a35–b21 and 1168b15–23.

71. Cf. *Ethics* 1148a22–32 and 1152b1–1153a14; *Politics* 1257a1–3, 14–19, 1258b9–11, 39–1259a6, and 1257b40–1258a14.

72. Cf. *Ethics* 1158b11–1159a12, 1170b20–1171a8, 1168b29–1169a6, and 1169b22–1170a13; *Politics* 1252a1–7 and 1253a29–39.

73. Cf. 1256a19–b26, 1254b16–23, 1254b27–1255b4, 1253a9–18, and 1253b1–14.

74. Cf. *Ethics* 1141a9–b8, 1094a18–24, and 1129a23–b6; *Politics* 1255a3–19, 1257b32–36, and 1259a6–21.


# CHAPTER 7

1. "Things exchanged-together" is a literal translation of *sunallagma* ("contract" or "dealings between men") that brings out the appearance of "exchange" (*allagē*) at its root (Liddell and Scott 1889, 767). As Finley notes, there is no easy translation of *sunallagma*, which he renders as "transactions" (1970, 6).

2. Cf. 1129a23–b6, 1168b15–23, 33–1169a6, 16–18, and 1170b20–29.

3. Cf. 1256b20–1257a1 and 1258a19–b5.

4. In Book V's inquiry into justice, "friend" (*philos*) only appears at 1130a6. In contrast, in the inquiry into friendship from Books VIII and IX, "justice" (*dikaiosunē*) appears at 1155a24–27, and "the just" appears either as *dikē* at 1162b30 and 1164b13, or *dikaios* within 1155a, 1159b–1160a, 1161a–1162b, 1164b–1165a, 1167a–b, 1168b, and 1173a–b.

5. Cf. *Ethics* 1155a12–28, 1158a10–b11, 1169b3–1170a13, and 1170b10–19; *Politics* 1252a1–7, b12–1253a6, 18–28.

6. Cf. 1152b1–1153a27, 1153b29–1154a1, b20–34.

7. Cf. 1252a1–7.

8. This argument includes a reference to Socrates' "second sailing" in Plato's *Phaedo*, 96a–100b.

9. Cf. 1111b20–30, 1112a13–17, and 1113a9–b2.

10. Cf. 1169b3–22 and 1170a25–b19.

11. Booth contrasts relations within the household (which he acknowledges derive from *philia*) with *pleonexia* ("holding-more") in the market, something he goes

on to characterize as "the invisible master" that is a threat to "the *oikonomia* of the soul" (1993, 8–9, 50–52). Despite this argument, he does not connect the problem of the one-holding-more in Book V to the true love-of-self (*philautos*) in Book IX.

12. Cf. 1139a31–b5, 1142a23–30, 1143a35–b5, and 1154a20–31.

13. Cf. *Politics* 1257a30–38 and 1323a14–1324a4, *Ethics* 1140a1–b30.

14. Cf. 1169b22–1170a25, 1163b1–5, 1148a22–32, and 1163b1–5.

15. Cf. 1105a7–13 and 1094a18–24.

16. Cf. 1152b1–12.

17. Cf. 1097a15–1098b12.

18. Given Eudoxus' argument that "each thing discovers the good for itself, just as food" (1172b9–15), it may be the case that the absence of "the good" from *Politics* I.8's account of the pleasant in the natural acquisition of animals and human beings refutes this analogy (1256a19–b7).

19. Cf. 1094a1–3.

20. Cf. 1096a11–17.

21. Cf. 1140a31–b21, 1142a7–30, 1143a35–b14, 1149a34–b1, 27–1150a8.

22. Cf. 1166a10–b2 and 1170a25b10.

23. Cf. 1171b29–1172a8.

24. Cf. 1172a8–15.

25. Cf. 1095a14–17.

26. Cf. 1097b14–1098a7.

27. Cf. 1102a5–6.

28. This translation owes itself to Burger's interpretation (2008, 200).

29. It is not clear if "the contemplative" (*tēn theōrētikē*) refers back to "self-sufficiency" (*autarkeia*) or "passing time" (*diagōgē*) at 1177a27, or "activity" (*energeia*) at 1177a24. Both Sachs (2002, 192) and Bartlett and Collins (2011, 224) insert "life," while Ostwald infers "activity" (1962, 289). It seems prudent to let the ambiguity stand, especially since Aristotle talks explicitly about "life" (*bios*) elsewhere. Plus, in Book X's account of pleasure, he uses philosophy to introduce the question of whether pleasure is something one needs to add into the contemplative activity.

30. The translation of the verb *chorēgeō* as "to resource" (as opposed to its definition of "to supply") aims to bring out its kinship with *achorēgēton* (without-resources) from Book I (1099a31–b9) (Liddell and Scott 1889, 891).

31. This lengthy translation is a literal rendering of the parts of *peripoieō*, namely, "concern" (*peri*) and "to produce" (*poieō*). In Book X, this verb appears in the middle voice, which means it carries the meaning of "to keep" or "to save for oneself," "acquire," "obtain," or "to make gain" (Liddell and Scott 1889, 630). The translation here avoids conflict with "gain" (*kerdos*) and "acquisition" (*ktēsis*). More importantly, by stressing the verb's root of "producing," Aristotle's criticism that the practical things lack self-sufficiency when held up against the contemplative life is stronger, for the practical things "produce" what is more or lesser besides the actions. This may resolve the ambiguity in Book IX over whether those who produce concern (*peripoieō*) for the noble to remain over and above themselves are unreproachable

lovers-of-self (1168b23–29), for their lives now seem to lack the contemplative activity's self-sufficiency.

32. Cf. *Politics* 1333a30–32.

33. Cf. 1099b9–25.

34. Cf. 1144b6–16.

35. Cf. 1152b25–1153a2.

36. Cf. *Politics* 1256a19–b7 and Ethics 1130a5–b5.

37. Cf. 1256b26–1258a19 and 1252b12–1253a1.

38. Cf. 1154b20–31.

39. Cf. 1172a34–1172b8.

40. Cf. 1103b26–1104a11.

41. Cf. 1138b18–34.

42. The literal translation of *methistēmi* as "to change (*meta*) the standing (*histēmi*)" departs slightly from its definition ("to place in another way, to change") (Liddell and Scott 1889, 493).

43. Cf. 1094b4–10.

44. Cf. 1094b23–1095a11 and 1094a18–26.

45. Cf. 1172a26–34.

46. Because he confines his interpretation to the *Politics*, Chan—like Arendt (2000, 186–187)—incorrectly argues that "household management ministers mainly to the body rather than the soul of man" (2006, 14). Nichols, in contrast, sees how the friendship and affection between parents and children fosters free care for the soul in the household (1992, 33–35).

47. Cf. 1102a26–31.

48. Cf. 1173a18.

49. Cf. 1253a7–33.

50. Cf. 1134b18–1135a5 and 1178a9–23.

51. Cf. 1137b5–1138a3.

52. Cf. 1172b35–1173a2.

53. Cf. 1129a3–21.

# CHAPTER 8

1. Among the interpretations of Aristotle's economic teaching, Finley comes closest to noticing the connections between exchange, community, and friendship in the *Ethics* and how they point to questions of political justice (1970, 7–15). But Finley errs when he claims, "That natural inequality is fundamental to Aristotle's thinking is beyond argument: it permeates his analysis of friendship in the *Ethics* and of slavery in the *Politics*" (1970, 13), for this keeps him from seeing how the *Ethics'* inquiry into friendship liberates human beings from the problem of worth, something Aristotle likely has in mind when he opens the master and slave to the possibility of friendship in the *Politics* (1255b9–15).

2. Cf. 1095a14–1096a10.

3. Cf. 1095a17–b4.

4. Cf. *Ethics* 1180a18–24, 1094a1–3, and *Politics* 1252a1–7.

5. Cf. 1257a19–28.

6. Cf. 1155a26–28 and 1137b5–1138a3.

7. Cf. 1157b17–21.

8. Cf. 1129a23–b6.

9. Adhering to the mathematical sense of this passage, translators usually render *logōn* as "ratios" (Ostwald 1962, 119; Sachs 2002, 84; Bartlett and Collins 2011, 96, though in Note 13 they alert readers to Aristotle's use of *logos*).

10. Cf. 1142a10–20.

11. Bartlett and Collins note *antipeponthos* carries with it the meaning of "to suffer in turn," and "can have the sense of 'an eye for an eye'" (2011, Note 19, 99). This fits an interesting characteristic of what Burger calls "the mathematics of justice," which "cover[s] over . . . political realities and passions" (2008, 95–99; cf. pg. 97 especially).

12. Though the proper meaning of *antipoieō* is "to do in return," the translation of "produce-in-turn" aims to stay consistent with the translation of *poieō* as "to produce" throughout this book (Liddell and Scott 1889, 80).

13. Finley also expresses a similar surprise at this form of justice's appearance (1970, 7).

14. Cf. 1257a19–28.

15. Cf. 1257a5–19.

16. Cf. *Politics* 1257a30–b4 and *Ethics* 1180a18–24.

17. Meikle also notices this competition between legal-currency and need (*chreia*) in *Ethics* V.5, and goes on in his next chapter to show the problems derived from mistranslating *chreia* as "demand" in the "subjective, utilitarian, or neo-classical value theory" (1995, 21–27, 28–42).

18. Cf. *Ethics* 1095b22–25 and *Politics* 1252a1–7.

19. Cf. *Politics* 1257b11–17 and *Ethics* 1134b18–30.

20. Cf. 1095b22–25 and 1096a5–10.

21. Cf. 1177a27–1179a9.

22. Cf. 1129a31–b6.

23. Cf. 1152b1–3.

24. Bywater's manuscript has *logos* in the main text at 1134a35, though he notes another manuscript has *nomos* (law) in its place (1894, 102). Both Sachs (2002, 92) and Bartlett and Collins (2011, 104, Note 32) use *nomos*, while Ostwald (1962, 130) uses *logos*. Though the immediate context is amenable to *nomos* (cf. Bartlett and Collins), the way Aristotle plays with *logos* in Book V and eventually declares *nomos* is *logos* in Book X suggests a need to draw attention to how he anticipates this conclusion.

25. Cf. 1176b11–1177a1, 1177b4–1178a26, and 1179b29–1180a24.

26. Cf. 1094b11–19, 1104b32–1105a13, and 1113a15–b2.

27. Cf. 1138b18–34, 1140a31–b21, 1152b25–1153a2, and 1181b1–15.

28. Cf. 1139a21–b5 and 1102a26–31.

29. Cf. 1166a1–b2, 1129a3–21, 1106b36–1107a6, 1108b11–19, and 1109a20–35.

30. Cf. 1253b1–8 and 1255b9–15.

31. Cf. 1254b2–34.

32. In his article "Aristotle's Rhetorical Strategy," Thomas Pangle notes the curiosity that the first mention of "regime" (*politea*) in the *Politics* occurs in Book I's inquiry into household management and the question of its education in virtue (1260b8–16) (2011, 89).

33. In *The Human Condition*, Hannah Arendt argues that "according to ancient thought . . . the very term 'political economy' would have been a contradiction in terms; whatever was 'economic' related to the life of the individual and the survival of the species, was a non-political household affair by definition." From this, Arendt argues that the "*polis* . . . was the sphere of freedom," not the household (2000, 185–187). For readers interested in a more thorough refutation of Arendt's argument, consider Judith A. Swanson's *The Public and the Private in Aristotle's Political Philosophy* (1992). Like Nichols (1992, 33–35), I argue that the household and the friendship within it provides a natural basis for freedom in Aristotle's political philosophy.

34. Cf. 1158b11–1159b21.

35. Cf. 1155b27–31.

36. Lorraine Smith Pangle observes this passage marks the only appearance of "common good" in the *Ethics* (2008, 98).

37. Cf. 1160a8–30 and 1156b7–1158a1.

38. Cf. 1131a10–33.

39. Cf. 1132b21–1133a31.

40. Cf. 1094a18–24.

41. Cf. 1162b21–31.

42. Cf. 1166a33–b2.

43. Cf. 1130b30–33. The only passing reference to the equal involves the question of worth between a laboriously-wicked (*poneros*) person making a loan to a decent person (1165a8–12).

44. Cf. 1257b32–38.

45. Cf. 1094b11–1095a11.

46. Cf. 1133a25–b23.

47. Cf. 1155b17–27.

48. Cf. 1155b27–31.

49. Cf. 1170a13–b14 and 1161b11–1162a29.

50. Cf. 1096a5–10, 1134a23–b8, and 1155a3–6.

51. Polanyi identifies community, self-sufficiency, and justice as the "focal concepts" in Aristotle's view of the economy. Though he notes *philia* resides in the household and city as communities and connects this to reciprocity in exchange in *Ethics* V.5, he does not consider where friendship and justice part ways. Furthermore, he does not think about how useful friendships bear upon the money-making art, and does not follow Books VIII and IX through to the discovery of love-of-self (*philautos*) as transcending justice (1968, 96–97). Finley also catches

the connection between community, exchange, and friendship, but like Polanyi, does not consider Aristotle's engagement of these ideas in Books VIII and IX (1970, 7–8).

52. Cf. *Ethics* 1168a25–b13 and *Politics* 1257a30–38.

53. Cf. *Politics* 1256b26–34 and 1257b8–25, *Ethics* 1172a34–b8, 1172b35–1173a2, 1140a6–23, and 1140b31–1141a8.

54. Cf. 1181b12–15, 1094a1–3.

55. Cf. 1131a10–33.

56. Cf. 1152b1–3.

57. A key part of Chan's interpretation is the argument that Aristotle favors "commercial Carthage" over "agrarian Sparta" (2006, 43–53). Yet while Chan addresses disputes over ruling offices in his account, he never connects these to Aristotle's account of political philosophy in Book III, which is a significant omission. For a more thorough criticism of Chan's dichotomy, see Dinneen (2015, 117–141).

58. Cf. 1134a34–b8, 1130a14–b5, 1168a15–23, 1176b11–1177a1, and 1177b4–1178a23.

59. Booth connects *philia* to leisure in Aristotle's teaching, but misses how this connects to the natural love-of-self (*philautos*) and *logos* (1993, 45–47).

60. Cf. 1178a23–1179a9.

61. A similar argument appears in the late Delba Winthrop's excellent book, *Aristotle: Democracy and Political Science* (2019, 89–97).

## CHAPTER 9

1. Cf. *Politics* 1252a1–7 and *Ethics* 1095a17–b4.

2. Cf. 1155a12–28.

3. Cf. 1279b7–1280a31, 1282b23–30, and 1258b9–27.

4. Liddell and Scott define *parastasis* as "a putting aside or away, banishing"; "a setting out things for sale, retail-trade" (1889, 603). The reading of "standing-beside" is a literal rendering of *para* ("beside") in composition (1889, 592–593).

5. Bartlett and Collins note this ambiguity in their translation of the verb *dokeō* (2011, Note 14, 197). Also note the kinship between the participle for this term (*doxanta*) and "opinion" (*doxa*).

6. Cf. *Ethics* 1167b17–1168a27 and 1129b11–19; *Politics* 1282b14–23.

7. Cf. 1094a1–3.

8. Cf. 1168b15–23, as well as 1148a22–32.

9. Cf. 1129a23–b6 and 1134a23–34.

10. Cf. 1168b29–1169a18, 1170a13–b20, 1171b29–1172a15, and 1180a18–24.

11. For a full exploration of a politics of the middle class in Aristotle's *Politics* and how this teaching applies to the American Founding, see the late Leslie G. Rubin's *America, Aristotle, and the Politics of a Middle Class* (2018).

12. Chan also compares Socrates' regime from Plato's *Republic* and Phaleas' best regime, focusing on the problems of unity and property (2006, 37–42), but not with an emphasis on friendship, political philosophy, and Aristotle's deeper sense of what is properly-one's-own.

13. Cf. Books II–V of the *Republic*.

14. Cf. 1142a7–10.

15. Cf. 1252a24–1253a1 and 1257a19–30.

16. Cf. 1132b21–1133a25.

17. Cf. 1252b27–1253a1.

18. Cf. 1172a34–b8.

19. Cf. 1155a12–28 and 1167a22–b16.

20. Cf. *Symposium* 189c–193e.

21. Cf. 1170b20–1171a20.

22. Cf. 1161b11–1162a29, 1166a23–33, 1169b3–8, and 1170b5–10.

23. Ross notes a discrepancy in the manuscripts between whether the term here is "character" (*ēthos*) or "habit" (*ethos*) (1957, 33).

24. Cf. 1256b26–30.

25. Cf. 1168a28–1169a6, 1148a22–32, 1146b24–35, 1147a10–24, and 1094a18–24.

26. In Plato's *Symposium*, Aristophanes describes *Erōs* as "the most philanthropic of the gods" (189c–d).

27. Cf. 1176b11–1177a1, 1178a23–1179a9, 1152b25–1153a2, and 1164a2–b6.

28. Cf. *Politics* 1257a28–30, 1257b5–17, and *Ethics* 1129b1–6, 1134a26–34.

29. Cf. 1263b15–1264a1.

30. Cf. 1159b12–21.

31. Cf. 1129a3–21, 1106b36–1107a6, 1108b11–19, 1109a20–35.

32. On his way to the argument that "the greatest thing" for regimes' preservation is education in Book V of the *Politics*, Aristotle argues the middle is not a single virtue for all regimes, for if one attempts to draw either democracy or oligarchy toward the middle, one ruins the regime (1309b18–1310a17).

33. Cf. 1141b2–1142a10.

34. Cf. *Ethics* 1141a9–b8 and 1095a17–b4, and *Politics* 1252a1–3.

35. Cf. 1257b36–1258a14.

36. Cf. *Politics* 1258b9–11, and *Ethics* 1146b24–35, 1147a10–24.

# Bibliography

Ambler, Wayne. 1984. "Aristotle on Acquisition." *Canadian Journal of Political Science* 17, no. 3: 487–502.

Ambler, Wayne. 1987. "Aristotle on Nature and Politics: The Case of Slavery." *Political Theory* 15 (August): 390–410.

Arendt, Hannah. 2000. "The Public and the Private Realm." In *The Portable Hannah Arendt*, ed. Peter Baehr, 182–230. New York: Penguin.

Aristotle. 1894. *Nicomachean Ethics*. Ed. Ingram Bywater. Oxford: Oxford University Press.

Aristotle. 1957. *Politics*. Ed. W. D. Ross. Oxford: Clarendon Press.

Aristotle. 1962. *Nicomachean Ethics*. Trans. Martin Ostwald. Indianapolis: The Library of Liberal Arts.

Aristotle. 1997. *Politics*. Trans. Peter L. Phillips Simpson. Chapel Hill: The University of North Carolina Press.

Aristotle. 2002. *Nicomachean Ethics*. Trans. Joe Sachs. Newburyport: Focus.

Aristotle. 2011. *Nicomachean Ethics*. Trans. Robert Bartlett and Susan Collins. Chicago: University of Chicago Press.

Aristotle. 2013. *Politics*. Trans. Carnes Lord. Chicago: University of Chicago Press.

Booth, William James. 1993. *Households: On the Moral Architecture of the Economy*. Ithaca: Cornell University Press.

Burger, Ronna. 2008. *Aristotle's Dialogue with Socrates: On the Nicomachean Ethics*. Chicago: University of Chicago Press.

Chan, Michael. 2006. *Aristotle and Hamilton on Commerce and Statesmanship*. Columbia: University of Missouri Press.

Chase, Alston Hurd, and Henry Phillps Jr. 1961. *A New Introduction to Greek*. 3rd ed. Cambridge: Harvard University Press.

Crespo, Ricardo. 2014. *A Reassessment of Aristotle's Economic Thought*. New York: Routledge.

Dinneen, Nathan. "Aristotle's Political Economy: Three Waves of Interpretation." *Polis* 32: 96–142.

Finley, M. I. 1970. "Aristotle and Economic Analysis." *Past & Present* 47 (May): 3–25.

Hanson, Victor Davis. 1999. *The Other Greeks: The Family Farm and the Agrarian Roots of Western Civilization*. Berkeley and Los Angeles: University of California Press.

Heilbroner, Robert L. 1986. *The Worldly Philosophers*. New York: Simon and Schuster.

Hobbes, Thomas. 1994. *Leviathan*. Indianapolis: Hackett.

Howland, Jacob. 2002. "Aristotle's Great-Souled Man." *Review of Politics* 64: 27–56.

Jaffa, Harry. 1963. "Aristotle." In *History of Political Philosophy*, ed. Leo Strauss and Joseph Cropsey, 1st ed., 64–129. Chicago: University of Chicago Press.

Liddell and Scott, eds. 1889. *An Intermediate Greek-English Lexicon*. Madrid: Oxford University Press.

Locke, John. 1970. *Two Treatises of Government*. New York: Cambridge University Press.

Mansfield, Harvey C. 1980. "Marx on Aristotle: Freedom, Money, and Politics." *The Review of Metaphysics* 34, no. 2: 351–367.

Meikle, Scott. 1995. *Aristotle's Economic Thought*. Oxford: Clarendon Press.

Nichols, Mary P. 1983. "The Good Life, Slavery, and Acquisition: Aristotle's Introduction to Politics." *Interpretation* 11, no. 2: 171–183.

Nichols, Mary P. 1992. *Citizens and Statesmen: A Study of Aristotle's Politics*. Savage: Rowman and Littlefield.

Pangle, Lorraine Smith. 2003. *Aristotle and the Philosophy of Friendship*. New York: Cambridge University Press.

Pangle, Thomas. 2011. "The Rhetorical Strategy Governing Aristotle's Political Teaching." *The Journal of Politics* 73, no. 1: 84–96.

Pascarella, John Antonio. 2015. "Friendship, Politics, and The Good in Aristotle's *Nicomachean Ethics*." PhD diss., University of North Texas.

*Perseus Digital Library*. 2014. http://www.perseus.tufts.edu/hopper/ (Accessed August 7, 2019).

Plato. 1968. *The Republic of Plato*. Trans. Allan Bloom. New York: Basic Books.

Plato. 1993. *Phaedo*. Trans. David Gallop. New York: Oxford University Press.

Plato. 2001. *Plato's Symposium*. Trans. Seth Benardete. Chicago: University of Chicago Press.

Plato. 2003. *Republic*. New York: Oxford University Press.

Polanyi, Karl. 1968. "Aristotle Discovers the Economy." In *Primitive, Archaic, and Modern Economies: Essays of Karl Polanyi*, ed. George Dalton, 78–115. Garden City: Anchor Books.

Rubin, Leslie G. 2018. *America, Aristotle, and the Politics of a Middle Class*. Waco: Baylor University Press.

Schumpeter, Joseph. 1954. *History of Economic Analysis*. New York: Oxford University Press.

Shulsky, Abram N. 1991. "The 'Infrastructure' of Aristotle's *Politics*. Aristotle on Economics and Politics." In *Essays on the Foundations of Aristotelian Political*

*Science*, ed. Carnes Lord and David K. O'Connor, 74–111. Berkeley and Los Angeles: University of California Press.

Smith, Adam. 1981. *An Inquiry Into the Nature and Causes of the Wealth of Nations.* Indianapolis: Liberty Fund.

Smith, Adam. 1982. *The Theory of Moral Sentiments.* Indianapolis: Liberty Fund.

Smith, Thomas W. 2001. *Revaluing Ethics: Aristotle's Dialectical Pedagogy.* Albany: State University of New York Press.

Swanson, Judith A. 1992. *The Public and the Private in Aristotle's Political Philosophy.* Ithaca: Cornell University Press.

Von Heyking, John. 2016. *The Form of Politics: Aristotle and Plato on Friendship.* Quebec: McGill-Queen's University Press.

Winthrop, Delba. 2019. *Aristotle: Democracy and Political Science.* Chicago: University of Chicago Press.

# Index

acquisition (as beginning of economics), 15–23; *hexis* and, 111; natural, 15–18; natural foundation for, 41; political community and, 301; and proper/improper use, 10, 39–40, 68, 167, 203; wealth and, 301; without-limit, knowledge of the good as preventing, 98, 109, 306, 309–10, 316. *See also* legal-currency; pirates; *specific topics, e.g.,* food

acquisition, art of, 17–23, 28, 34–35, 40, 48, 52–53, 87, 96, 112, 319, 335n11, 337nn44–45; household management and, 19, 132, 305; just, 34, 110, 148, 226, 232, 236; natural, 15–18, 20–21, 38, 53, 216, 237, 305, 335n13; unjust, 34; war as, 67, 81, 140, 181, 236. *See also* exchange, art of

action (*praxis*): aim of, 35; Aristotle's understanding of, 106, 108; art and, 90; choice and/choice as preceding, 240; and intellect, 106; noble actions, 133–34, 142, 199, 220–21, 278, 360n50; and production, 49–50, 108, 112; three things in the soul authoritative over, 106; and truth, 106. *See also* good-action

activity (*energeia*): and happiness, 180; *hexis* and, 147, 174, 255; and the human good, 154; and pleasure, 191, 206, 215–16, 238, 255, 263. *See also* motion

advantageous things/the advantageous, 56–57, 80, 105, 113–14, 119, 125, 129, 156–57, 168–69, 196, 217, 236, 299–300, 309, 314; sense-perception and, 59, 69, 88, 140, 154, 169, 232–33, 262

affection. *See* friendly-affection; friendship; love; *specific topics, e.g.,* family

Agathon (poet), 16, 112, 163

aim: "Every art and every inquiry, and likewise action and choice, seems to aim itself at some good", 35; good as "that at which all things aim," 44, 83, 89–91, 118, 135, 172, 187, 218, 244–46, 264, 267, 292, 300, 346n13

alliances, 209. *See also under* friendship, three forms of, the useful

Ambler, Wayne, 4, 334n9, 338n54, 340–41nn14–15, 341–42nn31–32, 342n37

Anaxagoras, 119, 129, 150, 174, 196, 257, 314

animals, 27–28, 37–38, 57–62, 71–72, 93, 103, 106–7, 118, 128, 132, 138–42, 154, 168–69, 179–81, 189, 194–